A Spanish Civil War Scrapbook

Lawrence & Wishart Limited
99a Wallis Road
London E9 5LN

© International Brigade Memorial Trust

ISBN 978-1-909831-98-8

British Library Cataloguing in Publication Data

A catalogue record for this book is available from the British Library

A Spanish Civil War Scrapbook

Elizabeth Pearl Bickerstaffe's
newspaper cuttings
of the wars in Spain and China
from August 1937 to May 1939

Published by
International Brigade Memorial Trust and Lawrence & Wishart
London 2015

On the Road That Leads to Safety. . . .
...country outside Tarragona. When they knew that Franco's men were coming they put all their goods into a waggon. The ...ay that they had to push. The road they had to go along was continually machine-gunned from the air. But they preferred to go.

...RAGEDY OF SPAIN

...from the war, a million human beings crowded into overcrowded Barcelona before it was cut off. As ...ged the roads, following a horse or mule if they were lucky, death came down on them from the skies.

PICTURE POST

SAFETY FIRST

"No, no, don't touch, we mustn't burn our fingers!"

RUSSELL RE... ...N SPAIN

MOV... ...ON ORKER...

CONTENTS

...A'S LAST DEFENCES L...

IN SOME PLACES M... ...STING AT THE TRENCH...

...Barcelona's defenders hung

...roads German warplanes di...
over the convoys of women and children, spray...
them with bombs and machine-gun bullets, as ...
sought safety during the battle for the city.

...OMEN TAKE THEIR STAND
...AGAINST DEATH DAILY

WORLD'S BATTLEFIELDS
...s, Germans, Poles and Britons
...y famous International Brigade
...to thank for his long wait
...hey get a few coppers for pay.
...s boots, breeches and khaki

...wo years ago when men from
...ntry in Europe were pouring
...a with a cry for freedom on
...e wer... ...ing ...
...ry th...
...ome

Those British nurses have seen men of
every country suffer bravely in this fight;
they have picked dying women and children
...ood; they have
Winifred Bates,
DAILY WORKER,

...they want help
...for life. Why
...ur leader see
...wounded, but

Co-op Aids Spain

...en collected in
...cal Aid Com-
...went out in

...and a large
...s have been
...here members
...units are not
...now numbers
...pharmacists,

...re 72 British
...surgical vans
...have gone to
...dical Depart-

...s every pos-
... to it in gifts

FIGHT FASCISM
HELP SPAIN

GIVE MEDICAL AID
...ST PANCRAS AND HOLBORN SPAIN WEEK 22-28 JAN

"TAKE CARE.
TODAY IT IS US—
TOMORROW IT
MAY BE YOU."

says La Pasionaria.
She is seen here at
the Birthday cele-
bration of the Inter-

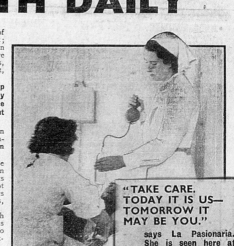

FOREWORD

Rodney Bickerstaffe

I first met Jack Jones in 1973 when I was an area officer of the National Union of Public Employees in Yorkshire. He'd travelled up from London to Sheffield to knock a few union heads together over a dispute involving hospital workers, including members of his own union, the mighty Transport & General Workers' Union. Like everyone else I was in complete awe of the man. What made him a giant was not just what he said and the way even governments listened. His deeds and achievements spoke much louder than any such words and gave him a special authority and integrity in the labour movement. Not least among these deeds was the fact that he had fought in Spain, had seen his comrades die on the battlefields of the Ebro and had himself been injured in that momentous fight against fascism that was the Spanish Civil War.

Perhaps more than many at the time, I was only too aware of the significance of the war in Spain and the important chapter in radical history written by Jack and the other volunteers of the International Brigades. This was thanks to my mother. The scrapbook she kept during the Spanish Civil War was one of her treasured possessions. I thumbed through its stark pictures as a small boy and as I grew older tried to make sense of the tragic defeat of democracy in Spain. I asked her questions about the war. Why did we lose? Why didn't Britain help the Spanish Republic? Why is Franco still the dictator of Spain? Her answers taught me many things and helped shape the beliefs and values I still hold today. For example, there is a time to fight in a foreign war, just as there is a time not to. And it's better to trust the decent values of working people than it is to be swayed by the self-interested arguments of the powerful.

Jack and I remained the best of friends until his death in 2009. I was proud to accompany him and youngest son Mick on his final trip to the Ebro four years earlier. He knew my admiration for the International Brigades and

ANDREW WIARD

Rodney Bickerstaffe (left) and Jack Jones at a pensioners' rally in 2003.

would tell me how fervently he hoped that their story would not be forgotten once he and the other surviving veterans had gone. I was especially proud therefore to be invited by him to be a trustee of the International Brigade Memorial Trust when it was founded in 2001 with that very aim of keeping alive the memory and spirit of the men and women who went to Spain.

In its own way I hope the publication of this scrapbook will help keep the flame alight. Jack and my mother were right. It's vital that future generations learn the lessons of what happened in Spain and know about the sacrifice of so many of the finest young people of their generation in the cause of freedom, social justice and democracy – a struggle that continues to this day.

December 2014

Rodney Bickerstaffe is a former general secretary of Unison and president of the National Pensioners Convention. He served as a trustee of the International Brigade Memorial Trust until 2012, since when he has been one of its patrons.

2010: Sam Lesser examines the scrapbooks, which include his despatches from Spain as Sam Russell.

Lasting Impressions of a War that Scarred a Family and a Generation

Jim Jump

The destruction of the Spanish Republic was felt as a "personal tragedy" by people around the world. It taught them "that one can be right and yet be beaten, that force can defeat spirit". So wrote French novelist Albert Camus ten years after the military uprising that sparked the Spanish Civil War of 1936-39[1]. Even seventy-one years on, the war's impact on a generation was remembered by Doris Lessing. Speaking after receiving the 2007 Nobel Prize in Literature, she recalled her friends in tears of rage and shame in the face of Britain's "heart-breaking" policy of non-intervention that allowed Hitler and Mussolini to secure General Franco's victory over the Republic[2].

The scrapbook kept by Elizabeth Pearl Bickerstaffe between August 1937 and the end of the war early in 1939 reflects that same visceral engagement with events in Spain and with the pain, mingled with defiance and diminishing hope, that accompanied the slow and agonising defeat of Spain's elected government.

---

1   'It was in Spain ... that men learned that one can be right and yet be beaten, that force can defeat spirit, that there are times when courage is not its own reward. It is this, no doubt, which explains why so many men, the world over, feel the Spanish drama as a personal tragedy.' From Albert Camus's preface to *L'Espagne Libre* (1946), cited in *Writers in Arms: The Literary Impact of the Spanish Civil War* by Frederick R Bensen (London: University of London Press, 1967), p.302.

2   See interview in *El País* of 21 October 2007, 'La guerra y la memoria no acaban nunca', in which Doris Lessing said: 'For those of my generation the [Spanish] Civil War was very important. It was so heart-breaking, so difficult, so impossible to understand the behaviour of our governments ... Maybe you've all forgotten, but Britain and France behaved deplorably: they allowed Hitler and Mussolini to help Franco because in Spain there was a government of the left. I would be with people who wept with rage and shame because of our governments.' (author's translation from the Spanish).

Born on 24 August 1920, Pearl was about to turn seventeen when she began keeping newspaper cuttings about the Spanish Civil War and that other great contemporary cause, Japan's brutal invasion of China. This was, incidentally, the same age as Lessing's at the start of the war in Spain. Pearl had just left school and worked as a children's nurse in Thorp Arch, some twenty-five miles north-east of her native Doncaster, south Yorkshire. Lessing was a nursemaid in Southern Rhodesia (now Zimbabwe): two teenage girls, worlds apart but united, along with countless thousands of their generation, in their emotional involvement in Spain's tragedy.

What made the young Bickerstaffe so assiduously stick to her task? She amassed many hundreds of cuttings, filling more than 170 pages of her scrapbook during the eighteen months leading up to February 1939 when, with the fall of Catalonia, the Republic arrived at the brink of final disintegration. There is only one more cutting after that date, a late addition that was no doubt included because of Pearl's special interest in the subject matter. It is a piece from the *Nursing Mirror* of 13 May 1939 about Lillian Urmston (1915-1990), a nurse from Tameside, Greater Manchester, who served in Spain in the International Brigades [on page 195 in this book]. There are no other clues to Pearl's feelings or thoughts. But you can sense – and still share – the mixed feelings of exhilaration, pride, anger, grief (imagine the effect these photos of dead and injured children had on a children's nurse) and despair conveyed in the reports from Spain and China as she pasted them on the page.

With their motif of playful – or are they fighting? – dogs, the covers of the scrapbook's two volumes belie their content. From the opening entries the tone is set. First, a carefully handwritten and matter-of-fact foreword announces: "This Scrapbook contains events concerning the War in China and the War in Spain from August 1937." Then on the facing page there is a picture of four Chinese soldiers above the slogan adopted by Spanish Republicans and anti-fascists worldwide: "They Shall Not Pass!" With doubtless intentional symmetry, the final page of the second volume has Pearl declaring: "The cry is still 'No pasaran!'" Above this stands a picture taken by Robert Capa of a Spanish soldier gazing from a bombed-out building and Pearl's caption, quoting the words of Dolores Ibárruri ("La Pasionaria") in the same neat script, says: "Dark as the hour seems, the loyalist Spaniards go on, for they remember the words of one of their leaders 'Better to die standing than to live on one's knees'."

Apart from the dates of the cuttings – mostly imprecise and not always accurate – along with a caption noting the death of eighty-two school-children in a Francoist bombing raid, a child described as "The hope of China" and a reference to the second anniversary of the Battle of Jarama, the printed words and pictures are left powerfully to speak for themselves.

The cuttings do not all appear in chronological sequence, suggesting that Pearl acquired batches of them and then pasted several at a time in her scrapbook. For example, a report of the 8 January 1939 rally at Earls Court, London, to welcome home the British Battalion volunteers of the International Brigades [pages 142–3] can be read before despatches describing their departure from Spain [from page 159].

It's worth noting that articles and pictures about the Spanish Civil War gradually become the overwhelming presence in Pearl's archive. By the second volume there is only one spread on the Sino-Japanese conflict. This is hardly surprising. The war in Spain was much closer to home, and the participation of British volunteers gave it a special relevance. Also, there is a sense of growing anguish and horror as, late in 1938 and into the following year, the scale of Spain's human disaster unfolds. Many of the images of refugees and other victims of the war are still today almost too harrowing to contemplate.

For a brief time, however, solidarity efforts in support of the Spanish Republic and China were a shared preoccupation on the left, particularly following the bombing of civilians in both countries in 1937. This is how Pearl's scrapbook begins, with collages of parallel scenes of suffering from China and Spain. But, as one historian has observed: "Though the conflicts were frequently presented in similar terms as 'fascist assaults' and 'people's wars' ... China never became 'China', a 'great cause' like that of 'Spain', instantly recognisable from one emotionally charged word."[3]

---

3 Angela Jackson reviewing *East Wind: China and the British Left, 1925-1976* by Tom Buchanan (Oxford: Oxford University Press, 2012) in *IBMT Newsletter*, issue 34/1-2013, p.23.

Pearl Bickerstaffe in about 1937.

Pearl and Rodney in 1949.

Pearl, top left, in her early twenties at Whipps Cross Hospital.

Pearl and Rodney (partly hidden on left) in about 1956 with a NUPE banner.

No foreign conflict in the twentieth century in which Britain was not directly involved had such an impact as the Spanish Civil War, another historian has noted[4]. Some have gone further, saying that the campaign in support of the Spanish Republic "was to become the most widespread and representative mass movement in Britain since the mid-nineteenth-century days of Chartism and the Anti-Corn Law Leagues, and the most outstanding example of international solidarity in British history"[5]. They stress moreover that the "Aid Spain" movement was largely a grass-roots phenomenon. It faced indifference and opposition from much of the established political class and, wary of the role of the Communist Party, often only luke-warm and conditional support even from some trade union and Labour leaders of the day.

For the 2,500 men and women who joined the International Brigades from the British Isles there was outright hostility and suspicion from some quarters, not least the Conservative-led government. The attitude of the Labour Party did harden in support of the Spanish Republic as the civil war ran its course and the dangers of the government's policy of appeasing the fascist powers became more apparent. Labour leader Clement Attlee visited the British Battalion in Spain in the summer of 1938 and greeted them at London's Victoria Station on their return home in December that year. However, only the Communist Party gave wholehearted support to the war effort in Spain and the "volunteers for liberty". The International Brigades were indeed a creation of the Communist International, and the Aid Spain movement's informal alliance of political, trade union, church and other voluntary groups exemplified the party's desire for a wider "Popular Front" against fascism.

It's difficult to imagine a seventeen-year-old girl in the early twenty-first century keeping such a scrapbook about a foreign conflict with which she has no obvious connection. But this probably says more about the deep impression that the war in Spain made on Pearl Bickerstaffe's generation than it does about

---

4   Tom Buchanan, *Britain and the Spanish Civil War* (Cambridge: Cambridge University Press, 1997), p.1.

5   Jim Fyrth, *The Signal Was Spain: The Aid Spain Movement in Britain 1936-39* (London: Lawrence & Wishart, 1986), p.21.

the nature of political activism by young people today. It also says much about the importance of the war reporting and photography that came out of the Spanish Civil War. Despatches, for example, by George Steer describing the bombing of Guernica by Hitler's Condor Legion and by Jay Allen reporting the massacre of Republicans in Badajoz occupy a special place in the annals of war reportage, as do of course the photographs of Robert Capa, Gerda Taro and others in Spain.

The potency of the images and written words that were sent from Spain are apparent in this scrapbook, though Pearl's cuttings, it has to be said, are taken from a fairly narrow range of sources. Some are of uncertain provenance but the main component consists of extracts from the *Daily Worker*, newspaper of the Communist Party of Great Britain. There are a few too from the left-leaning *News Chronicle*, the socialist weekly *Tribune* and *Cavalcade*, an illustrated weekly news magazine. Among others represented are the *Daily Sketch*, *Daily Telegraph and Morning Post*, *Picture Post*, *Weekly Illustrated* and Pearl's local paper, the *Doncaster Gazette*.

The importance of the Spanish Civil War for the Communist Party can clearly be seen in these cuttings, with the *Daily Worker* committing considerable space and resources to following the conflict and beating the drum for the Republic. Among its influential correspondents in Spain were Claud Cockburn (then known as Frank Pitcairn), party stalwarts Peter Kerrigan, Bill Rust and Rose Smith and a young ex-International Brigader from east London, Sam Lesser (1915-2010). Sam had taken part in the defence of Madrid in November 1936 before being injured in fighting at Lopera, near Córdoba, in the following month. Once recovered, he returned to Spain as a journalist, taking the pen-name Sam Russell. Under this by-line, first as a foreign correspondent and later as its foreign editor, he stayed with the *Daily Worker* (renamed the *Morning Star* in 1966) until retirement in 1984, reporting many of the great events of the twentieth century from, among other places, Budapest, Hanoi, Havana, Moscow, Paris, Prague and Santiago de Chile.

More than 70 years after the end of the Spanish Civil War, Lesser, then the chair of the International Brigade Memorial Trust, saw Pearl's scrapbook, containing many of his despatches from Spain – among them his dramatic accounts of the fall of Barcelona and Catalonia in January and February 1939. There was also a picture of the young Sam Russell himself [page 195]. And it was Pearl's son, Rodney Bickerstaffe, who showed him the scrapbooks in July 2010, just three months before Sam's death.

During the Spanish Civil War the circulation of the *Daily Worker* climbed from 30,000 to 50,000, with up to 80,000 copies sold on Saturdays[6]. Its influence on the left and in the trade union movement was disproportionately larger. From the number of cuttings in the scrapbook we can be fairly sure that the Bickerstaffe household, in the now demolished Victorian terraced house at 16 Oxford Place, Doncaster, read the *Daily Worker* – and Pearl, the eldest of ten children (one of whom died as a baby), was left to cut it up as she pleased.

Apart from the fact that she was born into a family radicalised by poverty and the social injustices of the inter-war years, we know little else of Pearl's formative political years. Her father, "Jack" (Charles Alexander Edmund John) Bickerstaffe was a mechanic and "strong union man", according to grandson Rodney, and became a Labour Party member[7]. He also chaired the National Unemployed Workers' Movement in south Yorkshire. Though never a declared Communist Party member, his activism in the party-dominated NUWM and his presumed readership of the *Daily Worker* suggest shared ideological leanings. He is pictured in the scrapbook [page 193] in a cutting from the *Doncaster Gazette*, with a moustache and in the centre of the photo, greeting the return home of a local International Brigade volunteer.

Pearl's mother, Mary Evelyn Inman, originally from Hull, spent three years in an orphanage until, aged nine, a rich spinster adopted her and took her to live in Chandler's Ford, Hampshire. Her benefactor died after three years and Mary was made a ward of court and adopted by another local well-to-do spinster. Whatever emotional privations she suffered during this unsettled

---

6 See entry for Bill Rust in Graham Stevenson's online 'A Compendium of Communist Biographies': (www.grahamstevenson.me.uk).

7 This and subsequent attributions are from an interview with the author on 29 October 2013.

childhood were at least partially offset by the benefits of a better education than she would have received as an orphan. This included time at a private school in Andover and, according to family legend, a spell at a finishing school run by nuns in France.

Perhaps it was a strong belief in the value of education that Mary passed on to her eldest daughter. Pearl won a place at the local grammar school, Doncaster Municipal High School for Girls, leaving at the age of sixteen to pursue her vocation in nursing. Soon thereafter, while living at home and commuting to work at a children's hospital in Thorp Arch, she compiled her scrapbook.

Franco declared victory in April 1939 and, as the supporters of the Spanish Republic had predicted would inevitably happen, the Second World War began soon afterwards when Britain and France declared war on Nazi Germany in September of that year. Pearl had meanwhile moved south to make progress in her career. That summer she worked as a children's nurse at the Sunshine Home in Shoeburyness, Essex. Then, aged nineteen, and in the early days of the world war, she was accepted as a student nurse at Whipps Cross Hospital in London's East End. There she trained and worked throughout the Blitz and for the rest of the war. It was also at the hospital that she met Thomas Simpson, a young carpenter from Ireland who had come to London with his father to find work. Pearl and Thomas courted for a few months before he returned to Dublin – where he subsequently married and raised a family.

Pearl, however, was pregnant as a result of the romance, and gave birth to a son at Queen Charlotte's Hospital in Hammersmith, west London, on 6 April 1945. She was faced with having to raise baby Rodney alone, at a time when having an "illegitimate" child was considered shameful. This was a view initially held by her father, a strict disciplinarian who ruled his household in rod-of-iron fashion. But with the help of the Child Welfare Workers' Committee, Pearl found work in nursing jobs that permitted her to keep Rodney with her. These began with a placement in Silchester Common, Hampshire, and included a posting at the Oxford House Settlement in Victoria Park Square, Bethnal Green.

In 1948 she was allowed to return with her child to live with her parents in Doncaster, staying there for several years until she married Norman Topham, a divorcee and family friend with a son, Peter. Rodney was then ten years old and the two families merged and moved to a two-up two-down house at 48 Somerset Road. There she and her new family remained, and she was able to continue her career, first as a school nurse and finally as a health visitor.

With Pearl and Rodney came a large trunk with her treasured possessions: a few gramophone records, souvenirs, books – and the Spanish Civil War scrapbooks. "The trunk had a blanket over it and served as a table most of the time," recalled Rodney. "But on special occasions it was opened. There was only one other picture book inside. So the earliest images I remember seeing as a child were those in a copy of 'The Wind in the Willows' and photos from the Spanish Civil War."

Soon the scrapbooks faded from memory as Rodney, after attending Doncaster Grammar School for Boys and then Rutherford College of Technology (now Northumbria University) in Newcastle, began his rise through the National Union of Public Employees. In 1981 he became the union's general secretary. Twelve years later NUPE merged with local government staff union NALGO and health workers' union COHSE to create Unison, Britain's biggest trade union. From 1995 Rodney was its general secretary. As a champion of low-paid workers, he was widely credited with committing the incoming Labour government of 1997 to introduce the national minimum wage. Following retirement in 2001 he took over from his close friend and mentor for nearly three decades and ex-International Brigader Jack Jones (1913-2009) as president of the National Pensioners Convention, a position he held until 2005. Jones, incidentally, is pictured with wife Evelyn in Pearl's scrapbook [page 135], in what must be one of his first headline appearances in the press.

Rodney's high profile successes in the labour movement were followed with special admiration by Pearl. Like her son, she was a staunch trade unionist and Labour Party member. She had joined NUPE in 1941 as a student nurse and remained a union member throughout her working life. "I wanted to join a real union," she would explain to Rodney, in a pointed

At the IBMT's annual commemoration in London's Jubilee Gardens on 3 July 2010, Sam Lesser (right) and Rodney Bickerstaffe look at Pearl Bickerstaffe's scrapbooks.

Rodney Bickerstaffe with Thora Silverthorne, nurses' union leader and former International Brigader, around 1995.

reference to the choice she was given at Whipps Cross Hospital between the Royal College of Nursing or the more militant NUPE. Half a century later it was her son, then NUPE general secretary, who, arriving unannounced at her branch meeting, had the honour of presenting her with her fifty-year union membership badge.

In 1986 Pearl and Norman moved into her son's family home in Catford, south London. Norman's health was failing and he died two years later. Pearl lived there until she died on 18 January 1999, aged seventy-eight. Her scrapbook thus ended up in Rodney's charge. He eventually deposited it along with his other papers at Warwick University's Modern Records Centre[8] – but not before having both volumes professionally scanned and then donating the images to the International Brigade Memorial Trust.

None of this is surprising. Rodney was one of the founding trustees of the IBMT, having been invited to join the trust's executive committee by its president, Jack Jones. The year was 2001, when the new organisation was created, uniting the remaining International Brigade veterans and their families, friends and supporters. From 2012 Bickerstaffe has been one of the trust's patrons.

So the Spanish Civil War – and a carefully handed-down teenage scrapbook – left its mark both on Pearl and Rodney Bickerstaffe. "She always used to say to me that, had everyone listened to the International Brigaders, we could have averted the horrors of the Second World War," says Rodney of his mother. "That made a lasting impression on me, as did the images of suffering and war that I grew up looking at in my mum's scrapbook."

He adds: "She passed on to me her values of solidarity and supporting the underdog, values that she learnt from and were reinforced by the war in Spain. As a nurse she was always gentle, caring and quietly sympathetic. But at home I saw her other side. She was outraged by injustice at work and in the wider community, in Britain or anywhere else in the world.

"I'm proud that she inspired me to do my union work, and I feel honoured that I was fortunate enough to meet, befriend and work alongside people such

---

8 MRC 907/33.

as Jack Jones and Thora Silverthorne[9], who went to Spain to fight for justice and who were a role model for my mother as a young woman and for me in later life."

Jim Jump is the secretary of the International Brigade Memorial Trust and author, with Richard Baxell and Angela Jackson, of Antifascistas: British & Irish Volunteers in the Spanish Civil War *(2010). He is the editor of* Poems from Spain: British and Irish International Brigaders on the Spanish Civil War *(2006) and* Looking Back at the Spanish Civil War: The International Brigade Memorial Trust's Len Crome Memorial Lectures 2002-2010 *(2010).*

---

9 Thora Silverthorne (1910-1999) was a Welsh-born volunteer nurse with the International Brigades. She founded the National Association of Nurses, which later merged with the National Union of Public Employees, and was also secretary of the Socialist Medical Association.

Correspondents Sam Russell (top centre, with beret) of the Daily Worker *and Willie Forrest (top right, in dark overcoat) of the* News Chronicle *accompany a delegation of British Battalion members at the British consulate in Barcelona in November 1938. Among the International Brigaders are (bottom, from left) Sam Wild and Bob Cooney; behind them are Alan Gilchrist (left) and George Fletcher (in peaked cap).*

Foreign Correspondents in the Spanish Civil War

Paul Preston

At the end of the Spanish Civil War, the American newspaperman Frank Hanighen, who had briefly served as a correspondent in Spain, edited the reminiscences of several of his companions. He commented: "Almost every journalist assigned to Spain became a different man sometime or other after he crossed the Pyrenees ... After he had been there a while, the queries of his editor in far-off New York or London seemed like trivial interruptions. For he had become a participant in, rather than an observer of, the horror, tragedy and adventure which constitutes war."[1] The well-travelled American correspondent Louis Fischer similarly noted: "Many of the foreign correspondents who visited the Franco zone became Loyalists, but practically all of the numerous journalists and other visitors who went into Loyalist Spain became active friends of the cause. Even the foreign diplomats and military attachés scarcely disguised their admiration. Only a soulless idiot could have failed to understand and sympathize."[2]

In the sense of becoming what Fischer called "active friends of the cause", there is a link between many of the writers and journalists who came to Spain and the thousands of men and women from all around the world who flocked to Spain to join the International Brigades. One of them was Sam Lesser, a young Egyptology student at University College, London. Injured early in the war while fighting with the Commune de Paris Battalion, he was invalided out of the International Brigades and went back to London. When he was

---

1   Frank C Hanighen, editor, *Nothing but Danger* (New York: National Travel Club, 1939) p.7.

2   Louis Fischer, *Men and Politics. An Autobiography* (London: Jonathan Cape, 1941) p.438.

fit enough to return to Spain, he made English-language broadcasts from Barcelona and, using the pseudonym "Sam Russell", became a correspondent for the *Daily Worker*. We can read many of his despatches describing the horrific bombing of Barcelona and fall of Catalonia in the cuttings reproduced in this book.

Lesser and the other volunteers believed that to fight for the Spanish Republic was to fight for the very survival of democracy and civilisation against the assault of fascism. At the same time, alongside the regular troops sent by Hitler and Mussolini to support Franco and the military rebels, a smaller number of volunteers also went to fight for what they perceived as the cause of Catholicism and anti-communism. A similar range, and breakdown, of sentiments could be found among the nearly one thousand newspaper correspondents who went to Spain.[3] Along with the professional war correspondents, some hardened veterans of Abyssinia, others still to win their spurs, came some of the world's most prominent literary figures: Ernest Hemingway, John Dos Passos, Josephine Herbst and Martha Gellhorn from the United States; WH Auden, Stephen Spender and George Orwell from Britain; André Malraux and Antoine de Saint Exupéry from France. Some went as leftists, rather fewer as rightists and plenty of those who spent brief periods in Spain were simply jobbing newspapermen.

However, as a result of what they saw, even some of those who arrived without commitment came to embrace the cause of the beleaguered Republic. Underlying their conversion was a deep admiration for the stoicism with which the Republican population resisted. In Madrid, Valencia and Barcelona, the correspondents saw the overcrowding caused by the endless flow of refugees fleeing from Franco's African columns and from the bombing of their homes. They saw the mangled corpses of innocent civilians bombed and shelled by Franco's Nazi and Fascist allies. And they saw the heroism of ordinary people hastening to take part in the struggle to defend their

---

3 A list of 948 men and women was compiled by José Mario Armero, *España fue noticia. Corresponsales extranjeros en la guerra civil española* (Madrid: Sedmay Ediciones, 1976) pp.409-36. The list is defective in many ways, not least in the omission of many correspondents known to have been in Spain but it is indicative of the numbers.

democratic Republic. Observation became indignation and sympathy became partisanship. As Louis Delaprée, the correspondent of *Paris-Soir*, wrote a week before his death in December 1936: "What follows is not a set of prosecutor's charges. It is an actuary's process. I number the ruins, I count the dead, I weigh the blood spilt. All the images of martyred Madrid, which I will try to put before your eyes – and which most of the time defy description – I have seen them. I can be believed. I demand to be believed. I care nothing about propaganda literature or the sweetened reports of the Ministries. I do not follow any orders of parties or churches. And here you have my witness. You will draw your own conclusions."[4]

It was not just a question of correspondents describing what they witnessed. Many of them reflected on the implications for the rest of the world of what was happening in Spain. What they saw and what they risked were harbingers of the future that faced the world if fascism was not stopped in Spain. Their experiences led them into a deep frustration and an impotent rage with the blind complacency of the policy-makers of Britain, France and America. They tried to convey the injustice of the Republic having been left defenceless and forced into the arms of the Soviet Union because of the Western powers' short-sighted adoption of a policy of non-intervention. They felt, in the words of Martha Gellhorn, that "the Western democracies had two commanding obligations: they must save their honour by assisting a young, attacked fellow democracy, and they must save their skin, by fighting Hitler and Mussolini, at once, in Spain, instead of waiting until later, when the cost in human suffering would be unimaginably greater."[5] Accordingly, many journalists were driven by their indignation to write in favour of the Loyalist cause, some to lobby in their own countries, and in a few cases to take up arms for the Republic. A small number of men – including Claud Cockburn and Louis Fischer came as journalists and ended up in the International Brigades. Without going so far, many of the correspondents

---

4   Louis Delaprée, *Le martyre de Madrid. Témoinages inédits de Louis Delaprée* (Madrid: No pub, 1937) p.21.

5   Martha Gellhorn, *The Face of War* 5th edition (London: Granta Books, 1993) p.17.

who experienced the horrors of the siege of Madrid and the inspiring popular spirit of resistance became convinced of the justice of the Republican cause.

In some cases, such as Ernest Hemingway, Jay Allen, Martha Gellhorn, Louis Fischer, George Steer, they became resolute partisans, to the extent of activism yet not to the detriment of the accuracy or honesty of their reporting.[6] Indeed, some of the most committed correspondents produced some of the most accurate and lasting reportage of the war.

Like many others, Fischer found his emotions deeply engaged with the cause of the Republic. Comparing the impact of the Russian Revolution and the Spanish Civil War, he wrote in terms which echo writings by other pro-Republican correspondents: "Bolshevism inspired vehement passions in its foreign adherents but little of the tenderness and intimacy which Loyalist Spain evoked. The pro-Loyalists loved the Spanish people and participated painfully in their ordeal by bullet, bomb and hunger. The Soviet system elicited intellectual approval, the Spanish struggle brought forth emotional identification. Loyalist Spain was always the weaker side, the loser, and its friends felt a constant, tense concern lest its strength end. Only those who lived with Spain through the thirty-three tragic months from July 1936 to March 1939 can fully understand the joy of victory and the more frequent pang of defeat which the ups and downs of the civil war brought to its millions of distant participants."[7]

On both sides, correspondents faced danger from snipers, the bombing and strafing of enemy aircraft. On both sides, there were difficulties to be overcome with the censorship apparatus, although what could be irksome in the Republican zone was downright life-threatening in the Rebel zone. The Rebels shot at least one, Guy de Traversay of *L'Intransigeant*, and arrested, interrogated and expelled over thirty journalists. About half were threatened with execution and imprisoned for periods ranging from a few days to several

---

6 Peter Wyden, *The Passionate War. The Narrative History of the Spanish Civil War* (New York: Simon and Schuster, 1983) p.29; Philip Knightley, *The First Casualty. The War Correspondent as Hero, Propagandist, and Myth Maker from the Crimea to Vietnam* (London: André Deutsch, 1975) pp.192-5.

7 Louis Fischer in Richard Crossman, editor, *The God That Failed. Six Studies in Communism* (London: Hamish Hamilton, 1950) p.220.

months. Only one was expelled by the Republicans and none imprisoned or executed.

There was physical risk from shelling and bombardment in both zones although the Rebel superiority in artillery and aircraft meant that it was greater for those posted in the Republic. Moreover, the close control exercised over correspondents in the Rebel zone kept them away from danger at the front. Within the Rebel zone, there were of course enthusiasts for Franco and fascism, and not just among the Nazi and Italian Fascist contingent. Nonetheless, they were in a minority. Many more of those who accompanied Franco's columns were repelled by the savagery that they had witnessed. Those in the Rebel zone were kept under tight supervision and their published despatches were scoured to pick out any attempts to bypass the censorship. Accordingly, they could not relate what they had seen in their daily despatches and did so only after the war, in their memoirs.

The correspondents in the Republican zone were given greater freedom of movement although they too had to deal with a censorship machinery, albeit a much less crude and brutal one than its Rebel equivalent. Nevertheless, given that the bulk of the press in the democracies was in right-wing hands, pro-Republican correspondents found publicising their views often more difficult than might have been expected. It was ironic that a high proportion of the world's best journalists and writers supported the Republic but often had difficulty in getting their material published as written. The powerful Hearst press and several dailies such as the *Chicago Daily Tribune* were already deeply hostile to the democratic Republic. Jay Allen, for instance, was fired from the *Chicago Daily Tribune* because his articles provoked so much sympathy for the Republic. There were cases of the Catholic lobby using threats of boycott or the withdrawal of advertising to make smaller newspapers alter their stance on Spain.

The Roman Catholic hierarchy in the USA would pressure advertisers to ensure that only "reliable" news of Spain be printed, making it clear to advertisers that they should not imperil their immortal souls or their

On the Ebro front on 5 November 1938, clockwise from left: Ernest Hemingway (North American Newspaper Alliance), photographer Robert Capa (pouring drinks), Vincent Sheean (New York Herald Tribune), Herbert Matthews (New York Times) and Hans Kahle. The photo was taken by Henry Buckley (Daily Telegraph).

pocket-books by dealing with supporters of "leftists, pinkos, and radicals".[8] Dr Edward Lodge Curran, president of the International Catholic Truth Society, boasted in December 1936 that his control of a large sum in advertising business permitted him to change the policy of a Brooklyn daily from pro-Loyalist to pro-Rebel. Other more liberal newspapers were subjected to pressure to prevent the publication of pro-Loyalist news. Herbert L Matthews, the meticulously honest *New York Times* correspondent, was constantly badgered with telegrams accusing him of sending propaganda. In 1938, the Roman Catholic Archdiocese of Brooklyn helped organise a campaign specifically aimed against Matthews and his reporting which led to the paper losing readers.[9] In Spain for the North American Newspaper Alliance, Hemingway also had cause for frequent complaint about his material being changed or simply not used.[10] He and Herbert Matthews were distressed to find that both the cable desk and the night desk of the *New York Times* were manned by Catholic militants deeply hostile to the Republican cause who edited or even omitted material deemed sympathetic to the Loyalists.[11]

The managing editor of the *New York Times* was the short, stick-toting Virginian Edwin L "Jimmy" James (nicknamed "Dressy James" by Damon Runyon because of his brightly coloured suits, which made him look like a bookie). A bon viveur, James was always keen to get off in the evening and so cultivated an irresponsibly hands-off management style which gave enormous freedom to the night managing editor, the deeply conservative Presbyterian, Raymond McCaw. In turn, McCaw gave considerable freedom to his deputy, Neil MacNeil, a fiercely partisan Catholic, and his assistant, the equally fanatical convert Clarence Howell. These night editors controlled the group of desks known as the "bullpen", in the southeast corner of the newsroom.

---

8 James M Minifie, *Expatriate* (Toronto: Macmillan of Canada, 1976) pp.53-4.

9 'To Aid Spanish Fascists', *New York Times*, 1 December 1936; Laurel Leff, *Buried by The Times. The Holocaust and America's Most Important Newspaper* (New York: Cambridge University Press, 2005) p.179.

10 William Braasch Watson, 'Hemingway's Civil War Dispatches', *The Hemingway Review*, Vol.VII, No.2, Spring 1988, pp.4-12, 26-9, 39, 60.

11 George Seldes, '"Treason" on the Times', *The New Republic*, 7 September 1938.

They had free rein in deciding what stories would get prominence and in the editing thereof.[12]

Matthews found that these men treated his copy with "suspicion, anger, and, at times, disbelief". They printed material from William P Carney, his counterpart in the Rebel zone, despite knowing that it was unashamedly partisan and sometimes even faked. In contrast, they cut Matthews's articles, tampered with his wording and buried entire stories because they were perceived to favour the Republican side. McCaw issued orders that, whenever Matthews wrote about the "Italian troops" who fought with the Rebels, the phrase was to be replaced by "insurgent troops". Matthews had gone to Guadalajara after the Italian defeat there. He reported what Italian prisoners had told him and what he had seen of captured Italian weaponry and documents. McCaw's device made nonsense of his despatches. Moreover, McCaw cabled Matthews, accusing him of simply sending Republican propaganda handouts. In mid-December 1937, with Sefton Delmer of the *Daily Express*, Hemingway and Robert Capa, Matthews courageously reported on the Republican assault on Teruel. His articles were ruthlessly cut while William Carney's fabricated despatches about a triumphal recapture of the city by the Rebels were printed. Hemingway was convinced that this was deliberate sabotage.[13]

As Hemingway recognised, Matthews, in fact, took enormous pride in his work and his personal ethic demanded that he never wrote a word that he did not fervently believe to be true. Over thirty years later, he concluded: "All of us who lived the Spanish Civil War felt deeply emotional about it … I always felt the falseness and hypocrisy of those who claimed to be unbiased and the foolish, if not rank stupidity of editors and readers who demand objectivity or impartiality of correspondents writing about the war … those of us who championed the cause of the Republican government against

---

12 Herbert L Matthews, *A World in Revolution. A Newspaperman's Memoir* (New York: Charles Scribner's Sons, 1971) pp. 19-20, 62; Leff, *Buried by the Times*, pp.165-9, 180-1, 399; Guy Talese, *The Kingdom and the Power* (New York: The World Publishing Co., 1969) pp.57-61.

13 Matthews, *A World in Revolution*, pp.19-21, 25-30; George Seldes, *The Catholic Crisis* (New York: Julian Messner, 1939) pp.195-9.

the Franco Nationalists were right. It was, on balance, the cause of justice, morality, decency."[14] The abuse that he received from Catholic propagandists did not diminish his passionate commitment to writing the truth as he saw it. "The war", he wrote, "also taught me that the truth will prevail in the long run. Journalism may seem to fail in its daily task of providing the material for history, but history will never fail so long as the newspaperman writes the truth."[15]

Writing the truth meant, to quote Martha Gellhorn again, "explaining that the Spanish Republic was neither a collection of blood-slathering Reds nor a cat's-paw of Russia". She would have no truck with what she called "all that objectivity shit", refusing to adopt a morally repugnant neutrality equidistant between two very different sides. She felt, as did so many, that those who fought and those who died in defence of the Spanish Republic "whatever their nationality and whether they were Communists, anarchists, Socialists, poets, plumbers, middle-class professional men, or the one Abyssinian prince, were brave and disinterested, as there were no rewards in Spain. They were fighting for us all, against the combined force of European fascism. They deserved our thanks and our respect and got neither."[16] A few who became Loyalist partisans went further than just writing the truth, indeed well beyond their journalistic duties. Hemingway gave an ambulance and dispensed advice to military commanders. Fischer helped both to organise the Republic's press services and to repatriate wounded International Brigaders. Jay Allen lobbied tirelessly for the Republic in America, then went into Vichy France to help Spanish refugees and imprisoned International Brigaders. In consequence, he suffered incarceration in a German prison. George Steer campaigned on behalf of the Basque government to get Britain to permit food supplies to get through to a blockaded Bilbao. The Russian, Mikhail Koltsov, wrote so enthusiastically about the revolutionary élan of the Spanish people that,

---

14 Matthews, *A World in Revolution*, pp.11-12, 17-18. For descriptions of Matthews, see Sefton Delmer, *Trail Sinister. An Autobiography* London: Secker & Warburg, 1961) p.328, and Carlos Baker, *Ernest Hemingway. A Life Story* (London: Collins, 1969) p.369.

15 Matthews, *A World in Revolution*, pp.30-2. Herbert L Matthews, *The Education of a Correspondent* (New York: Harcourt Brace, 1946) pp.130-1, 142-3.

16 Gellhorn, *The Face of War*, p.17.

in the atmosphere of the Soviet purges, he became an embarrassment and was executed.

The story of the foreign correspondents is fundamentally about the courage and the skill of the men and women who wrote about what was happening in Spain. It illustrates many of the differences between the harsh ambience of military dictatorship in the Rebel zone and the fact that, for all its difficulties, the Republic tried to function as a democracy despite wartime conditions. The fact that so many of the correspondents wrote and campaigned for the lifting of non-intervention underlines the extent to which the Spanish Republic was betrayed by the democracies – to their own very real detriment. The fact that the Western powers turned a blind eye while Franco destroyed the democratic Republic with the help of Hitler and Mussolini has been indirectly justified by two recent trends. In Spain a group of pro-Franco propagandists, styling themselves as "revisionists", and in the United States a number of neo-conservatives have resuscitated the idea that the Republic was a Soviet satellite.[17] The story of the independent-minded American, British and French radicals who fought with their pens against non-intervention is a valuable counterpoint to this narrow and ill-founded view.

The correspondents were right in arguing that non-intervention was deeply damaging to the Western democracies. For the duration of the Spanish Civil War, despite the reports of their own diplomats and of countless correspondents in Spain, the governments of Britain, France and the United States chose to ignore the fact that Hitler and Mussolini were sending unstinting help to the Rebels and tilting the balance of international power against the democracies. Despite the fact that it was normal practice under international law to permit an established friendly government to purchase arms and supplies, all three governments denied this right to the Spanish Republic.

---

17 For two examples of the Spanish 'revisionist' literature, see Pío Moa Rodríguez, *Los mitos de la guerra civil* (Madrid: La Esfera de los Libros, 2003) and César Vidal, *Paracuellos-Katyn. Un ensayo sobre el genocidio de la izquierda* (Madrid: LibrosLibres, 2005). The American neo-conservative literature is less prolific but has been influential. Two interesting examples are Ronald Radosh, Mary R Habeck, & Grigory Sevostianov, editors, *Spain Betrayed. The Soviet Union in the Spanish Civil War* (New Haven, Conn: Yale University Press, 2001) and Stephen Koch, *The Breaking Point. Hemingway, Dos Passos and the Murder of José Robles* (New York: Counterpoint, 2005).

Neither Anglo-French non-intervention nor the American "moral" embargo were neutral in their consequences.[18] They damaged the cause of Spain's legally elected government, limited the Republic's capacity to defend itself and threw it into the arms of the Soviet Union.

The fact that Leon Blum frequently burst into tears when reminded that, if the Spanish Republic was crushed, France and the rest of Europe would be next, suggests that he was tortured by regrets about his policy.[19] There is no record of Neville Chamberlain ever expressing regret for his betrayal of the Spanish Republic although it was a significant stepping stone on the way to his loss of power in June 1940. In contrast, when Claude Bowers went to report to Franklin D Roosevelt on Franco's victory, a crestfallen president told him: "We have made a mistake. You have been right all along."[20] In 1944, the assistant secretary of state, Sumner Welles, recognised that: "Of all our blind isolationist policies, the most disastrous was our attitude on the Spanish Civil War" and "in the long history of the foreign policy of the Roosevelt Administration, there has been, I think, no more cardinal error than the policy adopted during the civil war in Spain".[21] At least Roosevelt felt regret, but it can have been as nothing in comparison with the bitterness felt by the many liberals and leftists in America and Europe who had watched the policy of the democratic powers strangle the Spanish Republic and hasten the triumph of fascism.

Through their despatches, the correspondents, and in the case of Jay Allen, Louis Fischer and George Steer, through their campaigning activities, had tried to bring this home. Thanks in large part to the correspondents, millions of people who knew little about Spain came to feel in their hearts

---

18 Sumner Welles, *The Times for Decision* (New York: Harper & Brothers, 1944) p.59; Dante A Puzzo, *Spain and the Great Powers, 1936-1941* (New York: Columbia University Press, 1962) pp.149-60.

19 Dolores Ibárruri, *El único camino* (Madrid: Editorial Castalia, 1992) pp.423-5; Herbert L Matthews, *A World in Revolution: A Newspaperman's Memoir* (New York: Charles Scribner, 1972) p.75.

20 Dominic Tierney, *FDR and the Spanish Civil War. Neutrality and Commitment in the Struggle that Divided America* (Durham & London: Duke University Press, 2007) pp.1, 139-40; Richard P Traina, *American Diplomacy and the Spanish Civil War* (Bloomington, Indiana: Indiana University Press, 1968) pp.230-2.

21 Sumner Welles, *The Times for Decision* (New York: Harper & Brothers, 1944) pp.57, 61.

that the Spanish Republic's struggle for survival was somehow their struggle. The work of the correspondents and their letters to his wife Eleanor had an impact on President Roosevelt's thinking about the threat of fascism. In turn, the fact that he placed electoral interests before wider moral issues had an impact on them. It contributed to Jay Allen's plunge into depression and Louis Fischer's turn to Gandhian pacifism.

The Spanish Republic was a defensive bulwark against the threat of fascist aggression. But its appeal was not just negative. In the grey and cynical world of the depression years, the cultural and educational achievements of the Spanish Republic seemed to be an exciting experiment. However, for most of the correspondents, the most important element of their support for the Republic was the fight to defend democracy against the advance of fascism. To their disappointments in Spain was added vilification at home from those who believed that Franco was conducting a crusade in defence of true religion against Bolshevik bestiality. The consequence was what F Jay Taylor called "one of this generation's most impassioned political and religious controversies". Indeed, so intensely conflictive was the polemic provoked within the United States that the British consul in New York reported in February 1938 that the city was "almost assuming the likeness of a miniature Spain".[22] Nearly thirty-five years after the defeat of the Republic, Herbert Matthews declared: "No event in the outside world, before or since, aroused Americans in time to such religious controversy and such burning emotions."[23]

Yet despite vilification, defeat, and the bitter frustration of witnessing the culpable negligence of the democracies, almost all those who supported the cause of the Spanish Republic carried for the rest of their lives the conviction that they had participated in a struggle that mattered. It was a feeling shared even by George Orwell, whose memoir of his brief time in Spain has given much succour to those who wish to claim, whether from the far left or the far right, that the defeat of the Spanish Republic was somehow

---

22 Tierney, *FDR & SCW*, p.89.

23 F Jay Taylor, *The United States and the Spanish Civil War 1936-1939* (New York: Bookman Associates, 1956) p.7; Herbert L Matthews, *Half of Spain Died. A Reappraisal of the Spanish Civil War* (New York: Charles Scribner's Sons, 1973) p.173.

more the responsibility of Stalin than of Franco, Hitler, Mussolini or Neville Chamberlain. On leaving Spain, Orwell stayed for three days in the French fishing port of Banyuls. He and his wife "thought, talked, dreamed incessantly of Spain". Although bitter about what he had seen as a foot soldier with the semi-Trotskyist POUM, Orwell claimed to feel neither disillusionment nor cynicism: "Curiously enough the whole experience has left me with not less but more belief in the decency of human beings."[24]

As late as the mid-1980s, Alfred Kazin could still view the war in Spain as "the wound that will not heal". In words that could have been uttered by Jay Allen or Louis Fischer or Mikhail Koltsov or George Steer or Henry Buckley or Herbert Southworth, Kazin wrote: "Spain is not my country, the Spanish Civil War, like what followed, was my war. In the course of it I lost friends. I lost hope that Hitler could be stopped before the Second World War. The destroyers of the Spanish Republic would always be my enemies."

However, no one has summed up better the meaning of the Spanish war for so many of the writers and journalists who witnessed the heroic struggle of the Republic than Josephine Herbst. In February 1966, Josie went to see the Spanish Civil War documentary *Mourir à Madrid* by the French director Frédéric Rossif. She wrote that night to some friends: "I wouldn't have wanted anyone I knew to be seated near me, not unless they too had gone through the same experience. I not only felt as if I were dying but that I had died. And afterward, I sat in the lobby for a good while, trying to pull myself together, smoking, and the whole scene outside, and on the street when I got there, seemed completely unreal. I couldn't connect with anything or feel that it meant anything, somewhat in the same way that I had felt when I got down from the plane in Toulouse after I flew out of Barcelona and had expected to enjoy ordering a real lunch for a change and instead sat sobbing over an omelette – all I could bear to try to eat – and wine – and looking at people calmly passing by as if I had entered into a nightmare where the 'real' world had suddenly been wiped off with a sponge and vanished forever. And actually, sitting in the lobby, smoking, it came to me that in the most real

---

24 George Orwell, *Homage to Catalonia* (London: Secker & Warburg, 1971) pp.246-7.

sense my most vital life did indeed end with Spain. Nothing so vital, either in my personal life or in the life of the world, has ever come again. And in a deep sense, it has all been a shadow picture for years and years. In Toulouse, though the war had not yet ended, I knew it would end and with defeat. And that nothing was going to stop World War II. Nothing. And most of the time since then has been lived on buried treasure of earlier years, on a kind of bounty I could still take nourishment from. It is all too repetitive, and too terrible, with no lessons ever learned."[25]

Paul Preston is professor of Spanish history at the London School of Economics and Political Science, where he is also the director of the Cañada Blanch Centre for Contemporary Spanish Studies. He is the author of We Saw Spain Die: Foreign Correspondents in the Spanish Civil War *(2008) and many other books on Spain and the Spanish Civil War, including the biographies* Franco: A Biography *(1993),* Juan Carlos: A People's King *(2004) and* The Last Stalinist: The Life of Santiago Carrillo *(2014) as well as* ¡Comrades! Portraits from the Spanish Civil War *(1999);* Doves of War: Four Women of Spain *(2002);* The Spanish Civil War: Reaction, Revolution and Revenge *(2006) and* The Spanish Holocaust: Inquisition and Extermination in Twentieth-Century Spain *(2012).*

---

25 Herbst to Mary & Neal Daniels, 17 February 1966, Za Herbst Collection, Beinecke Library, Yale University. It is reprinted in its entirety in Elinor Langor, *Josephine Herbst* (Boston: Little, Brown, 1984) pp.ix-x.

SCRAPS

VOLUME ONE

SAVE PHOTOGRAPHS
AND PRESS CUTTINGS
FOR REFERENCE

This Scrapbook contains events
concerning the War in China and
The War In Spain from August
1937.

They Shall Not Pass!

Tuesday, August 17, 1937

The Spanish PATRIOTS Visit a COUNTRY TOWN

MONDAY was the weekly market day of Guernica, when the town existed. At about 4.30 the market, in summer, was at its fullest. The civil war had not made great difference to the Guernica farmers who brought in their animals and produce for sale from the rich valley.

Guernica remained a modest Vizcayan country town. The population behaved itself, the priests walked about in the cloth, mass was held in the churches all day and every day. There were no troops retreating through the town. Guernica lay well behind the front.

After four there were farm carts coming into Guernica, rolling on solid wooden wheels and drawn by oxen whose heads were shaded under fleeces of sheep. Basque peasants in their long puckered market smocks walked backwards in front of them, mesmerising the oxen to Guernica with their slim wands, with which they kept touching the horns and yoke gently. They talked to the oxen.

Others were driving sheep to market. There was an assembly of animals near the parish church, a stately structure cavernous and dark within, standing upon a flight of thin steps like leaves piled one upon the other.

It is improbable that anyone was thinking about the war, when at 4.30 the church bell rang out loud. All over Spain a peal on a single bell is an air-raid warning. The population took cover, and the sheep in the square were left to their own devices.

IN a few minutes a Heinkel III came over and dropped six medium bombs, probably fifty-pounders, near the station, with a shower of grenades.

A few minutes later another Heinkel III appeared, to bomb the same area, but near the centre. The telephone with Bilbao was now cut. The plane, from its slant and speedy sides, machine-gunned the town at random, then veered homeward.

The parish priest, Aronategui, left his church with the sacraments, for dying people were reported near the railway station. He went calmly through the deserted streets with the bread. No fires had yet started.

Fifteen minutes passed, and the people were coming out of their shelters. A heavy drumming of engines was heard to the east. It was what we called in lighter moments the tranvias—the trams —the Junker 52's, who were so clumsy that they seemed to clang rather than to fly. These were the heaviest bombers that Germany had sent to Spain.

*

OVER the town, whose streets were once more empty trenches, they dispersed their load a ton at a time. They turned woodenly over Guernica, the bombs fell mechanically in line as they turned. Then came the crack of the explosions: smoke stood up over Guernica like wool on a Negro's head. Everywhere it sprouted, as more heavy bombers came.

Besides many fifty- and hun-dred-pound bombs, they dropped great torpedoes, weighing a thousand. Guernica is a compact little town, and most of these hit buildings, tearing them to pieces vertically from top to bottom and below the bottom. They penetrated refuges. The spirit of the people had been good, but now they panicked.

An escort of Heinkel 51's, the same perhaps that had molested us that afternoon, were waiting for this moment. Till now they had been machine-gunning the roads round Guernica, scattering, killing or wounding sheep and shepherds. As the terrified population streamed out of the town they dived low to drill them with their guns. Women were killed here whose bodies I afterwards saw.

The little fighting planes came down in a line, like flashing, dancing waves on shingle. They burst in spray on the countryside as they merrily dived. Twenty machine-guns working together in line, and the roar of breakers behind them from ten engines. Always they flew nose towards Guernica. For the pilots it must have been like surfing. The terrified people lay face down in ditches, pressed their backs against tree trunks, coiled themselves in holes, shut their eyes and ran across sweet green open meadow. Many were foolish, and fled back before the aerial tide into the village. It was then that the heavy bombing of Guernica began.

It was then that Guernica was smudged out of that rich landscape, the province of Vizcaya, with a heavy fist.

> This vivid and moving description of the bombing of Guernica by planes of Franco's air force — an event which shocked the civilised world — is by a man who was a newspaper correspondent in the Basque country at the time of the raid. The article, slightly abridged, is reproduced by special permission of the editor of the London Mercury.

IT was about 5.15. For two hours and a half flights of between three and twelve aeroplanes, types Heinkel III and Junker 52, bombed Guernica without mercy and with system. They chose their sectors in the town in orderly fashion. Early bombs fell like a circle of stars round the hospital on the road to Bermeo; all the windows were blown in by the divine efflatus, the wounded militaimen were thrown out of their beds, the inner fabric of the building shook and broke.

On the shattered houses, whose carpets and curtains, splintered beams and floors and furniture were knocked into angles and ready for the burning, the planes threw silver flakes. Tubes of two pounds, long as your forearm, glistening silver from their aluminium and electron casing; inside them, as in the beginning of the world in Prometheus' reed, slept fire. Fire in a silver powder, 65 grammes in weight, ready to slip through six holes at the base of the glittering tube. So as the houses were broken to pieces over the people sheathed fire descended from heaven to burn them up.

Every 20 minutes fresh raiders came. And between the explosions and the spurts of flame as the burning metal seeped into curtains and beams, doors and carpets, while a grey pall stood over Guernica supported from below by white pillars where fires were starting, in the pauses of modern battle the population ran about the streets to clear away the doors of smothered refuges, to pull children and other small worthless belongings from houses afire.

There was much groaning in Guernica, much breathless work to dig out wounded people before the next planes came. Twenty minutes was the interval between fire, and the priests spoke to the people to keep them calm. By now something like a spirit of passive resistance had been built up in them. Guernica's face was turning to ashes, everybody's face in Guernica was ash-grey, but terror had reached a condition of submissive stubbornness not seen before Vizcaya.

*

IN the intervals out of the town, but the fear of the fighting plane and separation from their families persuaded many to remain in Guernica. And then the planes returned with their tinsel tubes to shower over Guernica and another part was destroyed, and more were buried in the refugios.

Soon there was little of the town to move about in. The Church of San Juan was burning fiercely, with a huge bomb-hole through its roof and its altar and pulpit rippling fire. Even a few isolated buildings were touched; at the old Parish Church of Andra Mari, in the corner of the square where the sheep had been gathered, the chapel behind the altar was aflame.

As the people not trapped in the refuges moved northwards before the general fire the planes that raided Guernica came very low. It must have been difficult for them to sight their target in the smoke and grit which rose from the spreading campfire below them. They flew at six hundred feet, slowly and steadily shedding their tubes of silver, which settled upon those houses that still stood in pools of intolerable heat; then slipped and dribbled from floor to floor.

Guernica was compact as peat to serve as fuel for the German planes. Nobody now bothered to save relatives or possessions: between bombardments they walked out of Guernica in front of the stifling smoke and sat in bewildered hundreds on the roads to Bermea and Munguia.

Mercifully the fighters had gone. They no longer glanced down to mutilate the population in movement and chase them across the open fields. The people were worn out by noise, heat, and terror; they lay about like dirty bundles of washing, mindless, sprawling, and immobile. There was nothing to save in Guernica but the few old mattresses and pillows, kitchen tables and chairs which they had dragged out of the fire. By seven-thirty that evening fire was eating away the whole of crowded little Guernica but the Casa de Juntas and the houses of the Fascist families.

These, being wealthier than the others, lived in stone mansions apart from the rest of the people: their properties did not catch the infection of the running fire, even when under pressure of the wind it stretched its savage arms to stroke them.

*

AT seven-forty-five the last plane went away. Guernica was finished, and when its people crept back to the town the soft breeze of the flames now blowing on every house, they saw what I saw later that night. In the centre of the town the smaller tongues of fire were turning into a single roar. The motorised police, with Monzon, the Minister of the Interior, stood helpless beyond the plaza, where streets tightened and intertwined to make the heart of our conflagtion. We tried to enter, but the streets were a royal carpet of live coals, blocks of wreckage slithered and crashed from the houses, and from their sides that were still erect the polished heat struck at our cheeks and eyes.

There were people, they said, to be saved there; there were the frameworks of dozen of cars. But nothing could be done, and we put our hands in our pockets and wondered why on earth the world was so mad and warfare become so easy.

Between cigarettes I played with three silver tubes picked up that evening in Gernica. The argent thermite distilled itself slowly from their bases; they came from the German RhS factory in 1936, said their stamp. And over the legend stood a symbol in miniature, the Imperial eagl with scarecrow wings spread.

The devastated streets of Guernica after the Fascist bombers had done their work.

THEY PRAY AS CITY FALLS

As Santander surrenders without bloodshed, Spanish Nationalist women, ringed by war-stained troops, offer prayer of thanksgiving for city's fall before temporary altar.

As you sit beside your fire in comfort, warmth and ease—Spare a thought of pity for the homeless refugees. . . . Fugitives from War—Old people—children—men and wives. Driven from the wreck and ruin—fleeing for their lives.

Driven from their little homes. . . . No food—no hope—no plan; victims of the folly and brutality of Man. . . . Seeking shelter from the death that rains out of the skies; many having seen their loved ones killed before their eyes.

God forgive this wicked world—its madness and its greed—and protect the innocent and those who are in need. . . . Soften now the hearts of men—May War's stark horrors cease—and the New Year bring us wisdom—sanity—and Peace.

Collecting money to aid Spain in France, they carry a sheet through the streets with a placard, "Spain is suffering, help Spain"—with obviously good results.

You Can't Trust These Fascists

STANDING in the white beam of a searchlight, on a tall tower in Berlin, Mussolini roared to over half a million people:—

"To the whole world, which is asking tensely what the result of this meeting will be, war or peace, the Fuehrer and I can answer with a loud voice: Peace."

Someone should then have led him away and told him the cautionary tale of Ananias and Sapphira.

◆ ◆ ◆

HE had just come from a visit to Krupp's colossal armament works in Essen, working at high pressure on the manufacture of materials for war.

Before that he had attended the biggest war manoeuvres ever held in Germany, witnessing the carefully staged triumph of the "Blues" over the "Reds."

His whole journey through Germany—in a bullet-proof train —had been one vast parade of armed men. But, says the Duce, "Our purpose is peace."

◆ ◆ ◆

HE goes on, in his speech, to introduce the whining note peculiar to the Fascist Big Men. He weeps at the cruelty with which their message of love is rejected by people who fail to appreciate Fascism's blessings. He protests at the injustice by which "a people of great military strength can fall a victim to an economic blockade."

"We have seen this defeat threatening us," he says, "when 52 nations gathered at Geneva determined on the criminal economic sanctions against Italy, those sanctions which were carried through in all their harshness . . ."

Harsh and criminal, cruel, nay barbarian, to withhold from the noble, culture-bringing Roman the means by which his armoured battalions could prevail over the calico-clad Abyssinian with his spear, shield and rusty 1878 rifle.

◆ ◆ ◆

BUT, with all respect to His Excellency the Duce, there is a touch of ingratitude in his whine. He seems to have overlooked the fact that, while sanctions were applied (I believe only half-heartedly) by certain Powers after the war had been begun, those same Powers had imposed an embargo hindering Abyssinia from arming for defence during all the months in which Mussolini had been shipping arms and men into Eritrea and Italian Somaliland.

Surely the Duce should give due recognition there to the helping hand of the British and French Governments—the same helping hand which is now extended, clothed in the glove of non-intervention in Spain. And if

"Peace now shouts MUSSOLINI. Abyssinia first, Spain Second; they know the value of Fascist pledges. This is a photograph taken by W. M. Holmes, on the Abyssinian War front.

these remarks seem to Fascist ears to come from a prejudiced source, let me recommend them to consult British diplomatic and active service men then on the spot in Africa, whom I know to have writhed in mental shame and to have openly cursed the Government at home which cleared the way for the barbarian.

◆ ◆ ◆

THE bitter fruit of the policy of 1935 is now ripened in Berlin, where the war lords howl from the midst of a forest of bayonets: "We bring peace." Dare you take the word of a Fascist?

I am reminded of a moment in the Abyssinian War. We had been encamped for three weeks at Kworem, awaiting the moment when the Emperor would go into the line, to lead his armies to stem the Italian advance from the north.

During those three weeks we had learned how Fascism wages war. Every day, half an hour before dawn, we had struck tents and taken cover. And every day, from dawn to sunset, Italian airplanes had circled overhead, raining bombs, machine-gunning and spraying corrosive gas.

Vittorio Mussolini, the Duce's son, had won himself the distinction of wiping out the British Red Cross camp (about which the British Government never made protest). The great plains, the undulating bush, the river valleys which we overlooked from the ridge where the Emperor and his staff held their position were strewn with rotting corpses and carcasses. Columns of smoke

rising daily told of the fate of village after village. The tilled land, under the tropical sun, returned into wilderness. Herds were blotted out by bombs or perished, driven mad by the devilish rain of burning gas from the sky.

The hinterland, through which we were ultimately to retreat, was being turned into a desert.

Then, one morning, when I took my usual ride at daybreak over the ridge to the cave where the Emperor's radio was hidden, the operator handed me a telegram from a colleague in Addis Ababa who was then my only link with the world. It said:—

"London reports Italian agreement cease further air bombardment pending negotiations. Please report immediately any bombardments."

◆ ◆ ◆

IT was a cloudless dawn. Thirty miles north, the high red ridge of Amba Alagi stood out against a perfect sky, the steel-blue waters of Lake Ashangi between. That was where the Italians were. And

━━━ ┈ ┈ ┈ ━━━

by
W. M. HOLMES

━━━ ┈ ┈ ┈ ━━━

over that ridge, from Makalle beyond, we were accustomed to watch the squadrons of Capronis and Savoias come wheeling and circling over our ridge, seeking out our hiding-places.

I showed the telegram to the little group of Abyssinian officers and secretaries already gathered on the rocky platform where stood the anti-aircraft gun which the Emperor himself operated in every raid. They smiled specti-

cally and all instinctively turned their eyes north, with ears alert for the distant drone.

But, strangely enough, that whole day passed in peace, with never a plane in the cloudless sky. In our camp at night we discussed the question; was something happening in Europe? But at dawn we took no risks. Tents were struck, fires extinguished, horses and mules scattered over the hillsides.

We made our way to the radio cave. No telegram. And again no aeroplane. Had the Italians agreed? Perhaps, but the Abyssinians' instinct was sound. Next morning the usual precautions were taken. And this time they were justified. Before I had reached the end of my usual ride to the cave, the warning bugles were sounding.

The bombers were coming over the northern ridge. That day we got a heavier dose than usual—bombs, machine-gunning and gas—in order that full advantage might be reaped by the enemy from any unawareness following the two days' holiday.

And the Abyssinians said, "The Fascists got their friends to send that story, so that they should catch us. You cannot believe them. They will never stop, for they mean to destroy us."

◆ ◆ ◆

IN this, we now know, the Abyssinians showed their wisdom—far greater wisdom than that of people here in England and in France who are beguiled by the idea that an understanding with Fascism is a possible way to peace.

There can be no understanding between Fascism and democracy. Therefore no way of peace lies in that direction. And we can put no faith in a Government which, like our present one, has aided the Fascist dictators in their lying and aggression.

Ambulance men remove the body of a victim after Fascists had shelled Madrid.

In September

Coming, in September, through the thin streets,
I thought back to another year I knew,
Autumn, lifting potatoes and stacking peats
On Mull, while the Atlantic's murky blue
Swung sluggishly in past Jura, and the hills
Were brown lions, crouched to meet the autumn gales.

In the hard rain and the rip of thunder,
I remembered the haze coming in from the sea
And the clatter of Gaelic voices by the breakwater
Or in the fields as the reapers took their tea ;
I remembered the cast foal lying where it died,
Which we buried, one evening, above high-tide ;

And the three rams that smashed the fank-gate,
Running loose for five days on the moor
Before we could catch them—far too late
To prevent an early lambing the next year.
But these seemed out of place beside the chip-shop
And the cockney voices grumbling in the pub.

In September, I saw the drab newsposters
Telling of wars, in Spain and in the East,
And wished I'd stayed on Mull, their gestures
Frightened me and made me feel the unwanted guest.
The burden on the house who having taken salt
Could never be ejected, however grave his fault.

In September, we lit the fire and talked together,
Discussing the trivialities of a spent day
And what we would eat. I forgot the weather
And the dull streets and the sun on Islay,
And all my fear. I lost my carefully-kept count
Of the ticks to death, and, in September, was content.
RUTHVEN TODD

Red Star Over China. By Edgar Snow
Gollancz. 18s.

From 1930 till last February a civil war raged in China which for ferocity, destruction of human life and scale of operations easily eclipsed the war in Spain. Of the war itself and of the Chinese Communists who were the cause of it the newspaper public in this country knew next to nothing. The demand for such news was small. The supply was smaller still. The cordon round the Soviet areas was so impassable that, except for one or two missionaries caught up behind the lines and later escaped or released, no foreigner could report at first hand on ' Red China'. In June last year a young American journalist seized an exceptional chance of slipping through the barrier and of spending several months in the Soviet Republic on the Shensi-Kansu borderlands.

After getting himself smuggled across the line (there is a touch of the *Thirty-Nine Steps* in his story of how he was told to stop at an inn ' to await the visit of a man who would call himself Wang') Mr. Snow found himself in what, when compared with conditions elsewhere in China, might be called a new world. His description in *Red Star Over China* of what he saw there may almost be classed as a historic document even though the vein in which it is written is frankly journalistic.

To what extent Mr. Snow's spectacles are tinted (he worked, by the way, for the *Daily Herald*) it is not very easy to judge. If he has a political bias he conceals it fairly effectually, and there seems no good reason against taking at face value what he says about the whole-heartedness and cheery enthusiasm of the Chinese Communists as a whole (who combine stern schooling in Marxism with folk-dancing, dramatics and basket-ball) or about the Soviets' really remarkable accomplishments—compared, that is, with the standards of Nationalist China—in organisation, education and above all in the elimination of 'squeeze'.

But the questions in most English readers' minds will be of a more general order. What *is* Chinese Communism ? Is it Communism at all ? What has it to do with Russia ? Where does it count in the present Far Eastern conflict ? To give Mr. Snow's replies in the fewest possible words, Communism in China is the real thing at the top ; at the bottom, among the masses, it is just a happy solution of the secular struggle between peasant and landlord. Russia is the spiritual home of the leaders (' Lenin is almost worshipped '), but in China the practice of Communism has taken a peculiar Chinese shape containing, as the author observes, an admixture of private capitalism. In illustration of this he states that the rule has been to expropriate absentee landlords, but that resident landlords, in some Soviet areas at least, have been left in possession of their properties. (Mr. Snow is writing of the conditions which he saw in the North-West ; in the early days, before the Great Trek from the South, such accounts as we had spoke of horrible massacres of the ' Gentry '). As to the question of Russian backing, Mr. Snow the gulf between Communist and Nationalist for the present, been bridged, the Communists having renounced their plans for a National Soviet State in favour of the ' united front'. This ' remarriage' of the two great forces in China—which had become divorced in 1927 and remained implacable enemies until a few months ago—gives, as *Red Star Over China* will show, the firmest basis for optimism to China and her friends in her present critical plight.

SADDEST GIRL IN LONDON

Should have been married to-day, but her fiance is missing in Spain . . . Lore Lons.

HER WEDDING DAY, BUT HER FIANCE IS MISSING, FIGHTING IN SPAIN

BY A SPECIAL CORRESPONDENT

SADDEST girl in London to-day is twenty-four-year-old Lore Lons. It is her wedding day . . . but her trousseau, collected for the past year from Europe's most fashionable cities, lies locked in a large brown trunk.

There will be no wedding bells for Lore after all. Her fiance, El Conde de Sierragorda, who is related to ex-King Alfonso of Spain, has not been heard of for six months. Lore, graceful, 6ft. tall Viennese dancer, is heartbroken.

" I cannot understand what has happened to him," she told me yesterday.

" We met in London last year, fell deeply in love and decided to get married on September 20." She turned away to hide her eyes, moist with sorrow, and then went on:

"Hard to Keep Smiling"

" He was so patriotic, and returned to Spain to fight in the war. We wrote to each other every day at first, but the last time I heard from him was six months ago. I just had a postcard from San Sebastian.

" Since we first met I have been dancing in Paris, Vienna and New York. I have spent all my money on my trousseau. I shall never wear it now . . . it is too much a reminder of what might have been.

" I must go now," she said. " It is hard to keep smiling, wondering where someone is, if he is dead, when inside my heart feels as though it is breaking."

Spanish refugees from Malaga, at Madrid

They Died For Liberty: Their Fight Goes On

THREE more men, young, courageous, ready to make any sacrifice for the cause in which they believed, have died fighting democracy's battle with the British Battalion of the Spanish People's Army.

Their names, which will be remembered long after Fascism has been defeated in Spain, are:—

HAROLD FRY, of Edinburgh, Battalion Commander.

ERIC WHALLEY, of Mansfield, Battalion Political Commissar.

EDWARD BURKE, of London, one of the first members of the International Brigade.

Fry and Whalley were killed while leading the battalion into action near Saragossa on October 13. Burke was fatally wounded much earlier during the critical fighting at Jarama, outside Madrid, but news of his death has only just been finally confirmed.

To these men and others like them the Labour and democratic movement of Great Britain owes a debt that can be acknowledged only by selfless, unceasing struggle to achieve the objects for which they gave their lives. It is a debt that must be paid by every individual member of a great movement—and it can be paid by struggle alone.

Behind that bundle on the Nantao station platform lie the mortal remains of a Chinese man. Widowed in the Japanese raid, the woman stares miserably at her husband's body. Fatherless, but not understanding either the personal tragedy nor the war horror, the baby finds something to play with amid the scene of death and devastation

DEFIED FASCISTS

HAROLD FRY was a fine leader and a fine man. He was wounded, captured, faced death with a shrug of contempt for those who sentenced him, but was rescued and brought back to the peace of Britain.

Yet within two months he had returned once more to the perils of the fighting line in Spain. He died at the head of the battalion he was leading. Of him the battalion newspaper, Volunteer for Liberty, said: "His death has robbed the battalion of an excellent military commander, and of a comrade whose whole life had been devoted to the anti-Fascist struggle."

Arm Broken

A member of the Communist Party since 1933, and of his trade union, the National Boot and Shoe Operatives, he first went to Spain in December, 1936. His military qualities and his ability to lead and inspire resulted in his rapid promotion to the post of lieutenant of the machine Gun Company of the British Battalion.

Fry was one of the 28 men who were captured on February 28 this

⋆ A tribute from Harry Pollitt, leader of the Communist Party:
"The loss of Comrades Harold Fry and Eric Whalley is indeed a heavy blow to the Communist Party. We have lost two of the finest comrades we ever had, comrades who would have developed into great leaders of our Party in Britain.

"We mourn their loss, but in our future work we will try to prove worthy of their selfless sacrifice and devotion to the working-class struggle against Fascism." ⋆

year at Jarama by Moors, who advanced singing the International and giving the Red Front Salute, thus creating the impression that they were joining the Government side.

Fry's arm had been shattered, but this is what Donald Renton, of Edinburgh, one of the captured men, writes of him:—

"His broken arm was swinging, and the agonising pain brought beads of sweat to his brow, but even then his quiet words of encouragement helped guarantee us against panic.

Their Pledge

"Forced to watch the cold-blooded murder of Phil Elms and Johnnie Stevens, later the execution of his friend Ted Dickenson, he nevertheless maintained that demeanour which during our period of training and at the front had made him more than simply our military commander.

"Even the Moors who bound his shattered arm in telegraph wire and beat him up could not make him forego his attitude of quiet contempt towards them. . . .

"When the Fascist military tribunal imposed the death sentence on him, his shrug of the shoulders was an eloquent testimony to the fact that he could die as Dickenson had died, with fist clenched and a defiant 'Salud!'"

The death sentences on Fry and 23 others were never carried out. They were exchanged for other prisoners and they returned to England to receive a great welcome at the Congress of the Communist Party in Battersea Town

Hall. But two months later Fry was back in Spain.

"We salute the courage of his wife," says Renton, "for she it was who proudly supported his desire to return to Spain.

"We pledge ourselves to his children to win for them that freedom for which their father so nobly died."

"VICTORY WILL BE SPEEDY"

Eric Whalley was only 23 years old, but he had crammed many years of political experience into a short life.

Energetic, eloquent, clear headed, he was one of the leaders of the working-class movement in Nottinghamshire and Derbyshire, and he had been in that movement since he left school. From Spain he wrote:—

"The more I see of Spain and the Spanish the more convinced I am that Franco's cause is lost. Spain will be won for democracy. The victory can be speedier and cost less if the British Labour movement will do something."

He became battalion commissar at the same time as Harold Fry

ERIC WHALLEY

was made commander, and the two died together at the head of an attack.

For some years Whalley belonged to the Independent Labour Party, working in that party for unity—"Unity in Britain must be established," despite the Labour chiefs," he wrote. "Get it locally —then unity will be here."

Cost His Job

Increasingly disappointed with the policy of the I.L.P., he left the party some three years ago and joined the Communist Party, where he worked with untiring determination.

When his convictions cost him his job he threw himself into the Unemployed Workers' Movement, helping to organise demonstrations and leading national and county hunger marches. Later he worked to ensure the success of the new united Nottinghamshire Miners' Union.

As long ago as last autumn he was impatient to go to Spain, and when this at last proved possible he quickly proved his great value to the British Battalion and the Spanish People's Army.

"He will be mourned," says the Volunteer for Liberty, "not only by comrades in the British Battalion, but also by the Notts and Derby workers, who knew him as an active and intelligent revolutionary worker."

ONE OF THE FIRST

When Fascism attacked the Spanish People's Government, Edward Burke learned that men were needed to aid the hastily formed militia. His response was quick and enthusiastic; he was one of the first to take his place in the group that later became the British Battalion of the International Brigade.

A professional actor of ability, he did much work for the Left Theatre, in addition to helping to build the Communist Party branch in North Kensington. When fighting broke out in Spain, Burke was a temporary member of the DAILY WORKER staff, and this work he left to go to Spain. Wounded as a machine-gunner, he died in the Federal Hospital at Madrid.

"In his opinion," a fellow-actor wrote to the DAILY WORKER, "the Communist Party was the Party which fought for the right of men and women to live, move and have their being in an ordered fashion, free from the shadow of unemployment and war, free to develop in leisure and security the richness of a common inheritance of culture...

"For this belief, in the fullness of his youth, he has laid down his life. I, who knew him, feel that the gift will not be in vain; and if what he stood for was worth his death, then it is worth the fight of we who are left and living."

THIS MIGHT HAPPEN HERE!
Death Rains Down on Shanghai

September 1937.

Have you ever thought what London would look like if, overnight, modern war 'planes, with modern bombs, came over and ravaged the city? These pathetic pictures from the Sino-Japanese war-zone show you how Shanghai is facing up to the most dreadful problem of civilisation. Although the streets are littered with war dead, Miss China, as you see in the picture on the right, has to go about her daily business. In the picture above is all that is left of the railway station at Nantao, one of the most congested districts of Shanghai. Between the metals in the foreground is the body of a child sacrificed to war. And, huddled on the far platform are two babes, who, by a miracle, escaped in the bombardment. Scattered around are the bodies of people who, a few moments before, were waiting for a train which would have borne them away from the peril of Shanghai.

Though the streets are littered with the dying and dead, Shanghai's daily life must go on. This picture was taken by a British Paramount News cameraman.

THESE RESISTED . . .
Bodies of Chinese soldiers mown down by Japanese machine-guns in the streets of Tien-Tsin, as they sought to prevent the Japanese advance.

CHINA: THREE WEEKS PUTS THE CLOCK BACK YEARS

. . . OTHERS FLED
Japanese soldiers search the ruined houses of a Chinese town which has been bombarded, in case any Chinese may have been left behind. Few Chinese soldiers have ever seen the invader at such close quarters. They are either killed at long range or else escape before the invaders come.

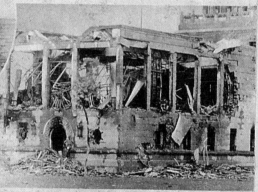

THREE WEEKS MADE THIS INTO THIS →
Above, the Civic Centre at Kiangwan—seat of municipal government for Greater Shanghai, home of a rare collection of Chinese books and works of art—shelled to bits by the Japanese.

SIDE by side with the destruction of life in China there is going on destruction of the means of saving life. In a few weeks buildings that took years to construct, and will take years to rebuild, have been destroyed. The magnificent Civic Centre Library at Kiangwan, shown in ruins on this page, is only one example out of hundreds. Here was housed the Municipal Government of Greater Shanghai—it was their County Hall. Here also were stored rare volumes and relics covering centuries of Chinese history. Japanese artillery and naval guns shelled the centre for three weeks, blowing it to pieces. Hospitals and schools — the attempts made by the still-young Chinese Republic to spread health and knowledge among its millions—have met with the same fate. Someone, some day, when the war which has never been officially begun, is ended, will have to start again from the beginning.

Chinese troops in Shanghai area wearing gas-masks. Japs deny use of gas, say Chinese wear masks for propaganda.

Chinese troops retreat across North Chinese river (name of river deleted in censored message).

Good-bye to all that—coffins prepared for victims of air-bombing carried out over the French Concession.

Cheering them off. Japanese planes set off with a load of death for mothers and children still working and playing happily miles away. Japanese high officer cheers them on.

Smoke rises from Shanghai over the U.S. warship "Augusta." Chinese aircraft are circling overhead. The American ship was hit in the confusion.

Another railway station, that of Shanghai South. It was crowded with Chinese refugees when the Japanese 'planes came over. They managed to kill 200, including many women and babies. 400 were wounded.

After the bombing—a Chinese mother left in the street. She has a baby and a roll of matting. That is all. She was lucky.

"ONLY HORS D'OEUVRE" say the Japanese..

PERHAPS the bottom level of human brutality was reached a few days ago when a Japanese spokesman described the killing from the air of thousands of Chinese men, women and children as "only an hors d'oeuvre" of what was to follow.

One or two "W.I." readers have written to complain of war pictures from China printed in these pages. "W.I." does not print war-horror pictures to horrify or affright. It prints them because these things are happening in the world to-day. If they had happened 30 years ago there would have been such an outcry throughout Europe that they would long ago have stopped. It may be impossible for ordinary people to stop such things to-day, but no good can ever come of our pretending they do not go on. It is better to see and to feel pity and regret and the wish for determined action, rather than not to see at all.

Left, just another few Chinese dead . . . Chinese Boy Scouts and Red Cross workers attending dead and wounded outside Nantao South railway station. Here 20 civilians (mostly women and children) were destroyed. Below, homeless crowds besiege a soup-kitchen.

—AND THE CHINESE KNOW WHERE THE PROFITS COME FROM

Good news for armament shareholders means bad news for someone. At the best it's only the taxpayer's pocket that's hit. At the worst it's the peaceful citizen and his wife—in China or in Spain.

Shot up in the lunch-hour—harmless people of Shanghai, machine-gunned and bombed from the air —and then in some cases run over by lorries during the confusion.

← **WHAT JAPAN SEES** Propaganda picture taken from a Japanese publication, was captioned, "a friendly Japanese army officer shares his sweets from back home with a group of delighted Chinese youngsters behind the lines."

WHAT CHINA SEES → Right, after a bombardment. Chinese man is now so familiar with death and destruction he holds corpse of killed child as casually as if it were a basket. While scenes such as this are common, propaganda pictures of sweet-sharers cannot mean much outside Japan.

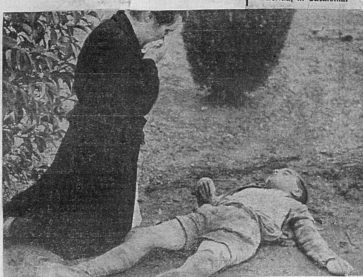

Scenes after the bombing of Lerida. All Saints' Day 1937. A school was one of the buildings bombed — 82 children were killed....

Pictures such as the above were inserted in Hollywood papers. Underneath was wording taken from Vittorio's book about his flying exploits in Ethiopia. . . . "War for us has been a sport." Below, further extracts from young Mussolini's book, printed as advertisements and paid for often by Hollywood stars, helped to drive him out.

WHY MUSSOLINI'S SON LEFT HOLLYWOOD IN A HURRY

MOST people look on Hollywood as the world's playground. Few believe that the people who make up the film industry have any other interests than picture making and extravagant enjoyment. The visit of Vittorio Mussolini throws a new light on this world-famous corner of the globe. When one remembers that Hollywood is easily the most hospitable place in the world, the reception given to Musso's son is doubly significant. In this country little has been said as to why Vittorio Mussolini left Hollywood after a short stay. His departure has been described as a mystery. The reason young Mussolini left Hollywood is simply that Hollywood—the stars and the working community—did not want him to stay.

Joan Crawford threatened to "walk off the set" if the man who boasted of bombing helpless Abyssinians showed his face on it.

TODAY—

Benito Mussolini confers with Hitler in Berlin . . .

TOMORROW—

Vittorio Mussolini arrives in Hollywood

He asked for—and received—the privilege of being the first fascist aviator to bomb helpless Ethiopians.

Anyone has the right to be in America, but we submit that his presence here is not an occasion for celebrations or social fetes. Those who welcome him are opening their arms to a friend of Hitler and an enemy of democracy.

"War for us has been a sport . . ."

"We received the order to repeat the bombardment. It was most diverting . . . It may be I had expected too much. I had anticipated terrific explosions such as in the American films whereas here the huts of the Ethiopians, made as they are of clay and brushwood, do not offer the bomber any satisfaction . . .

"WAR CERTAINLY EDUCATES. I RECOMMEND IT TO EVERYBODY . . . WAR FOR US HAS BEEN A SPORT, THE MOST BEAUTIFUL AND COMPLETE OF ALL SPORTS."

Excerpts from
"VOLI SULLE AMBE"
(Wings over Ambe)
Pub. in Florence, Italy
By VITTORIO MUSSOLINI
1936

And so young Vittorio Mussolini left Hollywood in a hurry refusing to answer queries as to whether his proposed operating film-producing company had been dissolved.

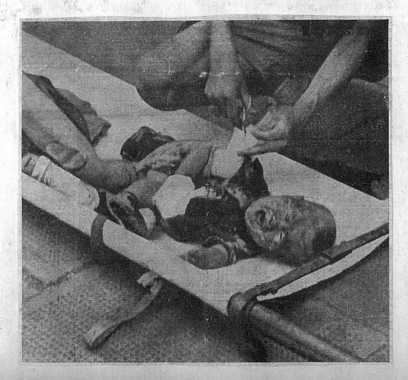

First picture to reach this country after the fall of Shanghai. It shows Chinese children begging for bread outside the French Concession when the Japanese had seized the area in which their homes were situated.—*Paramount News-Reel.*

October 1937.

BRITISH MEDICAL SUPPLIES FOR CHINA

CHINESE wounded are suffering far more than they need — through the terrible shortage of medical supplies. In this country a China Campaign Committee is hard at work raising money to buy badly-needed drugs, serums, and surgical necessities. The first consignment is seen leaving London docks. Further regular supplies will be sent off as fast as they can be got and paid for. Addressed to Nanking's Minister of Health, they will be distributed, as needed.

The Hope

of China

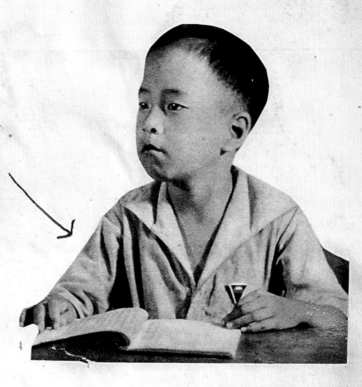

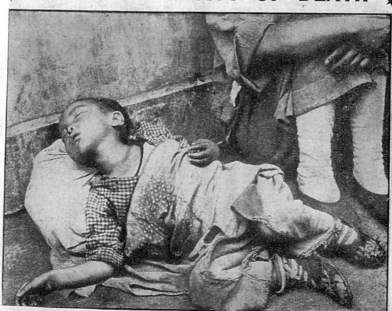

ASLEEP IN A CITY OF DEATH

Sleep gives a little Shanghai waif brief but blessed respite from the horror and torment of war as, pillowed on a bundle of rags, she slumbers, exhausted, on the pavement.

CHINA'S BRAVE

November 1937.

This is LIN-JUNG retrieving the mutilated body of a little girl from a bombed area. . . .

BOY SCOUTS

do their good deeds

Lin Jung, Chinese Boy Scout, wrote this letter from Wulhang, China, to a troop in Shirley, Surrey, appealing for help!

San Chu Middle School,
Wulhang, China.

Dear Brother Scouts,

I am sending you this letter because we are all Boy Scouts, wearing the same Baden-Powell Uniform, saluting with three fingers, and having exactly the same heart of serving mankind.

I am twelve years old and a member of the 2709 patrol of the 3 group of the 5 troop of Chinese Boy Scouts.

My name is spelled Lim Jung in English.

These are times of adventure and danger for B-P Scouts. The air raids have caused the killing and wounding of many thousands of poor helpless people.

After these raids, our older comrades go to the scene of the bombing with stretchers and First Aid Kits, and have good chances to carry out the second oath of our promise—" To help other people at all time."

All of us help in some way or another, visiting the hospitals, with comforts for the wounded, and writing letters for them.

I am trying to do my duty by helping the suffering and the homeless, and I am also trying to serve the Red Cross by sending this letter to you.

Asking you to do a good turn by sending money or medicines to Central China.

My Chinese brother Scouts and I have together written this letter. We all should be happy to have a reply from you and to know about the Scout work in your district.

Please help the Red Cross if you can. They need much money

Yours in scouting,
LIN JUNG.

Hero of China today. One of Shanghai's defenders waits with hand-grenade for a Japanese advance.

ORKER   Wednesday, November 3, 1937

Flaming Shanghai: the little dwellings of the working people burning after Japanese bombardment.

WAR!

REMEMBRANCE DAY. 1937

Nineteen years ago they came back to find that the promise of a land fit for heroes was a fraud. And scenes such as this, taken by Daily Worker photographer at Caledonian Market, London, this week, are still an everyday disgrace to our streets.

China

Spain

Chiang's Son Is Marching To Join Chu-teh

SHANGHAI, Tuesday.

INFORMATION has been received here that Chiang Ching-kuo, son of General Chiang Kai-shek, has arrived at Lanchow, Kansu Province in North-West China, at the head of a 100,000 strong column of crack Mongol troops, en route to join the famous Communist leader Chuteh and his Eighth Route Army in Shansi.

Chiang Ching-kuo is one of the strongest supporters of Chinese unity and last year strongly criticised his father for his failure to unite with the Communist Party and the Chinese Soviet Government against Japan.

There are thus now four Communist-led Armies operating under the new Chinese supreme military council. Others are the 4th Army, operating in Fukien, and the 10th, fighting in Anhwei province.

On the military council, alongside Chiang Kai-shek, sit three representatives of the Communist Party, including Mao Tse-tung.

This reorganised council is more and more adopting the military strategy and tactics advocated by the Communists as the only possible to defeat the Japanese invaders and win the war.

HANKOW DEFENCE

Meanwhile, it is learned from Hankow that while the Japanese advance in four columns on the

city, severely harassed by Chinese units operating in their rear, the city is adopting new measures for its defence against air attacks.

A big part in this defence, say these reports, should be played by the large number—more than a hundred — military planes received from Britain as well as anti-aircraft guns.

The international character of the defence of Hankow is further emphasised by the presence of American instructors there who are busy instructing Chinese pilots.

"WE SHALL FIGHT ON UNTIL VICTORY" SAYS CHINA'S COMMUNIST LEADER

(From Our Correspondent)

HANKOW, Sunday.

"OUR resistance is of revolutionary significance. We are supporting the supreme leadership of Chiang Kai-shek. The struggle will be carried on until the final victory is attained. There is no ground whatsoever for pessimism."

So declared Mao Tse-tung, former president of the Chinese Soviet Republic, now Governor of the Special Administrative Areas in China, in a special interview with a correspondent of the newspaper Takungpao, who has just returned from a visit to the former Soviet areas.

MAO TSE-TUNG

"Although the campaign of resistance has suffered certain reverses," Mao said, "these failures help us to draw important conclusions.

"The whole country now recognises our weak spots, spots which have led to individual defeats.

"In the future, therefore, we must undertake decisive counter-attacks, improve the quality of the army, develop the political consciousness of our fighters and draw attention to the independent partisan movement arising everywhere.

"The Japanese," he continued, "have up to the present shipped an army numbering 200,000 men to the North of China. While they penetrate deeper and deeper into the country the rear of their troops remains exposed all the time. This gives us a unique opportunity for crippling and driving out the enemy.

"We are straining all our efforts in order to strengthen the unity of the country for victory in the struggle to preserve the Chinese people.

"At present there is a lot of talk about defeat, but the entire people and the leaders are persistently organising resistance. There is no ground for pessimism whatsoever. We follow one path—the path of struggle and determined resistance.

"Our final victory is not in doubt."

GENERAL AND MADAME CHIANG KAI-SHEK
whose noble work in rousing their countrymen to repel the Japanese invaders has called forth world-wide admiration.

November 1938.

BLOODY, MANGLED REMNANTS OF HUMANITY, PRODUCTS OF A JAPANESE AIR RAID, ARE HEAPED IN THE STREETS OF SHANGHAI. THIS APPALLING PICTURE, TAKEN BY A PARAMOUNT CAMERAMAN, IS FROM THE NEWS REEL WHICH HAS HELPED TO AROUSE PUBLIC DEMAND FOR ACTION TO STOP THE SLAUGHTER IN CHINA. BOYCOTT THE BUTCHERS OF WOMEN AND CHILDREN!

December 1938.

ONE OF JAPAN'S VICTIMS

A Chinese mother, despair on her face, rests by the wayside in Shanghai with a child in her arms, after a Japanese bombing raid that destroyed her home.

Hollywood Aids Spain

December 1937

GIVING HIS BLOOD

Francis Lederer is buying Christmas stamps from Edith Fellows on the set of "Little Miss Roughneck," her first Columbia starring picture. The stamps are issued by the Motion Picture Artists Committee as part of the Christmas drive, sponsored by many famous stars, to aid the children of democratic Spain.

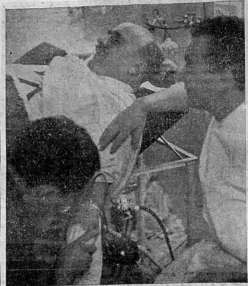

Professor J. B. S. HALDANE undergoing a blood transfusion operation during his recent visit to Spain.

Paul Robeson and his wife photographed during their recent visit to Barcelona.

BEHIND THE LINES

Schoolgirls behind the Spanish lines still carry on with their education despite Franco's bombers.

FASCIST BOMBS THROUGH EYES OF CHILDREN

Colonia escolar madrileña "Carmen Rojo" (Carlet)

WE have printed in past issues of the DAILY WORKER actual photographs showing the slaughter of children by air bombs in Spain and China.

Terrible as those photographs were, they reveal less of the ghastly effects of Fascist war methods on children than do the drawings we reproduce today.

Specially sent to the DAILY WORKER by William Rust, now in Barcelona, they are the work of schoolchildren who have suffered air bombardment in Republican Spain.

No. 1.—Emilio Blanco (age 14) shows bombs falling in the shape of Hitler and Mussolini heads, destroying school and hospital.

No. 2.—F. Rodriquez (age 13) shows Fascists bombing an ambulance column, with Government planes counter-attacking.

No. 3.—An anonymous child artist draws a little boy who says, while bombs crash, "Mummy, I'm hungry."

December 1937.

Spanish child refugees salute the Soviet Union as they arrive at Leningrad on the steamer Felix Dzherzhinsky.

THIS IS FASCISM!

These pictures show vividly the effects on peaceful Chinese people of the Japanese imperialist war of aggression. Above is a typical crowd of refugees awaiting some means of escape from the terror from the skies. Below, the ghastly result of a visit from the Japanese bombers, photographed shortly after a raid.

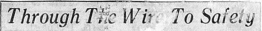

Major-General Telfer-Smollett (right) helping an old Chinese woman through the barbed wire into the safety of the British defence lines as the Japanese troops advance.

RED FLAG OVER CHINA
Chinese Communist soldiers such as are now fighting for the Nanking Government against the Japanese. Behind them is a red flag bearing the Star and the Hammer and Sickle, and an inscription in Chinese

MURDER—BY BRITISH CONSENT

FROM just after noon on Wednesday until midnight and on and on into the young hours of yesterday morning, emergency first aid squads were digging in Barcelona streets.

Twenty feet deep in broken stone, dusty rubble, twisted steel they dug, bringing, one by one, from their terrible grave the bodies of 300 men, women and young children, mangled beyond recognition.

From just after noon on Wednesday until midnight and on into yesterday, and still on while you are reading this, nurses, doctors in Barcelona hospitals are tending 1,600 men, women and children, injured with those who died.

For, within ninety seconds on Wednesday, six Italian Savoia bombing planes from the Fascist air base in Majorca, roaring high over Barcelona, dropped 11 500-pound high explosive bombs on the city.

Were they after some military objective? They were not. All but two of the bombs dropped in residential quarters of the city, of a city whose population is swollen with refugees from the Basque country from Madrid, from other towns and villages of the front line.

The object was sheer terror, plain frightfulness. Four hundred dead, 1,200 wounded. In ninety seconds.

Unable to stand up to the new People's Army of the Spanish Republic, Franco takes his revenge, his revenge for Teruel, on the helpless women and children in the rear, on the unarmed, the undefended, the little ones. That he should do so is no surprise. There was Badajoz, Guernica, Durango.

But Franco's blood guilt is shared by others. The bombers were new Italian Savoias. The peace policy of the gentlemen in Whitehall, of Chamberlain, Eden, the policy of "non-intervention" did not stop them any more than it has stopped the shells which rain on Madrid, the bombs "made in Germany" that shattered Guernica.

That is how "non-intervention" works, that is the "peace" policy of Messrs. Chamberlain and Eden, whose blood guilt is equal with Franco and Mussolini.

Three hundred defenceless men, women and children killed in 90 seconds, 1,200 maimed. That is the meaning of "non-intervention."

The Spanish War

"DETERMINATION" IN MADRID

YORKSHIRE M.P.'s VIEW OF THE STRUGGLE

Mr. Dobbie's Statement on Behalf of Labour Visitors

Mr. William Dobbie, Labour M.P. for Rotherham, and a former Lord Mayor of York, one of the seven British Labour M.P.s who are visiting Madrid, has made a brief statement to the foreign Press, on behalf of the whole party, says the British United Press.

Mr. Dobbie, praising the determination and confidence of the Spanish Government and people, remarked on the improving organisation, and the "handicap" of non-intervention.

MADRID, Thursday.

"We have been able to appreciate the great handicaps under which the Spanish Government has been, and is, labouring, because of the non-intervention agreement," said Mr. Dobbie.

"We have been impressed by the general attitude of Barcelona, Valencia and Madrid, which seems to us to represent a feeling of quiet confidence in the final result of the war.

"There is an air of definite determination to see the struggle through to the end, which, to the people, is victory for the Government.

"Deeply Impressed"

"We have been deeply impressed by what we have seen in the way of organisation, which is obviously improving day by day, indicating the spirit in which the people and the Government are meeting their difficulties.

"We can assure the Spanish people in return that it is with renewed conviction that we shall endeavour to aid in every way to secure for the Spanish Government, democratically elected, its legal rights under international law."

Speaking of Teruel, Mr. Dobbie said the heroism of the army typified the people's spirit, and that with that spirit victory was bound to come.

The Labour M.P.s would answer no questions, and of their departure they would only say that it would be "later."

The party consists of Lieut.-Commander R. H. Fletcher, Major J. Milner (Leeds, S.E.), and Messrs. J. Henderson, William Whiteley, J. J. Davidson, J. Griffiths, and Mr. Dobbie.

Madrid Shelled

While they were touring Madrid yesterday afternoon the city was heavily shelled for an hour and a half.

Shells arrived at the rate of three a minute, falling in the central districts at a time when many people were out shopping or walking.

The streets emptied rapidly, except for the food queues. Those waiting in the queues held on grimly, preferring to risk death rather than lose their places.

The M.P.s, who had already visited Barcelona, Valencia and Teruel, visited the Casa de Campo, the park on the western outskirts, which was a battlefield for months, the western suburb of Carabanchel, and other devastated areas.

They also visited some of the Madrid hospitals, went to one of the theatres, and dined with General Miaja and his staff at the War Office.—British United Press.

AIR RAID AFTERMATH in Barcelona—Rescue workers removing débris during a search for victims after a building had been hit by a bomb.

LETTERS FROM SOMEWHERE IN SPAIN

Being extracts from only a very few of the hundreds written by members of the International Brigade

January 1938.

DEAR Brother and Fellow Members, —Please accept my sincere thanks for the gift of cigarettes that I have received, I can assure you they were very welcome. I was very pleased to learn of the deep interest being shown by our members in the fight of the Spanish people and the International Brigade.

Whilst the mad dogs of Fascism have been beating their heads against the iron gates of Madrid in vain, our leaders have not been idle. Today the streets of Republican Spain ring to the tramp of the new People's Army. The sun glistens on the bayonets of our well-trained troops marching to the front to fight for world democracy.

It is a very inspiring sight to see them march singing, happy in the knowledge that they are fighting for freedom. There are many in Britain who might not understand the significance of the new People's Army, but to us who went into action in the early days of February ill-armed, ill-clothed and with very little training, we grasp the meaning of the new forces that have been created from the workers and peasants in Spain.

Our action in Spain in the early days of February is now known in Britain.

No matter what the sacrifice of the battalion, the honour of the British Labour movement had been saved. With their life's blood our comrades rubbed out the stain on the British Labour movement that had agreed to "Neutrality" and would not let us have arms to defend the peace of the world.

If there is one lesson that can be drawn from Spain, it is that unity of the whole forces of the working-class can stop Fascism.

The slogan of Spain has changed from " No Passaran " to Passaremos (we shall pass). Arms from Britain would enable us to pass with the least possible loss of life. Let us carry on the struggle with even greater intensity.

—*From a letter written by B. GOLDMAN to A. R. CARTER, London District Secretary of the Amalgamated Union of Upholsterers and to members of that union.*

NEWS FROM HOME HELPS US

THANKS for sending Comrade Rust out here.

It is amazing how quickly he has picked up the loose ends. We have been here for seven weeks and are only just beginning to see what needs doing.

Bill arrived at the battalion on November 28, and addressed us in the afternoon, and his statement on the political situation in Spain and at home and abroad was listened to with great interest the fact is that the boys are hungry for news of any kind. **News from home helps to keep up their morale considerably. The party groups should stimulate regular correspondence with all comrades.**

At a special parade with all the Brigade Staff present, the new Banner was presented to the British Battalion, after a speech by Bill, telling us that the Banner was a gift from the British people, and expressing the belief that the new British Battalion would more than maintain the glorious traditions associated with its name.

We presented the flag to General Copic, who in turn presented it to Sam Wild, the standard bearer. Frankly, the Guard of Honour was excellent, thanks to another Lancashire lad, Comrade Fletcher.

All the Lancashire lads pledged themselves to do all in their power to lift up to the highest level the fighting efficiency of the British Battalion.

In any case, we can look forward to the British Battalion in the future upholding its glorious traditions with the active assistance of the whole of the Lancashire contingent.

The Lancashire report which Comrade Rust brought with him was very enlightening and heartening, but the one significant feature (according to the figures) was the static position of the DAILY WORKER. The DAILY WORKER is certainly improving in news value and propaganda.

The question and answer series by J. R. Campbell is fine and the set-up of the paper is improving, but these improvements are not reflected in increased sales in Lancashire itself.

Increased sales of the DAILY WORKER are reported in almost every other district but ours. Nothing would more hearten the Lancashire boys fighting in Spain than to see the relentless champion of the Spanish workers and peasants, the DAILY WORKER, double its circulation in Lancashire.

We have just heard that young " Buck," of Nelson, is the first Lancashire comrade to receive the " Navilcarnero " Award for bravery on the field of battle. One of his numerous exploits was under heavy fire to seize the Fascist flag on Pulberrel Hill at Quinto, which incident shook the morale of the Fascist troops.

—*Signed by JOE NORMAN, SAM WILD, ALBERT MACINTOSH, G. FLETCHER, ROBERT CLARKE, FRANK BROWN, WALTER SPROSTON, ROBERT E. BLAIR, STEVE STOREY, WILLIAM JACKSON, H. W. SUTCLIFFE, W. M. THOMPSON, TOMMY MOORE.*

THE CHILDREN CHEERED

"YESTERDAY we had field manoeuvres. We had to attack an enemy town across an open field with no cover, only grass. We had each to run on the word of command from the officer about five paces and then drop flat, the machine-gunners first, and the ammunition carriers just after. I was an ammunition carrier.

Of course, it was pretty easy, with the only enemy being a blazing hot sun. (It's terribly hot.) It will be a hell of a sight different when there are machine-guns blazing at us in front.

Still, you get a great feeling of comradeship in the army, which I now understand quite well is the only thing that carries you through the real thing at the front.

This morning nine bombers flew over the village in formation, and we all cheered when we saw their red-tipped wings which meant they were ours. . . .

The people over here are all behind the Government, but I am most struck with the children.

Last night I went to the local village pictures, and the film was " Potemkin." It was half full of young children, and when the Russian sailors rebelled and hoisted the red flag, all the kids jumped up and began cheering wildly and shouting, " SALUD! SALUD! " It has left a great impression on my mind.

When you write, please give me NEWS and MORE NEWS.
KENNETH BRADBURY.

TODAY is one of the proudest of my life. As an International Brigade Staff Officer (Spanish Republican Army), I am especially detailed for escort duties to one of your old friends Harry Pollitt, who brings the greetings of the English workers to the British Battalion, the English-speaking comrades here and those brave sons of the Spanish people, who after 17 months of hard struggle are today stronger, more resolute, well trained, better equipped and solidly confident of a great victory.

We stand here, Black, White and Yellow from every land. We have stood together, forming a solid band, writing a new page in freedom's history, writing it in one common blood.

Do not fear for a moment that reaction is anything but shattered. I cannot give you any idea of what glorious scenes we have witnessed—in Madrid, the great battles of Jarama, Brunete, and Belchite. We have developed from riflemen and small squads to a modern, well-disciplined, trained army.

Today we have heard of the glorious offensive at Teruel. The Spanish Republican Army is delivering a smashing blow to Franco. While the world has waited for a great Fascist offensive, we have struck. Perhaps another page in history has been written.

Attlee, who came to Spain to see us, was firmly told that Spain is not the Abyssinia of Europe.

I am well, thanks to your sacrifices in the past. The education and technical training have proved to be the fine bullets against Fascism.

As you, Dad, fired your gun in the Great War, you now can fire again, through me—at Reaction. Have been wounded three times, spent one month in hospital and nine months in the line. Am going stronger and better every day. Why? In the mud and the ice, the blood and the hell, in life and death, is International Solidarity. **WE WIN.**

—*Extract from letter of Lieut. E. J. BEE'S letter to his father in December, 1937.*

TWO sorts of smile at Shanghai. Left, General Iwane Matsui, commanding Japanese troops, grins as he cracks a joke with reporters at his headquarters. Above, a famished refugee and his daughter, sleeping on an International Settlement pavement, awake eagerly to greet a charitable distributor of rice.

January 1938

Harry Pollitt being greeted by members of the International Brigade on his recent visit to Spain

FRANCO ON "LIVE FLESH" OPERATIONS

FRANCO means to go on bombing helpless civilians.

In a rebel broadcast, the amazing statement is made, "General Franco reserves the right to operate on live flesh as a surgeon amputates a gangrened limb when necessary" to end the war. February 1938

SOCIALIST M.P.s BRAVE GUNFIRE

Jan 21 1938

Machine-gun bullets whistled over the heads of the Socialist M.P.s touring the front line trenches of the Spanish Government forces, said Mr. E. Shinwell, M.P. for Seaham Harbour, Durham, arriving in Glasgow yesterday.

"I am certain that the Spanish Republic, in spite of the terrible adverse circumstances under which they are fighting—shortage of food and ammunition—are going to win. The new army they are creating is magnificent."

Mr. Shinwell spoke of the fine air-raid shelters in Valencia, saying that if Britain wished to create such shelters they should study the type erected in Spain.

"I should say they are the finest in the world," he said. "They have concrete roofing and are completely bomb-proof. They can hold 1,000 people and are air-conditioned. Special provision is made for children."

Co-op Aids Spain

A London Co-operative Society lorry takes part in the great week of effort in aid of Spain being held in St. Pancras and Holborn.

THE BATTLE ON THE
HEIGHTS of TERUEL

Fascists Driven Back by The Major Attlee Company

ON the heights of Teruel, the British Battalion, accompanied by Canadian and Spanish comrades, defeated a Fascist attack which had been preceded by one of the most terrific artillery borbardments experienced in the Spanish civil war.

British and Spaniards fought side by side in the ranks of the mixed British Battalion. They displayed military skill, cool officership and iron discipline.

The brunt of the fighting was borne by the Major Attlee Company, which suffered heavy losses. Eighteen British comrades fell in this action, and 25 were wounded. But their achievement will live in history.

The British Battalion has been specially commended by the famous Army commander Modesto, and Lt. Bill Alexander, acting commander of the Battalion, who directly led the most difficult fighting, was promoted Captain on the field.

The aim of the Fascist attack was to advance down the hill leading directly into Teruel. How to defeat this attack.

🕱 🕱 🕱

It was decided to send the British rifle companies down into the valley from their cliff-top position in order to stop the Fascist advance, and to relieve the Spanish troops who had been driven off to neighbouring hills by a sudden and overwhelming artillery and aviation attack.

These hills dominated the valley. In the valley there were also entrenched a company of Canadians, whose position was threatened.

This daring move achieved its purpose. The advance was held off, and from our positions on the cliff-top overlooking the valley, our gunners mowed down the Fascists when they attempted to move forward.

After two days of fighting, this Fascist attack on Teruel was smashed.

Our casualties were due almost entirely to the heavy artillery bombardment directed against the position taken up in the valley. The troops had no time to dig themselves in securely, with the result that the German and Italian gunners, firing very accurately, took a heavy toll, especially among the Major Attlee Company.

The first descent into the valley on January 19 was undertaken by the No. 3 Company, under the leadership of Lt. Sam Wild, who took his men down the gulley.

Then followed the No. 4 Company. The No. 1 Major Attlee Company brought up the rear, and ran down the gulley under heavy artillery fire.

Our boys continued with the Canadians, and during the night began to dig themselves in. Early next morning the Fascists advanced in great force from the village of Concud, against the Canadians on the left flank, and the enemy gunners also let loose a terrific artillery fire. The stand made by the Canadians prevented our boys from being encircled, and we performed a similar service to the Canadians.

🕱 🕱 🕱

The Fascists kept their artillery fire on the Major Attlee Company, who were but poorly protected by their hurriedly dug trenches. British machine-gunners on the cliff-top suffered the anguish of seeing their comrades being slaughtered in the valley below, by the long-range Fascist guns. Finally, the Major Attlee Company was compelled to retreat, but our machine-gunners had their revenge when the enemy infantry attempted to occupy the evacuated trenches.

Then followed a consolidation of our position in the valley, which was a test of steady nerves and powers of cool, military tactics.

We lost some of our best men in the hill, and were driven out of some positions, but we had not abandoned the valley to the Fascists. On the contrary, all our companies moved over to an abandoned blockhouse which controlled the entrance to the valley.

At night the blockhouse was feverishly fortified, and a number of trenches were dug in commanding positions around it. Fascists naturally opened up a terrific bombardment against these positions. Our trenches eventually became crumbled mounds of dust and rubble, but the men stood nobly to their work.

🕱 🕱 🕱

Lt. George Fletcher did not turn a hair but kept sighting his guns so that they killed the maximum number of Fascists and enabled our men in the valley time to reform.

In spite of all enemy efforts, however, this attack was completely repulsed.

People in Britain, reading a bare communique stating that another Fascist attack has been repulsed, know that behind the plain words is a wonderful story of human endurance and military skill for the cause of peace and democracy.

To those already mentioned, we must add the name of the Political Commissar, Wally Tapsell, whose coolness and close co-

They Died For The Cause Of The People

WE publish below the names of 18 comrades who gave their lives at Teruel to save the world from Fascism.

In the name of all readers of the Daily Worker and of all supporters of the fight for democracy and peace, we extend our deep sympathy and closest fraternal greetings to the relations of these men.

Their names will live in the undying scroll of honour of those who have saved the name of the people of this country by the part they have played in the first international army of fighters for freedom.

The truest tribute we can pay to their memory is for each and all of us to pledge ourselves to fight, with the same determination and steadfastness that they have shown, for the victory of the cause for which they have given their lives.

The following 18 comrades were killed in action in the battle of Teruel on January 20:

KENNETH BRADBURY - - OLDHAM
ALFRED CAPPS - - - - - - LONDON
J. FILLINGHAM - - - - - - - - BURY
F. FREEDMAN - - - - - - LONDON
PETER GARLAND
P. GLACKEN - - - - - - - GREENOCK
A. KEMP - - - - - - - - - GLASGOW
ALEC McGREGOR - - - - - LONDON
WILLIAM MACMULLAN - BELLSHILL
KENNETH MOORE - - MANCHESTER
CECIL MENNELL - - - - - LONDON
JOHN RILEY - - - - - - - GLASGOW
ANDREW THOMPSON
        GREAT LUMLEY, DURHAM
C. TURNILL - - - - - - - WORKSOP
DAVID WALSH - - - COUNTY MAYO
BERNARD WINFIELD - - - - NOTTS
FRANCISCO ZAMORA - - SWANSEA
SILVIO FRANCIS - - - - - LONDON
LESLIE MAUGHAM (great-nephew of Somerset Maugham), of Kettering, was killed on January 14.

operation with Alexander helped to keep the battalion moving in splendid organisation. Amongst such a heroic band, it is invidious to pick out this or that individual, but everybody feels that such comrades as Bob Blair, Harold Horne, Bernard Shields, Harry Sutcliffe and Bill Maccartney must receive special praise.

The last tribute to our fallen comrades was paid by the light of the stars only, on a hill-top overlooking the valley.

Moving stealthily through the darkness for fear of drawing fire from the nearby enemy, dele-

gates representing the four companies toiled up the hill, where Alexander planted a plain board dedicated to both the British and Spanish dead, and bearing the simple words: "In memory of the 21 men of the British Battalion of the International Brigade, who gave their lives around this spot in defence of Teruel."

We wanted to sing the Internationale, but the Fascists were too close, and would have answered with a hail of bullets.

Tapsell began softly to recite it, but broke down with a smothered sob. The men crept silently back to their positions.

AFTER THE BATTLE
January 1938

Spanish Government troops bivouac in the streets after taking Teruel.

December 1937

Some of the fighters of Spain's new People's Army now besieging Teruel.

ITALIAN BOMBERS' BIG ATTACK ON TERUEL

From Our Special Correspondent,
WILLIAM RUST

BARCELONA, Sunday.

FRANCO is trying once again to retake Teruel. Yesterday he launched his third counter-attack against the Republican positions in the centre of the town, and went into action with a great concentration of airplanes which were in the air during the whole of the day.

This air fleet not only bombed and machine-gunned the Government lines, but also attacked the communication routes and towns in the rear.

The Fascists have succeeded in capturing the village of Valdecebro, which lies to the east of Teruel, and during last night heavy fighting continued in the neighbourhood of the cemetery, which is only a few miles outside Teruel.

It appears that the Fascists are attempting an encircling movement, the main range of attack from the south-west.

A REPLY

The Republican Air Force, which engaged the Fascist 'planes, lost one of its chasers but succeeded in bringing down one, whose German pilot, a Meisserschmidt, was taken prisoner.

The recent rebel successes in capturing Perales and Alhambra have strengthened their communications on road and railway in the southern extremity of the Teruel salient, and have facilitated these new counter-attacks against the town itself.

But the chief reason for this advance is the big strengthening of the rebel air fleet which I have drawn attention in previous messages.

This technical reinforcement of Franco, and the new counter-attack at Teruel, may be regarded as the Hitler-Mussolini reply to the diplomatic negotiations now being sponsored by Chamberlain.

UNDETERRED

The feeling of the Spanish people in face of the new Fascist danger now confronting them can be gauged by the spirited display at two huge mass meetings held in the Barcelona Olympia this morning.

The meetings, under the President of Luis Companys, and addressed by all the representatives of the Popular Front Parties, were held to celebrate the Popular Front victory of February 1936. Enthusiastic audience loudly cheered all references to unity, and extended a particularly warm welcome to La Pasionaria, who spoke in the name of the Communist Party.

Pasionaria made a ringing appeal for the still further strengthening of the Popular Front, and said that the taking of Teruel by the Republic was now being answered by new and more desperate attacks of international Fascism.

At the conclusion of her speech, the entire audience rose and sang the Internationale.

Democrat Forces Evacuate Teruel

From Our Special Correspondent,
WILLIAM RUST February 23.

BARCELONA, Tuesday.

FOLLOWING heroic resistance lasting over four days, the Republican command last night ordered their forces to evacuate Teruel, in face of the pincers movement with which the Fascist forces threatened to encircle them.

The Commander-in-Chief of the 46th Division, which had been entrusted with the defence of Teruel itself, mustered his forces and succeeded in forcing an exit, together with all his men and material.

The present offensive, which is the fourth largest undertaken by the rebel command since the capture of Teruel by the Republican forces on December 22, 1937, began on Thursday, when the Fascist forces, supported by enormous numbers of planes, and a large amount of heavy artillery, forced their position to the left flank of the river Alsand, five or six miles to the north of Teruel.

The following day they continued the advance and occupied the village of Valdecebro, thus right-flanking Teruel on the east.

The next move was the storming of Mansueto, a height lying between Valdecebro and Teruel, in a commanding position.

From here the enemy advanced towards Castralvo, which lies to the south of the main road to Valencia, and, at the same time, began to press from their positions to the west of Teruel.

Here the Republicans retreated across the River Turia, and eventually, as the circle round it grew tighter, decided to abandon the city itself.

The Fascist advance was possible only as a result of the tremendous reinforcements of planes and artillery which Hitler and Mussolini have supplied to Franco in recent weeks.

It is necessary to point out that at a time when Italy talks of withdrawing "volunteers" from Spain, she did not withdraw, but actually increased technical aid in the form of the artillery and airplanes.

In spite of this, the Republican planes brought down 14 Fascist machines.

The offer to withdraw foreign combatants should deceive nobody, for Mussolini realises that the present Republican soldiers are far superior to the Italian "volunteers" conscripted to fight for an alien cause in a foreign land.

This concentrated attack against Teruel has been purposely delivered at a crucial moment in international politics, in order to give Italy a stronger bargaining weapon with the British Government.

This is the fourth counter-offensive the rebels have been forced to undertake in order to repair the moral damage given them by the loss of Teruel. Or, to put it more concretely, what the Republicans captured in one week, with the loss of only 200 killed, the rebels have taken two months to recapture, and in doing so, they have lost tens of thousands of men.

SPANISH NATIONALIST TROOPS IN TERUEL

A photograph taken in Teruel after the battered town had been recaptured by Spanish Nationalist troops. It is claimed that the Government forces sustained heavy losses in the action.

IN WAR-SHATTERED TERUEL.—A street in Teruel after the battered town had been recaptured by the Spanish insurgent forces.

Forty-two years ago today, in a little mining village of the Asturias, was born DOLORES IBARRURI—LA PASIONARIA . . .

December 9th 1938

Greetings To Pasionaria!
Victory To The People
Of Republican Spain!

HARRY POLLITT writes:—

FORTY-TWO years ago to-day, in a little mining village in the Asturias, was born Dolores Ibarruri, now famous all over the world as Pasionaria.

Daughter of a miner, wife of a miner, she has known all the suffering and sacrifices of the workers. Member of Parliament for the Asturian miners, foremost woman leader of the Communist Party of Spain, she has experienced all the struggles, defeats and victories of the workers' movement.

She is the embodiment of Republican Spain. No one understands better than Pasionaria the aspirations of the people, no one better deserves the love and respect that they give her.

LET US GREET THIS BRAVE AND SPLENDID COMRADE. LET US SAY WITH PRIDE, " SALUD, PASIONARIA. MANY, MANY HAPPY RETURNS OF THE DAY."

How well I remember her when we met shortly after the crushing of the Asturian Miners' Revolt in 1934. She recounted to me with flaming indignation all the terrible things that had happened to her people, and yet she was confident that they would rise again to fight once more.

Her Comrades Marched

And then again at the 7th Congress of the Communist International, we stood side by side on the platform and heard the Congress greeted by Spanish fighters who had found safety in the Soviet Union after the 1934 massacre in the Asturias. I can see her now, standing taut, her fists clenched, tears in her eyes, yet glowing with pride as these comrades of hers marched through the great hall.

I remember the enthusiasm with which she described the struggle for Unity of the People's Front in 1935, and her forecast of great victories in the 1936 General Election. That victory owes a great deal to the leadership of Pasionaria. And when in July, 1936, Franco struck, this magnificent defender of freedom was once more in the forefront of the struggle.

rallying the people to resist the vicious creed of Fascism. We can all remember the thrill with which we read Pasionaria's speeches, of how she inspired the masses during those critical days in July, August and September.

THROUGHOUT THE ENTIRE WORLD RANG HER SLOGAN: "NO PASARAN—THEY SHALL NOT PASS." IT HAS NOW BECOME THE DEATHLESS SLOGAN OF ALL PROGRESSIVE MANKIND.

Those first dangerous moments when the people responded so bravely to the sudden attack, soon developed into the long and anxious period of nation-wide war. Pasionaria never tired.

She faced the tremendous task of helping to achieve unity of the military command, the creation of a war industry, the formation of a broad People's Army. She also worked, without ceasing, to clear out the traitors.

She watched the bombing, the wanton slaughter of women and children, the destruction of irreplaceable art treasures, the food and milk shortage, the plight of refugees. Her suffering can only be imagined, as also the bitterness of her feelings over the agony of her beloved Northern Spain.

But Pasionaria did not flinch in the face of difficulties. She redoubled her efforts to accomplish that reorganisation which is essential to victory.

" We Have An Army . . ."

When we compare the splendid national army today with what existed a year ago, we can realise the pride Pasionaria must feel in this magnificent achievement of the Spanish people.

Some insight into her powers of leadership are expressed in her unforgettable speech made in the name of the United Socialist Party of Catalonia and the Communist Party of Spain, at the session of the Spanish Parliament on October 1 and 2 this year. I should like to quote it all, but perhaps these extracts will suffice:—

" . . . We, who first accompanied our militiamen in the hard days of the Sierra, and who have been since with our soldiers in the glorious days of Guadalajara, Brunete and Belchite. . . . We had no army. To-day we have an army which knows how to fight and how to conquer; an army which knows how to take ground from the enemy; an army which knows how to take the offensive, how to capture towns, which in a week has been capable of winning 400 square miles for the Republic.

" But the fact that we have this army puts before us, before the Parties and organisations, and even before the Government, a problem which we cannot let slide, a problem which must be given the deepest attention, the question of reserves. . . . The creation of these reserves leads logically to the development of another problem to which we also know that the Government is paying attention, but to which it should pay even more attention, the development of war industries.

" We had nothing in this respect. Now we have a great deal. Our factories are already beginning to produce what the army requires in order to take up the offensive, to fight successfully against the enemy. We have factories which produce airplanes, and the people should know it, so that they may have confidence in their Government. . . .

Faith In The People

" We believe that the wages of the workers in war industries and other forms of employment are not adequate to provide for the needs of their homes. We must offer them, not a distant prospect of improvement, but something practical and immediate, so that the workers see that something has fundamentally changed in Spain.

" We are living in the midst of war and we cannot afford to be sentimental because the enemy is not sentimental. The enemy is the enemy and must be treated as such. The more thoroughly we clean the rear of enemies, the sooner our victory is assured. . . .

" Faith in the people. We have had faith as nobody else in the will of our people to win. But at the same time, as we have faith in the fighting powers of our people, we must also make the people feel faith in the men who are guiding their destinies. Faith in the organisations which are ready to sacrifice themselves at every moment to win a life of freedom and justice for Spain.

" . . . It is also essential to say, against those who spread rumours to depress the atmosphere, that there is no possibility of compromise with the enemy. That there will be no shameful capitulation like that of Vergara. That we are determined that no solution can be reached except this one, to crush Franco.

" For the defence of the democratic Parliamentary Republic, for the defence of the liberties of the people, for the defence of democracy, for the defeat of Fascism, gentlemen deputies and Mr. Speaker, the unshakable sincere and profound adherence of the Communist Party."

When I met Pasionaria in Paris

on November 30 this year, she expressed the great appreciation felt by her people for what has been done in Britain for Spain. She asked me to convey her sympathy to all the families of our comrades who have been killed.

" *THEIR SACRIFICES CAN NEVER DIE,*" SHE EXCLAIMED. " *THE BRAVERY AND PROWESS OF THE BRITISH COMRADES IS KNOWN TO US ALL. THEY HAVE WRITTEN PAGES OF HISTORY WHICH TIME WILL NEVER ERASE. BUT, COMRADE POLLITT, URGE THE BRITISH PEOPLE TO DO EVEN MORE. WE NEED FOOD, MILK FOR THE CHILDREN, CLOTHING. WE SHALL WIN, BUT HELP US MORE AND THE VICTORY WILL COME THE SOONER. TRY AND GET THE BRITISH PEOPLE TO SEE THAT NO HELP IS GIVEN TO FRANCO. TRY AND DO MORE TO BRING ABOUT UNITY OF ACTION ON THE PART OF THE WHOLE INTERNATIONAL LABOUR MOVEMENT.*"

In Your Names . . .

I took Pasionaria's hand and promised in your names, comrades, that we will do still more.

THE BEST BIRTHDAY GREETING WE CAN SEND PASIONARIA IS AN EXPRESSION OF OUR DETERMINATION TO DO ALL IN OUR POWER TO BRING ABOUT THE VICTORY OF REPUBLICAN SPAIN.

Comrades, let us prove to this splendid woman, bone of our bone and flesh of our flesh, that her faith in us is not misplaced.

Republican Spain is indomitable in its determination to conquer, and conquer it will.

Once again, Pasionaria, we send you our greeting. Your name will stand out in the pages of history, foremost among all other women leaders. We raise our clenched fists and proudly cry: "Salud, Republican Spain. The victory will be yours and ours."

Let these lines echo round the world:—

Workers the world over,
Hear and Unite.
Keep ye the torch
We are burning, alight,
Carry it gleaming,
Still through the night.
They shall not pass!
THEY SHALL NOT PASS!"

"We Owe You A Debt..."

PASIONARIA, working - class mother, daughter and wife of Asturian miners.

Your tireless, fearless work in the cause of the liberation of Spain from the tyranny of Franco Fascism aided by Hitler and Mussolini is most gratefully appreciated by all women lovers of democracy here in imperialist Britain, where the National Government

For your great work on behalf of all oppressed workers we owe you a debt for which our best birthday tribute is a pledge to increase a hundredfold our solidarity action on behalf of your beloved country.

—ROSE SMITH

"Shame We Have Done So Little . . ."

I AM glad to join in greeting the women of Spain. The agony forced on them by the Fascist rebellion should stir the world. Their courage and fortitude is an example to all. The war from the air now shattering the life of Spain, Ethiopia and China has thrust the women and children into the line of battle to an extent never previously known in the history of the world.

I for one feel the deepest possible sorrow and shame that we in this country have not been able, despite our democratic constitution and the possession of adult suffrage for men and women, to insure that the great power and wealth of this nation should go to the aid of the constitutionally elected Government of Spain against a clique of adventurers supported by the gangster dictatorships of Italy and Germany.

In by-election after by-election, the Government has succeeded in returning its candidate and thereby has secured a verdict in support of its policy. Until we can change that, it is obvious that we have failed to arouse the people of this country to the true state of affairs.

In sending heartfelt greetings to the women of Spain in their heroic struggle from which a new and better life for all Spain will assuredly arise, let us pledge ourselves to do more than ever we have done to awake the conscience of the people of our own land.

—SYLVIA PANKHURST

Beyond Spain's Borders

DEAR fighter of an heroic working-class, with spontaneous urge, born of a miners' spirit of fraternity, I congratulate you on reaching another birthday stage in your life's service to humanity.

The daughter of an Asturian miner, it is, as would be expected, that you are with the people in their fight for freedom.

May your health, strength and mental clarity enable you to continue the struggle in which the success must penetrate beyond the borders of your native land.

I wish to you and yours all the best in life's creation.

—EBBY EDWARDS
(General Secretary, Mineworkers' Federation of Great Britain)

A recent picture of Dolores Irriburi.

From MARJORIE POLLITT

AMONG the many thousands of women who will send birthday greetings to Pasionaria on December 9 none will do so with greater affection and sincerity than the wives and mothers of the men fighting in the International Brigade.

Like Pasionaria, they have sent their loved ones to fight for democracy and freedom with the willing heart and quiet courage that arises only from supreme faith and belief in the cause for which the sacrifices have to be made.

Like Pasionaria, they follow with eager anxiety the achievements of the Spanish Government troops on all the fighting fronts.

Long be the brilliant life devoted since her girlhood to the goal of freeing the Spanish people from poverty and tyranny.

May the affection and regard of progressive and peace-loving people the world over cheer and support you in the task which you will never relinquish until every enemy of the Spanish people has been driven from the shores of Spain. Salud, Pasionaria!

* * *

From CHARLOTTE HALDANE

I AM proud to greet Dolores Ibarruri, daughter and wife of Basque miners; interpreter and symbol of all Spanish men and women who have suffered martyrdom by Fascist oppression and foreign intervention, but whose ultimate victory, under such inspired leadership, is certain.

I hope that London's democratic men and women will show their deep sympathy with Spain's heroic women by flocking to Pasionaria's Birthday meeting at Friend's House this evening, when they will have an opportunity to express their affection and admiration for this great working-class leader.

"HAS BEEN AN INSPIRATION"

I should like to congratulate La Pasionaria on all she has been able to do for the workers of Spain, in the darker years that lie behind and throughout the Civil War.

She has been an inspiration not only to her own people, but to all of us in other lands, who feel the cause of the Spanish Republic our own. May she live to celebrate its victory this year.

—CLAIRE LEIGHTON
the engraver and author

"THE FREEDOM OF US ALL"

I SEND the warmest greetings to La Pasionaria. As a member of a family which, before the war, played a prominent part in the fight for women's rights and women's freedom, I particularly rejoice to see a woman as one of the great heroes in what must be one of the most decisive fights for the freedom of us all.

—RUTH GOLLANCZ

"THE HEART AND VOICE OF THE NEW SPAIN,"
Says famous Novelist

I AM very glad to send a greeting to Dolores Ibarruri—La Pasionaria. Both as a Socialist and as a woman I respect and admire her deeply.

Her courage has long been proved, so has her gift of leadership, a rarer quality. There is no woman living, and not many dead, who have done what she has done and is still doing.

She is herself the heart and voice of the new Spain, and Spain will never forget her. Nor shall we others. There is no woman who does not owe her thanks for what she is doing, as much for us as for her own people. The proper thing to wish her on her birthday is what she would wish for herself—a free Spain.

—STORM JAMESON

"TAKE CARE. TODAY IT IS US— TOMORROW IT MAY BE YOU."

says La Pasionaria. She is seen here at the Birthday celebration of the International Brigade at Albacete.

Pictures of recent air raids on Barcelona. Above, civilians, being helped from wreckage, glance anxiously upward at still menacing airplanes; below, an ambulance man carries a child victim from the ruins.

AND MORNING POST, MONDAY, MARCH 21, 1938

AFTER NATIONALIST AIR RAID ON BARCELONA

Inhabitants of Barcelona searching among the debris of a building destroyed by a bomb during a Nationalist air raid.

A STEEL GIRDER TWISTED like wire when a bomb wrecked a building, in the ruins of which victims are being searched for. Right: Firemen raising an escape against another building, from which piles of household goods have been removed.

ABOUT 3,300 CIVILIANS HAVE BEEN KILLED OR WOUNDED in Barcelona by Nationalist air raiders. Above: Rescue work in progress in an area devastated by bombs. Flats in the background have been entirely destroyed.

STREET SCENE after a raid. On the left, the burnt-out shell of a tram. On the right, burning debris. The man in foreground has his head roughly bandaged, and the distance is obscured by clouds of smoke and dust.

STREET SCENE IN BARCELONA

A RED CROSS FLAG fixed to a traffic signal, near which stretchers have been placed for injured inhabitants trapped among wreckage.

TERROR-STRICKEN women of Barcelona flee for their lives as enemy bombers overhead shatter their homes and possessions.

THE BOMBING OF BARCELONA, WHICH CAUSED THE DEATH OF OVER 815 PEOPLE AND INJURIES TO 2200 OTHERS IN THREE DAYS: RESCUE WORKERS AMONG THE RUINS OF STRICKEN BUILDINGS.

THIS IS SPAIN!
THIS IS BARCELONA!
Italian and German warplanes in the service of Franco (non-intervention planes) have done this! If Spain is not saved, tomorrow it will not be Barcelona, it will be London.
ARMS FOR SPAIN! OUST CHAMBERLAIN!

March 29th 1938.

FARMACIA TAXONERA

OST, WEDNESDAY, APRIL 6, 1938

M.P.s See Air Raid Effects on Barcelona

Mr. Oliver Simmonds, M.P., Chairman, and Mr. Duncan Sandys, M.P., Secretary, of the Parliamentary Air Raid Precautions Committee, inspecting the effects of recent heavy air raids on Barcelona during their visit to Spain.

SPANISH REFUGEES IN FRANCE

APRIL 30, 1938

A SELECTION OF SPECIAL PICTURES from a DAILY TELEGRAPH AND MORNING POST correspondent in the Pyrenees, dealing with Spanish refugees in France. Above, left, is a group of refugees at the base of the pass leading to Aragnouet; and, right, Capt. Regad is assisting an elderly Spaniard over a rough section of track. In background is M. Maljean, Sous-Préfet of the Bagnères-de-Bigorre district.

WORKER   Wednesday, April 20, 1938

★ SPIRIT OF VICTORY ★

Weary and footsore, the Spanish Republican soldiers, who were forced to take refuge in France, line up before taking the train back to Barcelona. They are filled with but one desire—to return to their own country to fight Franco and his allies and to conquer in final victory.

BARCELONA "SYSTEMATICALLY RAKED" BY FRANCO'S BOMBERS FROM A GREAT HEIGHT: A STREET FILLED WITH SMOKE SHORTLY AFTER A RAID:
WITH (ON THE LEFT) AN ORDINARY LORRY BEING USED AS AN AMBULANCE. (Keystone.)

THE EFFECTS OF ONE BOMB IN A MODERN CITY: HOUSES, WITH THEIR FRONTS RIPPED OFF, LOOKING LIKE LIDLESS BOXES; A TRAM IN WHICH ALL THE PASSENGERS
WERE KILLED; AND THE TREES STRIPPED OF BRANCHES. (Wide World.)

 DEVASTATION IN THE STREETS OF A CITY WHICH WAS FORMERLY NOTED FOR ITS GAIETY AND ANIMATION : A TRAM-CAR COMPLETELY WRECKED BY AN EXPLOSION WHICH HAS ALSO BROUGHT DOWN HOUSE-FRONTS, A PHASE ILLUSTRATED ELSEWHERE IN THIS NUMBER.

What I Saw In Barcelona

Saturday, April 2, 1938

by R. W. ROBSON

I LEFT Spain on March 27 and immediately on entering France and particularly after securing English newspapers in Paris felt the tremendous contrast between the cool determination and confidence which exists among the Spanish people and the atmosphere of defeat which is being cultivated by the Press in this country.

For the Spanish people are responding to the wholesale murder and destruction systematically carried out by Italian and German bombing planes by intensifying the organisation of their still considerable resources for a supreme effort to drive the foreign Fascist army out of their country.

BARCELONA has suffered terribly in recent days from the cruel and inhuman bombing which Italian war planes, secure in the knowledge of their overwhelming strength, have reduced to a calculated and systematic orgy of mass murder and destruction. Mussolini undoubtedly believed that these Catalans could be frightened into submission by the terror from the air, but the result is the exact opposite.

Its main streets of magnificent buildings and shopping centres are dotted with ruins, heaps of broken glass swept into the gutters as in English towns snow is heaped up in winter. Miles of windowless buildings with the steel shutters of shops torn from their sockets by the concussion of the explosions gave general evidence of the destructive power of modern bombs. But the shops have been quickly cleared of wreckage, the windows it is true are empty of goods as of glass, but business is going on as usual.

In the centre where the most terrible destruction was wrought, volunteers work night and day over an area almost as large as Trafalgar Square, formerly occupied by great buildings, assisted by flood lighting by night, clearing away wreckage, and during the first hours feverishly attempting to extricate the bodies of hundreds of people including many children who were buried beneath the ruins.

TORTOSA, a small coast town immediately south of Teruel, is in ruins. Fallen trees which formerly lined the streets and have been uprooted by bombs have been pushed aside to allow traffic to pass.

Gaps mark the spots where houses were directly hit and many of the buildings have had the front walls destroyed, so that the interior of the rooms in which people lived are exposed to the street. There is not a window and hardly a door left in any of the houses, but only blank spaces. Pieces of masonry and broken glass crunch under foot.

Tortosa is the picture of desolation and ruin, a picture repeated in many other former Spanish villages and towns.

THE war planes of Hitler and Mussolini fill the sky by the hundred at the front. There cannot be less than eight hundred to a thousand first-line bombers and fighters at the disposal of Franco's Army. From the island of Majorca the Italian bombers make their raids on Barcelona and the Mediterranean costal towns, bombing the roads and machine-gunning anyone they see. THIS IS NON-INTERVENTION!

Its effect is quite the opposite to that expected by Hitler and Mussolini. Catalonia has great reserves, both in men and prospective war resources. For months after the Fascist insurrection began, anarchist illusions and romantic experiments prevented these resources being fully utilised and antagonised many middle-class people.

Trotskyism was able to make use of these errors to increase disunity and dishearten sections of the anti-Fascist masses. The Trotskyists not only sowed disunity and confusion, but actively sabotaged every effort to organise disciplined fighting forces and war industry. The Trotskyist traitors are destroyed, and the anarchist comrades have learnt from their first mistakes. The menace of the German and Italian invading armies has united the people more solidly than ever.

So far from being frightened into submission they are feverishly organising every possible weapon to resist and to defeat the invaders of their country.

FROM scores of towns and hundreds of villages resolutions are pouring in to the Press demanding the mobilisation of hundreds of thousands more men, the speeding up of war industry and the establishment of more efficient and effective control of the armed forces.

Trotskyist and hesitant officers whose contempt for the masses weakened the resistance of the Army in the first offensive at Belchite three weeks ago have been replaced.

Reinforcements are going to the front; the United Socialist Youth of Barcelona have recruited two new Divisions for the front, and the trades unions are taking similar steps.

All building workers in Barcelona not engaged in industry have been mobilised for the building of fortifications; everywhere the masses are confident and ready to make any sacrifice to defend Parliamentary institutions and democratic ideals against the Fascist army of occupation which is murdering men, women and children alike, under the protection of "non-intervention."

THE British capitalist Press is doing its utmost to create the impression that all is over in Spain. They hope that this defeatist propaganda will create pessimism among the people of this country and prevent us taking steps to compel the British Parliament to stop Italian and German intervention against Parliamentary institutions in Spain.

The gallant little Republican Air Force fights overwhelming odds and only asks that the great sister democracies of Britain and France allow them to purchase the planes so urgently needed to combat on more equal terms Hitler's and Mussolini's bombers.

And what of the International Brigades? One would imagine from reports in the Press that the men of the International Brigades had suffered enormous losses and were almost wiped out.

I saw many British members of the International Brigades a few days ago and William Rust had visited them just previously and met with a rousing reception. In spite of their retreat in face of massed bombers, tanks and heavy artillery, their losses have actually been relatively small. Their retreat had been necessitated by Fascist successes on their flanks which compelled them to fall back.

The men of the International Brigades are magnificent and we in Britain have every reason to be proud of those stalwart and unafraid who are members of the British Battalion. The Battalion had been scattered during the retreat and men had been lost for two and three days, but were reporting hourly, their first thought in spite of lack of food and weariness being that they must get back to the Battalion.

ONCE more it is necessary to emphasise that the Spanish Republic, hard-pressed, almost overwhelmed by the weight of foreign armaments, is fighting back heroically and still hopes even with its own slender resources to win the victory. The people are united and determined to an amazing degree. Their fortitude and courage is tremendously impressive and inspiring.

They are fighting only for the right to Parliamentary methods of Government and democratic ideas and ideals. Their victory will mean only a victory for these things and not as the millionaire Press in Britain would have its readers believe, to establish a " Red regime."

If they are crushed, the democracies of Britain will inevitably pay a heavy price in the not distant future for the policy of the British Government towards the Spanish Republic.

We must insist that Spanish democracy be allowed to purchase arms for their soldiers and food for the women and children. Liberals, Labour people and Communists combined would be a force easily capable of achieving this. Surely it will be accomplished.

Refugees pour into Barcelona from a countryside laid waste by Fascist bombers.

Young aviators of the Republican Air Force who fight against terrific odds in defence of the people.

SCENES IN STRICKEN SHANGHAI

Chinese refugees at Shanghai

A FAMILY arriving in Shanghai from the west. Women and possessions are carried on the single-wheeled Chinese truck.

A BRITISH POST in Brenan-rd., Shanghai. Between sentry and camera is a brazier.

A JAPANESE SOLDIER stabs the sack carried by a Chinese refugee at an entrance to the International Settlement, to make sure no contraband is being carried. The coins on table, right, are coppers paid on goods deemed to be dutiable. These photographs from the Shanghai area were specially taken by a DAILY TELEGRAPH AND MORNING POST correspondent.

CHINESE REFUGEES resting on arrival with their possessions in Shanghai. The police sign on the right reads "No parking."

SAFETY FIRST

They Paraded In London's West End

Jan: 1938

These supporters of China paraded through the heart of London's West End demanded a boycott on Japanese goods.

Inside the bag, wrapped up like a ham, is a tiny baby refugee in the Sino-Japanese war, rescued by the International Red Cross

Feb: 1938

A number of demonstrators who took part in the 1½-miles-long "Boycott Japan" march through London this week.

F. 26: 1938

Demonstrators in Paris demanding the boycott of Japanese goods.

Spanish children who escaped from Franco's bombs in Madrid exercising at Perello, Valencia.

ORPHANED BY FRANCO—This little fellow was photographed in the Spanish Government School for Orphans, near Alicante.

Republican Spain is caring for its children as shown by this picture.

March 1938.

ORPHANS OF THE WAR

Two little children from the School for Orphans at Benicasim, near Alicante, recuperate on the sunny beach there.

APRIL 1938.

ORPHANS OF THE SPANISH STORM

"AIR-RAIDS on Barcelona. Hundreds killed"—the heading is one of the commonest in our papers to-day. Every air-raid almost means more orphans to be cared for. In spite of the demands of warfare, Spanish Government is doing its utmost in caring for and educating children—and has established several large colonies for orphans in the orange-country near Valencia. Foreign missions help in some cases in caring for the children. Part of the day children do lessons, part they play games, for part they help in getting in the orange harvest or in work in the orange groves. Orange trade is vital to the Spanish Government, providing their chief means of paying for the war.

HOUSEWORK Life in one of the orphan-colonies near Valencia where Spanish Government cares for children whose fathers and mothers have been bombed, machine-gunned by Franco 'planes.

GATHERING ORANGES Chief contribution orphans make to Government is in the gathering of oranges—the Government's chief resource in paying for the war. Much of this work is done by children.

LISTENING TO STORY Young Spanish boys listen to a story read them by a teacher. Boy with bandaged head is healing from a wound—result of just one of those Barcelona air-raids.

March 1938.

EXODUS: *A picture from the Franco-Spanish frontier this week that expresses the pathos of the Spanish tragedy*

YES, from the beginning it was a bad day! I was the nightnurse and had spent the night taking care of fresh operation cases, giving intravenous injections of saline and glucose and helping with the blood transfusion. By morning all the cases except one seemed to be on the right road.

I felt a sense of satisfaction as I looked round. The patients were as comfortable as possible in the circumstances, housed in a large tent with a floor of sand. The worst cases were still under morphia.

ABOUT 6 a.m. I heard the roar of an enemy plane. I took off my white overall and stood by the door of the tent looking up. I kept very still, but my heart began to beat fast. A lone plane was flying right over us. On the faces of the patients who were awake was a look of intense expectancy and dread.

It is one thing to be killed while you are fighting and quite another to be murdered while you are in a hospital helpless and unable to move. The plane passed.

I breathed a sigh of relief, but I mentally registered the fact that it was probably an observation plane and that if it had seen anything to arouse suspicion it would certainly be back with bombers before long.

AT 8.0 a.m. I was relieved by the day nurses, to whom I gave my report.

Then Lola, the Spanish girl who had been helping me, told me that she knew of a good place for us to sleep in . . . . some sort of refuge where the planes could not get at us.

They had been over every day bombing a town half a mile away but so far had not spotted the hospital, and we were getting some good work done there.

She took me down by the side of the river, scrambling over rocks and slippery places for about a quarter of a mile to a square-shaped place. On each side were rocks and caves that certainly looked comfortingly good and solid.

In the middle women and children were sitting and standing. Some watched the sky with that same fearful look and some were frying pieces of meat over a fire.

LOLA led me along the rock to a huge cave with a small opening at the front and another along the side. Inside it was surprisingly large, enough to accommodate about 40 people. A few already sat knitting and sewing, some chatting animatedly.

ONE DAY IN SPAIN ★

May 1938.

by Winifred Bates

"We'll never be able to sleep here," I said.

At that moment people started to pour into the cave as that ominous burr of planes came again. A woman looking agonised ran out of the cave and snatched up her child. I noticed one child with head and another with leg bandages. "From the bombing at A—— yesterday," said one of the women, noticing my look.

"Ssh!" said someone suddenly near the entrance of the cave. "They're over."

EVERYONE huddled together, crouching, sitting and lying on the floor of the cave, silent and tense while the drone of a great many planes came nearer and nearer. Suddenly there was the dreaded, shrieking whistle of bombs falling through the air. Crash! Boom! They seemed to be on every side of us.

I remained as flat as possible on the floor, the beating of my heart accelerated by the thought that in a moment we might all be torn limb from limb by a violent, death-dealing bomb. Lola was chewing a handkerchief to keep herself from crying out.

Then the sound came nearer and we heard the sharp rpbrbrbr sound of strafing machine-gun bullets. An air battle was going on over our heads. The children began whimpering with fear, though one dear, little brown-eyed girl of about three years smiled enchantingly and put out her hand to play with my medical service badge.

EVENTUALLY the noise died away. I ventured to put my head out and look up. There were about 30 heavy Italian Caproni bombers in the distance and clouds of dense yellow smoke over an area of half a mile. By this time I could hardly keep my eyes open.

This bombing of the villages had been going on for the four days that I had been on night duty and I had not been able to snatch more than a brief sleep. That day I was all in and felt that whatever happened I must sleep. Lola preferred to stay were she was, but I started clambering over the rocks again.

Before long they came again. I made for the nearest shelter, which was very open and shallow. I lay very still and quiet and hoped for the best; and the planes passed over and bombed a village on the other side.

HOW long I slept, I do not know; but I suddenly awoke to a sense of danger and the noise of what seemed to be hundreds of planes above me. I pulled the mattress half over me and put the pillow on my head . . . . and waited.

In the seconds that each bomb took to fall, my imagination saw myself crushed with a split skull. The heavens and all the mountains seemed to be coming down on my head. I was breathing in little short gasps and my heart was pounding. Everywhere whistle, crash, bang.

I'm still alive, but the next one will get me; but the next one did not get me, nor the next, nor the next.

THE zoom died away. Comrades came dashing towards me, the last being Dr. Broggi, the Spanish surgeon with whom we work.

He stopped as he saw me, and at that moment my fear-sharpened ears caught the sound of returning planes. "Get down!" I shouted. I curled myself up into a smaller heap and left room for him to crawl under.

He, too, had been working all night and it was a long time since he had slept. "It's all finished!" he said suddenly. "What? The hospital?" I could not see anything. The grove was a cloud of smoke. "Our comrades," he said "must be in that."

Blood transfusion being carried out by a Spanish doctor in a Madrid hospital.

THE Spanish Republican soldiers take a rest after being in the firing line.

Nightmare In Spain

June 1938

Mision Sanitaria Britanica, 90,
Maria Blasco, Alberaya, Valencia,
Spain.

2.0 a.m.

LAST week we had a series of terrible air-raids here in Valencia, and last night we had two very severe raids, the details of which I am sending you in the hope that you will give them full publicity.

You will, of course, see by the above heading that I am a nurse, belonging to the Spanish Medical Aid, 24, New Oxford Street. I am in a hospital a good way from here, but last week I was sent for to come and nurse two comrades who were ill at the above address. I came down with another nurse, and we are doing day and night duty. I'm on nights.

THE first raid took place about 11 p.m. and was very severe, the second one at about 11.30 p.m. Bombs dropped about 50 yards away from this house, which is on the beach and between two anti-aircraft guns. The shrill barking of these guns shake our house to its very foundations, apart from the dull explosive thud of the bombs.

It is the practice, and considered the safest, for the people to run out of their houses and lie flat on the sands. They run out with the screaming children and the whole scene is pitiful . . . the awful ghastly drone of the air-plane engines, the sky ablaze with searchlights, and the shrill barking of the guns, accompanied by the dull death-dealing thud of the bombs.

Having two invalids in the house, naturally, my friend and I don't leave it.

When this second raid was over, we knew that the bombs had dropped pretty close and we ran out to be of service. It was just like a nightmare. We ran along the sands and came to a group of people shrieking and screaming.

Some of the men had formed a kind of rough guard in front of the figures lying prone. They said, "No Paras," but I said "Enfermeras Ingleese," and they took us to the prone figures. The moon was shining and it was like a scene of carnage. There was a huge bomb-hole with the people scattered round it. (They had previously been lying down together and the bomb had dropped right in the middle of them).

I went to an old man with a fractured arm who was babbling incoherently, and we rolled him

After The Planes Had Gone

in a blanket ready for the ambulance.

I next came to a woman, felt for her pulse, found she was just living, and started to feel and straighten the limbs, and, to my horror, was groping for a leg that wasn't there . . . there was just a bloody charred mass where her leg had been blown off just below her knee.

The next four were dead, with bulging, bloodstained cavities where their faces should have been, and then the ambulance came up.

They got the old man in, and a boy of about 14, and another woman, and were leaving the women without the leg.

I said "This one," and they said, "No meuerto." I said she was living, as I could distinctly feel her pulse, and so they took her. Idon't think she will live, but there is just a chance.

THE ambulance men then drove off, leaving the dead behind, as, of course, nothing could be done for them. They would be collected later.

The moon shone down on that ghastly scene, which I shall never forget. The dreadful screaming and hysteria all around was nearly more than one could bear. Poor, poor things, we couldn't help them, and so we made our way back to our house, sad and sick at heart, back to

our own invalids, whom we had left.

I can hardly force myself to write. If I once give way my teeth will chatter and I am forcing my feet to stay on the floor. My nerves are bruised and raw, and my heart is very heavy.

Our electric wires have been bombed, and I am writing this by candle light. Bear in mind we had only seen one little section of the raid. This was probably going on all along, and the docks certainly caught it, as they gave them hell.

Spanish youth on the march responding to the call of the Government for volunteers.

These Spanish mothers know the barbarities of Fascism.

EIGHTH ARMY MARCHES

THE MODERN, GERMAN-TRAINED CORE OF THE CHINESE NATIONAL GOVERNMENT'S "VICTORY" ARMY: A WELL-EQUIPPED MOTORISED UNIT BEING ADDRESSED BY ITS COMMANDER BEFORE A MARCH.

Troops of the Chinese 8th Route Army (formerly the main Red Army) moving up from their base somewhere in North China. This is one of a number of exclusive photographs just received by the Daily Worker from the North China war zone.

CHINA STRIKES BACK.
Some of Hankow's new mobile anti-aircraft equipment now in constant use against Japanese air terrorists.

A MOTORISED CHINESE UNIT: LINES OF WELL-KEPT MOTOR-CYCLES AND SIDE-CARS; WITH LORRIES AT THE BACK.

Summer 1938.

CHIANG KAI-SHEK

Chinese women soldiers behind the lines write letters for the wounded. They have more dangerous duties, but this is what they do when they are "resting."

THE ARMY THAT IS
Defeating Japan

THE CHINESE Eighth Route Army is important, not alone because it is the recognised Red Army and led by Communists, though that fact shows the strength of the new unity which brings together under one banner armies that have fought each other in civil war for the past ten years.

It is important also because it is the most efficient army of its size in China, in the opinion of foreign military observers—I have had opinions from American, German and British sources on that.

It has, furthermore, certain characteristics which the rest of the Chinese armies are increasingly adopting to achieve victory in the struggle against Japan.

Lacking airplanes, big guns and motorised equipment, it is none the less able to play in and out of the Japanese lines and operate confidently far in the rear of the enemy, taking back from their hands whole counties.

It achieves its success partly by long practice in mobile fighting, but still more by its close relations with the local Chinese population. It was this that ten years ago proved its potency by bringing the armies of the Kuomintang swiftly across half China.

Subsequently, however, the Chinese Government discarded the tactic of establishing close contacts with the people.

Today, on every front in China, the need of employing this tactic is increasingly felt, and its need will be greater as the war goes on. Steadily, therefore, though against the normal military and political jealousies, the ideas and methods of the Eighth Route Army are beginning to influence other fronts and armies in this war.

THE Japanese hold the main railway points in northern Shansi. Most military maps, therefore, credit them with holding the northern half of Shansi province.

If the inhabitants of Shansi province chose to be submissive, this claim would be a fact.

But the Shansi population is not submissive. It is organised by the Eighth Route Army, which serves as its fighting arm. Consequently, the Japanese are unable to go for more than a mile or two away from the railroad, except in temporary armed expeditions.

The railroads themselves have been made largely unusable by the Japanese. The north and south line from Tatung to Taiyuan has been completely put out of commission by the Chinese, while the other roads are daily raided and cut.

The Japanese situation in fact, seems a precarious one; it would not seem much of a trick to bottle them up entirely by seizing a few mountain passes, and finish them off at will.

The Eighth Route Army, in fact believes that this can be accomplished whenever the Central Government is able to release airplanes, large guns, and motor units for that purpose. These seem at present to be more needed elsewhere; China hasn't enough of them at best.

BECAUSE of the success of these tactics of mobile warfare, it is common in China to think of the Eighth Route Army as essentially guerilla fighters. Madame Chiang, in fact, so described them to me.

The Eighth Route Generals, however, reject this description.

"We are a regular army, and can also do positional fighting if we have the equipment. But with our present shortage of equipment and in the territory where we are operating, behind the lines of the enemy, mobile warfare is the best. With our present tactics we regularly kill more of the enemy—often very many more—than we lose ourselves. . . ."

THE five chief generals of the Eighth Route Army are no mere improvisors of revolutionary combats, but men of long military training and many years' experience.

Chu Teh, commander-in-chief, known as the "father" of the army, studied years ago in a Yunnan military school, became an officer in the Yunnan army, went to Germany to study the lessons of the World War, took part in the Northern Expedition of 1927, which established the present Chinese Government, participated in the Nanchang revolt, the seizure of Swatow, and later led the small group which eventually became the Red Army.

His chief assistant, **Peng Te-hwai,** graduated from a Hunan military school and was a regiment commander as long ago as the 1927 Northern Expedition.

Liu Pe-chun, a scholarly gentleman in spectacles, was a well-known Szechuan general, who

From an article by ANNA LOUISE STRONG in the New Masses

joined the Kuomintang forces at the time of the Northern Expedition.

Ho Lung, who of them all looks most like the traditional guerilla general, with his strong, stocky form and dare-devil air and a shabby tag, reading "120 Division," stuck to his grey, padded cotton sleeve with a safety-pin, led 20,000 men in the 1927 Northern Expedition, and later led the revolt in Nanchang.

Lin Piao, the youngster of the lot, who looks like a shy student, but whose division holds the largest area and has seen harder action than any, studied at Whampoa Military Academy, in Canton, before he led a company north in 1927.

As military men, therefore, the commanders in the Eighth Route Army have a past as competent as any men in China. They have also had ten years' experience in the Red Army. They differ from other generals chiefly in their relation to the common soldiers and to the common people. They are highly democratic, utterly accessible. Any common soldier, any ordinary peasant, can and does speak to them. In fact, you cannot tell them from an ordinary soldier except perhaps by their slightly greater age.

IF I were asked for the chief characteristics of the Eighth Route Army which differentiate it from others, I would mention three.

First, that they educate every ordinary soldier in what he is fighting for. Every day he attends three classes: military training, cultural training, political training.

The second characteristic of the Eighth Route Army is the comradely feeling between soldiers and commanders. Chu Teh is revered by his men as Chinese revere a father, not feared as they usually fear a general.

Last and perhaps of all characteristics the most important, is the relation of the Eighth Route Army with the people. Its soldiers are instructed in a series of homely rules, whose general purport is: leave every village in as good condition as you found it.

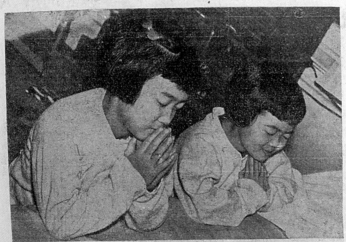

Chinese children at their prayers. Japanese bombers have no thought for such children.

At a meeting of Republican fighters in Spain: from left to right, Division Commander General Walter, Dolores Ibarruri (Passionaria), War Commissar Lizcano.

Summer 1938.

Spanish Republican artillery men operate one of the all too few pieces of artillery possessed by the Government.

MEMBERS OF THE BRITISH BATTALION PHOTOGRAPHED ON THE OCCASION OF HARRY POLLITT'S RECENT VISIT TO SPAIN'S FRONT LINE.

These brave fighters expect much of the British people. They are insistent that everything possible shall be done to end the farce of non-intervention and secure arms for the people of Republican Spain

Just a few yards to go and he'd have been in safety over the Soochow Creek bridge on Western border of Shanghai's International Settlement. Those few yards were too many. Japanese machine-gunners got him.

THIS IS AN OCCUPATION. With business of many kinds entirely at a standstill, Chinese must live as they can. One of the staple industries to-day is this—picking over the rubbish-heaps for anything edible.

THIS IS A HOME. Chinese woman keeps house as best she can on 10 square feet on a Shanghai sidewalk. Her possessions are a kettle, a basket, a plate, some mats, a sack.

IN MIDST OF WAR. Barbed wire, sand-bags, bayonets—and posters for a film . . . . but contrasts are too common to notice—and few have the heart to notice them.

ONE OF THE LUCKY ONES. Boat-dwellers have been lucky among Shanghai's unhappy people. They could move their homes with their crazy coverings of matting, to a region of comparative safety.

IT'S TOUGH TO-DAY BEING A CHINESE

THE generation that thought it had found the way to peace will be remembered in history chiefly for inventing a new form of war—the massacre of the innocents. For hundreds—in some parts of the world for thousands of years—it has been the tradition not to kill defenceless men, women and children. In Spain and in China that tradition has been flouted, treated as absurd, an out-of-date bit of sentimentality. Japanese airmen and machine-gunners are not fighting an army, they say, but a nation. So they bomb refugee trains, mow down peasants and their families running for safety down roads and across bridges. Franco's airmen on the road from Malaga, Japanese airmen and infantry round Shanghai and Nanking, will go down to history—but not perhaps in just the way they hoped.

"HOME-COMING 1937."

After the bombers came to Barcelona.

1938.

We watched these lads marching off to the Front—soldiers of Europe's newest army.

The little boy on crutches had his right leg smashed by splinters from an aerial bomb.
Yet he keeps his martial bearing.   He wants to look as much like Dad as possible.   His Catalan father is fighting
against the Fascists on the Aragon front.

"Are we downhearted?"   In Madrid where the Line goes through the Royal Palace.

1938.

Half a day's leave in Madrid . . . and a wrecked lorry for a seat in the sun.

International Brigade

Serving out bread for the Government troops in Barcelona.

FROM THE WORLD'S BATTLEFIELDS

Frenchmen, Italians, Germans, Poles and Britons make up the already famous International Brigade which Franco has to thank for his long wait outside Madrid. They get a few coppers for pay. Their uniform now is boots, breeches and khaki tunics—the Britons in early days were fighting in grey flannel trousers.

THEY KNOW WHAT THEY'RE FIGHTING FOR

A large part of the International Brigade is made up of so-called "intellectuals"—writers, professors, doctors, lawyers, teachers from all over the world. They are the best-trained and disciplined men on the Government side.

EACH day's news from Spain brings mention of the International Brigade. Since November 8, when the sound of their marching feet echoed through the streets of Madrid, the brunt of Franco's attacks have been borne by them. There were only 10,000 of them to begin with. They have lost 1,000 men killed already—but their numbers are soon made up again. The International Brigade is composed of men from every country. Its orders are issued in German, French and Italian. Its men have seen service in every continent. They are in Spain not for pay— some get a few coppers a day, some draw nothing—nor even for adventure. They are there to fight Fascism. They are the answer of individual democratically-minded men throughout the world to the battalions of Germans ordered to Spain by Hitler and to the flights of 'planes sent over by Mussolini. At least a hundred of these fighters come from our own country. Some have thrown up good jobs or cut short professional careers in order to help a democratically-elected government put down an armed revolt backed by foreign dictators. The International Brigade has already saved Madrid. It may easily save democracy in Spain, by holding up Franco until the Government can train its own many thousands of recruits. If it does that it may have saved democracy in Europe.

General Kleber, the Brigade's commander, is Canadian, has fought in Russia, Germany and for years in China.

Ludwig Renn, famous German author, officer in the world war, was imprisoned by Nazis for years—now fights in Spain.

"WE FIGHT TO SAVE SPAIN"—SAY THE GOVERNMENT TROOPS

This is a typical mountain position in the Guadarrama Range. Courage often makes up for skill and discipline.

"Don't fire, Comrades" reads the notice. Here's the result.

"Viva España!

"LONG Live Spain!" is the cry of both parties engaged in Civil War, and that cry is shouted to the accompaniment of murder and destruction.

Much has been written about the cruelty and savagery of the government supporters, but now comes the horrible story written by dispassionate observers of the behaviour of the rebels. It is sad to learn that these so-called "Saviours of Spain from Bolshevism for Christianity" are ferocious Mohammedan troops whose reputation for savagery is deliberately fostered. It is equally sad that these Moors who are pillaging and massacring the people of Spain were brought from Morocco under the shelter of Italian and German aeroplanes.

"Two words must for ever disappear from the Spanish dictionary," said the rebel general Queipo de Llano in a broadcast from Seville. "They are 'pardon' and 'amnesty'."

And the Legionaries from Morocco need little incentive. Outside new schools built by the Republic lie heaped the dead bodies of the teachers. It is not possible at this moment to obtain a clear and dispassionate view of the whole tragic business, but it is a sad misuse of a word to call these rebel generals patriots men whose avowed aim is "Fascism at what ever cost" to Spain.

Arms and ammunition being distributed to volunteers before advancing to meet the Rebels.

a recruit to the voluntary militia who are fighting for the Government against the rebels.

LIFE GOES ON

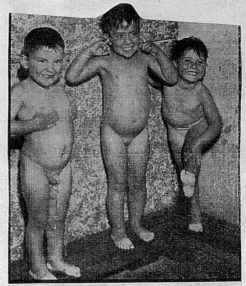

Happy children under the care of Republican Spain enjoy the new sensation of a shower bath in one of the modern nursery schools.

In the airy sunlit dining-room of the school the children get the best of the available food. But they need more milk.

BUILDING A

IT IS NOT ALL DESTRUCTION IN SPAIN. THE REPUBLIC'S CITIES AND VILLAGES ARE BOMBED BY ALIEN ENEMIES—BUT THE REPUBLIC BUILDS NEW SCHOOLS AND NEW MUSEUMS.

Fascism's high explosives destroy noble works of art—but many more are rescued from the cellars of great houses and the store rooms to which they were consigned by old officialdom.

The pride and vigour of Spain's manhood is decimated by bullets and shells on a dozen fronts—but a new, healthy childhood grows up even while guns roar. Spain defies destruction. The true Spain develops. Spain reaches through agony to a new life.

The art treasures of Spain are the heritage of the people. The Government has done work of immense value to the whole world in cataloguing and storing all works of art.

NEW NATION

August 1938.

THE RISING GENERATION HAS A RISING SCALE OF LIVING

HERE are some figures; and even if they are figures they are not dull. It does not take much imagination to see behind these figures an immense and noble national effort that has probably never been equalled in the history of Europe.

Remember during the Great War how all work on housing stopped, no new schools were built, every social service was restricted. Britain was at war.

Well, Spain has been at war for two years—and, unlike Britain, the whole country has suffered terrible devastation.

But since 1936 more than 10,000 new schools have been opened in Republican Spain. In 1937, when the Government was straining every nerve in its fight against Franco, Hitler and Mussolini, it set aside 142,969,000 pesetas for elementary education. In 1935 the reactionary Lerroux Government, during a time of peace, had spent only 9,000,000 pesetas on elementary education for the whole of Spain.

There are other schools, adult schools—for the old order had left 52 per cent. of Spain's population illiterate.

One of the most romantic and amazing stories in the history of the Spanish war is the work of the "Militia of Culture," which has held schools in dug-outs and trenches.

From the beginning of the war up to the end of last year 75,000 soldiers were taught to read and write in the trenches or immediately behind the lines. More than 800 trench and barrack libraries, containing 50,000 volumes, have been organised.

And among the army casualties have been hundreds of members of the Militia of Culture, who went to the fronts with no weapons but a few school primers.

The bombs of Hitler and Mussolini cannot reach these Spanish children now staying at the "House of Spanish Children" in Odessa.

AN
APPEAL
TO EVERY
BRITISH
CITIZEN
WHO LOVES
FAIR PLAY

Among the aliens who have found refuge in Britain are 2,000 Basque orphans In 52 camps in this country they are cared for by the Basque Children's Committee.

Each child costs the Committee 10s. a week. The older children help to look after the younger ones, but the Committee still has to find £1,000 every week to keep them here.

Under Spanish and British teachers they continue their education in a strange land. Many of them can now speak English fluently and enjoy English games as well as their own.

Their education is practical. Some day, when the civil war in Spain has ended, these poor war stricken children will go back to their native land and help to build it anew.

1938.

Although one reads little about nurses, this picture is evidence that the wounded are cared for whenever it is possible to do so.

Government supporters make a sandbag barricade near San Sebastian. The rebels have obviously been peppering this corner of the front.

Government forces "at the double" 34 miles north-east of Madrid.

The Major Attlee Company of the International Brigade on the march.

CANTON MAYOR ASKS AID: THANKS COMMUNIST PARTY

August 1938.

"**E**MBARGO on oil, raw materials and war supplies to the aggressor, and a complete boycott of Japanese goods are the most effective measures you can take to help our cause."

This is the message sent by the Mayor of Canton to the British people through the Communist Party.

Recently the London District Congress of the Communist Party passed with cheers a telegram of sympathy with the people of Canton, addressed to the Mayor of the city. The reply was received in London yesterday, signed by Tsing Yang-fu, the Mayor.

The response to the Mayor's appeal is clear. Everyone can take part in the boycott, and, more than that, everyone can support the campaign that will make an embargo on supplies to Japan effective.

"On behalf of the million and a half people of Canton I desire to thank most heartily members of your Party for their kind sympathy with our sufferings and their offer to assist us in our present struggle against the ruthless aggression and terrorism of the Japanese," says the letter, which is addressed to Ted Bramley, secretary of the London District Committee of the Communist Party.

"WILL NOT SUCCEED"

"The message which you sent us on behalf of the London District Congress has given our people encouragement and inspiration. With your sympathy and support we are confident that the aggressor will not succeed in getting his conquest dreams realised and that justice will eventually prevail over brutal might.

"The indiscriminate bombings of this open city by Japanese planes during the last three weeks have resulted in the killing of over 1,500 and the maiming of 6,000 of our civilians.

"Particularly deplorable was the fact that large numbers of our workers, men as well as women, were slaughtered while toiling in industrial establishments of entirely no significance.

MENACE TO HUMANITY

"Our suffering has been terrible, but I assure you that the enemy's barbarous methods have only achieved the massacre of our people and the destruction of our property, but have not succeeded in destroying our morale.

"The Cantonese people will neither surrender to terrorism nor yield to threats. We are grimly determined to continue our resistance to aggression and our fight for freedom and independence.

"The present Japanese aggression in China clearly is a menace to civilisation and humanity. We should, therefore, mobilise all resources to fight the common foe to make the world safe for peace and democracy.

EFFECTIVE MEASURES

"Embargo on oil, raw materials and war supplies to the aggressor and a complete boycott of Japanese goods are the most effective measures you can take to help our cause, and I hope that through the energetic efforts of your organisation, this movement for restraining the aggressor will become more and more widespread in your great country.

"We also welcome, of course, any concrete step you can take to secure for us material assistance which would enable us to strengthen our defence against further wanton killing and destruction."

This is the kind of thing the Mayor of Canton means when he says, "Our sufferings have been terrible." A wounded child, sitting in the gutter by wrecked buildings, weeps with pain, while a woman distractedly holds her head.

Shell-Delivered

A CASE unique in medical history has just been investigated and found true in war-torn Canton.

A pregnant Chinese woman was walking through the streets of the city when a squadron of Japanese planes flew over the city and dropped their cargo of bombs, one of which, exploding a few feet from her, blew the woman almost in two.

Red Cross workers found the baby lying just alive about five feet away from the mangled body of its mother.

Infant was rushed to the Sun Yat Sen Memorial Hospital. Dr. Wong Man, who examined it, said, although the child had been "born" about a month before its time, it had a good chance of sur-

Reported August 1938.

Students of the Chinese 8th Route Army at their studies. They are being told about their leaders and tactics in order to prepare them for service.

New York Daily Mirror

"LITTLE MAN YOU'LL HAVE A BUSY DAY"

Strange as it may seem to some people even these soldiers in Barcelona have wives and sweethearts to whom they say "Good-bye." These women have, in many instances, joined the Government militia and have fought side by side with the men.

The Children are Spain's Future

By ELLEN WILKINSON, M.P.

FIFTEEN HUNDRED children, each clutching a mug, stood in a queue. Two helpers, an Englishman and a Spanish woman, were trying to explain to mothers with babies in their arms why no more cards could be handed out. Each child had its cup of milk, dried powder and water, and a biscuit.

This week the funds sent devotedly by the Society of Friends were low, and only half the quantity could be given. For many of these children this would be their only meal that day.

Towards the end of the queue there was a strange silence. The big dark eyes of the children were fixed with a terrible anxiety on the arms of the helpers as they went deeper and deeper to get at the dwindling supply. I shared their anxiety. I felt I just could not bear it, if those sixes and sevens had to be told "No more to-day." And these were only fifteen hundred children in a city of a million souls.

Summer 1938.

In the main street outside "Asistencia Social," the great Government welfare organisation, some big lorries were parked. They contained tins of food sent by the women's committee of the French Popular Front.

A thin woman with a baby in her arms and another at her skirt stopped as she passed the lorry and stroked it, as though somehow it could understand her thanks.

"Will she have a ticket?" I asked the efficient young Catalan woman who was my guide. "That is all going out to the refugees in the villages. We have a million to feed," she replied.

A school in Madrid—a fine building, one of the fifty built in the short reign of the Republic—big windows, lots of light and air, and the children sitting happily round little tables. All children of the working class, keen as needles, but so thin. Every day they had to come to school through falling shells or casual bullets.

The school was only 2½ miles from the actual trenches. Bombs had fallen on schools just like this, wrecking them completely, blowing teachers and children to bits. That is how the Fascists bring civilisation to a country.

"How can you stand it?" I asked a young teacher. "It's all right if we can keep the children fed. That keeps up their nerves and it is wonderful then what they can resist."

"These children are Spain's future—if we can only get them through this time," said the courteous, elderly Head Teacher to Mr. Attlee. Our leader smiled, but his eyes were wet, as we passed through the school. "We'll send you milk, we promise we will," we said as we bade good-bye to these teacher-heroines.

We talked to the Premier, Dr. Negrin—the rock of his country's confidence in this crisis. Dr. Negrin is a specialist in physiology. He knows better than anyone what his children need.

He knows, too, that these children have to be defended. And the Non-Intervention Committee, which stops no Italian and German arms going to the Fascists, denies him the right to buy legally the means to defend these children. It denies even the anti-aircraft guns to keep off the Fascist bombing planes.

To get these—whether by making them in improvised factories in Spain, as they are doing, or from abroad—costs a lot more money than would be needed if ordinary orders could be placed. There is less money for food because of the Non-Intervention Committee. And Franco has the richest agricultural districts—and no refugees.

The Spanish Republic will win through. How soon depends on us. The soldiers of the Republic are fighting the battle of democracy—our battle. It is our task to see that their children are fed.

N.C.O.s in training at Castellon. Many of them joined the victorious brigades which took Teruel.

1938.

" A people who have stood this for eighteen months." Air-raid casualty gives the Salute while being carried out to the ambulance.

August 1938.

Off To Margate

Employees of Green and Hearn, Ltd., start the day well on their annual outing to Margate. During the day they gave 25s. to a collection for Spain.

NEW BOMBED SHIP DEMAND IS IGNORED

26.

(From Our Diplomatic Correspondent)

THE bombed ships situation becomes hourly more humiliating for Britain, inquiries yesterday revealed.

With the list of British ships attacked by Italian and German aircraft now standing at ONE HUNDRED AND SIXTY-TWO, the Foreign Office yesterday was still waiting . . . waiting . . . for a reply from General Franco to its latest "request."

And once again British seamen and shipowners are waiting . . . waiting . . . for a reply (a) from the General, (b) from the British Prime Minister.

The position is that the Foreign Office late on Thursday once again telegraphed to General Franco demanding an immediate reply to the question:—

"Will you or will you not agree to pay compensation for the ships you have deliberately bombed?"

This is the second request of the kind which the Foreign Office has been compelled to make.

It is a mark of the crawling humiliation to which this country is being brought by Chamberlain's pro-Fascist policy, that the British Foreign Office should have to repeat such a categoric request twice within a week.

The first telegram demanding a compensation promise said that Franco's reply must be in the Foreign Office by midday Thursday last.

The telegram was simply ignored.

Thereupon t h e shipowners pointed out that in these circumstances it was futile to continue discussions with the Foreign Office.

LETTER TO P.M.

As reported here already, they then wrote (Thursday evening) to Mr. Chamberlain asking whether, in view of the failure of Franco to reply, Mr. Chamberlain had or had not been lying to the House of Commons when he told M.P.s on July 26 that Franco had promised compensation.

That evening the Foreign Office wired to Franco again, demanding an immediate reply.

No reply has arrived.

Mr. Chamberlain, nursing his catarrh, has not replied either.

Meantime furious messages from captains and seamen of British ships in Spanish waters are arriving in London asking what the Government is up to.

RECALL AGENT

And in London the demand is growing for the immediate recall of Sir Robert Hodgson from Burgos.

Sir Robert Hodgson, the Government assured the House of Commons, was sent back to Burgos as British Agent, with the object of arranging details of the Inquiry into the bombing and the compensation.

Sir Robert Hodgson has apparently not even been able to get the Burgos authorities to read the urgent telegrams dispatched to them by the British Foreign Office.

What, then, people are asking, is the use of this futile individual's presence in Burgos?

If he cannot do even the elementary bits of the job he is supposed to be doing, why is he kept there at great public expense?

And if he is not doing that job, what is he up to?

---

28 Franco Still Silent

(From Our Diplomatic Correspondent)

SEVEN days after the last urgent and "final" request from the Foreign Office, Franco has still not replied to the question: Will you or will you not pay compensation for British ships and seamen you have bombed?

It was explained yesterday that Franco has sent "an interim reply."

It was to the effect that he may be sending a proper reply almost any time now.

It is explained further that probably he has not got around to sending a proper reply because he has been so busy working on his reply to the Non-Intervention Committee—rejecting the plan for withdrawal of his foreign troops.

Whether he will accept compensation or reject compensation nobody knows—despite the fact that on July 26 Neville Chamberlain assured the House of Commons that Franco had already promised to pay in cases of deliberate bombing.

If Mr. Chamberlain was telling the truth on that occasion, what is delaying Franco now? was the question still being asked yesterday.

August 1938.

"Victory Will Be Ours" writes SAM WILDE (above), Commander of the British Battalion

---

WAKE OF THE BOMBERS
—Ruin and Death in Tarragona tenement after Franco's planes had passed

---

FASCISTS MAKE UNHAPPY MISTAKE

FRANCO has got so much into the habit of shooting first and asking questions afterwards that he has now made a rather embarassing mistake.

His police at San Sebastian, it is learned, have shot at the car of the Italian Ambassador at Burgos, and wounded his wife.

The car, in which the Ambassador, Count Viola di Campalto, his wife and chauffeur, were travelling, was fired at by a police patrol when it failed to stop on request. The Ambassador and the chauffeur were unhurt.

ROME CONFIRMATION

On the surface the matter has been smoothed over. Rome publishes a semi-official statement confirming the report of the shooting and adding that it was an "unfortunate incident." The Ambassador's car, it states, was mistaken for another suspected of being engaged in smuggling. It denies that the Ambassador's wife was wounded.

San Sebastian is about an hour's drive from the French frontier, so that the explanation seems a hollow one. Screened from publicity, Mussolini will inevitably demand from Franco that severe punishment be meted out to somebody.

August 24, 1938

... Main roads .... Railways

BRITISH HEROISM IN GREAT BATTLE OF SPAIN WAR

From PETER KERRIGAN

BARCELONA, Tuesday.

ON a hill two thousand feet high, which forms part of the famous Sierra Pandols, I sat yesterday outside headquarters and listened to the latest stories of the magnificent quality and endurance of our lads.

You have to be on the spot to understand the character of the fighting which is at present ranging around this Spanish Sierra. To reach the line it is necessary to climb 1,500 to 2,000 feet up the mountain side along paths which only just qualify for the name. Footing is over bare volcanic rock or loose rubble that flies down from underfoot, and up these same paths have to come food and munitions for the men

The enemy have been furiously attacking in this region, but have been completely rebuffed, and the hill I have referred to was taken by our troops only a few days ago. Since then it has been held in the face of every counter-attack of the enemy.

On the night of August 15 our battalion was in reserve to another battalion of the same brigade. The reserve position was very difficult because of the constant use of aviation by the enemy, but when the other battalions attacked our machine gun company moved into action in support.

KEEPING CONTACT

During this period of the later fighting George Fletcher performed invaluable work in maintaining liaison under the difficult conditions.

On the night of the 17th our men attacked in absolute darkness over unfamiliar ground under the most difficult circumstances. Not only was there no moon, but there were clouds.

In this action Lieutenant Commander Johnny Bowes showed outstanding courage, rallying the men and driving against the enemy. In this action there were many incidents characteristic of the courage of the men. Comrade Miller and Bob Cooney, Adjutant, set out on a difficult task contacting the other battalions and informing them of our position. Cooney has a splendid record over this period.

A FINE AMERICAN

Miller was a very fine American comrade who was killed by the same shell that wounded Sam Wilde. After having his hand dressed, Sam returned to the line, where he remained in spite of suggestions that he should leave for medical attention.

Another comrade who did a splendid job and has been singled out for special mention is the Chief Battalion Observer, Ivor Hickman. His was a specially difficult task, carried through with a high degree of courage.

These incidents are typical of the men, but I want to quote one other told me by Bob Cooney. It concerned Malcolm Smith, of Dundee.

He was killed together with our crack machine-gunner, George Jackson, of Cowdenbeath, and Charles MacLean, of Dundee.

On the day previous to his death, Comrade Smith was speaking to Bob Cooney. During the conversation he remarked that he would soon have been a year out in Spain and that it had been the best and happiest year of his life.

August 1938.

COUNTER-DRIVES FAIL TO SHAKE REPUBLIC'S HOLD

BARCELONA, Tuesday.

FASCIST forces, vainly attempting to break through the defences of the People's Army on the Ebro Front, have suffered incalculable losses and all their attacks have been repelled.

The invaders attacked unceasingly, supported by large concentrations of foreign planes and tanks. Four tanks were destroyed by Government fire, and papers found on the bodies of the occupants indicated that the units to which they belonged were Italian.

Government anti-aircraft fire brought down a German Heinkel plane and its pilot, who descended by parachute inside the Republican lines, was taken prisoner.

An example of the intensity of the fighting and of the heroism of the Republican troops was the battle for possession of Hill 444, South-East of Villaiba de los Arcos.

An enemy attack was repulsed, and after intense artillery and aviation preparation, 12 tanks led a renewed offensive. The attack was again repulsed and a tank was destroyed. The Fascists, reinforced, succeeded in occupying the hill after two hours of continuous fighting, but a violent counter-attack by Government troops dislodged them.

ITALIAN PLANE DOWN

A Savoia tri-motored plane was shot down on the Teruel Front. Franco's forces occupied Nava, Malillo and Campillo, 20 miles south-east of Puente Arzobispo, but the People's Army captured a hill dominating Nava.

A carefully-planned night attack, aiming at crossing the River Segre near Camarasa, has been defeated.

The Fascists attempted to cross the river at one of its principal

dams, but the surprise element of the move was destroyed by the watchfulness of the Government forces. There were extremely heavy losses among the Fascist ranks as they were mown down at close range and not one Fascist was able to cross the river.

In a powerful counter-attack Government troops have recaptured El Cubillo, in the south of Teruel Province. The advance was continued and the heights of Lamarina were captured.

Bible sales in Republican Spain for the period from December, 1937, to February of this year were almost a record for any previous three months, states Señor Aranjo, president of the Spanish branch of the British and Foreign Bible Society.

◆◆ A STRIKING article by Peter. ◆◆
Kerrigan, describing the part played by the British Battalion on the Ebro Front, will appear in Saturday's Daily Worker.

New Spanish Pilots Beat Italians

From PETER KERRIGAN

BARCELONA, Friday.

WHAT is the secret of the heavy losses by the enemy and the relatively low casualties among the Government aviators? In two days no less than 33 bombers have been brought down by Republican planes. It is not the technical superiority of our chasers, because the enemy has many good machines, among them the latest German types.

In the main it is the pilots. The Spanish pilots are absolutely fearless and show splendid powers of manoeuvring. The Italians have the poorest pilots and the casualties are high among them, while there are many who have no heart for the struggle, as was seen when one Italian pilot flew his plane into the Government lines and handed it over complete.

Among the Germans also there is not the same heart for the struggle, and they cannot but be affected by the evidence of their eyes each day when they are on flights and get back with big gaps. None of these pilots have the enthusiasm and fearless confidence of the young Spanish army.

TRAINED HUNDREDS

Another all-important feature in these facts is the fact that the whole of the Republican Air Force has been trained by Colonel Ignacio Cisneros. His career has been so striking that only a full biography at least will illustrate the influence he exerts in the struggle against the foreign air forces.

He was a major at the outbreak of the rebellion in July, 1936, and from the beginning placed himself in the struggle. He was appointed Supreme Commander of the Republican Air Force in September, 1936, and has held the post ever since.

He has been able to train the youthful Spanish pilots on a really extensive scale and this, together with he splendid organisation of his military resources, has been a big factor in the Government successes.

Hundreds of these young pilots cannot make use of their training because the Government is not able to secure the necessary planes owing to the so-called " Non-Intervention " policy.

Nevertheless, the present factors are an augury of what can be done. Out on the frontiers the new Spain is trying to buy airplanes, and when they get them Franco is finished.

AFTER smashing through the front in the Aragon, Fascism succeeded in reaching the coast and cutting off Catalonia from the rest of loyal territory. In the South the enemy is slowly pressing down the coast and is threatening the vital centres of the Republic. But the confidence in victory remains unimpaired; a state of affairs in marked contrast to that distressing pessimism prevailing in Britain.

The threats to the Republic are being met by new superhuman efforts, like those that were made in March.

But all the heroism and solidarity of the people will be of no avail unless there is an army capable of organising a resistance and preventing the advance of Fascism. Can the Army do the job? It certainly can.

Now 900,000 strong the army is politically unified for the first time and, although still suffering from a shortage of arms, possesses sufficient to carry through the tactics of resistance.

TRAINING AND MORE TRAINING

There still remains, however, one basic weakness, the inexperience of many of the higher commands in face of the enemy troops directed by the German and Italian General Staffs. That is why training and yet more training is the order of the day.

The proof of this tremendous improvement in the Spanish People's Army is to be seen in the contrast between the retreat in the Aragon during March and the mighty resistance now taking place in the Levante.

Forced back by the heavy weight of artillery and tanks, and a sudden and overwhelming concentration of airplanes, the old militia system) the units did not always act together but because there was no fortified line to fall back on; their officers were inexperienced and because of political differences (remnants of Government troops retreated because there was treachery by Fascist agents, and in some places the opening of the front by Trotskyists.

And always there was the terrible shortage of airplanes, guns and munitions, the fruits of non-intervention.

These weaknesses, many of them inseparable from the building of a new regular army, are now being burned out.

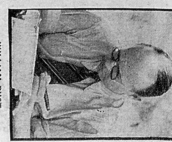

WILLIAM RUST

The Spanish people are prepared—if the democratic countries do not come rapidly to their assistance—to carry on a long war for their independence, a war in which there may be still further setbacks before victory is won.

What are the immediate military perspectives? The Catalonian front is quiet at the moment, it is solid and well defended. The Republic is in a position to launch an offensive, but the enemy is not likely to attack because their main forces, throw their main forces into the south, although there exists the possibility that they may attempt another push along the Pyrenean foothills with the object of cutting the rail and road connection at Puigcerda.

" TO RESIST IS TO CONQUER "

In the Levante the Republicans may have to fall back on Sagunto, but the enemy will not take Valencia, which is mobilising as Madrid did in November, 1936. On the other fronts there have been attacks, but the Fascist commanders, who lack man-power, are not in a position to launch a serious offensive on these fronts.

"To resist is to conquer" is the slogan of the hour. This slogan, issued by Negrin in March, sums up the whole present tasks of the Spanish people, because to resist means to wear down the enemy and to gain time, thus enabling the army to overcome its weaknesses. To resist now means to prepare for the future offensive. To resist means more time for the democratic countries.

which the capitalist Press has declared to be "the end." You see the "beginning of the end." You see the same tough development in process, as the democratic forces seek to pull themselves together to the point where their punch can tell.

It was within a few days of the outbreak of war that the Fifth Regiment—germ and core of the New Army—was organised in Madrid, with 200 men as the first full strength.

It was almost at the same time that the British Communist Party raised the demand that the carrying out of International obligations to the Spanish Republic, and the sending of arms, and called for the unification of all the forces of democracy in defence of democracy in Spain.

By the middle of the summer the Fascist powers had begun the real invasion of Spain.

THE first wave of the invasion of Spain brought the invaders all the way up the Tagus Valley. Neutral American correspondents, who were with the invading armies, have told the story of that frightful advance—with the bodies of murdered working men hanging from the trees or by the road sides of their villages, shot in the back of the head, with their hands tied together, lying there like monuments of the Fascist advance. On the other side, the Spanish

SUFFICIENT RESOURCES TO BRING VICTORY

I REPEAT that the situation is extremely grave. The independence of Spain is seriously menaced. But Spain possesses sufficient resources to enable it not only to check the enemy, but to repulse and completely defeat him.

Let us take a survey of our country. The districts with the densest population, with the highest industrial development, are in the hands of the Republic. The most advanced agrarian provinces, too, are ours: Madrid, Catalonia, and the Levante.

The countryside of the Levante, which is one of the most intensely cultivated and agriculturally productive provinces in Europe, is capable of feeding a considerable portion of Spain. Catalonia represents a powerful industrial basis, which supplied a part of the war material of France during the Great War.

We own the great Mediterranean ports and a considerable section of the Pyrenees frontier, securing for us freedom of communication and trade with the whole world.

The enemy has seized some very rich districts in Spain, especially the Basque country, Asturias, and a part of Andalusia.

But the difference between us and the enemy is that he encounters tremendous difficulties in his attempts to mobilise the resources of the country in the territory seized by the invaders.

It is difficult to make a people perform slave work after they have once known freedom.—PASIONARIA, Spain's woman Communist leader at a recent meeting of the Central Committee of the Communist Party in Madrid.

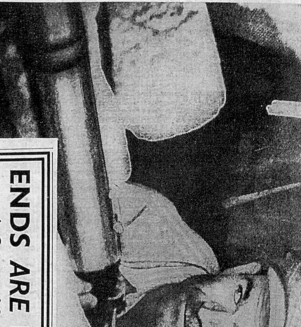

Rebellion crushed . . . and Revived by Dictators . . . the History of the Struggle . . . and the People's Capacity for Victory . . . Frank Pitcairn writes—

RUN your eye back along the news files of the spring and early summer of '36, and you wonder—now—that the Fascist attack that was coming in Spain was not more plain for all world to see and prepare against.

The provocations, the propaganda in the British Press, the visits to Berlin, the gun-running and all the rest of it were obvious enough, as it seems now.

Yet, as everyone knows, the fact is that at the moment when the conspiracy hatched in Berlin, Rome, and the Canary Islands broke into open military attack—from Madrid to Paris to London to New York—though they were much stronger, really, than the enemy, were less ready, less united, less prepared all round the democratic forces of the west spiracy.

The history of the war, in Spain and outside Spain, can be seen as above all the race between the constantly intensified Fascist attack and the organisation of the forces of democratic defence to a pitch where their real, latent superiority in strength can, and will, become victoriously effective.

At the gates of Madrid came in light the first magnificent results of what had been accomplished; above all by the people of Madrid who, despite the frightful pressure of the swift enemy advance, despite the Fifth Column, despite the shortage of everything from machine-guns to trained officers, united in the organisation of a defence which the world described as "a miracle."

Hundreds and hundreds of miles away, one people, and one Government, separated by the whole of a hostile Fascist Europe, the Soviet people and its Government, stood by the people of Spain.

side, it was the story of a people struggling against fearful odds to organise and unify its defences.

Arms were withheld from them. The British Government was responsible. Leaders of the British Labour movement supported the British Government in that. The real forces of British democracy were not united at that. The retreat went on.

But with it, behind it, went on too the organisation of the possibilities of defence.

At Guadalajara the largest Italian army engaged in infantry battle since the Great War, met and was routed by the newly trained troops of the new Spanish Army, with the Italians of the Garibaldi Battalion among the shock troops.

But Malaga had fallen. The Basque provinces were invaded. Trotskyist-Fascist agents were working unimpeded in Barcelona, organising disunity and blood-shed.

It was evident that despite all that had been done, there re-mained as much and more to do for the people of Spain.

Again they broke through, determined to put in order the machinery of defence and of ultimate victory.

Caballero was turned out and in his place the People's Front established the strong Govern-ment of Negrin, with a Mandate to do for all Spain what had already been done for Madrid.

QUICK on the heels of that ful Republican offensives—Brunete, on the central front, Belchite on the eastern front. And after that: Teruel. Those proved

That despite everything, the political and military organisa-tion of Spain—the People's Front Government and the People's Army—had advanced to the point where it was cap-able of taking the initiative, capable of actually overcoming the forces then available on the other side.

The fact was as obvious to Hitler, to Mussolini, and to Cham-berlain, as it was to people in Madrid, Valencia and Barcelona. The vast international counter-attack got under way. New Fascist

forces poured into Spain, new material on a scale which would have been fantastic only a few months before.

There began the drive outside Spain, and inside Spain which brought the Fascist forces to the sea, closed the French frontier at the orders of the Chamberlain Government, sank British ships one after another, killed and wounded scores of British sailors, to go ahead.

Once again the Chamberlain gave Mussolini the signal

Once again the capitalist Press —the people who announced in detail Franco's entry into Madrid, the people who every month saw the "end in sight"—had a rosy vision of Fascist victory.

ROUGHLY and method-ically and the organisation victory goes on behind the Republican lines and along the Republican fronts.

They look to other sections of the democratic front—above all to Britain—to accomplish advances as great as theirs.

WORKERS! PEASANTS! TRADESMEN!

THE GROWTH OF THE PEOPLE'S ARMY

"To Resist is to Conquer"

By WILLIAM RUST

(Daily Worker Correspondent recently returned from Spain)

FRANCO, in an interview with a French Fascist newspaper, admitted that if he had not in late July and early August, 1936, been able to use uninterruptedly the German and Italian planes to bomb the Republican fleet out of the straits of Gibraltar and also for the actual carrying of troops across, he might never have been able to begin the real invasion of Spain.

He was able to do just that because of the weakness of the international democratic front — meaning mainly Britain, where we were not strong or united enough to force immediately international action to stop the Fascist aggression against Spain.

Follow the war through all its grim stages and disasters, each one of the re-

United And Said "No Pasaran!"

THE International Bri-gade, symbol and weapon of the awakening of the democracy of Europe, was there to play its glorious part in the defence of the capital.

All through the winter and the early spring the battle for Madrid raged all around the city and ment, the Valencia road. Aided and abetted by the British Govern-ment, the Germans and the Italians hurled new forces against the defences of the city; and at Arganda Bridge 800 men of the British Battalion hurled them back.

the people of Barcelona flock in thousands to defend their liberty, their homes with Museum firing pieces (literally), household implements, bare fists, and an honest the tram tracks, bare fists, and an honest revolt in a few days.

WE thought the war would be over And so it would have been but for the whole-sale intervention of Germany and Italy, and other countries.

I appeal particularly to sportsmen and sportswomen to continue their support of the heroic defenders of Spanish democracy.

In sport the defeat of Fascism means the freedom to play with whom you choose, irrespective of class, colour or creed; the right to play for the love of the game—not as pawns in a vast military training cannon-fodder campaign; the privilege to build up by sport and recreation a strong and healthy nation prepared and willing to play its part in the progress of the world and not the destruction of your fellow-sportsmen and workers.
And that's worth fighting for!

★

PASIONARIA

Spain's Woman Communist Leader Says . . .

and . . . As Spain is today, it is only the calling up and enlisting in the army of all men able to bear arms which can bring an enhancement of enthusiasm and of the struggle.

Our superiority over the enemy consists precisely in the fact that we are invariably able to explain to the people for what they are fighting, and why the great sacrifices are necessary and indispensable, while the enemy finds himself faced by a resistance among the people which only grows with the amount of effort demanded of them.

It is clear that the formation of large reserves must not mean any slackening in the efforts to improve constantly the selection and efficiency of the army. These efforts must be intensified to the utmost.

All the World is singing
When the people are free at last.

But silent now the guitar,
And the jota aragones.
First comes the International,
Then the Marseillaise.

Red with the people's blood,
From the bombs of the enemy's raids,
Our flags are blooming like flowers
On freedom's barricades.

Girl of the People's Army,
Do not be jealous of me.
If to my heart I take
Both you and Liberty.

Translated by
LANGSTON HUGHES.

Send donations and contributions to Dependants' Aid Committee, 1, Litchfield Street, W.C.2.

WOMEN TAKE THEIR STAND AGAINST DEATH DAILY

NEARLY two years ago when men from every country in Europe were pouring into Spain with a cry for freedom on their lips, there were being organised also in every country the medical aid units that have since become famous.

The part played by the women of Spain in the Republican fight is a legend throughout the world; the work of those many other heroic women who went from the peace of their own lands to nurse the wounded of war-shattered Spain is not so well known.

In Spain today there are 20 British nurses, working night and day, risking wounds and death—for Fascist planes show no dis-crimination in favour of hospitals or ambulances.

Most recently wounded was nurse "Penny" Phelps, known to hundreds of fighting men in Spain as "English Penny," who was injured in a Fascist bombing raid on Castellon. Her wounds included concussion, fractured ribs, internal injuries and severe shock.

Another nurse, writing home with news of "Penny's" wounds, said :—
"The planes circle over our villa and Marguerite and I look up at them with our hearts in our mouths, although we both wear our 'old school ties' on the outside."

Those British nurses have seen men of every country suffer bravely in this fight; they have picked dying women and children from streets that ran with blood; they have seen hospitals bombed. And Winifred Bates, one of them, talking to the DAILY WORKER, summed up what they felt.

"You see it's urgent; they want help in Spain; they're fighting for life. Why can't every British Labour leader see that? We can help the wounded, but they can save Spain."

More than £56,000 has been collected in Britain for the Spanish Medical Aid Com-mittee since the first unit went out in August, 1936.

Nineteen base hospitals and a large number of front-line hospitals have been established; there is no front where members of the British Medical Aid units are not working. The total personnel now numbers 131—doctors, nurses, driver pharmacists, stretcher bearers.

In Spain today there are 72 British ambulances, lorries, mobile surgical vans and other vehicles. Supplies have gone to the Spanish Government's Medical Depart-ment almost every fortnight.

And the organisation needs every pos-sible support that can be given to it in gifts and cash. It is saving lives; it needs help.

British nurses on duty.

THESE HELP SPAIN.....

THESE ARE
THE REAL
BRITISH
FIGHTERS
FOR
FREEDOM

THE story of the heroic struggle of the Spanish people is linked up for ever with the story of the International Brigade. The people of Britain have more than a bond of sympathy with the people of Spain: they have an unbreakable bond of flesh and blood with them: their brothers in the British Battalion of the Brigades. Men from Ireland, Scotland and Wales, are now part of the very soil of Spain. They will not return to us: but as we are faithful to their memory, so we must not, betray them and their heroic deaths, by being faithless to the cause for which they died.

✳ Others, fortunately, have lived to return to us, in spite of their willingness to give their all in the struggle. But some of them, like Harold King,

Battalion Commander SAM WILDE (right) and BOB COONEY (left) pose for the photographer with smiling Spanish girls.

George Bisset, John Horner, have given their right hands and arms for democracy; like Ken White and Tommy Fanning, their right legs. Forty other comrades have received medical attention for nerve complaints, etc., in London alone, and have been attended by a panel of twenty doctors. Approximately ten doctors in the provinces have treated between fifty and sixty comrades. Fifty of the lads have been sent on convalescent holidays for periods ranging from one month to three months, to ten or fifteen friends in the country. Approximately five hundred men have received assistance varying according to circumstances.

✳ This has been the minimum that British democracy could do to show its gratitude to them. But, in addition, widows have been succoured; wives and children of men in the battalion have been assisted.

✳ How has this been possible!

✳ This entirely voluntary work has been undertaken by the Dependants' and Wounded Aid Committee, on behalf of the British people. The members and workers of the Committee have realised their responsibilities and their trust and have done their utmost to fulfil them faithfully, as is shown by the fact that the organisational expenses of the Committee since its inception have come to less than five per cent. of the monies collected.

✳ The Committee has been supported by National trade unions, Co-operatives, political parties, Spanish Aid Committees, factory collections, and by individuals of good will all over the country and even in the Colonies and Dominions and in foreign countries. The response to its appeals has been magnificent and continues to be so. Unfortunately, however, practically every

Charlotte Haldane

penny received has had to be spent immediately. The recent drain on human health and strength of the battles in the Aragon has brought the Committee face to face with a drastic situation. Much more money is now wanted to assist the wounded returning after putting up a heroic resistance to the Fascist onslaught; for the women and children cannot be dropped because the wounded must also be looked after.

✳ We owe a debt to the British Battalion that can never be repaid in cash, but cash is the first and most essential requirement. Pay tribute to the dead; honour the living; help the noble women who have never let their men down, but who have quietly and bravely stood up to the awful strain imposed on them by the absence of their loved ones, knowing them often to be in danger, rally to the support of the children and see that we can give them a summer holiday; people of Britain, the Dependants' Aid Committee is the channel through which you can pour your help to the men who did not count the cost when they went to fight for the

---

British Battalion Newsreel

ATHLETES against FASCISM

By GEORGE H. ELVIN,
(International Secretary, British Workers' Sports Association.)

IT is just two years ago since I was awakened in the early hours by the outbreak of the Spanish war. I had gone to Spain as manager of the British contingent to the People's Olympiad at Barcelona.

We did not see the Olympiad, but we saw

SPANISH FOLK SONG OF THE WAR

Frontiers that divide the people,
Soon we'll tear apart.
The masses speak a thousand tongues—
But have one heart.

For the workers no boasting Fatherlands,
Only freedom and peace,
So that through peace and freedom
All may find release.

The men sing as they work.
The women sing at their tasks.

REPUBLICAN DEFENCES FOIL BIG ATTACK

From PETER KERRIGAN
August 1938. BARCELONA, Wednesday.

FLINGING TANKS, PLANES, ARTILLERY AND MEN INTO A DESPERATE ATTACK, THE FASCIST FORCES ARE BATTERING UN-AVAILINGLY AGAINST REPUBLICAN DEFENCES ON THE EBRO FRONT.

The battle grows more and more intense, and the weight of arms possessed by the Fascists indicates that Mussolini is pouring fresh supplies from behind the line following Franco's rejection of the British plan for evacuation of volunteers.

Swarms of tanks are especially prominent in the recent attacks. Despite all their pressure, however, the Fascists have made only a slight advance.

Surprise attacks on the Republican positions at Bechi, north-west of Nules, have been repelled. The Fascists pressed in the Puente del Arzobispo sector, but Republican forces crossed the Zujar River and inflicted severe losses on the enemy.

Thousands of men have been flung into the attack. Numbers of enemy killed and wounded have been great because they have had to face troops who have maintained the utmost calmness and utilised their weapons and position with deadly effect.

The enemy Command has been utterly regardless of the lives of its soldiers. As a consequence the entire enemy division has suffered the same fate as the 4th Navarres Division and has been annihilated in efforts which have only gained a few yards of territory.

35th Division unconquerable on the Sierra Pandols.

In the words of del Vayo, during a visit to the Ebro line, "The Government and Republic are confident that you will repulse all the enemy attacks and will not allow a singe inch of soil to fall into the hands of the invader.

"Thanks to the action of units like the 11th and 35th Divisions the world has discovered that the Army of the Republic is the envy of any other army in discipline and enthusiasm."

EXPECTED BIG ADVANCE

In one attack on one small sector one of their battalions left the best part of three companies dead on the field when they retreated.

The foreign invaders were so confident that they had every preparation made for their expected advance. It was possible to see big concentrations of motor-lorries behind Gandesa waiting for the Government line to break. But the line did not break.

In addition, the enemy aviation had another disastrous day. The Government planes engaged in a whole series of fights with the enemy.

ENEMY PLANES DOWN

Seven of the Italian Fiats were brought down in flames in the Sierra Pandols. Three were destroyed near Mora de Ebro, and another between Mora and Miravet.

Later in the day a Messerschmidt was brought down, and all this without loss of any Government planes which were also able to bomb the enemy lines and troop concentrations very effectively.

A still bigger air battle was raging late in the evening and the news so far states that five more enemy planes were brought down.

In spite of Mussolini's supplies and the fact that the closed frontier continues, the whole of the People's Army is inspired by the same spirit that has made the 11th and

Food is very welcome after hours of fighting. Here are some of the fighters of the British Battalion gathering round for a meal.

CROSSING THE EBRO

August 1938.

RESTING

Taking a rest. Peter Kerringan, Daily Worker Correspondent, hatless and in his shirtsleeves, can be seen on the right.

BRITONS BATTLE FOR SEVEN DAYS WITHOUT A PAUSE

AUGUST 27, 1938

PETER KERRIGAN, Daily Worker Correspondent on the Ebro Front in Spain, tells of the Battle for Hill 481 at Gandesa

THERE is no man writing who can tell this story adequately. There is no one of you reading who can really understand it—for you were not on that hill at Gandessa. This is a record of such high and deathless heroism that to write of it is almost an impertinence.

When news came that the Republican Army had attacked along the Ebro River; was advancing, had relieved the Fascist pressure against Valencia, you in Britain must have been cheered and happy. When you heard that the British Battalion of the International Brigade had played a big part in the attack you must have been proud.

But you did not know then what the British Battalion had done. The glorious, heartrending details of those days are only just reaching England.

You did not know, for instance, how the Battalion hurled itself untiringly hour after hour, day after day against the key position of Hill 481. You knew nothing of how our men had stumbled, run, charged up the slopes of the hill against pill boxes, machine-guns and trenches that fortified the crest—to be thrown back and to charge again under a hail of bullets and shells.

You could not know then how young Maguire, of Greenock, found himself alone at the summit, shouted defiance to the entire enemy positions and emptied his rifle at them before he dropped to cover. You had not heard how the whole battalion, after seven nerve-racking days in action, calmly held a sing-song while Fascists shelled the position with artillery and trench mortars.

If after hearing these things the whole Labour movement of Great Britain does not—as it should have done long ago—adopt officially and with emphasis the British Battalion of the International Brigade as its own great responsibility, with all that such responsibility means, then the Labour movement is false to every tradition in its long history.

WHEN the Republican advance swept across the Ebro towards Gandessa through hilly country every height except one was taken. One held out; the most important of all—Hill 481, key position dominating Gandessa, heavily fortified.

Against Hill 481 the British Battalion was flung. Theirs was the position of honour, theirs also the post of danger; and theirs the greatest prize, to be fought for with unconquerable spirit, to be paid for with agony and wounds and death.

On July 25 the British Battalion crossed the River Ebro with the rest of the International Brigade; from that time until August 1—seven days—the Battalion fought without pause.

They fought in the heat of the Spanish sun without water; they marched over the hills and charged against the enemy almost barefoot, for their shoes had been cut to pieces by sharp rocks; they fought in clothes that were only rags. They fought with that rare heroism that passes into legend. And they kept on fighting.

From July 25 to July 30 they had nothing to drink but a little water, sometimes they went for a day without even a drop to moisten burning lips and parched throats. But they kept on fighting.

And late in the evening of August 1, exhausted—but did not—they were preparing yet another dash up Hill 481 when the order came from Brigade Headquarters for them to cease.

GREAT men. They didn't have to go out there to Spain. There were no bands or recruiting marches to rouse a romantic martial spirit in them; no jingoistic national newspaper campaign to dazzle them with the flashy glare of patriotism, no crowds to cheer their departure; no Government to send them out —only a Government to stop them.

They went away secretly to fight for things their Government no longer prizes—freedom, justice, democracy—and to oppose a tyranny which they knew would one day threaten their homes and yours if men failed to offer opposition.

The whole Labour movement of Britain knows why they went. There are some who would have the Labour movement shuffle the responsibility for these men and their dependents, even while it enjoys the reflection of their fame. For such meanness there is no measure of contempt.

THE two principal attacks against Hill 481 took place on July 31 and August 1, at the end of a gruelling five days when the men were already tired. The details of the attack and the behaviour of the men given here were told to me by the official Brigade Observer, who is not British.

Number 4 Company lost its commissar, Economedis, wounded. His successor, Brazell Thomas, was killed. Number 3 Company's Spanish commissar, Vano Vanos, was killed, and his deputy wounded. . . .

LISTEN again, all of you who would fail to give the men of the British Battalion and their dependants the support they have earned if ever men earned anything.

During the attack, young Maguire, of Greenock, reached the top of the hill and found himself alone. The Fascists shouted "Rendido," meaning that he should surrender.

He replied, "Rendido be d—, and facing them, emptied his rifle, at the same time stepping back until he dropped below their line of fire and got away.

Listen once more, any of you who recognise gallantry, and any who admire the steadfastness of men that can screw tortured nerves and weary bodies to the sticking point.

I sat on the night when the attack ceased and listened to Sam Wilde, Bob Cooney and George Fletcher start a sing-song. They sang choruses and songs, the other comrades joining in, while the Fascists shelled the position with artillery and trench mortars. No wonder the Brigade Observer turned suddenly to me and whispered, "What morale these men have!"

TWENTY-SEVEN members of the Battalion and 23 Spaniards who fought side by side with them were mentioned in dispatches after the battle.

It is impossible to quote the remarks that accompanied every recommendation, but here are a few of the British ones, taken at random:—

Corporal Michael Lehane: " He organised an attack on Hill 481 with some 25 of his comrades, and got to within 25 yards of his objective. . . . When he fell seriously wounded, he refused to be picked up by the stretcher-bearers, as he did not wish to expose his comrades to the danger of enemy fire."

Private A. Jamelson: " He carried messages for the Battalion Commissar beneath intense artillery and machine-gun fire. . . . He was wounded."

Private Michael O'Riordan: "He carried his machine-gun into every action, and when he was ordered to withdraw he waited until the whole of the company had done so. . . . When wounded, he refused to leave his position until the others had to leave it. Even then he did not leave until he was ordered by the Commander and Commissar."

Captain Sam Wilde: "For his untiring energy, efficiency, sang froid, giving an example of bravery to the whole battalion."

Private Alex. McLanders: "For having fulfilled his duty valiantly in exceptionally dangerous conditions, and in spite of his illness." (Specially commended).

And many more. Fine men. Real men. The salt of the earth.

THESE are men whose shadow overwhelms their Prime Minister, whose actions show the intrigues of their Government as a mean and muddy thing.

There were some who tried to tell these men that the fighting in Spain was not their quarrel. They knew better. For these men —Ted Edwards, Ivor Hickman, George Forbes, Tom Maguire, and many another—are the real Britain.

The plan was for No. 2 Company to attack on the left side of the hill while No. 1 and No. 3 attacked on the right. The Machine-Gun Company was to cover the advance with its fire.

On July 31 the men fought all day unceasingly until 10 p.m., despite heavy casualties. Frank Cyril West and five men of No. 1 Company reached the top of the hill and flung hand grenades into the enemy positions, but were driven back by grenades and rifle fire. They discovered that the hill was strongly fortified with concrete pill-boxes; in addition, it had four machine-guns at each end and a battalion of reserves waiting on the wooded slopes at the rear.

Next day the attack began again. A special letter, signed by Sam Wilde (Battalion Commander) and Bob Cooney (Political Commissar) was passed round. The letter emphasised the importance of Hill 481 as the key to success for the whole attack on this front. It said that courage, audacity, determination and rapidity of movement were needed to take the position.

"And," said the letter, "the British Battalion has all these qualities."

So into action they went again at 10 a.m. And all day, facing that terrible bombardment of artillery, machine-gun and trench mortar fire, they flung themselves against the hill. Time after time they got within bombing distance of the enemy, time after time they were forced back. At 10 p.m. they were preparing for yet another attack when they were ordered to stop.

AS I write this I look back for something to convey to you what was happening during those two days of fighting. There comes to my mind the ordeal of No. 2 Company. Listen!

Number 2 Company started out under the command of John Angus. He was wounded in the chest. The next commander was Gregory. He also was wounded. The third was Harrington: wounded. The fourth was Joe Harkins, of Clydebank. He was killed. The fifth was Lewis Clive; killed. Now the political commissar, John Powers, is in command.

Yes, listen! Let the whole British Labour movement listen. Let every man and woman in Britain who cares for selfless devotion to a cause listen.

Ben Richardson, George Fletcher, Lewis Clive, John Power, and a hundred more saw freedom attacked, justice threatened, happiness darkened—and sprang to defend the things they cherished, as their forefathers had done before them.

Jack Nalty, Henry Pearson, Cyril Scott, John Smith, Leonard Thompson, and all their fine company are not people who will ever be understood by those cold and cunning little men who sit in Whitehall and Downing Street today.

BUT they are Britain—in the best of Britain's tradition. They are more. They are humanity, as the International Brigade and the men of the Spanish Republican Army are humanity. They and all their comrades are today the highest hope of democracy and a decent life for the future. They have fought and suffered to save not merely Spain, but this country and all Europe from the barbarity of Fascist domination.

And the British Labour movement, whose name they have saved, must accept not merely the fame of them, but also the responsibility.

Cutting from "Daily Herald"

Republican Victory In The South

From PETER KERRIGAN

BARCELONA, Sunday.

STRIKING back hard at the Italian and German drive on the famous Almaden mercury mines, Republican forces have passed to the offensive on that southern front.

A large strip of territory, a dozen villages, and considerable war material have been taken from the Fascists.

Republican troops yesterday had reached the hills of Marroquin, more than ten miles south of the River Zujar.

The Fascist troops are retreating in disorder, losing considerable numbers of prisoners.

The significance of the battle is greater even than the above facts indicate. For it is a severe blow to high hopes and important ambitions of the German and Italian general staffs.

BLOW TO HITLER

They had concentrated a great deal of their strength on the effort to secure the rich Almaden mines, whose mercury is invaluable for war purposes.

Moreover, the action has demonstrated that the Government has now on the southern front forces as capable of decisive action as those on the Levante, on the Ebro, and at Madrid.

Drive On Mines Is Held

MADRID, Monday.

THE railway and road from Castuera to Cabeza del Buey have been cut by Spanish Republican troops in their advance on the Estremadura front.

As a result Castuera, held by the Fascists, is imperilled, while the Republican advance in this quarter is also holding back the attempted Fascist drive towards Almaden and the rich mercury deposits of that region, so coveted by the Italians.

HEAVY DAMAGE

Government planes bombed concentrations of enemy forces throughout the day yesterday and, according to reports received here, have inflicted very heavy damage.

Meanwhile, it is learned here, Dr. Negrin, the Prime Minister, has sent a telegram of congratulation to Captain Castro, commander of the destroyer Jose Luis Diez, which fought five Fascist warships in the Straits of Gibraltar on Saturday.

NAVAL CADET

Captain Castro is a Basque, twenty-four years of age. He was born in Tolosa, son of a former Republican Governor of the Province of Vizcaya. At the outbreak of the revolt he was a naval cadet. He was sent to Cartagena, where he served aboard the cruiser Mendez Nunez.

When part of the fleet was sent to the Biscay coast, he was placed in command of the Jose Luis Diez. He was later transferred to the Ciscar, aboard which ship he fought three engagements with the Fascist cruiser Almirante Cervera and distinguished himself in action. Later he was transferred back to the command of the Jose Luis Diez.

In the action fought on Saturday the Republican destroyer, whose tonnage is 1,566, which mounts five guns and has a complement of 175 officers and men, was opposed to five enemy ships whose tonnage is 26,920, mounting 40 guns and with a combined complement of 2,188 officers and men.

HARRY POLLITT greets a member of the Brigade. Picture taken on his last visit to Spain.

POLLITT VISITS WOUNDED BRITISH SPAIN FIGHTERS

From PETER KERRIGAN

BARCELONA, Wednesday.

ALTHOUGH he only arrived back here from his lightning visit to the Ebro front line at 3 in the morning, Harry Pollitt, now on his fourth trip to Spain, began immediately to visit the British wounded in the several hospitals.

Mataro—situated on the coast about 15 miles away—was the first hospital to be visited. With more than over seven hundred patients, the most seriously wounded, it is run by English and American doctors and nurses, with Dr. Tudor Hart as chief surgeon.

There are in all 35 Britons there and they are all doing well.

We were taken round the wards by Dr. Hart himself, who had just finished work in the operating theatre.

It would have done your hearts good to see the way each of the men looked up as Harry approached their bed. Crouched beside them, he talked to them and took notes of messages to be taken home and the requests to be fulfilled.

Mick Economides, John Angus, Gus Daubensbeck, young Benson of Leeds, Arthur Nicol of Dundee, and many others, including some boys who are recovering after a really tough time, all met and talked with Harry.

THE SMELL OF PINES

After a hasty farewell we set off on the long stretch to Santa Paloma Hospital, which is possibly one of the most beautifully situated in Spain, snuggled among tall trees at the base of the hills with its own natural mineral waters.

It was dusk when we arrived and the recent rain had brought out the smell of the pines as we threaded our way in the ghostly night down the long avenue to the hospital.

News of our arrival had preceded us and the Director and Political Commissar were waiting to greet us.

We went along to a common room with all the boys except four, who were in bed, following along behind us, and there Harry had a talk with them. This hospital has the less seriously wounded, and here is was possible for Harry to speak to the boys as he had spoken to the Battalion, but in much more favourable conditions

Councillor Jones, of Liverpool, whose arm is in a sling, was listening attentively with the others grouped around him. Dusty Miller, of The Vale, wounded again, Malcolm Sneddon, of Neath Hill, Lieutenant Morris Davies whom we had all been worrying about, because we had had no trace of him after he had been wounded, and all the others. . . .

LAUGHTER CAME EASILY

Laughter came more easily here. The tension that was inevitably at the Battalion was in no way evident. They were eager for news, and greedily drunk in every word as though it was something precious that had to be taken now, or it would be lost to them.

Then afterwards followed the personal and private talks with some of the comrades and the quick run round the wards where the others were. None of their wounds are serious—nothing more than the poisoned foot of Miles Tomalin.

One little incident happened yesterday—one which the older readers of the DAILY WORKER will appreciate. It was Harry's meeting with Ernie Woolley. They embraced like long-lost brothers, and Ernie, who is doing splendid work here, accompanied us on our journey, so that we were able to exchange views on many questions.

REPUBLICAN ARMY SUCCESS

MADRID, Tuesday.—The Extremadura front was once again the main scene of military activity yesterday and the villages of Gargantilla and Sevilleja, 20 miles south-east of Puente del Arzobispo were captured by the Republicans. North of Toledo hilly country is impeding the insurgent drive towards Almaden.

In the Zujar sector the Republicans continued their recent advance.

The insurgents made bombing raids on Benalcazar and Hinojosa, south-east of Castuera, during the day, but in the Ebro zone insurgent attacks near the town of Gandesa were repulsed.—Exchange Telegraph.

WHAT I SAW IN REBEL SPAIN

WHAT I SAW IN REBEL SPAIN

—Lady Chamberlain

By Our Own Correspondent

BURGOS, Monday.

LADY CHAMBERLAIN, widow of Sir Austen Chamberlain, is having a very pleasant holiday in rebel Spain.

When she arrived here after an inspection of the Auxilio Social—the Falange (Fascist) social-aid organisation at Valladolid—she told me:—

"I am extremely impressed with this organisation, which is likely to have a profound effect for good for future Spanish generations by improving the living standards of the masses and the teaching of modern hygiene, food values and caring for the destitute.

"I visited one of the Auxilio's children's dining-rooms, where there is plenty of air and bright colours. Here destitute children eat two meals of excellent food each day.

"Children have to wash their hands and brush their teeth and learn to appreciate clean tablecloths and table ware, with the consequence that they expect their parents to improve the hygiene and cheerfulness of the home.

"Thousands of Spanish girls do voluntary work in the Auxilio Social by creating a real feeling of social service, which scarcely existed before."

Editorial below.....

War Orphans

LADY CHAMBERLAIN is in rebel Spain, and she is highly delighted (quite impartially and non-politically, as she explains) with all she has seen.

In particular she is pleased with the thoughtful care given by the Fascists to the upbringing of the orphans.

If there had been no Fascists there would have been fewer orphans.

August 1938.

Republicans Still Advancing In The South

BARCELONA, Wednesday.—Republican troops, on the Extremadura front, now hold the greater part of the Zujar-Castuera railway and have advanced during the past three days to a line about seven miles north-east of Puerto de San Vincente. Communications between Castuera and Almorchon have been cut and the latter town is in danger of falling.

Operations are proceeding successfully and according to plan. The railway out of Almaden is under Republican artillery fire up to the point at which it branches towards Cordova. In the westward advance south of the River Zujar, Government troops are now approaching the Guadalatra river.

The offensive started by the enemy nine days ago was at first successful in one or two unimportant respects. It was stopped more than 60 miles to the north of Almaden and did not threaten seriously to penetrate the mountain chain north of the river Guadiana.

Counter-attacking, Republican troops recaptured a number of important positions and are now well in advance of their former line.

Meanwhile, the Ebro front line is being stabilised, more or less along the line reached in the Government attack of July 30.

INVADERS DRIVEN OUT OF HALF KEY NORTH CHINA PROVINCE

August 1938.

From Our Own Correspondent

HANKOW, Thursday.

EXCITING news has just reached here of the progress made in the struggle against the Japanese invaders in the extreme north of China.

It is contained in an appeal issued by the Hopei-Chahar Committee of the Communist Party of China, which has been sent, through Chu Teh, Commander-in-Chief of the Eighth People's Revolutionary Army, to all anti-Japanese organisations in the country.

Until units of the Eighth Army arrived in Hopei, Jehol and Chahar, these Chinese Provinces were under Japanese military rule, which was challenged only by isolated guerilla detachments.

After the coming of the Eighth Army units, however, the appeal states, heavy blows were dealt the enemy, with the result that several counties, including Shinglung, were cleared of Japanese and the whole eastern part of Hopei was covered by the anti-Japanese movement.

Now the Chinese national flag once again flies over Eastern Hopei.

When the Eighth Army arrived at the beginning of July and began to engage the enemy in fierce battles, there began an armed anti-Japanese guerilla struggle of the Chinese population in many counties in the Japanese rear.

JOINED BY DEFENCE TROOPS

These guerilla detachments then fused into a local anti-Japanese People's Army which was joined

by the "Defence Troops" organised by the Japanese in east Hopei.

So rapid was the advance of the Chinese forces that towards the end of the month detachments of the People's Army in Jehol succeeded in cutting the railway line between Peiping and Mukden, key Manchurian town.

They also managed to put out of commission iron and gold mines which had been seized and worked by the enemy.

MINERS FORM ARMY

On July 18 a big, new detachment of anti-Japanese troops was formed by seven thousand of the workers of the Tangshan mines, which immediately engaged the Japanese in two big battles in which they were victorious.

This detachment has now been incorporated into the general anti-Japanese Army, which is led, trained and armed by the Eighth Army.

UNITY IN STRUGGLE

Led by the Communist Party, the anti-Japanese struggle is thus developing in a very significant fashion in this part of China.

Members of the Communist Party and members of the Kuomintang are working closely together with wide sections of non-Party Chinese population against the Japanese. Especially close is the collaboration between the Kuomintang organisations and the Communist Party organisations, which is strongly supported by the Chinese masses.

The appeal concludes by declaring: "We shall fight for the establishment of a strong base for the anti-Japanese movement in Hopei and Jehol, in order, together with all the armies of China, to achieve the final victory."

CHINA: *Pen Picture of a Baby-Killing Raid*

JAPANESE naval expert Masamori Ito has attempted to justify the aerial bombardment of Chinese towns. (CAVALCADE, Aug. 27.)

"Military objectives were subjected to attack from the air" is the official euphemism which records a baby-killing expedition. Just what that means in terms of stark horror is indicated in the simple, unadorned account of a typical raid on Hankow written by Agnes Smedley, who was visiting the Chinese hospitals.

In the "Manchester Guardian" her dispatch records:

With the first death-like shriek of the sirens's warning Red Cross workers assembled, put on their first-aid kit, got their stretchers ready, and stood waiting for the bombs that might blow them into eternity.

In the hospitals for the severely wounded where the Red Cross had medical units the doctors continued their labours over the operating-tables, while the nurses took up their positions in the wards.

With the first siren warning the streets of the city were turned into scenes of mad tumult—and of organised action. . . . Then came the deadly drone of the 'planes, and all you could do was hold the hand of your friend and wait.

The streets were filled with the civilian rescue squads, pulling bodies from destroyed buildings. The primitive fire brigades fought the flames. The hand-pumps could throw water no more than fifty feet in the air. Yet by ceaseless labour with buckets of water the flames were extinguished. In the hospitals Red Cross doctors and nurses received the victims. . . .

Dead babies lay in corners and families squatted over the mangled bodies of their loved ones. The hospital receiving-rooms became an inferno, with men, women, and children dying.

One injured man went insane. But far worse than the dead were the living, searching—and finding —their loved ones. There was little demonstration or noise when they did find them.

One young woman with a baby in her arms found her mangled, blood-covered husband lying on the floor of a hospital corridor. Shocked, she began scolding him for being in such a condition, then fell on her knees and began weeping in a dirty cloth.

ORIENTAL AMAZONS: *Girls at Hankow Military Academy learn to click heels*

These two Chinese boys were arrested in the vicinity of Chowkaitu, and falsely accused of having taken part in guerilla warfare. They were both deliberately threatened and insulted before they were executed by the Japanese soldiers.

WHO ARE BETTER OFF—the little homeless victims bereft of parents, seared for life by the horrors they have seen (above), or those who sleep in death (below)?
Few hours before Franco's bombers rained death from the skies these boys and girls were at play in the street, which now becomes their morgue.

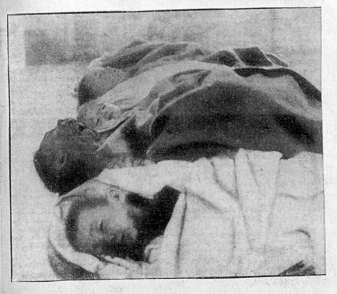

CAN IT BE STOPPED? These pictures are not pleasant to gaze upon, but CAVALCADE believes that they should be published in the interests of truth.

For it is only a realisation of the truth about war which will shock the conscience of the world into a resolve against it.

Tendency these days is to regard another war as something inevitable. Danger lies in thinking of war as some abstract thing; something which the politicians talk about and which in due time must occur.

There would be no war if the peoples of the world could be made to understand just what modern warfare means in terms of human savagery.

These pictures are but sidelights on war as it is waged to-day.

CAVALCADE has more horrifying pictures from China. (A vivid pen picture is printed in the Foreign Affairs section.)

But they are sufficient to indicate that no cause could ever justify such slaughter and misery.

Look at the row of little victims—some mutilated beyond recognition—gathered up like so much debris, after a raid on Barcelona.

Gaze also at the three dead babies lined up with the mangled corpse of a parent.

Look upon the unspeakable desolation and misery which

THIS IS WHAT THEY MEAN

THE SPOILS OF WAR might well be the caption to any of these pictures. The street scene in the centre has the silent pathos of a painting by some ancient master. Dumb grief of the two women who wander aimlessly amid the debris contrasts with the terrifying anguish of the bereaved wife (above) identifying her husband

haunt the centre photo; then turn to the hysterical grief of the woman at the right who has found the mashed remnants of her man (too horrible to include even here).

And remember these photos represent but a fraction of what is happening in Spain's war—which, after all, is only a civil war!

Power-drunk dictators put these pictures into civilisation's album.

German and Italian bombers, helping Francisco Franco (himself the father of two children), were the angels of death who cut down the little Spaniards seen above. They cannot hear the "patriots" cry, *Arriba Espana.*

For two years the world has looked on while the dictators

have made Spain a charnel house. Franco has carried out 1,167 bombardments on open towns; Barcelona has suffered 93, Madrid 151, Valencia 79. The non-combatant victims —women, children and aged—run into tens of thousands.

How can it be ended?

CAVALCADE'S guess is that if Madame Franco (mother of two), Signora Mussolini (mother of six), Madame Hermann Goering (mother of a new-born baby), and Madame Josef Goebbels (mother of three) were presented with enlargements of the pictures on this page, the rendezvous with death which their respective husbands are plotting might be put off indefinitely.

No mother is a Fascist at heart.

FILMGOING
under FIRE

THE B.B.C.'s Film Critic, recently returned from a trip to Government Spain, contributes this amazing description of filmgoing during a civil war

Summer 1938.

by F. ANDREW RICE

Madrid's Cine de la Opera—after being hit by an aerial bomb

"THE end is drawing near. There is no longer any hope for Madrid." So a war correspondent wrote in a London paper in November, 1936.

Today—nineteen months later—Madrid still holds out, though the front line stretches between the houses of its southern suburbs, and shells fall on the centre of the city from enemy field-guns barely a mile away.

There are twenty-five cinemas still open in Madrid—a fact which astonishes all to whom I have told it since my return from Spain.

Normally, I believe, Madrid supports about sixty cinemas—but twenty-five is a sufficiently remarkable number when you realise that a shell or bomb is always liable to come through the roof, and reduce the place to something like what you see in the photographs on this page.

I should say that the queerest cinema in the world just now is the "Hollywood," in Madrid. It stands half a mile from the line.

Sunflower Seeds

Its audience is more dramatic than almost anything you could see in a film.

The show begins at six p.m.; soldiers get an evening's leave from the trenches; walk up to the Hollywood to meet their girls; and spend an evening watching the Marx brothers, or Gary Cooper, or Garbo, before going back on duty.

Entering the Hollywood—or any other cinema in Madrid—you notice at once how clear the atmosphere is. Not because smoking is forbidden, but because—in Government Spain—there are practically no cigarettes to smoke.

Chewing sunflower seeds is the substitute—you buy paper bags of them quite cheap—and all over the cinema there is a curious rustling and cracking and spitting out of little shells. It's the audience chewing; it made me think of locusts.

You take your ticket from a box-office girl, who peeps at you over a wall of sandbags. The entrances of most Madrid cinemas are heavily sand-bagged. The darkness of the auditorium beyond seems like a large dug-out—without a dug-out's security.

Not long ago a box-office girl was wounded by a flying splinter. The manager was for closing down for the evening, but his audience set up a clamour. Most of them were soldiers, and what was a wound more or less? So the show went on.

But another evening, at another cinema, it was different. A shell came in through the roof, shrieked over the heads of the audience, and made its exit through the back wall by the projector. It burst outside. The audience thought it was time to go home.

It is queer to come upon, say, a Robert Taylor poster, or a Laurel and Hardy advertisement, pasted up on the only wall left standing of a bombed house, the gaudy illustrations flapping against the broken brickwork.

I noticed one small shell hole patched with a cinema poster. But rain had soaked the paper, and by now it was sagging through the hole.

Marx Brothers Preferred

Laurel and Hardy are great favourites in Madrid. They stick four Laurel and Hardys together and make a feature film of them. Nobody seems to mind the sudden changes in the story.

The Marx Brothers, too, go down well. Spaniards are cynical people, and the Marx Brothers make cynical films—and no doubt that's why they are so popular.

A visitor to Madrid noticed a long queue shivering in the cold; he expressed pity for these people lining up hour after hour for their food rations. Walking on a few yards, he came to the head of the queue. It was waiting to see *A Night at the Opera*.

Nearly all films shown in Madrid are pre-Civil War. New films, like other imports, need to be paid for in gold; and gold is wanted for more urgent purposes.

Only one or two recent Russian films have arrived—*Son of Mongolia*, for instance, an anti-Japanese propaganda picture.

I have beside me a Madrid daily paper of last week—about fifteen newspapers and weeklies still appear in Madrid, thin little sheets though they are—and among the cinema advertisements I find films which we were seeing about two years and more ago.

Desire, with Dietrich, a picture, incidentally, of a happier Spain; *British Agent; It's Love Again*, with Jessie Matthews; *Captain Blood; The Lives of a Bengal Lancer*, which had a long continuous run when it was first shown; *A Tale of Two Cities; Under Two Flags* (a sadly appropriate title in Spain just now); *The King of the Damned*, with Conrad Veidt; *Top Hat* (*Sombrero de Copa* is its Spanish title); and, of course, Disney cartoons and Pop-eye.

Forgetting the Gun-fire

They can't have too much of Pop-eye; he's just another cynic, ignoring manners and conventions.

These films, owing to the absence of new ones, are repeated every few weeks; *Mutiny on the Bounty* has been seen on and off for two years; they are becoming very worn and the sound is bad.

It was odd to find that *A Tale of Two Cities* goes down well in Government Spain. One might imagine that Sidney Carton's efforts to assist the aristocrats of France would be hissed and booed. But no—politics yield to entertainment, and Carton gets loudly cheered every time.

Even a few German films are shown without incurring hostile demonstrations. Russian films—especially *We from Kronstadt*—have a certain following, but American films are preferred. Spaniards are quick on the uptake, and relish Hollywood's slicker technique.

Madrid's extraordinary doggedness in this war has become a byword. It is within the four walls of a cinema that you may see something of that doggedness—an audience chuckling at celluloid antics, cracking their sunflower seeds, holding hands, forgetting for a while the threatening rumble of gunfire outside.

Another view of the interior of the Cine de la Opera

MUSSOLINI'S MILLIONS FOR FRANCO

By Our Diplomatic Correspondent

FROM the beginning of the civil war to the end of last June the Italian Government has spent 17,000,000,000 lire (over £180,000,000) on intervention in Spain.

These figures I have from what should be an entirely reliable source, and they tally well enough with rougher estimates made elsewhere.

Of the total of lire 4,500,000,000 were spent in 1936, 9,000,000,000 in 1937, and 3,500,000,000 in the first six months of this year.

* * *

During July and August I am informed 30,000 "legionaries" were sent to Spain. The wastage in the Italian army in Spain (killed, wounded, prisoners and sick) is estimated at 10,000, a net increase of 20,000.

The total number of Italian "volunteers" in Spain is now estimated at 70,000, of Germans at 8,000.

* * *

Lord Plymouth yesterday asked the various representatives for replies to the suggestion that Mr. Hemming, the secretary of the Non-Intervention Committee, shall go to Burgos and Barcelona, but no answers have apparently yet come in.

Nor (it is almost superfluous to add) have any answers come from General Franco about anything.

September 1938.

WHEN Franco began his revolt, he struck so that his troops could seize without delay some of focal points of Spain's rich natural resources. Glittering prize attracting the rebels in the North was the mercury mines of Almaden. Around the town of the mine (Al-Maden) the tide of battle surged; at one line General Queipo de Llano was only fifteen miles away. But the Government troops resisted all the rebels' assaults, and General Miaja erected one of his famous "Miaja lines" in the sector.

At the behest of Mussolini, Generalissimo Franco began, few weeks back, a determined effort to break through to Almaden.

The mercury mines of Almaden might decide the future of Spain, if not of Europe.

Mercury Mines

At one time Almaden and Italy produced all the mercury in the world. To-day, Almaden produces 51 per cent. of the world's supply Italy 36 per cent., the United States (where mines discovered in California in 1845 are called New Almaden) 6 per cent., Soviet Russia 2½ per cent., Mexico 1½ per cent., and the rest of the world 3 per cent.

If Franco wins Almaden, therefore, he and Mussolini will be able to control between them 87 per cent. of the total supply. That would be quite enough to enable them to hold the world to ransom and demand their own price, political as well as financial, for this essential metal.

Republic Holds Franco On Ebro

From PETER KERRIGAN

BARCELONA, Wednesday.

IT is five days now since the Fascists renewed their attack on the Spanish Government positions around Gandesa and on the Ebro front.

In spite of the most intense attack since the opening of the Ebro action they have failed to make appreciable progress.

Ten days after the opening of the Government offensive on the Ebro, around August 3, the enemy started his counter-attack.

As he brought up more men and material and mobilised additional planes for this sector, the strength of his onslaught increased, but after over three weeks he could only show a small advance in the Government lines north of Cerbera.

TERRIFIC LOSSES

His losses were terrific. His crack Fourth Navarrene Division was completely eliminated, and a stage reached when he was afraid to put into action some of his Italian brigades because of the character of the fighting and their loss of morale.

Frantic appeals to Mussolini, beginning at the time of the Government offensive in July, becoming increasingly urgent as the gravity of their situation became clear, resulted in the rapid dispatch of fresh men and huge quantities of arms.

A week ago the Fascists stopped their attack, and over a period of three days reorganised the whole of their forces.

ARTILLERY BARRAGE

A solid concentration of artillery, tanks and aviation also took place, and thus, heralded by a tremendous artillery barrage and accompanied by intense aerial attacks, on Sunday last he launched his great offensive.

What are the results so far?

Five small hills and a few hundred yards of territory were gained at the expense of really appalling losses.

The heroism of the Spanish troops who are defending their positions in face of these attacks is simply amazing.

Take this instance: In one small sector, north of Corbera, the enemy artillery put down a barrage lasting 24 hours.

During the day the enemy aviation bombed the Government positions time after time, although here they lost six planes in aerial combats with the Government aviation.

Time and again the enemy were repulsed, and at the end of all this struggle they had gained two small hills and 400 yards of territory, dominated from our heights.

Yesterday they made no progress at all, and it is clear that at that rate of progress they will use up all their new supplies and troops with no decisive outcome.

Will this happy British baby know the horrors of Fascist warfare? Picture below shows the blackened body of a baby killed by a Franco bomb in Barcelona.

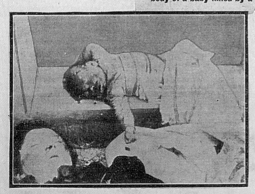

The Commissar General of the Spanish People's Army on the Ebro Front, Ossorio y Tafall, questions Franco prisoners at headquarters.

A Bomb Falls In China

THE CAMERA RECORDS in these three pictures what happens when Japanese bombers carry out their work of destruction. A bomb strikes in the crowded tenement district of Canton, China, and then—

—DESPERATE EFFORTS by soldiers and civilians are made in the hope that out of the wreckage a few lives may be salvaged. A hole is opened in the debris: a steel-helmeted soldier is lowered to investigate cries—

—and a frightened and injured child is brought to the surface. Her only crime for this punishment is that she was born Chinese.

CHINESE EIGHTH ARMY PUNISHES THE INVADERS

From Our Own Correspondent

Hankow, Sunday.

OVER 34,000 Japanese soldiers have been killed or wounded by the Chinese Eighth Army on the various battlefields in Shansi and Hopei provinces during the nine months from September, 1937, to May, 1938.

The number of Japanese war instruments, ranging from rifles and machine-guns to tanks and airplanes, which were either captured or destroyed by the former Red Army troops in the same period reached a total of 12,738 pieces.

These figures are given in a statement issued by the Commander-in-Chief of the Eighth Army, General Chu-teh, who also reveals that no less than 570 battles have been fought during these nine months.

In these battles Chinese casualties, killed and wounded, amount to approximately 20,000, of whom more than 7,000 were Chinese Communist Party members.

September 4 1938.

The following detailed list is given by Chu-Teh:—

Japanese wounded or killed, 34,007; Japanese and "Manchukuoans" captured, 1,094.

Rifles captured, 6,487; light machine guns seized, 171; heavy machine guns seized, 84; other type of machine guns seized, 212.

Field guns captured, 72; trench mortars captured, 25; hand-grenades seized, 80.

Mules captured, 1,584; horses captured, 1,783.

Anti-aircraft shells seized, 5 boxes; high explosives seized, 20 boxes.

Airplanes destroyed, 24; tanks destroyed, 5; armoured cars destroyed, 5; motor-cars and trucks destroyed, 901; motor-cars captured, 190; mule-carts captured, 847.

Radio and receiving sets seized, 10; telephone sets seized, 19.

Liquid poison gas, 5 boxes; rifle bullets seized, countless numbers; foodstuff, large quantities; fur coats, large quantities.

TROOPS MUTINIED

The number of "Manchukuoan" troops who mutinied and surrendered to the Eighth Army are given as follows:

Number of soldiers, 1,366;

Machine guns taken along for surrender, 6;

Rifles taken along for surrender, 995;

Mules brought along for surrender, 30.

JAPANESE WOUNDED

Meanwhile it is learned here that from one thousand to three thousand wounded Japanese soldiers arrive daily in Shanghai from the Yangtse front, while on August 30 and 31 ten Japanese warships on the river were seriously damaged by Chinese artillery fire.

On this front, despite continued Japanese attacks, the Chinese are holding their basic positions.

From Honan province comes the news that after a hard-fought battle the Japanese have been driven from Tsyuan on the north bank of the Hwangho river, north of Loyang.

China's Fighting Fishermen

THE FISHERMEN of Kwangtung, China's southernmost province, have formed their own militia to repel landing parties from Japanese warships which constantly bombard the shore villages in the area. The pictures show a party just as they have dashed from their nets to answer an alarm, two of their sons, mere boys, who have been pressed into service, and some of them in action.

FRANCO PRISONERS HAVE TO BUY THEIR OWN COFFINS

WOMEN'S VITAL PART IN SPAIN: AID NEEDED

From PETER KERRIGAN

BARCELONA, Sunday
September 1938.

OVER the signature of Prime Minister Negrin, the Spanish Government has published an order recommending the following tasks for the anti-Fascist women of Spain:—

(1) Provision of homes for children whose parents have been killed fighting for the Republic.

(2) Organisation of effective help for women working in the war industries and for their children.

(3) Visits to hospitals to help the wounded.

(4) Equipment of the soldiers with those things not included in the kit provided.

Behind this order lies an epic story of the way in which the women of Spain are taking their part in the struggle for freedom.

But the dry order does not indicate the part played by that wonderful woman Pasionaria, herself the embodiment of the heroic womanhood of Spain, the inspiration and example for all this splendid work.

THEIR SLOGAN

Six weeks after the military revolt—on August 28, 1936—the Government officially endorsed the work then being undertaken by a Women's A.1 Committee in Madrid. This work has developed until it has covered the whole of Government Spain.

In the first days of the principal tasks of the women was to provide clothing for the militiamen who had stepped into the breach against the foreign invaders. In Madrid workshops involving thousands of women were set up for this purpose.

Then came the transfer to Valencia and the first sewing factory employing 1,800 women was created. Naturally, it was named the Pasionaria Workshop and everything produced here and in the other workshops were handed over to the Ministry for National Defence.

The struggle transformed the women of Spain and when the extent of the foreign invasion became clear, the women of Spain issued the slogan—" Men to the front, women to production." And throughout Republican Spain, women marched in the streets demanding that they be allowed to take their places in struggle.

GIGANTIC STEP

They succeeded and one has only to know a little of the previous attitude to women in Spain to realise what a gigantic achievement this was.

All over the Republican Spain, women have efficiently replaced men in agricultural work, and in some places have even increased the amount of land under cultivation. And in the factories and offices thousands of Spain's women have replaced men now at the front.

At the same time, the Women's Aid Committee has as one of its principal tasks the assistance of women in industry, and help for their children. Never forget that factory workers in Spain—whether in the war industry or not—are working day and night, often with insufficient food and always with the threat of bombardment from the air by foreign airplanes.

What do they say of international help? They proudly report that since May 1 until the present time more than 500 tons of food has been sent to factory workers by international effort.

"The result of this contribution has been magnificent," says the official report. "Workers see that the anti-Fascists of the whole world are doing what they can to contribute to our victory against criminal Fascism."

Five hundred tons of food in three months. How pitifully little it appears in the face of such enormous need. Of course, it has an effect out of all proportion to the amount sent. No one knows better than the women who direct this work over here how much the consignments of food represent in personal sacrifice on the part of anti-Fascists throughout the world.

But I think they have the right to ask for more — and that speedily.

UP TO YOU

It is up to you to give Pasionaria and her comrades the support they need. Milk, food, clothing cannot be distributed if they do not exist.

We should always remember that the people of Spain have chosen to face hardship and privation rather than capitulate to Fascism. In making this choice they are fighting for the people in every democratic country of the world.

They have every right to expect supplies and support from us in this battle. I have always been proud of my country, but I cannot walk through the streets of Barcelona and look any Spanish mother in the eyes. Always in my mind is the thought: "My children are all right, but I know that my country-men are not doing what they could for the mothers and children of Spain."

I hope that is the kind of thought you will have after reading this; and that you will go and do something to get a stream of foodships going out to Spain at once.

PASIONARIA

AMERICAN prisoners in Franco concentration camps have had to club together to buy coffins for their dead comrades. This story was told in the New York Times by the newspapers' correspondent, W. P. Carney, notorious for his sympathy with the Franco forces.

Carney told how he visited 80 American prisoners at the camp of San Pedro de Cardena, after he had been continually delayed by the Burgos authorities.

Talking to a New Yorker named Ornitz, Carney learned that those men who refused the rites of the Catholic church when dying were not provided with coffins, but "just dumped in a hole in a field by the river."

If the other prisoners wanted to buy a coffin for the dead man the guards fleeced them for it.

NO SURGICAL AID

Another prisoner, Acker, also an American, told Carney that the greatest need was competent surgical attention in the prison hospital.

"One fellow," he said, "who has already lost an eye, still has a tiny piece of shrapnel in his face near the other eye, and the doctors here say that unless it is removed by a surgeon soon, a hard jolt may cause him to lose his sight altogether.

"Several others have bullets still in their hands, arms, legs or feet, which only a surgeon can take out, and meanwhile they are developing festering sores.

"Since we have been here one American died of pleurisy and two died of appendicitis, because there are no surgeons in this camp. Another died from too many iodine injections, and still another from dysentery, before we arrived here."

The Major of the camp admitted the lack of medical attention, although he claimed that a surgeon had been promised.

STOP CHURCH PARADE

It was also admitted by the major in charge of the camp that the men had been able to force the withdrawal of compulsory church parades designed "to soften their antagonism."

Nearly all the men talking to Carney were proud of the aid they had given to the Spanish people.

"Several," he says, "indicated proudly that they were veterans of labour conflicts in the United States, and that therefore they felt that they should be fighting on the side of the Spanish workers.

"Ornitz and Acker evidently voiced the collective sentiments of their companions in declaring that they all hoped they might be allowed to return to the Government Army in exchange for an equal number of prisoners held on that side. . . . All 80 now affirm that they enlisted primarily because of their political convictions."

SPAIN PEN PORTRAITS No. 7

Enrique Lister

By W. RUST

THERE is something heavy and tenacious about Lister. At 15 he struggled laboriously to read and write; at 29 he grappled with military strategy, beginning with the storming of the Montana barracks and becoming the commander-in-chief of the Communist Party's "Fifth Regiment."

Today the former stone-cutter is a Lieut.-Colonel, Commander of the 5th Army Corps, and one of the most romantic figures of the war. He looks a military leader; strongly built and large featured, he has a granite sternness which frequently disappears in a ready smile.

Lister was trained in a hard school. In and out of prison in his

LISTER

native Galicia, he finally fled the country in order to escape a thirty years' sentence, but returned to live illegally finding himself in Madrid when the rebellion broke out.

Since then he and his men have passed over half the war map of Spain. The "Listers" are shock troops who are thrown into every front.

I sat opposite him when he entertained Nehru to lunch in a little cottage on the Mediterranean coast not far behind the lines. "We are facing hard days," he said to Nehru," and our difficulties may increase, but you can tell the people of your country that the final victory will be ours."

This burly fighter personifies Spain's will to victory. His four brothers were killed by the Fascists in the North. In their name Enrique will fight on until Spain is free and independent.

BRITON'S BIG PART

IN PRESERVING EBRO GAINS

From PETER KERRIGAN
BARCELONA, Monday.

THE splendid Spanish People's Army crossed the Ebro a little over two months ago.

In spite of weeks of continuous counter-attacks with hundreds of planes, guns and tanks, and with casualties amounting to over 50,000 among his best troops, the enemy has made practically no progress in his frantic efforts to force the Government troops back across the river.

These two months have demonstrated to the world the gigantic progress of the People's Army. They have also brought forth examples of heroism that history will find it hard to parallel.

The story of one unit which I will call the Special Machine-Gun Battalion, is an outstanding example. It has the added interest that in its ranks were groups of Britons and Americans who played a worthy part in all its work.

Two days after the successful crossing, I met one company of the Battalion at the Ebro. It was entrusted with the task of guarding the Ebro Asco Bridge, while another company has performed a similar service at Flix, further north.

BOMBING TARGETS

Naturally these crossings were the principal objectives of the enemy bombers in their efforts to cut our communications.

Equally naturally, the companies became transformed into anti-aircraft units, using their machine guns and showing remarkable ingenuity in the process. What I want to bring out here is quality of the courage required for this kind of job.

In his book "A.R.P." Professor Haldane says:—

"The true military effects of a number of raids is terrific. Any brave man can stand one raid. To stand a number requires military discipline, mass heroism such as is found in Madrid or a philosophy that makes it clear why it happened and why the final victory of Fascism is impossible."

These boys had all the qualities that Haldane laid down and a cold courage that I will never cease to admire.

RUSHED TO HELP

The enemy counter-offensive was at its height. The Battalion was again split up, single companies being rushed to the aid of separate battalions sorely pressed at different points of the battle front.

Tributes were paid from many quarters to the men of the Battalion and I was delighted to know the high regard in which the British comrades were held by their Spanish and American comrades.

These are the men whom Dr. Negrin has publicised before the whole world at Geneva. They will

PETER KERRIGAN (in shirt sleeves) here seen with members of the International Brigade on the Ebro front.

soon be back in Britain, invaluable forces defending democracy in new spheres.

They have no fears at leaving the Ebro. They realise how strong the true Spain really is.

Faced with a fresh Italian intervention and a ferocious offensive, the Government can calmly take out of the line these magnificent soldiers, supremely confident that the glorious Spanish People's Army is certain of victory.

With sufficient weapons, airplanes and food, its victory will be a matter of weeks.

EXAMPLE OF FASCIST PROPAGANDA

The picture above appears in a recent edition of the "Corriere della Sera," of Milan, as an example of the "bestial ferocity of the Bolshevists in Spain."

The Republican troops are supposed to be holding the heads of their decapitated prisoners.

Picture below exposes the fake. The photograph is actually taken from the book, "The Memoirs of Abd El Krim," published in 1927, and depicts Spanish soldiers in Morocco holding the heads of executed Riffs.

German and Italian planes still continue to bomb Spanish cities. This picture was taken following a recent bombardment on Barcelona when a number were killed and many injured.

In an effort to aid Spain organised by the Kirkcaldy Trades Council, members of trade unions, Co-operative organisations, Labour Party and Communist Party recently collected £35. An envelope collection among trade unions affiliated to the Trades Council brought in another £35.

Picture shows the Aid Spain van and some of the collectors. Councillor J. Kay is holding a floral horse shoe presented by an anonymous Spanish woman living in Edinburgh, "as a token of esteem to Kirkcaldy people for assisting my countrymen in their struggle for freedom." In 20 months the local Spanish Aid Committee has collected £500.

**SPANISH KIDDIES
ARE AS LOVELY
AS OURS**

Franco's Air
Terror Fails

From PETER KERRIGAN

BARCELONA, Thursday.

THE last few days has seen a considerable increase in attacks on the civilian population by Italian and German aviation, in the small towns and suburbs as well as large towns.

On October 2 a German plane dropped bombs on a school in Codella, near Valencia, killing one and injuring seven of the children.

The main attention, however, has been concentrated on large cities like Barcelona. Here is an outline of the attacks over the period from October 2 to October 5.

On the night of October 2 there were five attacks on the town. One of the bombs hit the British ship Lake Geneva, wounding one sailor. Another bomb struck the British ship African Mariner.

The raids ended at 3.30 a.m. on the 3rd. On the 4th there were two raids. In the evening the first alarm went at 5.30 p.m., and there were recurring attacks during the night, until 6 a.m. on the morning of the 5th.

There was another raid a little later, and then, at 9.35 a.m., 10 enemy planes made an effort to penetrate right into the town itself. In the aerial battle which followed one of their planes was brought down into the sea.

A significant feature of these attacks is that if the enemy planes are driven off from their objective they turn their attention, wherever possible to other easier objectives, which means unloading their bombs on the civilian population in small, undefended towns and villages.

Yesterday this happened at various points in the province of Lerida and that of Tarragona. Thus more deaths were added to the mounting total of innocents murdered by order of Hitler and Mussolini.

But despite all the terror from the air, the citizens of Barcelona are continuing their work in the factories, in the shops, on the railways, trams, etc. The children still go to school, the housewife goes on with her shopping.

Under this terrible strain, and with insufficient food, the determination of the people is greater than ever.

The rearguard is proving itself worthy of the heroic deeds of the Army of the Ebro, which, at this moment is not only defending its gains but actually counter-attacking and regaining positions.

In a world which is witnessing the ghastly betrayal of democratic Czechoslovakia, Spain continues to hold aloft the banner of liberty.

MUST SHE HOLD IT ALONE?

Franco Fury
Leaves Ebro
Keys Intact

BARCELONA, Friday.—After two months of Fascist counter-offensive on the Ebro front, Government positions remain almost as they were when the Republican six-day offensive stopped on July 30.

Only 11 square miles of the 300 square miles then captured by the Republicans have been regained by the Franco troops, at an estimated cost of 42,000 casualties.

HILLS RETAKEN

The Republican forces have counter-attacked in the last two days, in the sector north of Gandesa-Corbera, and have retaken two hills that the Fascists had previously gained in ten days' hard struggle.

All key positions on this front have remained in Republican hands since the end of July.

With the coming of winter, Fascist activity on this front is likely to be slowed up, as the intensive air and artillery action on which the counter-offensive is largely based will be affected by bad weather.

Fascists
Surrounded
In Spain

BARCELONA, Tuesday.

ON the Estremadura front, north-east of Cordova, the Republican forces have successfully completed a series of important operations to isolate Fascist divisions in the bend of the River Zugar. During last week they were cut off, having previously been encircled on the north and east.

RAIL LINES CUT

The only lines of supply and communication between these enemy divisions and their base are the two main railway lines.

The line from Bon Benito to Almaden has been cut for several weeks in three places, near Campanario, at Castuera, and between Castuero and Cabeza del Buey. Only the Cordova railways remained open.

UNDER FIRE

Now the Republican forces have succeeded in bringing the second railway line under artillery fire for a considerable distance between Sepill and Oviejo. There remains only a narrow gauge railway between Penarroaya and Fuente del Arco.

October 1938.

September 1938

POLLITT'S PLEDGE

The following is the pledge given by Harry Pollitt at the memorial service to the members of the International Brigade who have fallen in Spain.

Comrades,—On behalf of this Congress, on behalf of all the thousands you represent, I here and now give a solemn pledge that we Communists shall not cease to fight for the principles for which these men laid down their lives—that we shall stand by the struggle of the Spanish people until their victory is won, and until the cause of peace and democracy is triumphant.

While peace came to other parts of Europe last week the war in Spain still went on. Scene shows Barcelona citizens watching Government machines patrol the sky after a new raid by Franco's machines on Monday

Fascists Fought To Standstill

September 1938.

The following message, telephoned by Peter Kerrigan on Friday evening, was read to the Communist Party Congress at the memorial service for those who have fallen in the fight for democracy in Spain.

From PETER KERRIGAN

BARCELONA, Friday.

ON the Ebro front each succeeding Fascist offensive utilised increased material as it developed with greater intensity than its immediate predecessor. But each is shorter in duration, and this last great onslaught was brought to a complete standstill more speedily than any previous one.

The Spanish People's Army is demonstrating its ability to withstand the most intense pressure and come through successfully.

Yesterday I was with our boys in the reserve position they now occupy after their third major battle since they reached the outskirts of Gandesa at the end of July.

The front was completely quiet. Desultory shelling, compared with the terrific barrages of the previous week, passed almost unnoticed.

ONLY THREE AIRPLANES

During the whole day only three airplanes were in the air. One of these was an early morning observation airplane, and the two in the afternoon were on the same mission.

From our comrades in the battalion, and the Brigade, I was given a first-hand story of how we fared in this latest great battle of the Sierra Caballos.

As each successive chapter comes to be added to the saga of our army on the Ebro, it becomes increasingly difficult to convey a full understanding of what these men are doing, together with their Spanish brothers-in-arms.

CONTINUOUS BOMBARDMENT

At 2 o'clock in the afternoon of September 6, the Brigade went into action, as part of the Spanish army, which was flung into the breach to stop a threatened break-through.

Under continuous artillery fire, the huge lorries, with their tireless drivers, drove back and forward along the road, taking up a battalion and rushing it forward, then dashing back to hasten ahead with the fighters.

At 6 p.m. our American and Canadian comrades contacted the enemy and stopped the advance. The next day we counter-attacked. And in this advance the Canadian comrades covered themselves with glory.

Concentrated on the flank, they drove home such an amazing attack that the whole enemy advance was stopped because of a threat to its flank.

Special mention has to be made of our comrades in the Spanish battalion. Under terrific enemy fire they dashed forward with utter disregard of danger, and held them from gaining ground.

BRITISH IN ATTACK

The British were also flung into the attack, and occupied a very important field in brilliant style.

Following this they were brought back to a reserve position, but left one company to reinforce the Spanish battalion, and another to assist the Lincoln, who had lost men in their gallant advance.

Every section of our Brigade was subjected to the merciless pounding of the enemy artillery and a 6.5-inch shell landed right in front of the Brigade Staff, wounding eight men, including Captain Malcolm Dunbar.

Here is what one of the staff, who was also wounded, and refused to be evacuated, writes about Malcolm:—

"Dunbar received about 15 fragments in his face, chest and legs, but refused to be evacuated and carried on. This is the fourth time he has been wounded—or is it the sixth? A good officer Dunbar. He keeps calmly puffing on his cigarette while his wounds are being dressed."

Are you not proud of men like this? Believe me, there is hardly a man of those in our battalion who does not measure up to a similar standard.

EIGHT CAME, FIVE RETURNED

This was on the 10th. Eight Heinkels came over and dropped bombs, but only five went back. Two white points in the sky slowly developed into parachutes, and a little later two men from the British Battalion appeared at Brigade Headquarters with a Fascist airman.

He was a Spanish lieutenant, one of the few Spaniards in Franco's Air Force, and was in tears at the thought of the torture and shooting which he supposed awaited him.

His plane was brought down by rifle fire, and every battalion in the Brigade is claiming that it was their rifles that did it.

Our boys are firmly confident that it was they who had the honour, and they had the added argument that it was they who captured the pilot.

In this battle the enemy used more than a hundred tanks and scores of motor-cycles carrying heavy machine-guns.

CAVALRY ROUTED

At one place they even flung the cavalry into action, but our artillery landed shells in their midst, and their disordered retreat completely disorganised the enemy lines.

Our artillery also disposed of a Moorish Tabor in the same way.

On the 9th three deserters came into our lines. When asked the routine question: "How did you get over here?" they replied: "We came over through the 'Cotas de las Viudas Orfanos y Novias' "—Hills of the Widows, Orphans and Sweethearts.

This is the name given to our position and the hills in front. They are named so by the Fascists because of the appalling casualties they have suffered.

This salient which we have gained along the Corbera road and the area around Corbera has been named by them "the death sector."

INTENSIFIED AIR BOMBING

On September 11 the enemy intensified the air activity. Twenty-one to 24 bombing planes at a time, accompanied by the fighters, came 12 times in one day and each squad is capable of dropping 50 tons of high explosives.

Think of what that means, and realise that when you read of artillery and airplanes changing the shape of hills, that it is actually happening.

Think of the men who have emerged from their trenches and trained their rifles and machine-guns on the advancing enemy, and once more demonstrated the unconquerable courage of the Spanish People's Army by hurling back the infantry and tanks of the invaders.

In the ranks of this army are Britishers, flesh of the flesh, and blood of the blood of some of those who read this, brothers of all of you. Nothing that can be said in their praise is too extravagant, because only a few today fully appreciate all these men have done.

THOSE WHO HAVE FALLEN

John Smith, of Irvine, and Ernest Sim, of London, fell on the 8th. With them we also lost Ben Glazer, of London, who was attached to another section of the division.

This represents a loss of some of the finest cadres in the army of democracy, but it also signifies a triumph of democracy over the brutal beasts of Fascism.

Side by side on the Sierra Caballos, Spaniards and Britishers are hammering out a new humanity on the forge of war.

Events are showing that these heroes of the Spanish People's Army, sprung from the people and forced in battle, are equalling, and, I think, surpassing their brothers-in-arms.

Together, these men are speeding the day when Fascism will be utterly crushed, and when that day comes, with it will come the full appreciation of their services to humanity.

Salud to the heroes!

COMMUNIST CONGRESS PAYS TRIBUTE TO HEROES OF SPAIN

Sept 1938.

(From Our Special Correspondent)

BIRMINGHAM, Sunday.

A MEMORIAL SERVICE to members of the International Brigade who have fallen in Spain concluded the opening session of the Communist Party Congress on Friday evening. The ceremony was most moving in its extreme simplicity.

In a voice racked with emotion, Fred Copeman, ex-Commander of the British Battalion of the International Brigade, read a letter which he proposed Congress should send to the members of the Brigade now in Spain.

When he came to the sentence: " We remember Bill and Charlie, Harry, George and Jim and all those hundreds more . . . ," he could go no further, the poignancy of his recollections was too strong, the memories evoked of all the fine comrades alongside whom he had fought and who had since given their lives.

In a moment the organ broke into the magnificent strains of Chopin's " Funeral March," softly at first, then swelling into a mighty volume of sound which stirred every man and woman in the hall, then dying down again. The notes of the organ stopped, all was silence, save for an occasional repressed sob.

Then as one man the audience rose as the notes of a bugle sounding the Last Post were heard. The whole hall was on its feet, with clenched fist held shoulder-high in salute of the dead.

Gradually the lights were dimmed, and the rest of the ceremony was conducted in a half light.

POLLITT'S PLEDGE TO SPAIN

While Congress remained standing Harry Pollitt came forward to give the pledge printed in another column of this page.

Every comrade present was silently making Harry's pledge his own, when once again the strains of the bugle were heard. This time it was the " Reveille " that was sounded.

As the bugle notes died away, John Goss sang " Far From Their Homeland," a song dedicated to the boys in Spain, set to the tune of " Whirlwinds of Danger," that splendid revolutionary hymn of the Russian Revolution.

" Far from their homeland our comrades are lying," he sang, and in a moment everyone present was singing, too: " Yet as they died 'twas with brothers they stood." And above the massed voices arose the pure tenor notes of John Goss.

THE INTERNATIONAL

As the last words of the song were concluded, the organ could be heard once more. This time it was the " Internationale " that was being played. A great volume of sound swept through the hall as the historic hymn of struggle was sung again and again by all present.

PASIONARIA

SPAIN : Parliament Adopts £22 Million War Budget ; "No Truce with Fascism" ; Unrest in Morocco

MEETING for the first time in the third year of war, the Spanish Parliament, Friday, approving the lead of Premier and War Minister Juan Negrin, refuted entirely the many rumours of imminent armistice.

Orated Premier Negrin: " So long as Fascists remain in Spain there is no prospect of peace. No treaty with Fascism will ever be made by the Government in which I am included."

After reviewing the history of the war and observing the recent improvement of the Government's military position, he emphasised the need for common objectives, said, " Complete unity to continue the struggle to successful conclusion is essential."

" Betrayal "

Followed Communist Deputy " La Pasionara." Elected one of Parliament's vice-presidents, she supplemented the Premier's call to solidarity, denounced the " black betrayal of Czecho-Slovakia by the democracies."

Unanimously endorsing Government policy, the assembly passed a £22,000,000 Budget, then dispersed having empowered the Cabinet to suspend the half-yearly convocation and to convene Parliament again when circumstances make it necessary.

With the aim of speeding up arms production the powerful U.G.T.—Spanish Workers' Union—informed deputies it was departing from the one-wage practice and going over to production bonuses, thus, in the exigencies of war, dropping the Utopian ideal of a single rate of pay.

In coming weeks the Government expects to implement the recent decision to withdraw the International Brigade, and hopes " volunteers " on the Insurgent side will be withdrawn by the Non-Intervention Committee.

By League of Nation's Council decision an International Commission is to supervise withdrawal of foreign combatants on the Government side, but there is no indication yet that a similar commission will be accepted in Insurgent territory.

Pessimism

Britain, France, and Iran are to select the commission and direct its operations. When the commission was mooted originally, it was believed a truce would be arranged. Though accepted by the Government it was turned down by the Insurgents after consultation in Rome.

Rejection was said to be due to Government successes on the Ebro front, where since crossing the river three months ago Republicans have held on with grim determination despite Insurgent assurance that the crossing would prove a trap.

" Reds " Indexed

Unexpected Government resistance against the counter-attack has spread pessimism among Insurgent forces, caused further rumblings of revolt. In Morocco, especially, Arab agitation against conscription for General Franco's armies is increasing. " Subversive " tribes are kept in order by squadrons of warplanes.

Official information from Saragossa says the Insurgent authorities have a card index of 1,500,000 persons in enemy territory, the majority " of Red tendencies." Others are Insurgent sympathisers. The index is added to daily with information from captured documents, and the testimony of prisoners and deserters.

October 1938.
Published by 'Cavalcade'

"WE MAY WELL BE PROUD"

September 1938.

This is the message of greeting sent by the Communist Party Congress at Birmingham to the British Battalion of the International Brigade in Spain.

WE send to the members of the British Battalion in Spain our sincere love and pride, and an assurance that their well-being is forever in our hearts. We may well be proud of you. No party has more right to voice its pride in your great work than this Communist Party.

Many of those who have given their lives and limbs came from our ranks. We know you as good comrades. We shall forever remember you as such.

Over two years now war has ravaged Spain: thousands of true Spaniards have given their lives in defence of their country, for peace and progress.

From the beginning of the present G vernment of our country has used every method to obtain victory for the rebels and those whom they serve.

If the history of the present generation of Britons were to be written with this as our contribution to world progress, then it would be truly said we had betrayed the future generations of our people, ourselves and all humanity.

SAVED HONOUR OF BRITAIN

But that will not be so, for men have gone, to save for our people their honour. Yes, men have gone to die on the soil of Spain, that the world may live and society progress according to the will of the people.

The history of our generation will be written, and will include pages telling of the glorious sacrifices of the men of the International Brigades, and none will have a greater place than that gallant band of Britishers who today carry the standard of our people in the vanguard of the Republican Army.

To all those who have gone, we say on behalf of the people of Britain, who will one day come to understand the great and glorious task you have undertaken, "Thank you, comrades! We shall not forget your work; your sacrifice is, and shall for all time be, a glorious example to us all."

We assure you that we have not forgotten the days at Boadilla, or Las Rosas, or in the Casa del Campo, when as a small body of fighters in the first militia groups, you, countrymen of ours, gave great service to Spain and to peace and progress by assisting in the defence of Madrid.

GREAT RECORD

Our memory recalls the first organised British Battalion which won for itself and for our country the everlasting gratitude of the people of Spain.

At Jarama, you played your part with the volunteers of all nations and the new Peoples' Army in defending the road to Madrid. Your sacrifices on April 17, 1937, helped in the rout of the Italian Army at Guadalajara. At Brunete and Villa Nueva de Canada you proved your worth. Belchite and Quinto will remember your valour. In the defence of Teruel you were not found wanting, and during those terrible days of April and March of this year when the Republic was hard pressed you were with her sons prepared to die in order to stem the tide and throw back the barbaric Fascist invader. During the last few weeks on the front you have again proved your worth.

FIGHTING TOGETHER

Comrades, we, as you, are of the common people; we understand how these things were done; we have shared your sorrows whenever you have lost a pal; we have wept, too, when news came through of those killed in action.

We remember Bill and Charlie, Harry, George and Jim, and all those hundreds more; they were our pals, too. They once worked with us, in our branches and workshops. We remember how very human they were. We felt proud the day they left to go to Spain; though they are gone, you still remain fighting on for the greatest of all causes.

As we are here are fighting, we have no rifles, comrades, no trenches, no tanks; our hardships are not as yours; though we only sell a paper, or collect a penny, we feel we are with you. We know we are together, each in his or her way fighting for a better world, free of war and poverty, full of happiness and peace.

VICTORY EVER NEARER

We follow with intense interest every action taken by the Spanish People's Army to which you belong. Every day we see an improvement in its ability, bringing victory ever nearer. Your experiences with these gallant people of Spain will be to our movement, as fertiliser to the soil.

Once again, comrades, we thank you for all you have done, for our people, for Spain, and for peace.

We send to you all our sincere love and admiration. Be assured that our Party will forever treasure the memory of the fallen, and will work with the same willing sacrifice to carry on the struggle for the liberation of mankind.

We will do all in our power to ensure that none may regret having offered their services to the cause, by seeing that those who are near and dear to you will not suffer by your absence.

The Movement has seen many great tasks carried through by the working people. Many have gained the thanks and pride of our Communist Party. You, comrades, join that great band of workers of whom we are justly proud. May your efforts end in victory, that you may return to your people and to our Party to continue in the struggle until the final victory of the people.

We have the honour to be, your Comrades of the Communist Party of Great Britain.

SPAIN'S FAREWELL TO MEN WHO KEPT FAITH

From PETER KERRIGAN

October 4 1938. BARCELONA, Monday.

DRAWN up on the field was the whole International Brigade with the British Battalion, as the oldest in Spain, honoured on the right flank.

Next to them the Lincoln Battalion, then the 59th and the MacKenzie-Papineaux flanked on their right by the Brigade Engineers. The Transmissions were drawn up in the rear.

Facing them on the high bank were the Brigade Staff. Alongside the Staff stood the Battalion Commanders and Commissars of the Brigade.

Here was the setting for the moving ceremony, bringing to an end the magnificent career of the International Brigade here in Spain.

HISTORIC CEREMONY

All round were the spectators—the villagers and their children, soldiers from other units—watching the historic ceremony.

First Major Valledor and then Johnny Gates, emotion in their voices, made their speeches.

Spanish Republican flags made a splash of colour at the head of the Battalion. I noticed our Major Attlee flag, and the 15th Brigade banner proudly held by the British on the right.

The sun rays were striking Valledor from behind as he spoke, passing over the soldiers in the shaded field and transforming the tops of the Catalan hills in the background into blazing masses of light.

The International Brigade is leaving Spain. This was Spain's farewell.

Valledor said: "We pledge to fill the places in our ranks that you leave vacant, and go forward under the banner of Spain to liberty."

SPAIN NEVER FASCIST

"Tell your countrymen that when a people is determined to be free no power on earth can enslave them. Spain will never be Fascist, while there is an anti-Fascist left in Spain."

When Jonny Gates spoke of the last Brigade meeting I recalled that it was not the same Brigade. Now my eyes turned involuntarily to the British.

Behind the new Commander and Commissar stood Johnny Power, Alan Gilchrist, Ben Richardson, Hooley Walker, Jim Brewer and Cypriano Escuidera. Over at the back with his men I could see Jim Ruskin. Beside him were Sam Wild, George Fletcher, Bob Cooney and Malcolm Dunbar.

Then I didn't hear any more of what Gates was saying because

I was looking at a procession passing before me.

Arnold Jeans, Ralph Fox, John Cornford, Hyndman, George Brown, Bill Meredith, Charlie Goodfellow, Fry, Tappy, Jack Nulty, James Pollock, Gregory, Tony McGuire. . . .

I saw them all—all dead—and dozens more. I thought: "This is the price we pay."

Then Johnny Gates' voice was clear again in my ears. He was telling how we had fulfilled our promise and crossed the Ebro to the very gates of Gandesa.

CERTAIN OF VICTORY

"We go away with the certainty that victory is assured. We go away with no pessimism. We leave behind the army and the people determined on victory."

The sun had left the hill tops and only the sky was red. Dull thunder of guns across the Ebro sounded. The men stirred uneasily.

A young Spanish girl, representative of the youth of the delegation, stepped forward. For a few minutes she poured her very heart forth, then stepped back with her throat throbbing, to rest against the side.

A bugle sounding the last long salute to the dead, the ranks to attention in homage to the bravest of the brave; the band's stirring notes of the Internationale and the Spanish National Anthem; vivas—and the ceremony ended.

The British Battalion of the 15th Brigade will go, but will leave its great tradition in the hands of our Spanish brothers alone.

Oct. 1938.

Lady Layton casts on first stitches in the Duchess of Athol's Knitting Competition, assisted by Dame May Whitty. The competition is to help provide aid to the Spanish people.

THE MAKING OF A MODERN HERO

THE day after his 21st birthday, John Cornford was killed in action, in the autumn of 1936, in Southern Spain.

His short life and his death are both of them, I think, typical of the new kind of intellectual fighter for liberty the post-war world has brought into being.

In the past Byron and Shelley evolved their opinions and fought for them, chiefly on the basis of their emotions.

Cornford, on the other hand, fought in the most practical way possible (with a machine-gun) after having gradually evolved a thoroughly workmanlike, rational outlook on the world.

His scientific, Socialist ideas were the stimuli which incited him to ever more practical, ever more decisive, action.

◆ THAT this is so is shown very clearly in this intensely interesting and very well-edited account of his life,* which deserves to be very widely read.

The first article is a description by Cornford's father, Professor Cornford, of Cambridge, of some incidents in his son's childhood.

To begin with, for example, the small boy was far from practical. John "lived in thought without needing to translate it into action. In his eighth and ninth years he produced some remarkably bold drawings, illustrating stories which he had in mind, but found it too laborious to write out.

"They were war-like and adventurous, with terrific battles of the hero with Indians, Eskimos, bears, etc. There were also some designs for making things, but he would never make them himself.

"One is headed 'MAKE THIS GUN.' Get three feet of elder then get piece of wood six inches long, an inch thick, then nail (see figure three). Then get piece of Meccano four inches long. Nail it on piece of wood, and so on. His mother said this was splendid: if she got the materials would he try to make the gun? But he was quite content with the directions."

◆ THE second chapter is written by Christopher Cornford about his brother's schooldays.

He says: "The most remarkable, the main thing about John, was his terrific rate of development, his burning energy. If I am

*John Cornford, A Memoir. Edited by Pat Sloan. (Cape, 7s. 6d.

JOHN CORNFORD

AN APPRECIATION BY HUGH SLATER, WHO WAS IN SPAIN FOR OVER 18 MONTHS, AND WAS FORMERLY COMMANDER OF THE BRITISH ANTI-TANK CORPS IN THE INTERNATIONAL BRIGADE.

to say anything about him, I must say this, at the risk of repeating a conclusion which the rest of this book will make obvious. 'Forging ahead' is a well-worn expression, but it is the best I can think of to describe his life. Trying to know him was like standing on a railway embankment trying to grab an express train."

◆ IN this essay Christopher Cornford suggests that the starting point for John's political ideas are to be in his early criticisms of literature.

At school he wrote an essay on Eliot's "Waste Land," and this essay, says his brother, "leads me to think that it was partly through the search for a sociological or historical explanation for the nature of a poem that he came to consider contemporary society, and so politics, and so Communism."

But don't get the idea from this that John Cornford was a "wonder-youth," or a "martyred sensitive soul."

◆ JOHN CORNFORD was a real person who grew out of the conflicting needs and aspirations, the doubts and fears of the educated middle classes.

He was intellectually arrogant and personally modest. A reluctant member of his school O.T.C. and an enthusiastic militiaman in Spain. A humanitarian with the ability to fight the enemies of liberty and progress violently and physically.

Sometimes lonely and homesick, he fought bitterly and doggedly until he was killed leading a brilliantly successful counter-attack near Lopera, in Andulucia.

◆ FROM Aragon John Cornford wrote home: "Up till now this letter has been very miserable. For this reason. I came out with the intention of staying a few days, firing a few shots, and then coming home. Sounded fine, but you just can't do things like that. You can't play at civil war, or fight with a reservation you don't mean to get killed. It didn't take long to realise that either I was here in earnest or else I'd better clear out.

"I tried to avoid the dilemma. Then I felt so lonely and bad I tried to get a pass back to Barcelona. But the question was decided for me. Having joined, I am in whether I like it or not. And I like it. Yesterday we went out to attack, and the prospect of action was terribly exhilarating . . . Going into action. Thank God for something to do at last. I shall fight like a Communist if not like a soldier. All my love, Salute."

◆ I REMEMBER very vividly going to see John just after he was wounded by shrapnel in the University city.

I found him in bed in hospital in Madrid. There were two or three of us arranging to spend the evening together in the Miami Bar.

John was not going to miss anything and refused to stay behind. He walked slowly up the tall dark Gran Via, John a bit shaky with a touch of concussion. The screaming crashes of enemy shells inside and round the skyscraper telephone building opposite the bar we were going to, made us rather less interested in seeing the sights of the town than we had been when we started. But Cornford insisted upon pushing on towards the explosions and whining splinters, slowly, unsteadily.

I thought at the time how like him that was. In everything he did, important or unimportant, there was the same indomitable purposefulness.

He died as he had lived.

FAREWELL TO SPAIN
—International brigade parades for the last time before being disbanded

SPAIN

FOLLOWING the discussions between Chamberlain and Mussolini at Munich and those between Lord Perth and Count Ciano in Rome, Franco has announced his decision to withdraw a number of his Italian mercenaries from Spain.

This decision is being played up by Mr. Chamberlain and his friends as "clearing the way" for the ratification of the Anglo-Italian Pact concluded in April.

That Pact is an agreement that underwrites a defeat for democracy in Spain. As such it is in direct keeping with the policy pursued by the representatives of the Four Powers at Munich, and its ratification becomes the first step necessary if a deal similar to that concluded at Munich at the expense of Czechoslovakia is now to be attempted at the expense of Republican Spain.

Now Mr. Chamberlain gave his pledge in the House of Commons when the Pact was debated that he would not ratify the Agreement until certain conditions had been fulfilled. The most important of these was that either there should be a "settlement" in Spain or there should have taken place a "substantial withdrawal" of foreign combatants.

SPAIN FIGHTS ON

Today the prospects of a Franco victory in Spain—the meaning of a "settlement"—are more remote than ever before. Not only has the Spanish Republic withdrawn all the foreign anti-Fascist volunteers but, militarily and politically, it is in a stronger position than at any time since the war began. Unlike Czechoslovakia it is fighting and will continue to fight.

Does then this latest manoeuvre of Franco and his Italian and British friends constitute what could be called with justification a "substantial withdrawal"?

Certainly not. The troops to be withdrawn are a mere fraction of all the interventionist forces on Franco's side. The 10,000 men who, it is believed, will be shipped back to Italy are composed of wounded, sick and war-weary men who are in any case due to return.

Not a single airplane, not a single tank, not a single pilot or military technician is to go. Simultaneously, let it be remembered, more than 10,000 men have been shipped to Franco Spain since the beginning of this year and more are still being sent in.

The whole plan for this "token withdrawal" then is a monstrous manoeuvre designed to give Chamberlain an opportunity to push through the ratification of the Anglo-Italian Pact, which means in fact an intensification of the blockade of Republican Spain, open British endorsement of Italian intervention.

ACTION NOW

British democrats, many of whom were taken by surprise by the Munich betrayal, although the DAILY WORKER warned against it, will realise, therefore, that all the shouting about Franco's decision is in fact part and parcel of a new plan to sacrifice Spain.

Today there can be no excuse for failure to take action before the deal gets under way.

Spain becomes more than ever the centre of the whole struggle for peace and freedom against the Fascist counter-revolution. Militarily and politically, the Spanish Republic is capable of settling the Spanish problem itself and the democrats of the world must now see to it that nothing is allowed to prevent its doing so, that everything is done to assist it.

FOOD FOR SPAIN

That is why the true nature of this "token withdrawal" must be exposed, why nothing short of the complete evacuation of all foreign combatants, technicians, war material and planes from Franco Spain can be accepted.

That is why at this present moment British democracy must prevent the ratification of the Pact with Rome, must prevent any intensification of the blockade against the Republic.

That is why a supreme and sustained effort must now be made to break the embargo and blockade imposed on Republican Spain, why every effort must be made to increase a thousandfold all the forms of aid to Spain and especially to increase the food supply.

Here, indeed, is the vital issue. The Spanish Republic is strong, it is united, it has all the prerequisites for victory. But, because of the blockade, it lacks food with which to feed its people and its army. Chamberlain and Mussolini are proposing to intensify that blockade in the hope of putting over a deal and crushing Spain's democracy.

Today, under the slogan, "Food and Freedom of Trade for Republican Spain," the last outpost of freedom in Europe can be saved, and the disastrous treachery of Munich itself defeated.

WORLD ARMY MARCHES ON LAST PARADE

October 11 1938 **From PETER KERRIGAN**

BARCELONA, Tuesday.

SUNDAY, October 16, will be one of my most cherished memories, because then I witnessed the last parade of the Internationals of the famous 35th Division.

Drawn up, three deep in a long line, were the Guard of Honour of picked companies from the Division across the river. They had just come in full battle order from the front, and the distant thunder of the guns was a reminder of the job to which they would return shortly after this ceremony.

The white ribbon of the road stretched flat and straight in front of me for half a mile. About 70 yards back were the troops, and behind them, sharply stepped hills. On the terraced sides fine vines, hazel and fig trees were growing, and I could see a mule moving high among the trees near the top.

THE RANKS PASS BY

In the open space between the road and the guard of honour, Andre Marty and Luigi Gallo were conversing with the officers of the Division. Marty was seeing the passing of the great epic organisation of which he had been one of the foremost creators.

The piercing note of the Spanish bugles called the ranks to attention. Valledor ordered them to salute arms, and the rifles swung up along the ranks. Down the road came the Divisional Staff, and I saw Malcolm Dunbar, just promoted Major, with the bandages still on his head.

The bugles called again: the arms went to the present; the band started, and away in the distance I could hear the shrill note of the bugles and the stirring roll of the drums. The 35th Division Internationals were marching as a military unit for the last time. Round the bend of the road, rank on rank they came, men whose memories will never die.

cards of honour were issued to a number of comrades of the Division.

Sam Wild received one, and I was amazed at his efforts to escape the embrace of Jose Maria, the Political Commissar, who was making the presentations. Andre Marty made a short and telling speech.

"The front will now be for us in London, Paris, Washington, and in our countries we will struggle harder than ever," he said.

"Not Messrs. Chamberlain and Daladier represent the people of Britain and France. It is the volunteers from these countries who represent the peoples of France and Britain."

Let London be the first to give the men a reception worthy of the work they have done. Remember, also, that they will continue this work in Britain, and it is our duty to help them to do so."

GERMANS AT THE HEAD

At the head of the famous 11th Brigade marched the remnants of the immortal Thaelmann Battalion. With eyes right they saluted the Spanish colours, and Andre Marty and the others returned the salute.

In quick succession they passed, Germans, Czechs, Poles, Austrians, Bulgarians, Yugoslavs, Scandinavians, men of all Europe, who had come in democracy's hour of need.

The 11th and the 13th Brigade had passed. Now our Brigade was coming. First, Sam Wild, George Fletcher, and the officers of the Brigade, then the saluting boys; then the flags of the Brigade, with the British Battalion first, followed by the Lincoln and the Mac-Pap.

Then they were all drawn up, facing the platform in front.

A PEOPLE'S THANKS

Lt.-Col. Lerino read the last Army Order to the men he had so ably led and with whom he had just gained promotion.

The Order thanked the volunteers for their magnificent work as members of the Spanish People's Army. Commencing with the heroic defence of Madrid in 1936, the Order listed every action in which the International had participated, right up to the epic crossing of the Ebro and the magnificent defence of Pandois and Caballs.

The beautiful Spanish language caressed and at the same time inspired us as phrase by phrase, the official document set out the thanks of the Spanish people, while at the same time it assured us of Spain's indomitable will to victory.

SPANISH TROOPS TAKE OVER

Again the bugles swelled and again the men marched past. This time they continued on down. As the last of the Internationals passed the platform and the first Spanish troops came abreast, they broke into "Vivas!"

Here was something not merely symbolical. The International Brigade were replaced by the army of the Republic, the army which is the Spanish people itself.

Afterwards at a dinner and further celebrations, during which

"STILL MEN LEFT IN ENGLAND"

From FRED COPEMAN

Yesterday the office boy at the International Brigade Dependants' Aid Committee's headquarters came in to me and told me that there was an old lady downstairs who wanted to "see someone."

I went down to find a real picture book old granny. At first I did not know what to say, she looked so frail and tender. Then in a very soft voice she explained that she had 10s. to give to "those grand laddies who had shown that there are still some men left in our country."

KILLED AT BRUNETE

Her grandson, she said, had been killed fighting with the International Brigade at Brunete and tears formed in her eyes as she looked up to me with her white-lined face and her white hair.

Incidents like this are daily occurrences in the lives of those of us who work for the men of the International Brigade and their relatives. They give us inspiration and they show that the work of those men who fought in Spain will never be in vain.

Franco To Make "Token Withdrawal"

By RICHARD GOODMAN

WHILE Mr. Hemming, Secretary of the Non-Intervention Committee, was over the week-end travelling to Burgos to explain to General Franco Mr. Chamberlain's plan for a "settlement" of the Spanish war, an official communique issued in Rome contained the following announcement from Salamanca:

"Gen. Franco is preparing for the immediate repatriation of Italian volunteers who have been in Spain for more than eighteen consecutive months."

The communique does not say how many men this will involve, but the number is given in Rome circles as 10,000 and is openly characterised as a "token withdrawal."

As I forecast on Thursday, this plan for a "token withdrawal" admittedly affects none of the specialist services, particularly aviation, and does not provide for the withdrawal of any of the war material or planes which have been poured and are still being poured into the Peninsula.

On the very day it was announced that this withdrawal was to take place, reports from Cadiz stated that an Italian ship loaded with 200 light armoured cars, each manned by its own crew had arrived at that port.

Meantime at the London end preparations are being further speeded-up to push through the ratification of the Anglo-Italian pact of April on the basis that this "token withdrawal"—of infantrymen who are either wounded, sick or in any case due to return—can be regarded as that "settlement" in Spain without which the Agreement cannot be implemented.

COMPLETE WITHDRAWAL

Simultaneously there is a hardening of opinion in all democratic circles that it is today more than ever necessary for there to be.

(1) a complete withdrawal of all foreign troops, technicians, war materials and airplanes from Franco Spain;

(2) complete freedom of trade with Republican Spain, and

(3) the raising of the embargo on arms for the Spanish Government.

The Spanish Government has made its position perfectly clear. It has itself withdrawn all the volunteers fighting in the International Brigade and it insists on a complete withdrawal of all Italian and German forces and material on Franco's side.

This was amplified over the week-end by a joint manifesto issued by the Socialist and Anarchist trade union federations of Spain and the Spanish Socialist, Communist and Anarchist Parties warning against the intrigues of the Four Powers, Britain, France, Germany and Italy, for a deal at Spain's expense.

October 10 1938.

WE OWE A DEBT TO SPAIN

October 18 1938.

ROSE SMITH

By ROSE SMITH

I AM going to Republican Spain to try to discharge a debt which I feel I personally owe to its people.

Nearly half a million refugee children and thousands of others in that country are in urgent need of food.

Hungry children are turned away day after day from the food distributing centres because supplies are exhausted.

Milk has to be watered down to meet increasing demands while supplies diminish.

Bread rations for the civilian population have unavoidably been cut to the barest minimum.

Franco and his Fascist allies hope to starve out the defenders of world peace and democracy.

FEAR OF WAR

During the past few weeks, while the Chamberlain Government has been working overtime harnessing Britain to the Fascist warmakers, I have watched the fear of war visibly ageing Englishwomen.

And I have realised more and more intensely the debt we owe to the women of Spain who are holding the front line trenches.

I remember, too, how, in our times of need, help has always been freely given by workers of other countries.

AID FOR LANCASHIRE

In 1929, '30 and '31, when Lancashire textile workers were fighting against wage reductions and speedup, food supplies sent by our friends abroad raised our spirits in that bitter conflict.

Workers of Britain, including myself, have an outstanding debt to pay.

I hope that what I write of what I see will help to pay off some of that debt.

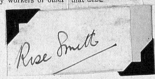

October 20 1938.

AMAZING SPIRIT OF SPAIN'S BRAVE MOTHERS

"RUN, children, run !!

"But senorita, this is the seventh time . . ."

"That seventh time took a toll of, oh, how many women and children that were waiting in long food queues in a market place in a thickly populated part of Barcelona.

"So many were never found again, and with a group of kiddies I saw a thing I never want to see again and which those little mites saw—it was the passing of a lorry load of 'remains.'"

These grimly moving words appear in a story issued as a special supplement to the Labour Press service and written by Mrs. Adams de Puertas.

"My fifteenth visit to Spain," Mrs. Puertas continued, "leaves me more than ever convinced that the spirit of the Spanish people can never be broken. . . ."

During the recent crisis, Mrs. Puertas said, little children of twelve were asking, "Senorita, if a war begins with England won't you ever come again, and won't we get any more milk and food?"

"God knows they are getting little enough now," Mrs. Puertas adds, "but that little must be made more with the winter coming on. It makes one dread to think how terribly we are handicapped with never having enough to go around."

"Every little village throughout has its many privations, but patient faces on all sides tell of heroic resistance for a cause that is going to win.

PARENTS' HEROISM

"One is amazed at the fight the parents put up to deal with the sickness and food shortage.

"Clothes, too, are getting a great problem, as the cold nights have begun and wool is scarcer than ever before.

"Boots and shoes are getting non-existent.

INTO ACTION

The facts here revealed by Mrs. Puertas should galvanise the whole British Labour and Trade Union movement into action.

In the next few weeks there should be a continual stream of ships to Spain laden with food and clothing.

At the recent Blackpool Congress of the T.U.C., Sir Walter Citrine said "The need in Spain is increasing every hour . . . in these coming months, particularly with the advent of winter, it may well be that the contributions of trade unionists will constitute one of the principal factors in maintaining the morale of the Spanish people in face of the terrible odds they are fighting against."

Need more be said, except to urge that every effort will be made NOW to assist the heroic fight of the Spanish people.

October 15 1938.

"FIGHT OR BE CRUSHED"— SPAIN WARNS

"WE do not regret that we faced war to save ourselves from slavery and to save our country.

"Democracies of the world, fulfil your duties as we are fulfilling ours. Only thus will peace and democracy be saved."

In these stirring words, leaders of all Spanish political parties and trade union organisations join in an appeal, issued from Barcelona, "to all democracies and to all who wish to save peace and civilisation."

"Democratic and working-class Spain," says the appeal, "which for 26 months has been struggling for its independence and in support of democratic principles, feels itself, in view of recent events in Europe, obliged to launch an appeal to all the honest consciences of the world.

TREACHEROUS SLANDERS

"While we are struggling for democracy, so-called democratic Governments are giving every credit to rumours which slander us; are trying to abandon us to the imperialist aims of the totalitarian States.

"There are those in Europe who wish to put an end to our tragedy by the same method as will ensure the lasting dishonour of the Munich Agreement. This fact is the concern of all free men who wish to prevent Spain from being crushed by the demand of dictatorship for a new colony, the encirclement of France which the author of Mein Kampf is trying to achieve, and finally the imposition on the whole world of the Nazi hegemony.

"This is not a cry of anguish from Spain, but a vigorous cry from liberal people. The liberals of the world—those who do not wish to be transformed from citizens into slaves— can, if they are willing but to try, save humanity, peace and liberty.

DRIVE OUT INVADERS !

"The Spanish Republic will soon make an end to bloody strife and establish normal life, if the forces of invasion leave our soil.

"It is the duty of the democracies and of all those who love peace and civilisation to aid the Spanish people—by prohibiting the export of arms and food to the aggressors, by applying the most rigid sanctions against them, and by putting an end to the sinister activities of miscalled "Non-Intervention."

The signatories are:—

Emilio Baeza Medina, Left Republican Party.

Mateo Silva, Republican Union.
Ramon Lamoneda, Socialist Party.

Jose Diaz, Communist Party.
Jose Rodriguez Vega, General Workers' Union.

Mariono R. Vasquez, C.N.T. (National Labour Confederation).
Terminal de Sousa, Iberian Anarchist Federation.

MILK MAKES NEWS THAT CHEERS IN BARCELONA

From ROSE SMITH

October 20 1938.

BARCELONA, Tuesday.

TODAY, WHEN I VISITED THE BOQUERIA MARKET PLACE, A SMALL BOY WHO WAS THERE SUDDENLY BEGAN TO DANCE WITH JOY, SHOUTING, "THERE'S MILK! THERE'S MILK!", AND REPEATING THAT FAMILIAR AMERICAN EXPRESSION, "WHOOPEE!"

At his cry, a wave of relief swept along the queue of waiting women and old men. Some of them had been standing for six hours, tortured by the thought that perhaps after all there would be no supplies.

They were relatives of invalids, of old and young to whom milk is an urgent necessity. Some were obviously sick people themselves.

As they waited, everyone talked "food"—mainly as to who should receive the first supplies.

No pushing aside, no harsh words, just a grim realisation that, urgent as the need of each was, circumstances necessitated that some should get precedence over others.

Milk is a life and death matter for their loved ones.

Most of them had left their homes before daybreak, knowing full well that the early morning food queues are the special object of the German and Italian bombing planes.

The ghastly crime of a few mornings ago still fresh in their minds, they braved the risk in order to attend to the needs of the sick.

CONVERSATIONS IN THE QUEUE

With the aid of a Spanish friend I talked with them as they waited.

Here is a middle-aged woman: "I am waiting for milk for my sick brother and sister, who are older than me. I was here at 4 o'clock." It was then 10 in the morning.

"I came early because I was too far back in the queue last week and all the milk was gone before it got to my turn," said another. "My sister has had only one small tin of milk in a fortnight and the doctor said she should have three pints a day. If only she could get milk I am sure she would be well again."

"It is the war which none of us wanted. We only want Spain for the Spanish people."

I turned to a young mother nursing a small child who, she assured me, was three years old.

It had the body of an English child of about half its age. They had been in the queue for about five hours, and the mother looked ready to collapse.

ONE SMALL TIN FOR A WEEK

Their turn to receive the milk ration arrived, and they were handed one small tin of condensed milk. The mother said:—

"It will be gone in four days, yet it is supposed to last the baby a week. My baby can never get strong and well on such a little milk."

I thought of the milk being made at that moment into buttons in England, and felt that surely the most thoughtless woman would feel it her duty to see that milk was made available for the sick and young children of this country. If they could only picture for one moment the tragedy of the empty milk can.

Accompanied by my Spanish friend, I went on to another part of the market.

Here groups of women stood about discussing the failure of the fresh fish supplies. Rumour had run round that there was fish to be had.

BOMBERS MENACE FISHING BOATS

I sensed the deep feeling of disappointment, understanding that German and Italian planes lie in wait off the fishing grounds, menacing the lives of the fishermen, and the food of the women, children and invalids.

Again I thought of Britain and the many thousands of herring that will be thrown back into the sea during the next few weeks. One per cent. of this would provide a feast in many a Spanish home!

We talked of the worry of trying to feed a family. One housewife said:—

"Every morning I go out to seek food. I have six to feed. We cannot remember when we last had meat. And there is so little bread to eat," she added, as she placed her right hand across her left, indicating the length of the top two finger joints.

I sat beside her as she bargained for some vegetable marrow.

"It is too dear," she said, turning to me explaining that it was nearly all water, and of very little food value.

Her husband, I learned, was a lorry driver and got one good meal a day in the factory restaurant, a system which is easing a little the acute food problems.

But for that this and many other families would literally starve.

" Milk is a life and death matter for them," writes Rose Smith, of the Spanish babies whose mothers stand in the queues braving the Fascist bombers every day.

October 27 1938.

From ROSE SMITH

BARCELONA, Sunday.

TODAY I have witnessed an unforgettable scene. Fascist war as it came to the market place of a working-class area. The war which has as its object not the armed men and fortifications of the battle front, but the women and children, the houses, shopping centres and food depots.

War specifically designed by Franco and his allies to destroy the food and spread terror among the civilian people. To destroy both human life and the wherewithal to sustain it.

A few days ago, like hundreds of my own countrywomen, I would say when reading of this barbarity : "It's terrible. Can't anything be done about it?"

Today I feel like a criminal that we in England have done so little.

ATTACK IN EARLY MORNING

After a night of repeated raids, the Italian bombers made a concentrated attack at 6.30 a.m. dealing death to the workers hurrying to their factories, to the young mother sleeping beside her baby, to the mother of the family who was about to rise and begin her daily search of the shops and stalls for her growing family, and to the women engaged in the preparing of the market place for the day's sales.

More than 100 people lie injured and 20 dead. Some who are reported missing will never be found again for Fascist bombs have wiped out all trace of them. Scores of homes are destroyed.

Families are engaged in a desperate endeavour to retrieve their scattered and buried belongings.

Aged women with sons at the war push trucks piled high with bed linen, seeking some new shelter, knowing that within a few hours the Italian murderers will return to deal death and destruction.

Young women scarcely started housekeeping collect their household treasures and, with huge bundles balanced on head and hip, begin a weary pilgrimage away from the wreckage.

SHATTERED TREASURES

As I walk through these streets of tragedy I pass a child's wooden horse, broken by the force of the explosion from a Fascist bomb, the wreck of a sewing machine, once a woman's treasured possession, mute emblems of a once happy home.

High up on an exposed corner, I see a plate-rack complete with dishes, just as a careful housewife had left it.

Imagine a war coming to the back streets of Battersea, of Burnley, of Bradford, Glasgow or Cardiff. I realise that, if the courage and resistance of these people break down, this will certainly come to Britain.

Meanwhile here every day children are rendered homeless and parentless. The problem of finding clothing and houses daily becomes more acute.

BOMBERS ARE COMING AGAIN

As I write this the electric current is cut off. The enemy is once again going to bomb the crowded dock area.

From the windows of my room, only a few minutes ago, I watched a mother preparing her child for bed. Now, scarcely asleep, he is hurriedly aroused and is on his way to the refugio or bomb shelter.

I think of the anxious mothers in the dock area, with last night's tragedy still fresh in their thoughts. And now they will spend another tortured night.

Women wait for the all clear signal. They will leave the shelter fearful of what awaits them in the homes they have left.

At best it will be a day of scouring the shops for scanty food supplies to be followed by another night of terror. Twin evils, death and hunger, haunt them night and day, while imperialist Governments calmly deliberate.

But working-class neighbourly sympathy is quick to act. Not one of us would knowingly allow a child to go hungry. Here are tens of thousands who need your aid.

As I finish this by the aid of candle light, I learn that the same ruthless bombing of women and children is taking place in all large cities of Government Spain.

Tomorrow and tomorrow this will be repeated unless much more aid is forthcoming.

October 1938.

Spain's Food Supply Must Be Guarded

—Demand To Government

A DEMAND that the British Government should afford protection to the supply of food and other civilian necessities to Spain and should not ratify the Anglo-Italian Agreement unless and until all her soldiers and technical experts are withdrawn by Italy was made yesterday by the Executive Committee of the League of Nations Union.

Yesterday, too, reports from the various democratic countries of Europe received by the DAILY WORKER show that everywhere Labour and progressive organisations are engaged in the biggest effort so far to send aid to the people of the Spanish Republic.

Here is a summary of the main reports:—

NORWAY

More than 1,200,000 crowns have been collected by the Norwegian Aid Spain Committee, and it is estimated that by the end of the year this sum will have exceeded one and a half million crowns.

Another 12 ambulances are to be sent out together with 12 lorryloads of salted fish and regular supplies of food for the children's home at Alcoy.

SWEDEN

Support for the idea, now under discussion, that Sweden's surplus harvest yield, which includes 100,000 tons of wheat, should be sold to Republican Spain is growing especially among the peasants.

Many trade union branches are urging the Swedish T.U.C. to put itself at the head of a nation-wide campaign for Spain.

FINLAND

An appeal to all their members and followers to support a Spain aid campaign has been issued jointly by the Finnish T.U.C., Labour Party and Labour League of Youth.

FRANCE

Two hundred thousand francs and 8,500 tins of milk were collected in Paris by the Young Girls of France during their special Milk for Spain day. Putting the milk at five francs a tin, this represents a total of 2,500,000 francs. It is expected that this amount will be quadrupled when the results from the provinces are received.

Sailors at Le Havre gave 4,000 francs and 600 tins of milk.

BRITISH BATTA

By

By
PETER KERRIGAN
Daily Worker Correspondent in Spain

THE STORY OF

MEN OF IMM

MY STORY IS ABOUT MEN. BRITISH MEN, IMMORTAL MEN, WHO, WHILE CHAMBERLAIN WAS BETRAYING THE HONOUR OF THE BRITISH PEOPLE IN MUNICH, WERE TRYING TO SAVE IT IN REPUBLICAN SPAIN.

My story is about the last battle our comrades took part in, before arrangements were made for their evacuateion from Spain.

If my story is jerky and a little disjointed, that's because it is being written under the stress of emotion and the stress of experiences I hope from the bottom of my heart none who see this will ever have to undergo.

Consider, you who read this by fireside, in train or workshop, the circumstances under which the British Battalion went into its last action.

On September 22, President Negrin announced the decision of the Republican Government to withdraw all foreign volunteers.

The Battalion knew of this decision. But the men also knew they had received a call to go into a final battle because of a critical situation that had arisen in a vital part of the Ebro front.

The Battalion had been in a reserve position for nine days.

But what a reserve position! I saw them on one of the only two days when they had complete quiet. All the rest of the time they were under continuous artillery and aviation fire.

One bomb dropped on a small house, where our transmission and communication comrades were working. Alas, when the men were dug out, life had gone.

GREAT RESPONSE

Another bomb dropped almost on top of the dug-out where the Battalion headquarters were, the concussion affecting every man there, but fortunately the earth protection saved serious damage.

One night the men were moved up to the line to occupy their old positions, but were taken back again, only to move up on the evening of September 22 for the last terrible action.

Imagine how the men felt. The last battle. Who would come through? Some more than 18 months from their homes and loved ones, some many times wounded before; now they were going home soon.

And yet, despite circumstances which it is not possible to write about, these comrades of yours and mine responded unflinchingly to a call from the Higher Command of the Spanish People's Army, even though they knew that for some it would be the last call.

DROVE ENEMY OFF

Here let me quote from Bob Cooney's report:—

"On September 6 the Brigade again went into action, our Battalion remaining in reserve. Two days later we received an urgent call. The Fascists had captured Hill 356 and the line was broken.

"We moved up in record time, and were just in time to close the break. The boys, despite their tiredness, fought splendidly and drove the enemy off 356.

"On September 11 the entire Brigade went into reserve. Before long, however, we were called into action again, as the line was wavering. Day after day, our comrades had to make a dash to this or that point in order to strengthen the line. We succeeded in holding all positions, but the strain was tremendous.

"On the evening of September 22 our Brigade relieved the 13th, which had suffered severely. Our forces had not slept for three nights, and were in a very exhaused state.

"We knew that we were due to be relieved the next night and that this would be our last action, as the Internationals were to be withdrawn.

TERRIBLE SHELLING

"You can imagine how we felt. None of us could help but speculate on our chances of coming out alive, especially as we knew we were going into a very dangerous position. Owing to various delays, it was daylight before we moved into the line, and we had no time to take stock of our positions.

"What a day it was! Such artillery bombardments as I have never seen before. They literally churned up our position. Under cover of the artillery, the Fascists advanced with infantry and tanks. They were on top of us before we were aware of their advance. Our boys suffered heavily. We retired in as good order as possible, and formed a line on the next ridge. The artillery bombardment, with continuous bombing from airplanes, continued.

"Somehow or other we managed to hold on till dusk, when we went out to get our wounded. It took us four hours to do this, and then we were relieved.

"The following morning we crossed the Ebro."

These simple, matter-of-fact words of Bob Cooney hide an epic story that will live as long as history. When you read the Official Orders paying tribute to what they did, you will see the kind of men that really represent Britain.

Not the kind that sit in Downing Street, or crumple up in Parliament when Chamberlain tells them he's going to fly to Munich. But working men from Scotland, Lancashire, London, South Wales, Ireland and the North-East Coast.

Let me tell you of George Fletcher. He has been in command in the last two actions, while Sam Wild has been in hospital with his wounds. George was the last man to leave the valley. He saw all our machine-guns safely out, and then, at 1.10 p.m., he tried to leave. He was under machine-gun fire, and dropped behind a vine, while the machine-gunners fired bursts at him.

After two hours, during which he lay without moving a finger, the snipers gave up, assuming they had killed George. He could not move from the spot until dusk, which means he lay for seven hours before getting back to our lines.

Then George came back into the valley and, with Bob Cooney, organised the evacuation of some of our wounded, who had lain there all the time because it was suicide to try and move, never mind reach them, during the daylight.

Johnny Powers, the Commander of No. 1 Company, used all the bullets in his revolver against the Fascists, except one, which he kept for eventualities. Fortunately, he managed to get out and reach our lines with a handful of other comrades.

Bob Cooney is another, about whose work it is impossible to speak too highly. Through the whole of this last terrible two months he has been without a break of any kind, and in every action. His steadfastness has been a sheet anchor for others.

I was in at the formation of the British Battalion in November, 1936. I saw the first battle at Jarama our comrades were in. We thought nothing could ever equal the valour of our comrades then, but, with the greatest respect, it now has to be said that nothing will ever equal the last battle in Spain of the British Battalion of the International Brigade.

If our deep-felt grief can be assuaged and consoled with pride it is surely in the knowledge of the unforgettable deeds that have been done by our comrades.

HARD TO LEAVE

I have just seen a further report from Bob Cooney, dated September 26.

"Yesterday we moved to—and entered billets for the first time since last December. We have fought our last action in Spain. We expect to remain here about a week, after which we will move to the security of Barcelona. We have had a Battalion meeting to explain the reasons for our going home. Both British and Spanish were sad.

"We love our homes and our people. We will be glad to see them once more. But it is hard to leave the soil in which we have fought and helped to liberate, the soil under which so many of our loved comrades sleep. It is hard to leave our splendid Spanish comrades.

"Tomorrow our Battalian is to give its extra bread rations to the civilian population in the little village where we are billeted.

"There will be many sad leavetakings. Each of us will leave with the address of a Spanish comrade to whom we will write and send fags.

"The 57th Battalion of the 15th Brigade will remain, and we will follow its struggle with pride. It will always be our Battalion. A pact is to be drawn up between Spanish and Internationals pledging all comrades to fight to the death for the liberation of Spain."

I said I would write about men. You see they have written for themselves.

But now, reader, the challenge is to you. As you read this, I ask you wherever you are, to pause in silence as your solemn tribute to the living and the dead of the British Battalion. Then, inspired by what they have dared and done, I appeal to you to dare and do for Republican Spain.

Our heroes will soon be home. For them the welcome they have earned and desire is for us to see that their families are looked after; that jobs are found; that the Dependants' Aid Fund is increased so that all obligations can be discharged with honour and with thankfulness.

ION 1936-37-38

ORTAL GLORY

THE LAST EPIC

WE OWE THEM THIS MUCH

The following statement has been received from the Wounded and Dependants' Committee:—

LAST Sunday, on the left bank of the Ebro, the Spanish Government, with ceremonial honours, carried out its decision to disband the International Brigade.

As the big guns boomed in the distance and the warplanes circled overhead, the volunteers and their Spanish comrades in the Brigade marched towards their commander. The Spanish soldiers went forward and the volunteers laid down their arms. To the cries of "Long Live Spain" the volunteers marched away.

From the Universities and technical colleges of Britain, from all classes and professions, the factories, mines and workshops, over 2,000 men went to Spain.

Four hundred and thirty-two have made the supreme sacrifice—killed in action.

Many more have been reported missing and are now presumed dead.

One thousand, two hundred and three have been wounded. Most of these returned to the Brigade after treatment, but 494 have been invalided home, many incapacitated for life.

WHILE the men were in Spain, their wives and families were maintained by funds contributed by the democratic movement in Britain and administered by the Wounded and Dependants' Aid Committee.

Lately this Committee has also assumed responsibility for the returned wounded men. Since its inception the Committee has collected £45,574, all of which has been spent on the above purposes with a minimum of administrative costs, which amounted to less than 5 per cent.

At present the Committee has to provide £550 a week for the dependants of the volunteers. An additional £100 per week is needed to provide the wounded in this country with sustenance and treatment.

THE dissolution of the Brigade and the return of the wounded creates a financial liability which must become a charge on the whole democratic movement of Britain. By this means we shall be giving very practical help to Spain at the present time.

To meet this new situation the **Wounded and Dependants' Aid Committee has inaugurated a National Memorial Fund.**

The Fund has the support of representative people and all organisations. The Blackpool Trades Union Congress, through its General Secretary, appealed to all affiliated organisations to assist the Fund.

The Communist Party of Great Britain decided at its Birmingham Congress to ask every member either to donate or to collect £1.

A National Appeal signed by representative leaders of all sections of the democratic movement has been issued. Its 66 signatories include Sir Norman Angell, C. R. Attlee, M.P., Alfred Barnes, M.P., the Dean of Chichester, Vernon Bartlett, Professor Crossman, Milner Gray, C.B.E., Lord Parmoor, Will Lawther, Dr. Maude Royden, J. B. Priestley, W. J. R. Squance, Harry Pollitt, Victor Gollancz, H. G. Wells, Arthur Horner, A. J. Cummings and G. Maurice Hann.

MEMORIAL meetings for the Fund are being organised in the main provincial centres, culminating in a national memorial meeting in London in December. The Fund was officially launched at the great Liverpool memorial meeting on September 22, when, under the chairmanship of Prof. Lyons-Blease, representatives of all sections paid a tribute to the men who had fallen. This was followed by Manchester, where 3,000 people packed the historic Free Trade Hall to pay homage to those who had died for the cause.

The first donation came from a miners' branch. The second came from the Duchess of Atholl. This is symbolic of the response which must be obtained if the widows and children of the men killed in Spain and the returned wounded men are to be fully cared for.

The greatest tribute that can be paid to men who have borne the brunt of Fascist aggression is to see that their dependants are provided with all they would have had if their loved ones had lived, and that those incapacitated should be able to live as full a life as their disabilities will allow. We cannot do less than this.

Get busy inside every organisation of which you are a member to make a success of the Memorial Fund to the British Battalion. Demand as never before that the Spanish Government gets its international rights. Force the withdrawal of the Fascist invaders. See that food and yet more food is sent to Republican Spain.

All are not called upon to look death in the face and be unafraid like the men of the British Battalion.

Yet all can help in the way I have suggested. It is as little as you can do. I know you will do so.

In these days, when the shame on our country's name is world wide, when in Czechoslovakia the people must hate Chamberlain for his contemptible treachery, never let it be forgotten that on a dozen battlefields of Spain, British men, your comrades, your men, have carried forward the finest traditions of our people, and have written pages of history, whose lustre will not illuminate the world with their grandeur and will yet see victory brought to Republican Spain.

FROM PETER KERRIGAN

BARCELONA, Thursday.

AT midnight, in heavy rain, the men of the International Brigades marched to the waiting train, and by 9 a.m. on Tuesday reached the place which had been chosen for the Government's farewell fiesta.

The spot chosen had once been the country home of some rich Spaniard. There was a big square enclosing a large sunken courtyard, overlooked by a balcony, broad and spacious, which ran round three sides.

The heroes of the two famous international divisions were drawn up in close formation in that square.

Through the guard of honour, and along the overlooking balcony, while the band played the Song of the Republic, came Dr. Negrin. Big of frame and forceful of personality, he is a man who inspires confidence.

With him on the balcony were the leaders of the People's Army, come to pay their farewell to the men who had helped to forge their army, and, in the process, had become a living part of it—General Rojo, Colonel Modesto, Colonel Lister, Andre Marty, and representatives of the Republican Navy and Air Force.

FATHER OF THE BRIGADES

The "father of the Brigades," Andre Marty, spoke first. He said:—

"In a few days we shall be leaving Spain, which we consider as our fatherland. We shall always be proud of the fact that the Spanish Government allowed us to come here. To the President of the Government, who has always maintained his faith in the people, we solemnly promise to continue the struggle."

These words were greeted with tremendous applause, and in homage to the hero of the Black Sea mutiny the band struck up the Marseillaise, which was taken up by the whole parade.

It was indeed a memorable occasion.

No sooner had he finished than the men broke into storms of cheering, crying "Viva el Commandante!"

The applause reached its crescendo when Dr. Negrin drew near to the microphone.

Addressing the volunteers as "International Brothers," Dr. Negrin said: "You came to Spain of your own will, prepared to sacrifice your lives."

MADRID

"I remember," he said, "those grave moments in the month of November, when the whole world thought that Madrid would fall, Madrid, a defenceless city, except for the breasts of her sons. Never shall I forget the impression that I received at the sight of that solid, marching column, resolute and determined, as the first of two thousand international volunteers marched through the streets of Valencia on the way to Madrid."

Before wishing them a final farewell, Dr. Negrin made this solemn declaration:—

"The Government of the Republic has recognised the right of the Internationals, who have fought so valiantly at our side, once the war is over, the right of Spanish citizenship."

As the final words were pronounced, the whole parade sprung to attention, the Spanish comrades presented arms, and the band struck up the Song of the Spanish Republic, while the Internationals stood with clenched fists raised in salute.

A moment of wild cheering, and then, spontaneously, the full assembly burst into the Internationale.

END IS BEGINNING

I looked down on the scene. The red scarves of the famous Garibaldi Battalion caught my eye at the back. Just below me were the British and Americans, with their banners. On their left the Germans and to the right the French and Belgians.

What men! What deeds! And now, we were witnessing the end. But only the end of a phase, which is at the same time the beginning of a new chapter.

Oct 28 1938.

SPAIN HAILS BRIGADE IN LAST FAREWELL

From PETER KERRIGAN

Who sends his last message as Daily Worker correspondent in Spain, as the International Brigade in which he fought gives its final salute.

BARCELONA, Sunday.

YESTERDAY BARCELONA SAID FAREWELL TO THE INTERNATIONAL BRIGADE. OVER A QUARTER OF A MILLION OF HER INHABITANTS HAD ASSEMBLED TO SAY IT PERSONALLY.

I watched it from a balcony overlooking the Avenue 14th April, the world-famous Diagonal.

Far out at the Western end was the saluting base, where the President of the Republic, Don Manuel Azana, and the Premier, Dr. Negrin, took the salute.

At 4.30 p.m we heard the beat of the drums, and the first of the 10,000 troops, who were parading in honour of the internationals, came in sight.

The Navy had been given the honour of leading the parade. They marched jauntily along behind the battery of motor-cycles who signalled their approach.

After them came the motorised forces and machine-gunners. Then, greeted by an extra loud burst of hand-clapping and applause, came the Air Force.

There was a gap in the procession. Then all along the tense crowd on each side of the street swept stormy cheering, which grew and swelled into a mighty roar.

Now they were in sight. the flags of the first ranks of the Internationals. No longer did the troops carry rifles, their arms were filled with huge bouquets of flowers. Flowers were rained on them from all sides.

Breaking through the ranks of the guards on the pavements, women and girls and little children rushed to rain more flowers, and then to stand to clap, to cheer and cry.

Tears rolled down the cheeks of many. The emotional effect of the moment was terrific. The sounds reached a great crescendo as the men who had comprised the immortal 11th, 12th, 13th, 14th and 15th Brigades of the Spanish People's Army appeared before us.

It was as though they were borne onwards on the crest of a great wave of love, devotion and gratitude that all of us will remember so long as memory is with us.

BRITISH BATTALION MARCHES PAST

Then our 15th Brigade came abreast, and as I saw our proud Battalion banner, with the names of every battlefield. from Madrid to the Ebro inscribed on it, I thought:—

"Will the British workers, who are soon to be reading these names, understand that the men who died in each of these battles, died fighting to save our liberties in Britain?

"Will the British people realise that the men who survive are worthy of a welcome in Britain no less great than this mighty farewell in Barcelona today?

"These are the men who saved the good name of our country."

The last of the Internationals had passed, and pouring along behind, not waiting to permit the last of the procession to join up, came the workers of Barcelona—men, women and girls in spontaneous demonstration.

SPAIN FACES WINTER'S FIGHT

The sun was setting in a great fiery orb. Its almost horizontal rays picked out the marching workers, while a strong, cold wind, precursor of the winter, swept the leaflets and flowers up and chased them along the street.

As we joined the masses of people below, the chill of the night was ever more pronounced, because of the previous excitement.

The Spanish people are facing the rigours of their third winter as the Internationals leave. But we know that their promise will be made good. They will make good the promise, emblazoned on their banners along the route: " Brothers of the International Brigade, come back; Spain will ever be your home!"

With our help they are going to fling back the foreign invaders, defeating Chamberlain and Daladier, as they will defeat Hitler and Mussolini.

Beloved, unconquerable Spanish brothers and sisters, we will come back to Spain some day to thank you for all you have taught us, and to partake once more, in happier circumstances of your boundless hospitality. Speed that day! Salud!

October 31 1938.

When the news of the departure of the International Brigade was announced in Spain, spontaneous demonstrations took place in their honour. Here local people entertain the lads with an impromptu " Sardana."

Resting by the wayside. This group includes Bob Cooney, Paddy O'Dare, George Fletcher, Sam Wilde, Ted Edwardes and Peter Kerrigan.

Some of the first batch of 40 British men who have returned home on Tuesday after being prisoners in Franco territory.

98,000 MEN LOST BY FRANCO

BARCELONA, Wednesday.

SEVEN or eight divisions of his best troops have been lost by Franco in the past three months' fighting on the Ebro front, according to Spanish Government military authorities.

During the six-day Republican advance on the 100-mile front from Fagen to Cherta, which started on June 25, Franco's casualties were 11,000 dead and wounded, and 7,000 prisoners were taken.

COUNTER-ATTACK FAILS

The first series of counter-attacks against the new Government positions started on July 30. Despite the use of ever increasing numbers of aircraft and of artillery batteries, the line held.

During August, the offensive against Sagunto was abandoned, and men and material were transferred to the Ebro, where soon 300,000 men were face to face in the comparatively small sector of Gandesa.

The insurgent counter-attack, which has been sustained almost ceaselessly for more than two and a half months by picked troops and concentrated tanks, aircraft and artillery, has had this result at the cost of 80,000 dead and wounded; some 20 square miles have been re-taken on the whole front.

WINTER APPROACHING

The Government advance of three months ago yielded them 420 square miles, and of that territory they retain 95 per cent.

No reason other than the urgent necessity of trying to force the issue before the coming of winter could have persuaded the insurgent command to pursue so costly an operation.

SCRAPS

VOLUME TWO

SAVE PHOTOGRAPHS
AND PRESS CUTTINGS
FOR REFERENCE

CLIVE BRANSON joined the International Brigade, was captured, spent several months in one of Franco's Prisons. He arrived in London with the batch of Prisoners just released, came into the DAILY WORKER Office yesterday and—

THIS IS WHAT HE SAID . . .

WHEN news came through about the exchanges the Spanish prisoners were all lined up in twos, and those who wished to be exchanged had to stand out.

There were only a very few who stood out, and after they were dispersed we asked the others why they did not stand out also.

They said: "How can we? Our wives and families will be left in Franco territory and they will all be shot. . . ."

* * *

◆ THE food in prison was vile.

In San Sebastian prison, where we had to stay for two days before coming home, we got boiled water in the morning slightly coloured to make it look like coffee; for dinner, a small plate of lentils; and in the evening bread steeped in boiled water.

In the cells next to ours there were 200 girls who had been in the prison for over two months. There were little girls three and four years old among them.

A week before we were to be exchanged we were all made to sit out in the sun so that we could get a good tan to show the people in England how well Franco treated his prisoners . . .

* * *

◆ I SAW Italian soldiers walking about and talking to the women, and the Spanish soldiers were doing all the work.

In Palencia there were two statues, one of Christ and one of the Virgin Mary. A little over a year ago a section of Fascist soldiers—t h e Phalangists—came and bombed the statue of the Virgin Mary to smithereens. The Italian guards themselves armed the Spanish prisoners in readiness for a fight with Spaniards who were very angry at the bombing of the statue. The relationship of forces there is really extraordinary. It is really not one side fighting Barcelona. . . .

* * *

◆ AT San Pedro 4,000 prisoners were concentrated, and were used for work in the labour gangs which were run by a sergeant-major who simply used a stick on the prisoners as if they were cattle.

There were no sort of regulations at all, and no time tables. If the guard didn't feel like letting the prisoners out, he didn't.

The sanitary conditions were simply terrible. There were two broken-down lavatories for 650 prisoners and the water supply came in through the same pipes as used for the lavatories, there were no medical supplies.

All medical cases treated went to the hospitals, where they were treated very well, and there was plenty of good food. . . .

* * *

◆ THE Spaniards themselves were starving, and the guards, as at San Pedro, hadn't any new equipment at all or clothes.

My trousers were completely ripped when we were captured, and one fellow had gone into battle with no trousers at all. But the Spanish guards bought our clothes off us in order to clothe themselves, and this will give you some idea of how well off they are.

When Franco's Spanish contingents went out to fight they looked an even funnier sight than the first International Brigaders—and that's saying a good deal!

* * *

◆ THE Italians are completely fed up with fighting, and most of them just don't know what they are there for.

When they were asked how long they had been in the army they said three years, and when asked where they were before, they answered "Abyssinia."

Volunteers in both places! It became a good joke, and we were thinking of writing to them, asking them when they were going to be released. . . .

The Italian guards on the whole were good friends of the prisoners. The guards had practically the same food as the prisoners.

* * *

◆ ALL the talk about there being few Italians left or Franco sending them out is absolutely ridiculous. The only Italians being sent out are the caballeros, t h e better-class Italians, members of the Fascist Party, who are sick of fighting and have been there for about 18 months.

We were driven from our camp to San Sebastian, and the driver of the taxi who took us was an Italian who could speak a little English He had been in Spain a fortnight. As fast as they were being shipped to Italy, they were being brought into Spain.

There are two lines of Italians at the front. The front line are the peasant lads, who, it is quite obvious, hate fighting and just don't know why they are in Spain. Behind them are the machine-guns, behind which are the caballeros, so that if the Italian peasants should want to make a break for it, they must either run into the fighting or into the caballeros.

The caballeros are mostly the sons of hotel keepers; slightly lower middle class. They are the only men who who are keeping the organisation behind the Franco lines together.

It is the Italian peasant that is getting it in the neck and really suffering in Spain. . . .

* * *

◆ WHILE we were fighting we were simply having steel flung at us in every shape and form, and they just go on doing it for four or five hours, and then the village or whatever they are attacking is reduced to smouldering ruins, and the Italians take the town.

We were simply astonished at the tremendous equipment of the Italians. Just rows and rows of heavy artillery.

Gandessa, for example, was blown to smithereens before the Spanish left, and the Italians occupied it. They have to blow every single village to smithereens because the Italian infantry do no fighting, rely entirely on their equipment, and just occupy the ruins . . .

Any organisation at all in Franco Spain is Italian, but the few Germans there are, hold executive positions.

October 1938.

The British Battalion of the International Brigade taken immediately after the demobilisation. These lads will be back home soon and London is preparing a monst welcome.

BARCELONA'S WAR ORPHANS

A NURSE AND SOME OF THE WAR ORPHANS IN BARCELONA'S CHILDREN'S RESTAURANT No 1. THEY WANT FOOD AND MILK. *November 1. 1938.*

100,000 TINS OF MILK FOR WAR BABIES

FOLLOWING the serious news that 4,000,000 Spanish children are nearing starvation point, the British Youth Peace Assembly has launched an appeal for ONE HUNDRED THOUSAND TINS OF MILK FOR SPAIN during November.

Sponsoring the appeal are 30 National Youth Organisations, including the National Council of Girls' Clubs, the League of Nations Union Youth Groups, the Civil Service Clerical Association Youth Committee, the Y.W.C.A., etc.

Individual support comes from the Archbishop of York, the Duchess of Atholl, Sir Walter Layton, the Earl of Listowel, Megan Lloyd George, H. W. Austin, and many others.

From November 5 to 13, the committee has arranged a **Spanish War Baby Week**, which aims to bring to the British public the Spanish baby in all its tragedy and need.

On November 19, the Youth Organisations affiliated to the British Youth Peace Assembly are to meet in conference to plan the next stages of the winter campaign.

FOODSHIP

Twenty-five representatives of French youth movements will be present, and will discuss the project of sending a **Youthship** to Spain in the New Year.

To coincide with the conference a drive for milk will be made, and November 19 will be **National Milk Day**.

A **Milk Club** has been started whereby the public can donate small sums for milk regularly. For 7s. per month a child can be maintained with milk in a home in Spain.

Back From Franco's Jails

RELATIVES, friends and comrades cheered loudly when the train bringing a further batch of twenty Britons, freed from Franco's prison, drew in at Victoria Station, London, last night.

Twenty more will arrive today and a further twenty tomorrow.

Taken from Palencia to San Sebastian on Monday, they spent their last night in a Fascist jail on Monday.

Before they left, however, the British Consul asked the men not to demonstrate as they passed over the bridge and not to have anything to do with the Press representatives.

Ernest Savage, a young Lancashire shop assistant, told me how the Italians staged a mock air battle to keep the people off the streets, while a train, filled with wounded soldiers, came into the station.

All the freed prisoners remarked how when they spoke to the Italians of Spain, the Italians would con-

Fascist Enemy Driven Back

MADRID, Monday. — Colonel Ortega, Commander of the Jarama Sector divisions of the Republican Army, said today he considered the Fascist attack on the sector had come to an end.

The enemy, he said, numbered 10,000. Furious efforts had been made to break through and 20,000 shells fired along a two-mile front, but the enemy was driven back with huge losses.

Killed and wounded totalled 3,000.

VALENCIA BOMBED

Valencia port was raided this morning by five Fascist planes, which dropped 50 high explosive bombs.

The raided district was uninhabited and there were no casualties, but damage was caused to some of the wharves.

YESTERDAY THE FOODSHIP, LADEN WITH THE GIFTS OF THE SCOTTISH PEOPLE, AND DESPATCHED TO SPAIN BY THE SCOTTISH TRADES UNION CONGRESS, WAS BEING UNLOADED IN THE PORT OF VALENCIA.

She had succeeded in evading the Fascist fleet which, it was known, lay in wait to send the ship and her cargo to the bottom of sea.

Today it is possible to reveal that the Prime Minister refused to allow any protection to this British ship.

The facts are as follows:—

On October 10, Mr. Arthur Brady, Secretary of Glasgow Trades Council, wrote to Mr. Chamberlain and to the Secretary of the Admiralty informing them that the ship, with British captain, officers and crew was to sail within a week of that date.

He continued:—

"I am directed by the Joint Trades Council of Glasgow and Edinburgh to inform you of this humanitarian project,

and to ask that you take the necessary steps for protection of the crew, the ship and the precious cargo of food it is carrying.

"I have to ask also that such protection be extended to the ship, not only on the high seas, but within the three-miles limit as well."

Four days later a reply was sent by the Secretary of the Admiralty, saying:—

"While the provision of naval escort is not possible, the vessel can, of course, expect to receive such naval assistance as is available, while she is on the high seas, if the circumstances should require it.

"With regard to your request that protection may be expected inside territorial waters, your Council will be aware that His Majesty's Government have persistently maintained that they cannot undertake to give naval protection to ships which enter the territorial waters of any part of Spain."

BRADY'S RETORT

Mr. Brady's reply was short and to the point.

"If the British Government cannot protect the lives of their seamen and the cargo of food so necessary for humanitarian purposes in Spain," he wrote, "I am afraid the whole of your communication is pointless.

"It was our belief, unfortunately, that if British subjects were murdered in any part of the world, the authority of the British Empire would be immediately evoked.

"It is regrettable that the Prime Minister and His Majesty's Government takes a contrary view."

Spain Will Fight Till Victory

BARCELONA, Monday.—In a broadcast speech the Spanish Prime Minister, Dr. Negrin, said:—

'The Spanish people will fight until it wins, and it will not rest until it has won. If the enemy does not agree to recognise the principles of reciprocal tolerance and a common life based on service to Spain, the war will be long and it will be hard. But neither the length nor the difficulty of the war will discourage this people.

TRAITOR

"He who speaks of compromise or mediation is a traitor to his country and, consciously or not, an agent of the enemy.

"After the war it will be necessary to choose between a powerful Spain as a friend and a powerful Spain as an enemy. Spain will not disappear, although other States will tumble."

November 1 1938

Franco Will Not Pay For Bombed Ships

(From Our Diplomatic Correspondent)

FRANCO has refused to pay any compensation to British shipowners whose vessels have been sunk or damaged by his Italian and German air-pirates.

One reason for this is that the Fascists maintain that their present financial position makes it impossible for them to guarantee in the future the payment of unascertained sums in sterling.

Nevertheless, through their office in Rome—the address of which is known to Mr. Chamberlain—they have been offering large sums in British currency to bribe British captains to commit barratry.

(Barratry is a very wide term covering running away with a ship, sinking it or stealing the cargo.)

These facts were revealed at a meeting of shipowners trading with Spain held in London yesterday. The meeting heard the result of the discussions which have been proceeding between the Shipowners' Committee and the Foreign Office over the proposed inquiry into the bombing of British vessels.

It was also reported that the Foreign Office and the committee's legal advisers were agreed that no liability would lie against the Spanish Republic at the conclusion of hostilities and, in the event of Franco being defeated, there would be no authority from whom they could claim compensation.

Among the Spain volunteers who will be welcomed back to Dundee is James Colman. Jimmie, as he is popularly known in the city, was for a considerable period manager of the Workers' Bookshop at 34, Hawkhill.

Vatican And Spain

From Our Diplomatic Correspondent

DIPLOMATIC relations between the Vatican and the Spanish Republic have, I learn, now been restored.

This very important decision follows the receipt by the Vatican of a very satisfactory report on the religious position in Government territory.

The report was made to the Primate of Catalonia, Cardinal Vidal y Barraquer, by Mgr. Salvador, Vicar-General of Tarragona and Apostolic Administrator or Lerida, who entered Italy with a Spanish diplomatic passport.

NEGRIN'S SPEECH

Relations between the Vatican and Barcelona have been improving rapidly ever since June, when the Prime Minister, Dr. Negrin, declared:—

"We are struggling to secure the rights of conscience and respect for religion. We will have no interference in the life of the State by the Church as an institution, but we will guarantee freedom of worship."

That declaration of policy has been put into practice.

The British people will, no doubt, realise that by permitting Chamberlain to ratify the Anglo-Italian Pact and grant belligerent rights to Franco, they will be allowing themselves to become accomplices in the destruction of those rights and liberties which as even the Vatican now recognises exist in and are the essence of Republican Spain.

CITY WATCHES AIR BATTLE

(From Our Own Correspondent)

BARCELONA, Tuesday.

SHORTLY after 10 a.m. today two squadrons each of five Savoia bombers raided the working-class quarter near the port here.

Striking demonstration of the efficiency of the air raid warning system was given by the sounding of the sirens fully four minutes before the bombers were seen.

This gave the population ample time to take cover and heavy casualties were thereby averted.

Immediately the raider appeared, anti-aircraft batteries opened fire and caused them to break formation.

CHASER GIVES BATTLE

While firing was still going on, a Government chaser, disregarding the risk of being hit by our own guns, went up and engaged the enemy.

We could see the small chaser diving in at great speed among the big bombers, preventing them from regaining their formation.

In doing so, however, the chaser collided with a bomber, and both went into a spin, falling in the sea. Search for them is now being made by Government airplanes and gunboats.

As we lifted our eyes from the falling planes we saw another Savoia, evidently hit by the chaser's fire, making off seaward and losing height rapidly.

Some 30 bombs were dropped in the port area. Known casualties at the moment are one dead, 20 wounded.

I visited the workers' dwellings to inspect the effect of the bombs. Comparatively small ones had been used, but the upper two storeys of four-storey buildings had been completely destroyed.

A long chain of workers was helping to clear away debris from one totally-wrecked house, in which a number of workers had been buried.

SLEEPERS BURIED

Among these, I learned, were young girl munition workers, who had been sleeping after their night shift.

Sam Wild, who was with me, recognised one of the girls as one who, at the July 19 celebration, before the Ebro offensive, had presented the British Battalion with a banner from the Barcelona youth organisation.

A brief nod of recognition was all that time allowed. The work of rescue had to go on.

This is the spirit which defeats the invaders. With every raid the efficiency of the defence increases and the determination of the people rises.

November 2 1938.

This Spanish girl is now in Moscow studying. She is one of the many children from Spain being cared for in the U.S.S.R.

WOUNDED BRITONS HELD UP BY FRANCE

From Our Own Correspondent

PARIS, Tuesday.

THREE HUNDRED AND SEVENTY-SEVEN members of the International Brigade, of whom 40 are very seriously wounded, are being refused permission to leave Spain by the French authorities.

The men have all taken part in the recent Ebro fighting and are being held up at Cerbere.

There are 27 Englishmen, 63 Americans and 16 Canadians among them.

Direct intervention by the American Ambassador in Paris has not secured any modification of the French attitude.

In spite of an official Government statement issued today which claims there are technical reasons for refusing to allow the men to pass through France, it is clear from the full facts of the case that it is intended to make it impossible for the Spanish Government to evacuate the International Brigades from its territory. This then will be used as justification for continued Fascist intervention in Spain.

PASSPORT DEMAND

Up till now, the French authorities have allowed the British and Americans to pass through France in agreement with the Embassies of the two countries. This they now refuse to do, even if the men have transit visas and are vouched for by the Embassies, unless they have passports.

The American Embassy in Paris yesterday made a direct representation to the Minister of the Interior. He was told bluntly that nothing could be done unless the Embassy could guarantee each individual was going to America. This was, of course, impossible.

AMERICAN PROTEST

David Amriglio, the representative of the Friends of the Abraham Lincoln Battalion, told me today he is making the strongest protest to the American State Department, urging Government action to lift this ban.

"The Spanish Government," he said, "is paying the Brigaders' fares to New York and is even ready to charter a ship to pick the men up at some Spanish port, if the French government will protect it. This the French Government refuse to do.

"I urge strongest possible protest in Britain and in America."

There are in addition 600 demobilised American volunteers who were due to leave on November 6. If the present French attitude continues they will be unable to leave.

So, too, will the many hundred British volunteers who are waiting in Barcelona.

REFUGEES FIND PEACE IN CONVENT HOME

From ROSE SMITH

BARCELONA, Tuesday.

HERE in Barcelona, behind the battle area, there are those other soldiers of this Fascist war.

The old men whose sons are fighting for the Republic; old women once more mothering families of little children; women with minds unhinged by the terror of Fascist bombings—these are some of the people I have met here at the Pasionaria Refugio home of 500 refugees.

SEARCH FOR PEACE

An old convent has been turned into a retreat for the refugees, many of whom have been tossed by the war from Spain to France and back again to Spain in search of peace.

One old grandmother from a village near Santander has brought up five children of her own and seen them set out into the world. Now here she is starting her motherhood all over again with a family of three—one her own grandchild, the other two orphans.

Outside she showed me her garden. She had tomatoes, peas, mint and cauliflowers.

She had achieved this on a tiny patch of soil spread four inches deep over less than a square yard of concrete pavement. Here was a woman who would make a desert bloom.

One of the 170 children in a refugees' centre in Barcelona.

FRANCO FAILS IN SEVENTH EBRO PUSH

From SAM RUSSELL
BARCELONA, Wednesday.

FOR three days now a battle has been raging along the Ebro as the invaders make their seventh desperate attempt to regain the territory conquered by the Republican Army in three days more than three months ago.

For the most of last week it was quiet on this front, while the enemy reorganised his badly beaten troops who have suffered some 8,000 casualties, killed, wounded and prisoner, since July 25 last.

On Sunday morning the attack was launched, and it is already quite obvious that it is meeting with the same successful resistance as the previous six attacks.

In this seventh counter-offensive, the enemy is using 15 to 20 fresh battalions, totalling some 20,000 troops, against two Sierras—Caballs and Pandols.

After tremendous artillery preparation, and incessant bombing by hundreds of planes, these troops were thrown against the Republican positions on Sierra Caballs. Cet, after a whole day's fighting the enemy only managed to occupy six hills, and three of these were regained that very night in a brilliant night attack by our troops.

While the battle was raging on land, in the sky, too, the Republican pilots were showing their prowess, in spite of the enemy's numerical superiority.

BATTLE IN THE SKIES

Time after time our planes gave battle to the masses of the enemy bombers and chasers, and, at the end of the day, five Fiats had been brought down, without the loss of a single one of our planes.

On Monday the attack continued in all its forms. Yet, although the enemy put 300 German and Italian planes into the air which bombed and machine-gunned the hill all the morning, it was midday before they attempted to send over their infantry. And when they did come it was only to be cut to bits by concentrated machine-gun fire from the hundreds of posts with which these hills are covered.

Yesterday the enemy attacked again in the Sierra Caballs. After continuous attacks they managed to occupy two hills, one of which was immediately retaken.

FRESH BATTALIONS

With the attack against Caballs showing such little results, the enemy transferred their efforts to the Sierra Pandols, and the whole day wave after wave of these fresh battalions were sent over behind a formidable artillery barrage.

Every attack was repulsed, and the Republican posts are maintained intact.

Film Stars And Doctors Spain Push

CARRYING with it a cargo of 5,000 tons of food and a personal gift for Dr. Negrin, American Relief Food Ship will sail on October 30 for Republican Spain.

The gift takes the form of a portrait of Dr. Walter B. Cannon, Professor of Psychology at Harvard University, who was a former colleague and a life-long friend of the Spanish Premier.

The portrait is being sent by graduates of the Harvard Medical School and with it goes a further gift of money presented by the majority of the school's graduates.

Among those who have contributed to the campaign for food for Spain are the Hollywood Motion Picture Artistes' Committee, the American Federation of Teachers, the Student Christian Conference and many other progressive organisations and individuals.

NORWAY CREDITS FOR SPAIN

IMMEDIATELY the Norwegian Parliament reassembles it will discuss a motion that the Government shall grant special credits to the Spanish Government for the purchase of agricultural products from Norway.

Negotiations are to be started with the Spanish Government immediately.

This decision is given in Premier Nygaardsvold's reply to a question put to him by the Communist daily paper, Arbeideren, which has been pursuing an energetic campaign to ensure supplies of foodstuffs to the Spanish Republic.

Mme. Palencia, Spanish Ambassador to Sweden, has told the Arbeideren that her country is keenly interested in the proposal.

NEW AMBASSADOR?

It is learned that a new Spanish Ambassador will soon be appointed to Oslo, but meantime the Spanish Foreign Office will be in charge of the Spanish end of the negotiations.

Two thousand crowns have been sent to Spain by the Norwegian General Workers' Union, as a result of a decision at its annual congress, recently concluded. At this gathering a resolution was adopted, expressing support for the Spanish people and urging international unity to defeat Fascism.

"The first task now," the resolution concludes, "is the realisation of one trade union movement and one workers' party."

IN SWEDEN

In Sweden, too, there is widespread activity for Spain.

In response to a special appeal made by the Stockholm Spanish Aid Committee, the Metal Workers' Union of Hofors, one of the largest branches in the country, has agreed to subscribe two crowns for each full-paying member and one crown for each part-paying member.

The Iron and Steel Workers' Union has sent 2,000 crowns to the Spanish Aid Committee, while a nurse has sent 1,000 crowns to the Swedish Women's Committee for Spanish Aid.

Similar support is also forthcoming from working-class organisations in France.

FRENCH AID

Here, in response to its recent appeal for money to buy hard-wearing shoes for soldiers in the Spanish People's Army, the Federation of Shoeworkers has already received 30,000 francs. The Association of Ex-Servicemen has collected 58,000 francs, enough to buy 350 pairs of shoes.

Agricultural workers, affiliated to the French T.U.C. have proposed to other organisations of agricultural workers the organising of a joint Agricultural Week for the Spanish Republic.

Hundreds of local committees have been set up for next Sunday's Milk Day for Spain, organised by the Association of Young Girls of France. Last year's Milk Day brought in 600,000 francs worth of milk, and still better results are expected next Sunday.

November 5 1938

Children from the Spanish Government merchantman Cantabria, sunk off Cromer by a Franco Q-ship, caught by our photographer on their arrival in London yesterday.

Paris Stands By Spain

From Our Own Correspondent
PARIS, Friday.

IN thousands of meetings in Paris and greater Paris, tonight, the workers of the French capital, answering the call of the Paris Trades Council, demonstrated

against the granting of belligerent rights to Franco;

for the complete withdrawal of all foreign combatants from Franco's forces; and

for the opening of the Spanish frontier.

These demonstrations, it was made clear, are the reply to the pro-Fascist manœuvres of the Chamberlain Government.

SOCIALIST ATTACK

A further indication of the strength of feeling in France against the granting of belligerent rights to Franco is seen in the article of the Socialist leader Leon Blum, in Le Populaire.

Associating himself with the speech made on Wednesday by Anthony Eden, the French Socialist leader declares France can have nothing to do with the Anglo-Italian Agreement.

"The operation of this agreement can neither concern nor engage France in any way," he writes. "The question of belligerent rights cannot be regulated, and is not regulated, by a pact to which Italy and Britain are the sole parties.

"There exists no relationship between the Anglo-Italian Pact and the London Plan. The duty now facing the French Government is immediately to oppose anything which tends to establish a connection between the two.

"The French Government must watch this with the greatest vigilance and firmness. It would be intolerable if the Spanish Government were submitted at the same time to invasion and blockade."

TRADES COUNCIL APPEAL

The statement issued by the Paris Trades Council says:—

"In spite of international law, Britain is prepared to grant belligerent rights to the traitor Franco, agent of international Fascism.

"You will not allow the French Government, trailing behind the lamentable policy of the British Conservative Government, to renew the scandal of Munich, and after Czechoslovakia, to sacrifice, with Republican Spain, the security of France and the peace of the world.

"Against the granting of belligerent rights to Franco!

"For the opening of the Republican Pyrenees frontier!

"For the complete withdrawal of foreign troops from Spanish territory, including German, Italian, Moorish soldiers and technicians, as well as all foreign war material!

"For free trade with Republican Spain! Spain for the Spaniards!"

Speakers from the three great political parties of France, the Radical Party, Socialist Party and Communist Party, spoke at tonight's meetings, together with the leading trade unionists, who represented the Trades Council.

DUCE SENDS FRANCO MORE TANKS: FOOD NEEDED BY REPUBLIC

WHILE yesterday Rome official circles were demanding the immediate ratification of the Anglo-Italian Pacts, reports received by the Daily Worker from Spain showed beyond the shadow of a doubt that Italian intervention on Franco's behalf is continuing unchecked.

A constant stream of war materials, including lorries, anti-aircraft guns, tanks and armoured cars, is pouring into Cadiz and other ports in the possession of the Fascists.

Meanwhile the Government troops on the Ebro front continue to hold the Fascist attacks, which can now only be made with the help of reinforcements withdrawn from other fronts.

Only the food situation in the Republic continues to give rise to anxiety. But already indications are that the democrats of the world are moving into action to remedy this. Foodships are on their way from America, and further steps to rush food from Britain are being taken.

No Peace With The Invaders

BARCELONA, Monday.

THE entire Press here is unanimous in rejecting the idea of a "settlement" in Spain just to allow Chamberlain and Mussolini to operate the Anglo-Italian agreement.

"The only possible settlement," writes El Diluvio, "is to leave the Spaniards to themselves," and adds that Mussolini's withdrawal project is only a pretext for applying the Rome pact. Even complete withdrawal of Italian infantry, "which has hardly any military value," would not solve the problem if intervention continued in the form of aviators, military specialists and arms.

TO BE FREE

Similar comment is made by El Dia Gráfico, which adds that "No one can any longer doubt our firm resolve to be free and to be masters of our own fate."

La Vanguardia declares: "Whatever the price Mussolini will demand for mediation, we—the Spaniards—are not at all inclined to pay it."

"Only Spaniards can decide the destiny of Spain," writes Frente Rojo. "The policy of our Government is to fight without hesitation until the invasion has been defeated and national unity restored."

300 Britons Will Fight On At Home

From PETER KERRIGAN

I HAVE just arrived back in London after five months as correspondent of the DAILY WORKER in Spain.

Left behind in Spain are 300 Britons of the International Brigade, waiting for the completion of arrangements for their transportation home to England.

I have come back with mixed feelings. It is good to be home again, but I can't help feeling how the boys quartered in the village near the French frontier are chafing at the delay in their transfer home.

It is not because they want to leave the Spanish people. For three weeks the Spanish people have been feting the boys of the Brigade in a last expression of gratitude and goodwill towards the men who stood by them.

CONFIDENT

The men know the conduct of the war can be left with complete confidence in the hands of the people of Spain themselves, and quite naturally, their job in Spain completed, they are anxious to get back home. Their return has been held up by the tactics of the League of Nations Commission, which was in Spain for three weeks before setting to work.

During their stay in the frontier village, the boys are receiving political education under the direction of Bob Cooney, who has recovered from his recent illness. Sam Wild, Commander of the Battalion, is also about again on recovery from his wound.

When these men come back to England they will not be merely 300 fighters for Socialism back on the home front.

The things they have lived through in Spain, the first-hand political experience they have had, will make them a force in the British Labour movement that will have the widest possible effects.

Their return will, I hope, bring the Labour movement as a whole to realise the debt it owes to these men.

If the work of these men does nothing more than make British democrats realise their responsibility to the people of Spain, it will not have been in vain.

The members of the International Brigade are coming home because they are no longer needed in the fighting line.

The need now is for food—food to enable Spain to hold out against Franco's attempt to starve the people into defeat during the coming winter.

Britain no longer has men in Spain upholding British honour. The responsibility is now one lying directly on the people of Britain themselves.

They must reply to the callous destruction of foodships by Franco's bombs and shells. Chamberlain refuses to act in defence of Spain or of British foodships—but he can be made to act, or get out.

IN WHITEHALL

The wreath shown above was placed on the Cenotaph in Whitehall on Sunday.

It bore two inscriptions. One read: "In loving memory of Democracy"; the other, "In loving memory of our Comrades who have fought a just cause in vain and have been betrayed."

The wreath was placed there by Mr. W. E. Higgins, of Willesden, a delegate to Willesden Trades and Labour Council and to Willesden Aid for Spain Committee.

Mr. Higgins was a member of a deputation to the Prime Minister that expressed opposition to National Government foreign policy. Deputation was from members of the National Society of Painters, the Amalgamated Union of Building Trade Workers and the Amalgamated Engineering Union.

No Persecution

Here is the answer to any talk of religious persecution by the Spanish Government. It is a picture of the Catholic funeral procession in Barcelona of Captain Vicente Eguia, killed fighting for the Republic. In the funeral procession was Senor del Vayo, Foreign Minister, and other representatives of the Government.

NEW SPAIN AIR TERROR
Result Of Anglo-Italian Agreement

Martyred People Appeal To Britons

From SAM RUSSELL

BARCELONA, Sunday.

NOW THAT THE ANGLO-ITALIAN PACT IS TO COME INTO FORCE, THE FASCIST INVADERS OF SPAIN HAVE STARTED A NEW WAVE OF ATTACKS ON THE CIVIL POPULATION OF THE REPUBLIC.

At 10.25 yesterday morning the sirens here sounded in that mournful wail which heralds the approach of enemy warplanes.

Five Savoia bombers, big, black, murderous, were approaching the city.

I was in the Plaza Catalunya at the time and I watched the people run quickly, but orderly, to the underground shelters.

A soldier, bronzed with the sun of the Ebro, helps an old lady with a bundle of cabbages from a tram. Then the anti-aircraft guns open up.

Together you hear the boom of the guns and the whistle of the bombs. Then comes the explosion.

The women who have taken shelter in a doorway cannot withhold a shriek of terror as explosion follows explosion—the Italian murderers dropping their load of death on the peaceful population.

Then everybody is looking up to see the planes as they circle over the town before making their way back to Majorca, their foul work done.

The guns blaze away at them, but, at more than 17,000 feet, there is not much chance of hitting the vast bombers, the latest production of Mussolini's war factories experimenting in Spain.

"Non-intervention" prevents us from getting the guns and planes which could protect Barcelona and assure the lives of our women and children.

Once more the bombs have fallen in the thickly-populated port area and in the old town. Many people have been killed and buildings destroyed.

Again this morning at 9 a.m., ten Savoias, divided into two squadrons, bombed us. Over 40 bombs were dropped on the port area alone, and the British ship, Lake Hallwell, was hit and seriously damaged.

TWENTY BODIES

Forced to fly off by the intense anti-aircraft barrage put up, the planes dropped the majority of their bombs on a small village on the outskirts of the town, and so far 20 bodies have been recovered and 20 people have been taken to hospital seriously wounded.

In the last fortnight the whole length of the Catalan coast has been bombed time and time again. Tarragona has been bombed nine times in one night and a hospital and school destroyed.

993 ARE KILLED

From August 10 to November 1 the German and Italian bombers have raided us 64 times. Some 668 buildings have been destroyed, 993 people, mostly women and children, have been killed, and large numbers have been wounded I have been down the Ramblas. Though a few bombs had fallen

on the actual port itself, most of them had fallen on houses, six and seven storeys high, in the narrow streets of Barcelona's Old City, streets very often less than 15 feet wide.

In one street a lorry had been completely destroyed by falling masonry, and, as I watched, the whole roof of the house crashed into the street.

Going further on I came to a street which seemed familiar. Of course, it was only a week ago that I had been there with Peter Kerrigan in search of a present for his wife. I remembered we had gone into a small shop, where Peter bought two small Toledo-work brooches, beautifully engraved.

From the street it looked as if the house and shop had escaped damage; the windows were intact. But, when I looked through the door,

THE WORK OF THE FASCIST BOMBERS.

the November sun was shining on the tremendous pile of ruins which was all that remained.

The entire back of the house had been blown out, and the pools of blood on the doorstep told their own grim story.

Scattered over the floor were those tiny Toledo trinkets, fashioned so lovingly by Spanish hands, hands that have been crushed by Mussolini's bombs.

Nearer the port, a tenement house stood with its third and fourth storeys shattered by a bomb which had crashed through the walls.

Two firemen climbed up the dizzy escape, and entered the ruins. As they stepped off the ladder a young woman, who could not have been more than 28, pushed her way through the crowd, panting, her hair dishevelled, gripping under her arm a shopping bag.

She lived on the third floor, and had left her only child with her young sister there while she went out.

She held her breath. The look of anguish on her face was indescribable. The men were now out of sight searching the back room. Beneath her breath the young mother muttered: "Mi Nina, mi Nina!"—"My child, my child!"

PRECIOUS MILK

The men reappear carrying a form covered in a sheet. Behind them is a Red Cross volunteer, carrying another form, smaller, in a blue-striped blanket.

The woman shrieks out, "It cannot be!" and as if transfixed, she waits as they descend slowly, so slowly.

They reach the bottom. The woman rushes forward, shaking off those who try to hold her back. Perhaps there is still a hope, and with shaking fingers she tears away the covering. Her sister, not more than 13 years old, lies there horribly maimed. The child in the blanket is waxen-white, with the tiniest trickle of blood still oozing from its mouth.

The Red Cross doctor shakes his head, and as he does so, with a ghastly and frenzied shriek, the mother falls on the two bodies.

The bag falls from her arm, and on to the pavement roll a few tomatoes and two tins of milk.

Yet Barcelona, and the whole of Spain, carries on.

As I turned to go back up town I saw that, barely a hundred yards away, a queue had already formed outside the Liceo, Barcelona's largest theatre, for the afternoon opera show.

Further up, in a clothing factory, the girls had already returned to the machines, and were singing as they continued their work, doing their job like their brothers and fathers at the front to hasten the day when Spanish mothers will not have to leave home in the morning with fear in their hearts.

Beneath the bombs of the German and Italian warplanes Spain fights on. In the rearguard as in the front there is only one thought and one determination—to win the war, to drive out the invaders.

As the sirens shriek through the city the all-clear signal, Barcelona goes back to work, confident in victory, confident in its army, confident in its heroic womenfolk, confident that all decent-minded people and, above all, the British people will do their job to stop this massacre of Spain, and by their united action cast out that man who disgraces Britain's name, Neville Chamberlain.

...ing-class in France and England will take up their weapons of struggle, including the use of strike...

The defeatist attitude of the rulers of France will be overcome by the vigorous action of the French people. It will, no doubt, take time for the reaction of the working-class and the people against the criminal policy of those who are betraying them to positive results. But, Diaz concludes, "I believe it will not be..."

Every mouthful's precious. Spanish shelter in Barcelona, and in other will starve unless the foo...

...espondent

BARCELONA, Monday.

...ny is going to throw into ...sposal in order to obtain a ...to consolidate the conquest ...s of Europe."

General Secretary of the ...in an article in the Party ...he defence of Madrid.

...e continues:—

We must be prepared for difficult days and hard struggles on all ...ts and be prepared to meet...

MASK IS OFF

Diaz shows how, with its decision to operate the Anglo-Italian Pact, the Chamberlain Government has definitely thrown off the mask behind which it has tried for some time to conceal its true intentions towards Spain.

The most reactionary section of the British capitalist class, he says, intends Spain to lose its freedom and its independence. It wants to see Spain a colony of German and Italian Fascism, because its objective is first and foremost to help

Franco Gets New Aid From Mussolini

From Our Own Correspondent
BARCELONA, Monday.

TODAY, on the second anniversary of the siege of Madrid, Alvarez Del Vayo, Spain's Minister for Foreign Affairs, received representatives of the Press in Barcelona.

It is seven months today also since Del Vayo received the Press on that fateful April 7, when the whole world had given up the Spanish people for lost after the Italian advance in Aragon. At that time, when even the friends of Spain resigned themselves to the defeat of the Spanish people, Spain's Foreign Minister voiced the people's confidence—and that confidence has been justified time after time during these seven months.

In the course of his remarks Del Vayo revealed that the Government of the Republic has had further information about the arrival of new Italian reinforcements, which showed up quite clearly the farce of the so-called withdrawal of Italian troops.

The information, received from reliable sources, shows the existence of a new Italian division in

DEL·VAYO

Spain. The forces already in the country have been added to by the 'Green Arrow' division. Large numbers of troops are also being placed in the Spanish Foreign Legion in an attempt to disguise their existence.

This brings the Italian forces in Spain up to six regular Italian infantry divisions, in addition to large numbers of technicians, artillerymen and engineers—and not counting the huge quantities of war material which Mussolini has sent in his attempt to conquer the Spanish people.

Dealing with the position of Spain and international considerations, Del Vayo said:—

" Spain is not prepared to allow now less than ever before that anyone outside Spaniards should decide the fate of Spain. We are firmly determined to continue the fight for our national independence as long as the foreign invasion continues.

" We are equally determined to reject any so-called solution to the Spanish problem which is not based on the undeniable right of independence and of sovereignty of our nation. This is the permanent position of Spain in the struggle which we are waging for our very existence."

His last words were devoted to Madrid.

" Never before has history given us the example of a city surrounded and attacked at its very gates which has resisted with the dignity which is Madrid.

" Madrid today enters on its third year of resistance, with the prospect of an exceptionally hard winter.

" It is for this reason that I make an appeal for solidarity to all those countries where an abundance in food supplies and, above all, in wheat, enabling them to increase ever more the mighty current of aid to the civil population of Spain."

November 9 1938.

ACT TO SAVE SPAIN!

The following statement was issued by the Political Bureau of the Communist Party yesterday :—

THE Chamberlain Government is preparing a new betrayal.

The Spanish Government has demonstrated to the admiration of the whole world the will and the power of the Spanish people to hold its own in the military field against even the unlimited intervention of the Italian and German forces, and to drive the Fascist invaders out of Spain.

It is in this situation that the Chamberlain Government is hastening to the assistance of Franco and Mussolini, and preparing, by way of the Anglo-Italian Pact and the granting of belligerent rights to Franco, to impose starvation on the Spanish people.

The granting of belligerent rights to Franco means that Franco's piracy will be legalised with the support and consent of Britain. Franco and Mussolini are to be given the right to establish " legally " the starvation of Spain.

British ships, engaged in peaceful commerce with the Spanish Republic, are to be driven off the seas by the decision of Chamberlain.

The Issue
Before Britain

This is the issue before the British public : shall the power of Britain be used to starve the heroic Spanish people?

The Labour Party, leading all the Opposition forces, can defeat this infamous plan. Already universal indignation has been roused at the piratical outrages of Franco, the murder of British sailors, and the extension of these outrages to our own doorstep.

There is discontent even in the ranks of the Government's supporters over the shameful consequences of Chamberlain's policy.

Surely, in this situation the great Labour movement of this country will not fail the Spanish people.

Ready To Co-operate

The Communist Party declares its readiness to co-operate in any campaign which the Labour Party and Trades Union Congress may undertake to defeat this betrayal.

A united mass campaign throughout the country, led by the Labour movement, and uniting all supporters of democracy and peace, can still force Chamberlain to abandon his aims.

Such a campaign should voice the demand :—

That no belligerent rights be granted to Franco;
that all Italian and German troops and war materials should be cleared out of Spain;
that protection should be accorded to ships trading with Republican Spain; and that credits should be opened for the purchase of necessary provisions for the civil population of Spain.

November 11 1938.

SPANISH ARMY ENDS BATTLE ON EBRO FRONT

From Our Own Correspondent,
SAM RUSSELL
BARCELONA, Thursday.

WITHOUT the loss of a single man or a single rifle, the Spanish Republican Army on the Ebro withdrew to its positions on the right bank of the Ebro.

By a perfectly organised retreat, the General Staff put the final touch to their great offensive on the right bank, where four months fighting has had results, for Spain and for the whole world, which cannot yet be calculated.

The battle of the Ebro falls into three phases.

The first was the attack, carried out by night on June 25, that swept clear of enemy troops over 200 square miles of territory on the right bank. It threatened Franco's rear and stopped the offensive he was conducting against Sagunto and Valencia.

ENEMY LOSSES

The second phase was the defence of these positions, forcing Franco to divert all his available men and material on this front.

Not only was the offensive in the Levante stopped, but also the attempt to take Almada. Entire divisions of the enemy were smashed in their attempts to take the heights of Pandols, Cabals and Laval de la Torre.

The strategic diversion caused by the crossing of the Ebro was intended to last for one month. The fact that four months have elapsed, in which the enemy has continued to waste material, is a measure of the success of the operations.

The persistent enemy attempts to drive us back to the left bank have cost them dearly: some 80,000 casualties, among them the finest of the enemy shock troops, 214 German and Italian planes brought down, and large quantities of artillery and other materials destroyed.

OBJECTS ATTAINED

The Republic has obtained a further space of time in which it has continued the work of the reorganisation of resistance.

The battle of the Ebro entered its third phase, the withdrawal to the left bank. This was made in perfect order, without the loss of men or materials.

The object of the Ebro battle was to stop the enemy offensive against Valencia, and frustrate their international plans, which were based on the hope of a smashing success in the Levante.

All the objectives had been attained, and the Republican higher command considered that the time for withdrawal had come.

The state of the rebel rearguard bears witness to the damage inflicted by the Republican troops on the enemy in Spain and abroad.

November 11

LORRIES RUSH FOOD TO SPAIN

(From Our Own Correspondent)
PARIS, Thursday.

French Socialists and trade unionists are responding solidly to the urgent appeals for food for the Spanish people.

The twelfth convoy of lorries carrying foodstuffs and other gifts has left Toulouse for Republican Spain, and will shortly be followed by a thirteenth convoy.

BREAD WEEK

A Bread Week for Spain begun four days ago by the Popular Front parties in Alsace has already brought in 10,000 francs.

Brenot, secretary of Paris Trades Council, has issued a stirring appeal for the six million francs needed by the Council to buy French wheat for Spain.

Only Brenot and two other members of a French delegation have returned from a National Solidarity Congress held in Madrid. Mme. Agnes Dumay, of the Women's Committee Against War and Fascism, was killed by a bomb there, and M. August Bonet, of French People's Aid, was badly injured.

Five hundred pairs of shoes for men of the Spanish People's Army are on their way from here, and another 400 pairs are being made by the Federation of Skin and Leather Workers. The Federation has received 63,000 francs from members in response to an appeal.

Big donations from Swedish workers are reported. Money has been given to support Spanish children and to provide food and milk

---

90,000 ITALIANS IN SPAIN

(By Our Diplomatic Correspondent)

INFORMATION on the extent of Italian intervention in Spain at the present moment in the possession of the Spanish Government has been handed to the Foreign Office by the Spanish Ambassador in London.

Summarised, this information shows that—

there are in Spain about 90,000 Italians in Franco's service, composed of 60,000 infantry, artillery and tank troops and 30,000 technicians, including pilots, radio operators, aviation mechanics, lorry drivers, engineers and police agents.

None of the four divisions of 12,000 men each have been dissolved as a result of the withdrawal of the 10,000 Italians who left on October 15, while a new division—the "Nine of May"—is being organised.

INCREASING

Thus Italian intervention in Spain is actually increasing instead of diminishing.

According to information reaching the Spanish Government—and couting only confirmed reports—the figures of recent Italian arrivals in Spain are:—

Pilots, 325; soldiers, 3,374; technicians, 600.

Recently, too, there have arrived in Franco territory from Italy, by direct flight, bombing of a new type not previously seen in Spain—twin-engined Capronis with double tail (CA.135).

The total of Italian planes noted in flight on the Ebro front during the first fortnight of September is as follows:—

Savoia S.81, 420; Broda -65, 18; Romeo RO-37, 65; Fiat Br.-20, 19; Fiat CR-32, 779.

These figures do not, of course, represent the total of all the Italian machines in Franco territory.

FRANCO LOSES POWER STATION

From SAM RUSSELL

BARCELONA, Tuesday.

AT dawn yesterday morning the army of the Republic crossed the River Segre at a number of points south of Lerida.

By 6 p.m., the advancing troops had consolidated their positions on the right bank of the river, taking the towns of Seros, Aytona and Soses, crossed the Fraga-Lerida road, and were advancing on to Alcarraz.

The attack is being made along a 12-mile front, and has already resulted in the recapture for the Republic of the important hydro-electric power station to the north of Seros.

In this new offensive the tactics which brought such splendid results on the Ebro three months ago have been repeated, and with equal success.

Although the Segre is, at the moment, a swiftly flowing river, due to the snow which has fallen on the hills during the past few days, it was crossed at a number of points.

ENEMY SURPRISED

How surprised the enemy were can be judged from the fact that immediately the Republican troops had crossed the river they took over 700 prisoners.

As our units advanced this number was added to, and large quantities of war material and transport were captured.

This new offensive is a further proof of the strength of the Republican Army today. For ten days now, with the support of large quantities of German artillery, the Fascists have continually attacked the Republican positions on the right bank of the Ebro.

At the cost of losses even greater than those sustained in three months of constant counter-offensive, they have managed to make slight advances.

ARTILLERY FIRE

These advances, however, have only been made after intense artillery preparation had actually changed the outline of the Sierras. Even then, when the barrage lifted, the Legionaries and Moors were cut to bits before their total advance of 200 or 300 yards had been achieved.

As a result, the enemy "successes" in this seventh counter-offensive are actually one of the biggest defeats they have suffered.

Twenty battalions of enemy shock troops have been decimated.

November 9 1938.

REPUBLIC'S TWO-WAY ADVANCE

From SAM RUSSELL

BARCELONA, Thursday.

YESTERDAY the forces which crossed the Segre so successfully devoted their energy to consolidating the positions taken, resisting the enemy counter-attack, and enlarging the bridge-head on the right bank.

The forces employed were small and relied entirely on the surprise effect obtained by crossing the river at five different points.

THROUGH FOG

There was no artillery preparation and, once on the other side, the troops advanced without tanks or artillery covering fire through a thick fog, which enveloped the whole of the Segre valley at the time.

In the whole of the action the Republican losses, killed and wounded, were less than the total number of the enemy taken prisoner. An area in some places 6¼ miles deep along a 12-mile front has been occupied.

ATTACKED FROM REAR

The attack on, and capture of, Seros was particularly well executed. This town was protected from frontal attack by a bridgehead. Our troops crossed the Segre, attacked the town from the rear, captured it, and at the same time captured the enemy Colonel-in-Chief of the sector and his staff, as they were crossing the bridge.

This is the third time in three months that the Republican command has undertaken the difficult military task of crossing of a river which the enemy defended in depth on the other side.

Yesterday the Republicans on the Ebro front were already counter-attacking, and near Venta de Camposinos, two important heights were recaptured.

In the Levante, too, the Republican attack continues, and the troops have advanced up to the outskirts of Nules.

Nov. 11 1938.

LOST SIX PLANES IN ONE DAY

BARCELONA, Monday.

AFTER eight weeks of furious counter-attack on the Ebro front Franco's troops have only managed to win a few thousand yards of ground.

So great has been the drain on men and materials that Franco has had to fill the gaps in his divisions with companies withdrawn from other fronts and to obtain fresh supplies of artillery.

During the first eight days of this month the rebels have lost eight Fiat fighter planes, four Messerschmidts, three Savoia-Marchetti bombers and a number of other aircraft. In yesterday's battle alone they lost six planes to the Republicans' two.

UNTENABLE GROUND

Even the ground which has been won is rapidly becoming untenable owing to the concentration of Republican fire from both the unbroken flanks. More and more, in the bend of the river the position approaches stalemate.

In yesterday's battle the Republican system of fortifications that has been built since the Ebro was crossed in July, proved its worth. Using 35 tanks in a violent attack, the net result to Franco was a few yards of open ground and heavy losses of men and material.

British Battalion Trains For Bigger Job

From SAM RUSSELL

BARCELONA, Wednesday.

THE British Battalion is once more in training. Since October 25, 300 of them with comrades-in-arms from Canada, the United States and South America, have been training in a small village of Catalonia near the French frontier.

This is the last village in Spain which will see our British boys training for battle, led by their Commander Sam Wild and Commissar Bob Cooney.

The training they are undergoing is the most important in their history as a fighting unit of the Spanish People's Army.

They are training to be standard-bearers of the truth about Spain's struggle for independence, and it is only fitting that in this final training they should be led by the man who has led them so steadfastly in battle against the invading hordes.

When I visited them the other day I found the town a hive of activity. Commanders and commissars, officers and men, together with the local townspeople, are all doing their job.

Sam Wild, in command of all the troops here, is ably seconded by his adjutant, George Fletcher, by Commissar Johnny Gates, and by that staff which proved its mettle time and time again on the other side of the Ebro.

In the British Battalion itself, Johnny Power is acting commander. Bob Cooney, Bobby Walker, Alan Gilchrist and Ernie Woolley are seeing to it that the thirst for information is supplied.

IMPATIENT TO GET HOME

Everybody is looking forward to going home, and speaking to the boys, I understood the reason for this impatience. They are anxious to let the people at home know what they have learned here in Spain.

Above all is the lesson that they have learned so well on every one of Spain's battlefields—the lesson of unity.

Every day there are at least three or four lectures on the various aspects of Spain's life and organisation. Delegates leave the town daily for Barcelona and nearby villages to visit schools and children's colonies. Every minute is being utilised to the full.

Nor is the lighter side forgotten. Bobby Walker is keeping up the family tradition, arranging football matches and playing in them, too. Dances and concerts are also arranged, and the other night it was the turn of the British to entertain the Brigade, and a good job they made of it.

AUTHORS OF THE DELAY

Star turn of the evening was a skit on the visit of the League Commission to check up on the volunteers, but I am afraid the law of libel prevents me from dealing with this act in detail.

The boys are under no illusions as to who is responsible for the long waiting.

Before returning to Barcelona, Sam Wild walked with me a good way out of town. He spoke eagerly and proudly of the work that was being done, the hopes of our boys and their impatience to return to the towns and villages of Britain.

"The boys are as fit as they ever were," he said. "Although they have been demobbed from the first day of their arrival here, they demanded to continue as a military unit, under the officers who had served them at the front.

"Every morning the Battalion parades for inspection and orders for the day are read, details assigned, and the general working of the Brigade assured.

THEIR DEEDS LIVE ON

"The British Battalion is prepared to carry on the work begun here, to see to it that our 500 comrades who sleep for ever beneath Spanish soil shall serve as an example to the entire British people in the struggle against Fascism.

"I know that these boys who are going back will be worthy. It is for those at home to be worthy of their aims."

This is the message which Sam Wild gave me, and it is one which should be understood by all those who are waiting so impatiently for the arrival of the Battalion.

Commissar JOHNNY GATES, of the International Brigade, making his final speech before the Brigade left the Ebro front.

November 18 1938

MEMBERS OF THE BRITISH BATTALION OF THE INTERNATIONAL BRIGADE PHOTOGRAPHED TOGETHER BEFORE THEY LEFT THE EBRO FRONT TO PREPARE FOR HOME.

CHILDREN FIND PEACE, BUT NEED FOOD

PEPITA was a 15-year-old refugee from Bilbao, orphaned by Fascism, with only one relative in the world, her seven-year-old sister. I met them in what from its furnishings, might have been an English private school, a haven of peace and happiness.

They were typical of some 400 refugee children I met at the Herzborg Children's Colony in Barcelona.

As we arrived within the high walls surrounding the three houses comprising the colony, the older girls were sitting in the garden sewing—most of them, we learned, embroidering garments for their small sisters or knitting woolly suits for the smaller boys.

It appeared just such a peaceful scene as could only be encountered in a remote English village on a late summer afternoon.

YET all through the night and for many nights previously, Italian and German bombing planes had zoomed overhead, prevented from carrying out their deadly destructive work only by the efficiency of the Republican anti-aircraft squad.

These children had witnessed the destruction of their homes by a pitiless rain of bombs and shells; fathers, mothers, sisters, brothers, all slain before their eyes. Scenes enough to break the nerve of a strong man.

Homeless wanderers, they had migrated or had been evacuated from their homes in Bilbao, the Asturias, Madrid, Valencia, to find a refuge in Barcelona.

THE younger children about the grounds or indoors engaged in their scholastic tasks were already taking on the appearance of normal, healthy children.

They were eager to show us their toys and their drawings and to give us an exhibition of community singing and dancing. Trained as a teacher, I was amazed at the standard of their work, their complete absorption in what they were doing, especially as many of them had never received any educational training until the last few months.

Here was a high standard of easy discipline, courtesy, consideration, obvious love for the adults in charge, and happiness in communal expression—singing and dancing.

HERE in the midst of invasion was a community pursuing the arts of peace, in a way which would reflect high credit on any Western European nation isolated from war.

Yet this colony is only one and typical of a number I have visited.

In Catalonia alone, 600 children's settlements have already been established. Plans are under way for the creation of Children's Cities, in well-protected areas, which will each accommodate 1,000 children.

This province has the huge task of dealing with 200,000 child refugees from Franco - occupied territory.

AS I talked with the guardians of the children, I found myself caught up in the prevailing faith that democratic Spain will rise triumphant and build a social order by united effort which will be a model to Western democracies.

Of the 600,000 child victims of Fascism, 150,000 are definitely suffering from starvation, a further 150,000 from under-nourishment, and the remaining 300,000 from malnutrition.

These children also obviously suffer from all the illnesses attendant on such conditions—both of the body and the nervous system.

SO the former palaces of the wealthy have been dedicated to a new purpose—rest, healing and culture for the children.

To visit these colonies is to realise something of the high motives which inspire the children.

For already it is obvious that here in the midst of barbaric Fascist war the Republican Government carries out a creative work, which with peace, will mould a new generation of men and women with high ideals, and which will be an outstanding contribution to world progress.

I found that this work is the fruit of unity. The Republican Government, the trade unions, and even divisions of men at the front are determined to make this one of their joint and primary concerns.

They are assisted by a gallant body of men and women, many of them war victims, who have sunk all thoughts of self in a life dedicated to the children.

Not only are the needs of the 1,750,000 children normally living in the present Government occupied territory met, but the pressing needs of 600,000 child refugees receive strict attention.

I WOULD ask my friends in England to try and visualise the conditions in which the work goes on, with the combined forces of Franco, Hitler, and Mussolini, ranged against the Government, with food supplies for the normal use of the people held up.

Try to visualise what is means in these circumstances to attend to a vast army of terror-stricken, homeless, parentless children. Spanish people to endure great hardships in their defence of democracy and their beautiful country.

Children who have passed days and nights in bitter tears learn to smile again. The savagery of war is replaced by loving kindness. Meals are regular and as plentiful as supplies augmented by gifts from humanitarian people in other countries will allow.

THE older children find comfort in service for their younger orphaned brothers and sisters. They take advanced education courses and fit themselves to become the citizens of tomorrow.

When I express my amazement that this is going on in the midst of war my Spanish friends say, "But you must never forget that Republican Spain only took up arms in order to ensure that Spain should be reserved for the Spanish people that they might work out a full and happy life."

This article, sent by ROSE SMITH, Daily Worker special correspondent in Spain, from Barcelona, comes at a time when a big campaign for sending food to Spain has just been opened.

In a kitchen of children's restaurant N.1 in Barcelona.

November 16 1938

November 18 1935.

Remember "Potato" Jones?

From Our Own Correspondent
LIVERPOOL, Thursday.

CAPTAIN David ("Potato") Jones, first British skipper to run Franco's blockade at Bilbao, will be in command of the Mersey foodship leaving Liverpool for Spain in December.

Mr. J. L. Jones, of Stormont-road, Aigburth, Liverpool, who married, three weeks ago, the widow of his best friend, killed while fighting in Spain, will probably spend his honeymoon on the ship.

Mr. Jones was himself wounded on the Ebro Front while fighting with the International Brigade. When he returned two months ago the first person to greet him at the station was Mrs. Brown, to whom he had to break the news that her husband was dead.

Now with his wife he is helping to run the appeal, which has the support of influential Merseyside citizens. In 12 days over £1,200 has been raised, while many of the city stores have promised parcels.

CONVOY PLAN

Mr. Jones told me: "To make sure the ship will get through safely we are trying to make arrangements for a convoy."

Mrs. Jones said: "Naturally my husband's interests are mine, and if he goes I shall go with him. I am not afraid of running Franco's blockade."

Mr. Jones, who is 26 and one of the youngest members of the City Council, is a Labour representative for Croxteth ward.

November 18 1938.

Wounded in Spain —will honeymoon there

LIVERPOOL Councillor J. Lakin Jones, who was wounded fighting for the Spanish Government, dictates a letter to his bride, widow of his greatest friend, Mr George Brown, of Manchester, killed fighting in Spain. They were secretly married three weeks ago, are pictured here at work in the office of the committee organising the departure of a Merseyside food ship for Spain. It will be their honeymoon ship. They sail on December 6, and will tour war zones.

SPAIN'S PEOPLE ENDURE ON DIET OF STARVATION

AFTER five months in Spain as special correspondent of the DAILY WORKER, Peter Kerrigan is back home in Glasgow.

He still has news for the people of Britain, but it isn't news of armies and their battles. It is news that comes nearer home to the British people than that.

The Spanish Republic's most vital need is food, said Kerrigan in an interview with the DAILY WORKER.

"The standard of living of the Spanish worker has always been lower than that in Britain," he said, "but I'm not exaggerating when I say the people there are living on about a fifth of the food available to the family of a low-paid or unemployed worker in Britain."

"Since I came home," he went on, "the conviction has been forced home to me that in general there is a complete failure on the part of the people of Britain to understand what the civilian population of Republican Spain is enduring.

"You really will have to live with the people to realise their heroism fully, but perhaps I can convey an idea of what they are suffering.

"The average meal in the popular Government restaurants in Barcelona costs five and ten pesetas, according to the grade, and only workers or employees can secure a card entitling them to eat at mid-day and in the evening.

"The mid-day meal usually has two courses. The first is either lentils or garbanzos (chick peas) and the second is either meat (horse flesh or stewed "bully") or bacalao (salted dried codfish).

"A round of bread about the size of a Vienna roll is issued to each person, although sometimes this ration is halved. The beverage is water.

"At night the first course is sometimes replaced by a clear watery soup with dried bread crumbs floating in it. Otherwise the meal is the same."

RICE OCCASIONALLY

The Press from time to time will announce an issue of garbanzos or bacalao and, occasionally, rice, Kerrigan continued.

These are purchased at fixed prices in rationed quantities. Sometimes an issue of tinned or powdered milk is made to mothers whose children have been prescribed a special diet.

"Butter, milk, eggs, jam, margarine, potatoes, wine and fruit disappeared from the table months ago. Green vegetables are almost unobtainable.

"It is no wonder scurvy and skin troubles are common, especially among the women and children. It is a plain truth that unless there is a great increase in the amount of assistance forthcoming from Britain and France, thousands of Spanish children are going to die before March.

"On top of this," he said, "air raids on Barcelona have averaged five per week between August and November.

AIR RAID EFFECT

"Apart from the death and destruction they bring, consider the effect of these raids on the nerves of an undernourished people, and remember they have been intensified all over Catalonia since the ratification by Britain of the Anglo-Italian Pact.

"When faced with these facts some people have asked: 'Wouldn't it be better to end it all rather than that this suffering should continue?'

"The bestial pogrom in Fascist Germany is the answer. Franco's declaration that he has 2,000,000 names on his lists marked for punishment 'when he wins the war,' is the answer.

"The Spanish people have declared, in the words of Pasionaria: 'It is better to die on your feet than live for ever on your knees.' Their army is unvanquished; their spirit is unconquerable.

HORRIBLE WEAPON

"That is why Chamberlain is now trying to operate the horrible weapon of the blockade against them by granting belligerent rights to Franco," went on Kerrigan. "If this man and his ministers are allowed to carry through their foul deed, it will besmirch the honour of Britain for all time and it will bring disastrous consequences on our own heads.

"Two things are paramount," he concluded. "First, no belligerent rights for Franco. Next, food, by ship, by road, through credits, loans, collections—any way, but food, thousands of tons of food, to the people who are holding the front-line trenches of democracy."

November 18 1938

MINERS' GIFT OF COAL FOR SPAIN

BRITISH miners are to send 2,000 tons of coal to Spain.

The executive of the Mine-workers' Federation in London yesterday decided on this course and will charter a ship to convey the coal to Barcelona.

It was explained that 6,000 tons of flour are being dispatched from the United States and the British miners' gift of coal is to be used to bake the flour.

The executive passed a resolution expressing grave concern at the general concessions made to the Fascist Powers by the Chamberlain Government and declaring, in particular, that it regarded the proposed granting of belligerent rights to Franco as a betrayal of the democratic Government of Spain.

November 16 1938

"This executive committee requests all the peace-loving forces throughout the country," the resolution continued, "to unite in repudiating the Chamberlain policy and urges the combined Labour movement to oppose the recognition of Franco with all the forces at their disposal."

Yesterday's meeting of the executive was the last over which Mr. Joseph Jones will preside. In consequence of his appointment as a member of the Coal Commission, on which he will take up duties at the beginning of next month, he formally announced his retirement from the presidency and also his consequential resignation from the general council of the Trades Union Congress.

Mr. Will Lawther, vice-president, will act as president of the federation until the next annual conference.

Mr. Arthur Horner, a member of the executive, who is president of the South Wales Miners' Federation, was nominated to succeed Mr. Jones on the T.U.C. general council.

November 17 1938

Spanish aircraftsmen at work on an invading Italian bomber shot down by Government anti-aircraft gunners.

Students' Help For Spain

GIRL UNDERGRADUATES of Newnham and Girton, Cambridge, are trying out a novel method of collecting funds to aid destitute Spanish people. They are selling (as seen above) hot sausages and bread in the streets of Cambridge—and helped by the cold weather are doing a roaring trade.

NURSE ADDY

November 29 1938

NURSE MADGE ADDY, who returned to England with the International Brigade, provided nearly all the Spanish goods in the Spanish medical aid shop which opened in Shaftesbury-avenue, London, W., yesterday.

She brought several hundred pounds' worth of pottery for Valencia packed in fruit cases, as well as Spanish dolls.

Miss Addy, a 34-years-old masseuse who threw up her practice in Chorlton-cum-Hardy, Manchester, to go to Spain 18 months ago, told the "Daily Herald": "It took me three months to get the goods across.

"There were no packing cases or straw in Valencia, and in the end a fruit company packed them in cork for me.

She was nursing at an evacuation hospital with 800 beds between Madrid and Valencia, built by the Spanish Medical Aid Committee.

In Valencia she got a bomb splinter in her arm while looking after two wounded nurses.

"Before Christmas I hope to be back in Spain, not as a military nurse but as a civilian. I can teach the Spanish girls nursing."

ONE OF SCOTLAND'S NATIONAL HEROES

JIMMY RUTHERFORD, of Leith, would have been 21 years old today.

He was a fine boy—as fine as any Scotland has ever produced. But six months ago Franco's men took him out of prison and shot him.

Shooting Jimmy Rutherford, the Fascists not only killed one of the bravest of men, but showed once again that cold brutality which is the accompaniment of their creed. Against that deed and against the danger to the men who still remain in Franco's hands every person of decent human feelings, whatever their politics, should protest.

JAMES RUTHERFORD had himself revolted against the Fascist creed and Fascist methods. To his father before he went to fight a second time in Spain he said:—

"If all the young men had seen what I saw out there they would be doing as I am doing."

He came of fine old stock. His family had been associated for generations with the Society of Free Fishermen of Newhaven. And the Society of Free Fishermen dates back 400 years to the time when King James was building a Scottish navy and the fishermen freed themselves from feudal obligations by volunteering for service. A Rutherford is secretary of the society today.

Jimmy followed the fishing trade himself, working with David Dryburgh, the Newhaven trawlerman, who is president of the Society of Free Fishermen and Parliamentary candidate for Labour in Leith.

WHEN he was just 19 years old—November, 1936—Jimmy went to Spain to aid a cause which had always been dear to his heart.

When he was fighting at Jarama for the Spanish people and their Government, he was captured. In his pocket was a licence for machine-gun study and a special military pass. So a Fascist "court" passed sentence of death on him. Jimmy's interpreter at these proceedings could only speak some 20 words of English.

Jimmy's impending fate caused gloom to settle over the other prisoners, but it was he who helped to dissipate their depression, even while the death lorry was going to and fro with Spanish prisoners and he was expecting his own turn at any moment.

Escape came when Jimmy was at the last moment released with prisoners for exchange.

HE came back to Britain to campaign for several months in an effort to increase support for the Spanish people.

Then he returned to Spain again, knowing well what his fate might be—and indeed a comrade said to him: "If there is any danger of being captured again you had better keep a bullet for yourself."

Said Rutherford: "I'll give them the very last one I have, and that will make sure they finish me off quickly."

He did very well in Spain when he returned, going to an officers' training school and being made lieutenant. The authorities, knowing that he had been captured once, wanted him to keep away from the front line, but he persuaded them to let him go back.

IT was at the end of March that he was captured again with a number of other men in the British Battalion by a sudden advance of Fascist tanks.

Jimmy assumed the name of Small—to have given the Fascists his own name would have meant instant death. An official, formerly associated with the Spanish Embassy in London, recognised him, but was unable to recall his name—"I have seen you somewhere before," said the man.

Jimmy's fellow prisoners denied that he had given a false name, but he was interrogated by a member of the German Gestapo, accustomed to such occasions, watched closely and took notes. Then Jimmy's fingerprints were taken by the Gestapo agent and compared with previous records. His identity was established.

Jimmy's fellow prisoners saw him led away in handcuffs to be shot.

It is men like this who represent the finest traditions of Scotland. Jimmy Rutherford was as great a hero as any Scotland has produced.

He deserves to remain in Scotland's memory for ever.

Jimmy Rutherford

Was among the first men from Britain to fight for the Spanish Government.

Was captured by Franco and sentenced to death. Joked to keep his fellow-prisoners cheerful even while he expected his own death at any moment.

Was released at the last moment in an exchange of prisoners.

Returned to England to conduct a campaign of aid for Spain.

Went back to fight in Spain, knowing he would be shot if recaptured.

Was recaptured, recognised and shot.

"GAVE HIS LIFE FOR AN IDEAL"

by DAVID DRYBURGH, Labour Parliamentary candidate for Leith and President of the Society of Free Fishermen of Newhaven.

JIMMY RUTHERFORD'S many friends in Newhaven were sad when they learned of the death of one of the promising young men of the old fishing village on the Forth; but their regret is tinged with a pride that he gave his life for a great ideal.

Jimmy Rutherford was full of enthusiasm for the cause of freedom, liberty and justice. It was no sudden impulse that took Jimmy to Spain to fight on the side of democracy. It was the practical working out of his own theory of life.

Although as a lad he was cheery and full of fun, yet from his earliest youth he took a serious interest in the problems of life as he found them all about him. Even as a boy he was known among his workmates as a keen student of social and economic conditions.

He was a great favourite in Newhaven, especially in the Fish House, where he worked in my employment.

He was a very active member of the League of Youth in West Leith and was shaping to be a live member in the cause of Socialism.

Jimmy came of a real fighting stock. His forbears were seamen and fishermen. His uncle, Bob Rutherford, has been for years the secretary of the Free Fisherman's Society of Newhaven, the oldest society of its kind in Great Britain. His grandfather's working days were spent on a fishing yawl. His grandmother, with whom he lived, carried the creel in her working days along with other Newhaven fish wives, who from time immemorial have gone round helping to sell the catch for their menfolk.

We in the village who knew young Jimmy so well mourn his loss and express our deep sympathy with his father and other relatives.

November 19 1938

AN HONOURED NAME

THE story of James Rutherford is told on Page Seven of this paper. It should be told again for many, many years to come as long as men and women have tongues to tell of brave deeds well done; or ears to hear of ideals nobly defended; or spirit to admire sacrifices finely made. So long as these qualities are held in esteem, so long should Jimmy Rutherford be one of Scotland's national heroes.

Rutherford went to Spain in 1936—at the age of 19. His defence of democracy came temporarily to an end when he was captured. Sentenced to death, he kept fellow prisoners cheerful by his jokes and courage. When at the eleventh hour he was released, Rutherford came to Britain, helped for several months in the campaign for the Spanish people, and then returned, knowing that he ran a twofold risk—death in battle and death by shooting if he was again captured. He was captured; this time there was no reprieve—he died at Franco's hands in 1937.

No wonder the working-class movement is proud of men like this. There have been none braver in the whole history of man's defence of liberty. The British Battalion will soon be home now; its welcome should be the greatest London has ever known. Above all, the best way of showing admiration for Rutherford and others like him is by contributing to the National Memorial Fund of the Wounded and Dependants' Aid Committee. For that is not only a tribute, but practical aid to those who have fought.

THE BRITISH BATTALION ON THE MARCH SOMEWHERE IN SPAIN.

EVERYONE CAN FIGHT FASCISM WITH FOOD

HERE IS PRESENTED A FRONT LINE VIEW OF EVENTS IN SPAIN. REPUBLICAN SOLDIERS IN THE TRENCHES EFFECTUALLY COMBAT FASCISM AND DEFEND DEMOCRACY. IN THE REAR FASCISM — THANKS TO THE NON-INTER-vention policy of European Powers, carries the war into the lives of innocent women and children. Aerial bombardment has killed or maimed hundreds of thousands of civilians and rendered more homeless. The care of refugees are making bigger and bigger claims on the Government.

The lives of countless women, children and old people depend on the amount of help that can be received from outside during this, the third, winter of invasion. Food is a vital issue if democracy is to survive.

December 3 1938

by ROSE SMITH

TO see at first hand the events in Spain is to view two opposing forces at work in the most dramatic manner, the one using the weapons of slaughter and starvation to impose its reactionary policy, and the other, while fighting back tenaciously, concerned simultaneously with the de-velopment of the peaceful arts and higher standards of life for the common people.

Whilst the Fascists daily shower death from the skies, the united democratic forces explore new ways of bringing health and happiness.

THE problem of orphan children is met by almost superhuman efforts to establish a special children's city where the terrors of war may be shut out, and a new way of life created which will blot out memories of past experiences.

Ill-health, caused by nervous strain and continued under-feed-ing, is met by an extension of the maternity and child welfare ser-vices. New clinics and creches are coming into being in all the principal centres.

Every possible building—pal-aces, convents—is commissioned for accommodation of the refu-gees.

THE arrival of each food-ship, Red Cross ambu-lance and consignment of medi-cal supplies gives a new impetus to this constructional work.

Carefully tabulated records show that the supply of even one ration of milk per day over a period of a month brings a big advance in the health of the children.

The supply of warm clothing and footwear to clothe these under-nourished bodies, brings an immediate result in general happi-ness, comfort and health.

The arrival of packages of soap and medical supplies means that the clinics and Welfare Centres can push ahead with their task.

A proper wash as a prelude to medical treatment becomes pos-sible for the countless numbers of children covered with skin eruptions, as the result of under-feeding.

Soothing ointments, coupled with doses of cod-liver oil, assist to restore the helpless victims to normal health.

BRITAIN, amongst the children of Spain, has become known as the country where there is lots of food.

The queues outside the Spanish depots fed from various aid com-mittees in this country are a pathetic testimony to the belief of the people that there are enough supplies forthcoming to meet their needs.

One of the most touching sights is to see children turn away when the word is issued: "All supplies finished."

In Spain 300,000 children suffer from malnutrition.

Shall we allow Fascism to gain on the Spanish home front what it has been unable to achieve in the front line trenches.

Ten Point Charter for Food for Spain

(1) Grant from British Government.
(2) Co-operative Credits.
(3) Trade Union Levies.
(4) Every Co-op. Store a Food Centre for Spain.
(5) Convoy of Foods' ips.
(6) Food Parcels—Regu-lar Service.
(7) Care of Spanish Orphan Children—Patronage Groups.
(8) Youth Peace Foodship Campaign.
(9) Milk Centres.
(10) A Spanish Relief Committee in every Town.

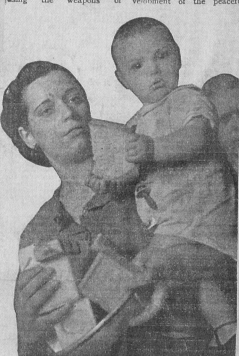

Women queue up outside a food canteen in Barce-lona. There may be a little for them—there may be nothing.

An everyday street scene in Barcelona. . . . bombed buildings, shattered homes . . . but the people of Spain stand firm.

Franco warships in line outside Catalan Bay wait for chance to capture Spanish destroyer Jose Luis Diez, crippled in battle with them when she tried to leave Gibraltar at 1 a.m. last Friday.

January 3 1939

NAVAL BATTLE OFF 'GIB'

EARLY last Friday the Spanish Government destroyer Jose Luis Diaz, which had been undergoing repairs at Gibraltar, tried to run the gauntlet of Franco warships which were waiting for her outside the harbour. After a fierce battle she was hit and driven ashore in Catalan Bay. Above, the Jose Luis Diaz aground. (Right) a roof at Catalan Bay damaged by rebel shellfire. (Left) Mr. and Mrs. Stagno and their daughter, British subjects, who were injured by a shell.

Food, Fair Play, To Restore Peace

BARCELONA, Tuesday.

"**T**HERE are two things above all that the Government of the Republic needs in order to restore peace in Spain: food and fairplay," announced the Reverend Father Michael O'Flanagan in a broadcast speech last night. "In the matter of food help is arriving, particularly from the United States, France and Britain, but the help is still inadequate."

"Above all, the people of Spain want fairplay. They need the benefits of international law, out of which they have been cheated by the hypocritical policy of non-intervention.

"I wish also to protest against the cruel injustice done to the Republican Government by the campaign of falsehood, largely carried through the agency of Catholic organisations. The Government has been called a persecutor of religion. I have seen with my own eyes the truth that the Government protects religion.

"Any fairminded person who would see and hear what I have seen and heard would long for the triumph of the Republic in Spain. With a feeling of unbounded admiration I hail Republican Spain, glorious defender of both the old and new civilisations of Europe."

January 4 1939

ITALIAN ATTACK CHECKED BY BIG LOSSES

From SAM RUSSELL
BARCELONA, Monday.

THE latest phase of the fighting on the Catalonian front provides striking evidence of the heavy losses inflicted on the enemy by the Republican resistance.

While the battle in the lower Segre Valley was continued with great ferocity, in the upper Segre enemy activity was reduced to shelling and exchange of fire. Neither in the sectors of Balaguer nor of Tremp did the enemy make the slightest attempt to advance.

Further south a very slight advance was registered which only extends the line reached previously at Pobla de Granadella and Bisbal de Falset by some 2½ miles south of the hamlet of Cabaces.

The latest news speaks of enemy attack in the direction of Borjas Blancas.

After ten days of fighting and using all the materials and troops at their disposal, including troops which it had been intended to hold in reserve until the third week of the offensive, the enemy can only show an advance of little more than a third of the distance to Igualada. This territory is strewn with the bodies of their killed and wounded.

FASCIST DIVISIONS WITHDRAWN

The position at the moment is that of the 21 or 22 enemy divisions concentrated here, at least 17 have already been employed in the attack. The famous First Navarrese Division has lost from 30 to 40 per cent. of its effectives, and what is more important, almost all its officers.

The Littorio Division has had to be withdrawn temporarily from the line because of heavy casualties. In the air, the Republican aviation has more than held its own against the hundreds of German and Italian planes that continuously bomb the lines and

villages of the rearguard.

Since the opening of the offensive, 26 enemy planes have been brought down, including a flight of three Dornier planes not used before in Spain.

In their first flight over the Republican lines the three of them were brought down by the same anti-aircraft battery that was awarded the medal of valour for its work during the Ebro battle.

The greatest defeat, however, which has been inflicted on the invading forces has been the immobilisation of the Italian mobilised columns and tanks with which it had been intended to smash right through the Republican lines.

This plan has failed miserably. The anti-tank units in every company and battalion has shown that the Italian tanks are very vulnerable, and the Italian tankists more so.

At the front and in the rearguard, however, preparations are being made for more difficult days ahead. Although there is confidence, there is no false optimism. The enemy is not beaten yet, and further efforts will be needed before the back of the Italian offensive is finally and completely broken.

REBEL PLAN DAYS BEHIND

BY OUR OWN CORRESPONDENT
BARCELONA, Monday.

FRANCO'S latest offensive on the Catalonia front, now in its 12th day, is falling far behind the time-table drawn up beforehand by the rebel general staff.

Information in Government hands shows that the attackers planned to take Borjas Blancas, south-east of Lerida, in two days, and Igualada, on the Lerida-Barcelona highway and 64 miles from the start of the offensive, in three days.

Actually the rebels were still pouring troops towards Borjas Blancas to-day, while the farthest point they have advanced, Bisbal de Falset, is only 21 miles from their starting point.

Too Costly

A Government military observer who returned from the war front to-day told me:—

"The rebel offensive cannot last for more than a further few days; it is costing too much.

"After eleven days of appalling expenditure of men and material, their total advance at the greatest point is less than two miles daily. Franco must break the Loyalist ranks in the next few days or face ignominious failure.

"Four or five days will exhaust the force of his offensive and leave the Spanish Government in a position to counter-attack."

Fine Morale

That the offensive is still making headway is frankly admitted here. But it is emphasised that there is unbroken morale and discipline and organisation among the loyal troops against unprecedented artillery and aviation attacks.

On the other hand, Franco's crack Littoria division has been withdrawn for reorganisation after heavy losses.

To-day intensive rebel attacks were loosed towards Borjas Blancas, centre point of the present fighting zone in the Segre River valley.

Three fresh divisions were thrown into the lines by Franco.

January 3 1939.

A PLEDGE ON A HILLSIDE

By CHARLOTTE HALDANE

WE were on a bare hillside — the rock pounded into powder by Fascist bombardment — a little above the trenches outside Teruel. Bill Rust was there, and Sam Wild; George Fletcher; Bill Alexander and Walter Tapsell. There was no light but starlight and the occasional glimmer of the headlights of a Fascist truck passing along the road the other side of the valley.

Tappy told us all to squat down on the ground; no need to offer the Fascists a free target. We all squatted. The boys came up from the trench in small groups and squatted with us, until we were all there. Then a comrade brought along a wooden board, on which were inscribed the names of the members of the Major Attlee Company who had given their lives in repelling the Fascist counter-attack a few days previously.

When Tappy started to speak there was absolute silence. He told of the action; of those who were no longer with us. The wooden board was set up on that bare hillside under the stars.

Singing was, of course, prohibited; Tappy said he would recite the first verse of the International instead. But emotion overcame him; he could not go on.

PLEDGE TO BATTALION

I pledged ourselves once more to the Battalion. I told them:—"As long as you on, we go on." Tappy has gone on a long way ahead since then.

Do we, British democrats, for whom he gave his life, keep that pledge, The pledge to our truly glorious dead: Wally Tapsell, Wilf Jobling, Harry Dobson, workers and fighters? To Ralph Fox, John Cornford, Christopher St. John Sprigg, Lewis Clive, the flower of England's intellectual youth; to the five hundred irreplaceable men who have left us a sacred trust?

They go on forever; their memory can never die in the hearts and minds of British workers. We go on, until we have accomplished our task of raising £50,000. That is the sum we need to keep our promise to the dead. The promise to care for the widows and the orphans. The promise to keep a roof over their heads and food in the kiddies' tummies, and shoes on their feet.

All the time the airplane was bringing me back to London from a visit I later made to China—at the rate of 2,500 miles a day—I wondered: "Shall I be there in time to meet the Battalion?" And I was thinking of the great memorial meeting to our dead at the Empress Stadium on Sunday. I felt I must keep a promise to five hundred dead comrades; take the opportunity once again to reaffirm that promise.

At Victoria, when the Battalion came back, a distracted mother came up to me and grabbed my arm.

"Where's my boy?" she demanded. "He should have been here with the others." Her boy, badly wounded, had had to take the journey in easy stages; I hope he is back by now. But, having had my boy in Spain for ten months, I knew what she was feeling. And not a mother among us whose boy is now back does not count herself lucky. We know the anguish of those mothers whose boys will never come back. It might have happened to any of us.

MESSAGE TO CHAMBERLAIN

We who have worked in the office of the Denpendants' Aid Committee have sometimes had a terrible time. Some weeks we thought we could not meet our obligations.

And it wasn't "they" we thought about; it was Mrs. Dobson's rent or Mrs. Gibbons's baby's woollies we thought about.

We wished all you thousands of other democrats could have been with us for a day now and then. The money would soon have come rolling in then.

Because of our dead, because of our living, because of ourselves, we have got to send a very definite message to Neville Chamberlain from the meeting on January 8, to take to his friend, Mussolini. That message is: "Hands off Spain! No belligerent rights for Franco!" The Battalion will send it. But the Battalion is the vanguard of British democracy, and a vanguard without a solid backing is, unfortunately, not enough. You and I have got to send this message with the Battalion.

I was asked to write about the attractions of the meeting. Here they are:—

(1) A supreme opportunity to honour our dead.

(2) An opportunity to fulfil our pledge to them; to start that £50,000 fund with a swing; to put their wives, mothers and children in the way of security.

(3) An opportunity to honour these women, whose heroism, though less spectacular than that of their men, has been every bit as great.

(4) An opportunity to send a message to Chamberlain that will resound through Britain and throughout Europe.

Of course it will be a magnificent ceremony. Such an occasion demands fitting celebration. The Battalion will be there with bands and banners. Paul Robeson will sing. Leaders in all political parties, in science, art, drama, in all spheres of cultural activity will be there.

But unless you are there, brother, friend and fellow-worker—then when, on that starlit hillside at Teruel I pledged British democracy to Walter Tapsell, Political Commissar, and those other four hundred and ninety-nine who gave their lives for us, I shall have taken your name in vain. Somehow I don't think I did!

January 6 1939

Students Speak On Spain

THE delegation of British students which arrived home on December 30 after spending eight days in Barcelona, gave a Press reception yesterday.

The object of the delegation has been to investigate the food situation, and discuss with Spanish students how best the British colleges could help Spain, both with regard to food and educational needs.

Questioned as to the value of the world solidarity effort on behalf of Republican Spain they vigorously attested to the value of this work. There had recently been a sensible increase in the rations of refugees. The Government relies to a great extent on the foodships to supply milk to children in the big centres.

CHILDREN'S COLONY

Generally the delegation was greatly impressed with the constructive efforts which the Government is making to cope with problems. At the same time they clearly saw the need for greatly increasing all forms of aid.

Last term colleges collected over £2,500 for Spain. It is planned to greatly increase this sum in succeeding terms by an adoption scheme.

A children's colony of 500 was visited which was under the patronage of a British group. Boots, shoes, clothes, chocolate, milk, all came from England and was tremendously helpful in keeping the children healthy and happy.

January 3 1939

Returned members of the British Battalion of the International Brigade meet to finalise plans for a tour through Britain to secure support for the Spanish people.

January 9 1939

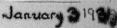

SPAIN: *Insurgents Raise Nuisance Value in Twelve Days' Push; Republican Destroyer, Ejected from Gibraltar, Registers Naval Epic, Is Interned by British Admiralty*

PREDICTING "victory before the end of 1939," Insurgent General Francisco Franco serenaded Madrid on New Year's Eve with a salvo of shells, poured in a dozen in place of the traditional grapes passed among friends as the clock struck twelve.

Similar gifts greeted midnight at Valencia, but at Barcelona Christian courtesy extended to a dozen bombers, which, approaching under cover of cloud, swiftly spread disaster among the celebrating New Year crowds.

Raids were by way of punctuating eight days' battle on the three fronts, and notifying Il Duce that though some small advance had been achieved at enormous cost, it was perhaps sufficient to enhance nuisance value when Premier Chamberlain shows up in Rome.

Sunday morning Insurgent batteries resumed operations on the Lower Segre sector, where by Monday the two leading Italian Divisions, among them the Littorio, supposed to have been withdrawn under the Anglo-Italian Agreement, got into difficulties between Alfes and Aspe owing to a surprise Republican counter-attack.

Italian Regulars

Tuesday they were on the run, Republicans recovering positions lost under a blizzard of Insurgent shells in preceding days.

Sum of twelve days' battle on a 100-mile front showed an Insurgent gain of some 300 square miles by Wednesday morning, most of it unimportant territory, as in the Tremp mountains, and rendering communications liable to assault.

Assessing their losses as the conflict waned, Republican Headquarters also assessed the value of Il Duce's promise to withdraw 10,000 "volunteers." Prisoners taken on the east front, glad to be out of the fray, confessed that they were Italian regulars, part of 10,000—in batches of 150 from various regiments—sent in at the

"Cavalcade"
January 7 1939

very time the others were being taken out.

Sergeant Pascualo Estoni, corroborated by others, declared they were selected for service in Abyssinia, only discovered their real destination when they arrived in Cadiz.

Leonatino Camino and his compatriots admitted they had volunteered from their regiments under subtle pressure, gave as personal reason the belief, significantly enough, that "France and Britain are the great enemies of Italy."

Formerly, said another, Corporal Allesandro Cassiano, Italians had been enlisted to fight "Bolshevism," but when he was sent in September the emphasis was on "the British imperialists," against whom a footing had to be created on the Spanish Peninsula, ultimately "to smash both British and French."

Whitehall Aware

British Consuls in Republican Spain are fully aware of these assertions, and it is unlikely they have failed to inform Whitehall. In this latest—the eighth—Insurgent offensive, six Italian divisions—72,000 men—have taken part.*

Contributing a naval exploit reminiscent of days before Prime Ministers scurried by aeroplane, umbrella and all, to lick the pants of dictators, Republican destroyer Jose Luis Diez early Friday morning slipped out of Gibraltar harbour, leaped epically into the newslight.

Insurgent eyes had watched her since she limped into port with thirty dead last August after an encounter with vastly superior forces in the Straits. Prior to that she had fought the whole Insurgent navy off the Basque coast and, disabled, put into Havre for repairs.

All day Friday her commander, Juan Antonio Castro, had requested permission to remain in Gibraltar for further adjustment of machinery and check of repairs; but he was ordered to leave that night under penalty of internment—by the non-intervening British Admiralty.

"Rock" Signals

So Commander Castro, seasoned, coatless on the bridge, knowing the enemy watched, promptly at the 1 a.m. time limit gave orders to cast off, swore as one of his men splashed overboard, waited until he was hauled aboard, then under a half moon crept round the sea wall, swung sharply to port and raced for the Mediterranean.

As the destroyer, lights extinguished, pulled away, from a window high on the Rock signals flashed. Then a rocket soared into the sky.

*Six Italian Divisions are: Littorio, whose commander arrived in Spain early December; Black Arrow, commanded by General Pichone; Green Arrow, under General Batiste; Blue Arrow; Black Flame; March 23rd Division. All are under High Command of General Cambara, who recently replaced General Berti.

Patrolling Insurgents switched on their searchlights. They were all around—nearest the sloop Saturno, against which the Jose Luis Diez launched a pair of torpedoes and raced on.

She dodged Insurgent destroyer Calvo Sotelo, and a half-dozen armed trawlers, out-distanced the cruiser Canarias round the bend, fired another brace of torpedoes at the approaching sloop Vulcano, scattered a dozen lightly armed motor-vessels with her 4.7-in. guns.

At that stage a Tennyson might have hailed her escape, but, like his Revenge, she ran straight into the heart of the foe. Rounding Europa Point, funnels aglow under forced draught, she met the 2,000-ton Jupiter emerging from the shelter of British waters, trying to head her off into Canarias' gun range.

Unhesitating, Commander Castro signalled the engine-room her full 36 knots, steered her 1,800 tons directly at the Jupiter, rammed her, forced her aground.

Losing speed in the impact, the Jose Luis Diez then caught a salvo from the Vulcano, fractured a boiler, dropped to eight knots, and grounded in Catalan Bay to avoid capture.

Refloated, Held

There she again fell into the hands of the "neutral" British Admiralty, which put aboard Gibraltar Governor-General Sir Edmund Ironside, followed later by Assistant Adjutant Currey, and a military escort.

Refloated in the afternoon by Admiralty tugs Rambler and Rollicker, she was taken back to Gibraltar for internment, escorted by H.M.S. Vanoc.

While General Francisco Franco next day decorated Vulcano Commander Don Fernando Abarzura with the Military Medal, Commander Castro buried five of his men at sea from the British warship Glowworm. Eleven others were in Gibraltar Hospital.

Remainder of his 150 crew had been taken to the Military Detention Barracks. "We do not know why we are interned," said Commander Castro. "We only defended ourselves against superior forces—and in British waters."

"Non-Intervention"

Enjoined to silence by the Spanish Government, he gave no account of the battle, but an official statement from Barcelona confirmed its cause.

"British authorities refused to extend the period allowed for repairs, and the Jose Luis Diez was obliged to put to sea under penalty of internment, and thus run the gauntlet of Insurgent blockade."

In connection with this cynical episode of non-intervention, the statement might have added that of all the Insurgent warships engaged only the Canarias was Spanish when the war broke out in July, 1936.

Catholic Priest Hits At Mussolini

FATHER MICHAEL O'FLANAGAN, famous Irish Roman Catholic priest who was once Advent preacher in Rome, hit out against Mussolini's intervention in Spain, when he spoke to members of the International Peace Campaign deputation which went to Downing Street on Saturday to express the view of the British people on the Prime Minister's visit to Rome.

He had just returned from a visit to Barcelona.

He said:—

"I saw a country in a profound state of internal peace, and ruled according to the highest ideals of Christian democracy. My own church is in a healthier condition than I have ever seen it in any other part of the world.

"It is not enough to tell Mussolini and Hitler that they will not have our friendship while they continue to help Franco. You will have to send a sufficient amount of help to the Republic, and to send it soon."

DEPUTATION

Members of the deputation represented over 300 constituencies throughout the country, 367 trade union branches, 52 trade councils, 83 co-operative organisations and many other democratic bodies.

Thirty-nine Churchmen were present.

They adopted unanimously a resolution which

opposed the granting of belligerent rights in any circumstances;

demanded the recognition of the legal rights of the Spanish Government; and

demanded protection for all British ships and British sailors inside and outside territorial waters while conducting lawful business with Spain.

An amendment that Chamberlain should call off his visit altogether which had the support of the majority of the deputation was, however, not adopted, following an angry intervention by the Chairman, Lord Cecil, who said that it was outside the scope of the meeting.

TO DOWNING STREET

The resolution was then handed in at 10, Downing Street, by Lord Cecil, supported by the entire deputation, which marched from the meeting place.

The same afternoon 270 delegates met in Bridgwater for a "Food For Spain" Conference. This was followed by a meeting in the Blake Hall, addressed by Vernon Bartlett, M.P., Sir Stafford Cripps, Victor Gollancz, Valentine Ackland and Alderman Hennessey.

TO VISIT SPAIN

Meantime it is announced that Mr. Alfred Barnes, M.P., and the Rev. George Woods, M.P. (chairman and director respectively of the Co-operative Press), are to visit Spain. They will discuss with the Spanish Government authorities questions involved in raising in Britain a credit loan for Spain.

January 9 1939

Brigade Widows At The Cenotaph

THERE was a deeply moving scene at the Cenotaph in Whitehall yesterday, when widows, mothers and relatives of fallen members of the International Brigade went there to lay two wreaths at its foot.

Among them, too, were comrades of the fallen men, and women whose husbands and sons are still prisoners in Franco's jails.

At this spot, the goal of so many noble and tragic pilgrimages and tributes, there are already many wreaths in memory of hundreds of thousands of "unknown soldiers" who died in the hope of securing a free and happy England.

Fresh tributes came yesterday from the relatives of men who died in the certainty that their sacrifice was in the cause of British freedom and security, and the freedom and peace of the world.

PROTEST TO FOREIGN OFFICE

Among those present were Mrs. Carmel Haden Guest, Mrs. Leppard, Mrs. Ivor Hickman, and Mrs. Kath Gibbons, whose husband is a prisoner.

After laying the wreaths, four women went on to the Foreign Office to protest against the continued imprisonment by Franco of their relatives, and against the failure of the British Government to take action to secure their immediate release.

January 10 1939

Counting the collection at the Empress Hall Stadium.

General view of the platform when the "Internationale" was being sung.

As the trumpet call dies the men of the British Battalion march into the arena headed by their banners and carrying flags of the world. They were met by deafening cheers. With them (below) are some of the courageous nurses who tended them.

IMAGINE 9,000 people sitting tense and expectant in a huge hall, their eyes fixed on the entrance to the arena in front of them.

They are restless, though a band is playing steadily and receiving their applause after each number.

Suddenly there is a trumpet call. And then dead silence. People stare fixedly at the entrance. The trumpets sound again.

Then you see the head of a column of men, with flags. The men begin to march. They come out, the first of them, into the arena's blaze of light.

This is the moment you had been waiting for. This is what everybody is cheering so wildly about. This is what you came to see.

Minutes later you find you have been standing and cheering with the rest. The whole vast crowd is on its feet. The arena is filled with ranks of men and masses of flags and banners.

The men are the two British Battalions of the International Brigade —what is left of the Battalions after two years of war in Spain. The flags are those of all peoples—and the banners of the Battalions.

The Empress Hall at Earl's Court, London, is packed for this meeting of memorial to the comrades of these remnants of two Battalions. Nine thousand people come to honour Britons who died in Spain.

Eyes are glistening as people sit down again. Tenseness is gone: things are happening now.

In the arena ranks of men with flags are still standing to attention.

Thrills And Highlights

Here was the setting for one of the most impressive ceremonies ever carried out by the democratic movement in Britain.

From this moment until the end of the evening, thrills and emotional highlights followed fast upon each other.

The commentator's voice came through the amplifiers, explaining that the Company Commanders were taking the roll of their men.

"Now the Company Commanders are reporting to the Battalion Commanders," the voice went on, "and now they in turn are reporting to the Brigade Command."

Then Fred Copeman, former Commander of the Battalion and chairman of the meeting, announces:—

"From Britain went 2,762 men," he said. "Of these, 1,747 were wounded, some of them several times. Five hundred and forty-three gave their lives in battle; and here tonight are 412 men."

Nearly one-fifth of the men who went to Spain lie dead there. These parading survivors, many as they were, were outnumbered by over a hundred by their dead comrades.

The ceremony moved on swiftly. People stood again as the band played Republican Spain's anthem. The Brigade Staff stood at the salute.

Tribute To The Dead

Then the band switched to the Funeral March, and flags were lowered as the deeply significant moment of the ceremony arrived. Representatives of Britain's pro-gressive movement were paying their tribute to the dead.

There followed the sounding of the Last Post, a silence, and the reciting of a poem.

In the trenches near Jarama, scene of the British Battalions' bitterest fighting, Alec McDade, of Glasgow, wrote the words of a song.

Members of the Battalions took it as their own, and they sang it now, accompanied by Clapham Accordion Band.

As the notes of the Reveille died away the voice came from the amplifiers again.

"At the call of freedom these men will march again," it said.

The men were still standing in their ranks, serious, and a little abashed by the weight of the acclamation they had received.

To Action In The Country

They went from the arena to an honoured place near the platform, and later from the hall to posts of action all over the country, there to lead in the struggle for a better country and a better world. With them marched in well-known costume nurses of the Medical Aid Committee, who got a special cheer to themselves for their magnificent work.

On the platform were representatives of every section of the Labour, trade union and progressive movements.

Father O'Flanagan, the first speaker, roused the meeting's applause by a vigorous speech exposing the falsity of the attacks made on him by Catholic newspapers, and declaring that Republican Spain—from which he had just returned—was completely free for all forms of religion.

Harry Pollitt Speaks

Harry Pollitt, greeted by prolonged cheering, said the Communist Party Congress had in September given the pledge that:—

"We shall not cease to fight for the principle for which these men have laid down their lives. We shall stand by the struggle of the Spanish people until their victory is won and until the cause of peace and democracy has triumphed."

"If reality is to be given to that pledge, if we are to prove worthy of all that the Battalion has done, we must make this demonstration a starting point for a new nation-wide effort on behalf of the Spanish Republic."

MEN WHOM ILL NEVER FORGET

Chairman of the Empress Hall meeting was Fred Copeman, former commander of the British Battalion of the International Brigade.

"BROTHERS of the International Brigade, come back. Spain will ever be your home."

This was Spain's farewell to the men who for two years had fought with her people against invaders. It was a farewell tinged with sadness at the parting with brave men Spaniards had grown to love.

And Britain's welcome home to these same men?

Pictures here show you something of the magnificent spectacle staged at Earl's Court, London, on Sunday. It was a welcome to the survivors of the Battalions —and a memorial to the men who died.

Sadness in the farewell from Spain and sadness in the welcome to their own country; for 543 of the men who went from Britain made their farewell in battle.

THE ROLL CALL.—Fred Copeman, the chairman, announced the roll call figures. " From Britain went 2,762 men. Of these 1,747 were wounded. Five hundred and forty-three died, and here tonight are 412 men."

The giant memorial banner (shown below) which hung in the Empress Hall bore the inscription:—

" Man's dearest possession is life. And since it is granted to him to live but once, he must so live as to feel no torturing regrets for years without purpose; so live as not to be seared by the shame of a cowardly and trivial past; so live that, dying, he can say : ' All my life and all my strength were given to the finest cause in the world —the fight for the liberation of mankind.' "

LAST ROLL CALL

With heads high, flying banners picked out by brilliant arc-lights, survivors of the British battalions of the International Brigade marched into the darkened arena at Earl's Court to a bombardment of cheering for the last Roll Call.

Over 2,000 men left England to fight for the Spanish Government, 543 now lie for ever in Spanish soil.

Packing the mighty Empress Stadium, 8,000 people shared the grief and pride of the 412 war-weary fighters, stood in silence when flags dipped in salute to Spain, while bugles sounded the Last Post.

MARCHING SONG

Marching song, "Jarama Valley," composed by a British soldier (now dead), named after an action in which 294 Britons lost their lives, stirred the crowd deeply.

From a raised dais spot-lit, silver-haired Father O'Flannagan warned Catholics of Britain not to take their politics from the Church, saying that the Pope is now in the power of Benito Mussolini.

ADDED EMOTION

Messages from the Duchess of Atholl, Labour's Attlee, speeches from Liberal M.P. Wilfrid Roberts, Communist Harry Pollitt, songs from giant, dark-skinned Paul Robeson added emotion to the meeting.

Swayed by the eloquence of veteran appeal-maker Isabel Brown, the crowd dug into their pockets, raised £3,000 towards £50,000 to aid International Brigade's wounded and dependants.

FRED COPEMAN (Formerly Commander of the British Battalion of the International Brigade)

REVIEWS →

IN the beginning of the 19th century, the history books tell us, the British army under the Duke of Wellington fought the long and bitter campaign of the Peninsular War on behalf of the Spanish people against the invading armies of Napoleon.

The victories they won, Badajos, Salamanca and the rest, are famous in history, but they were fought by unwilling men for a cause they did not understand.

From 1936 to September, 1938, British men were again fighting for the Spanish people, against other invading armies, the legionaries of Mussolini and Hitler's airmen and gunners. And again they won victories—Jarama, Brunete, the Ebro—which are already famous in the history of democracy. But there the likeness ends.

THE men of the British Battalion of the XV International Brigade were not led by famous generals; and the British Government, far from supporting them, did everything in its power to hinder them by the cowardly tactics of "non-intervention."

But the greatest difference between Wellington's troops and the men of the Battalion is this: that the latter were in the fullest sense of the word volunteers—free men, freely giving up the safety of home and the security of jobs in defence of a great cause, which they realised to be their own and that of all civilized humanity.

This was the spirit that enabled the Brigade to play its historic part in the struggle against Fascism, and it is of the first importance that the real nature of that achievement should be fully understood by all progressive people, particularly by the working-class movement.

RUST'S book* is a first-class beginning towards that understanding, for, though it deals mainly with the British Battalion, their experiences are typical of those of the Brigade as a whole.

Rust has excellent qualifications for writing this history. For eight months he shared the life of the Battalion as special correspondent for the DAILY WORKER; he has had full access to the official documents of the Brigade and, what is most important, he has been able to quote freely from the accounts of the volunteers themselves contained in hundreds of letters home.

The result is a real contribution to history, an honest, straightforward account, and, just because it is a first-hand description of unity in action, the book can be a powerful instrument for welding together all the forces of progress for the urgent struggle that confronts them.

DON'T let it be imagined, however, that for this reason "Britons in Spain" is simply a political tract. On the contrary, its political value lies precisely in the fact that it is a lively narrative of things being done, of men getting on with the job, under conditions of great danger and difficulty.

January 9 1938.

The book begins with an account of the formation of the Brigade, and no one can read of the tremendous obstacles overcome —the babel of languages, the acute shortage of arms and clothing, the opposition of bourgeois Governments—without a thrill of pride in the grit and ingenuity and drive of workers when there is a job to be done.

As the veteran revolutionary, Andre Marty, who himself played a big part in the organisation of the Brigade, wrote at the time: "What the bourgeoisie called a miracle actually happened." And miracles of the same kind were to go on happening for the next two years; miracles of inventiveness, of adaptability and, above all, of sheer endurance and courage.

ANYONE who has actually taken part in modern warfare knows it is extremely difficult to describe; and here, in my opinion, Rust has been particularly successful.

In the descriptions of the various actions, helped by a number of useful maps, he has managed to combine a clear explanation of the military objectives with a real feeling of the horror and savagery of modern war; he has succeeded in conveying not only the main movement of particular battles, but also the experiences of individual men and units.

If I have any criticism to make it is that he tends to overstress the part played by those of us who were in positions of leadership.

For the outstanding thing about the Battalion, what made it the tremendous fighting force it became and earned for it the proud title of "the shock battalion of the Brigade," was the morale of the rank-and-file, the true comradeship that bound together these men from many trades and occupations, from different social classes and different political parties, in a voluntary discipline far more effective than the wooden obedience of the Fascist regulars.

BUT it is impossible here to give a full account of the book. All I would say is that, to anyone who wants to understand something of what the Battalion experienced and what they achieved, and of the spirit that kept them going, I heartily recommend it.

It is a book that no one can read without seriously taking stock of the part they themselves are playing in the mighty struggle for civilisation. More than this, it is a solid memorial to the five hundred gallant comrades whose bodies lie buried in Spanish earth.

Not only will its sale materially benefit the Fund for the Dependants and Wounded, but it will be a constant reminder of our tremendous debt to those who, having lost their dear ones, can still write like Wally Tapsell's parents:—

"We deeply sympathise with all those other mothers and fathers, wives and children and sweethearts, who have had to make the great sacrifice, and hope that comfort will come to them when the war is over and the Spanish Government reigns supreme."

In this book will be found expressions from various men and women who gave all that human beings can; it expresses the soul of a great people in the midst of a bitter struggle for all that is life to them.

* BRITONS IN SPAIN. A history of the British Battalion of the XV International Brigade. By William Rust. (Lawrence and Wishart, Ltd. 2s.).

Miners' Six Months In Franco Lines

HAVING performed the astonishing feat of living hidden for nearly six months just behind the enemy's main lines in Southern Spain, hundreds of miners dramatically appeared from their hiding places yesterday to greet and join the advancing Republican Army.

The story of the "lost battalion" of the miners as told by them yesterday is one of the most dramatic episodes of the war.

Many of them are men who at the very beginning of the war escaped from the mines of Rio Tinto, where Fascists were rounding up and killing those they caught.

CUT OFF IN HILLS

The escaped miners reached the Republican lines, fought on the Madrid front at Navalcarnero, later returned to the southern front.

When the Italians last summer made their big drive for the mercury mines at Almaden, these men were cut off.

They took to the hills. By day they lived hidden in peasant huts. By night they crept out to raid food supplies, ambush isolated enemy patrols, obtain munitions.

RESCUED AFTER SIX MONTHS

For nearly six months they endured this perilous and arduous existence. Two days ago they heard the noise of battle coming nearer, knew the Republican Army was on the move.

They saw the fleeing remnants of the enemy passing along the roads westward. Yesterday their scouts told them "our people are here." Now they have reformed their battalion and joined the advance.

January 11 1938.

Sam Wild, Commander of the British Battalion of the International Brigade—supported by a large contingent of Welsh volunteers—lays a wreath on the Welsh National War Memorial, Cardiff, in memory of Welshmen who died fighting for democracy in Spain. The International Brigade convoy, of which he is a member, has just concluded a successful stay in South Wales.

January 16 1939

ANGELA GUEST
Home From Spain

CHRISTMAS EVE, 1937. Harry Pollitt and I arrived at the Benicasim Hospital of the International Brigade after a tiring ride from Madrid. We were both cold and hungry.

"You must see Angel," said the head doctor, meaning Angela Guest. And a real angel she turned out to be. We were soon warm and well fed.

Now, after two years in Spain, Angela is back again in England to give a laughing denial to the story that she had been killed in a Barcelona air raid.

Her extraordinary life during these two years would make many a suburban Miss sit up and shudder. Death has been near all the time since she started to work with the artillery in September, 1936, in the Aragon up till she left a hospital in Catalonia a short time ago.

WHEN Angela took her degree of Bachelor of Science in Economics and Sociology at the London University, she little thought tha' its first practical application would be as a first-aid worker with an artillery unit on a battle front. She stayed with the gunners for months before leaving for a front-line hospital in Cordoba in the South.

Then came the big Government offensive at Brunete, where she was the only girl in the front line. The Czechish and Austrian doctors needed an interpreter for their orders to the English ambulance drivers and so Angela, who speaks German, Spanish and French, was roped in. She also did first-aid work in odd moments. But what odd moments!

"WE were bombed and shelled the whole time," Angela told me, " and one day a shell dropped within five yards of us, but fortunately being a dud it only ploughed up the earth and smothered us in dirt. I was bombed out of one village and then bombed again in the fields."

"You were afraid then," I challenged. Her blue eyes flashed. "Of course I was. Wasn't everybody?" she retorted.

After Brunete Angela went to Benicasim as the secretary to the hospital. It was a lovely spot. A long row of detached villas on the Mediterranean coast with a high range of hills behind. She did all kinds of jobs. And riding up and down the front perched on a bicycle and wearing her overalls she was a familiar figure to all the Brigaders.

THE Fascists have got Benicasim now. The hospital was evacuated by the Republicans, but Angela did not know she was leaving. She was in a high fever at the time and only regained consciousness in Barcelona. But soon she was busy again doing those hundred and one jobs that fall to the lot of a hospital secretary in Spain.

"How did you feel about leaving?" I asked. Angela hesitated for a moment and her face dropped. "I was very sad and did not want to go," she replied. I know that she was also thinking about her brother David, that brilliant young intellectual, who died when the Ebro was crossed last July.

What will Angela do now she is back? She should continue her studies and take her Ph.D., but I would not be surprised if she were to attempt something much more thrilling. She is one of the virile spirits of the new generation who are fighting for the brave new world.

—WILLIAM RUST.

Jan. 1938

ANGELA GUEST takes a meal somewhere in Spain.

SPAIN'S MAIN BATTLE IS IN CATALONIA
—Says The General Staff

By Our Diplomatic Correspondent

AN estimation of the present military position in Spain has just been made by the Republican General Staff. Of considerable interest and importance, it insists that

the main battle is being and must continue to be waged in Catalonia; and that

the Estremadura offensive of the Republican army of the Centre must be seen as part of Spain's defence against the Italo-German invasion.

Franco has concentrated 300,000 troops, including over 100,000 Italians, Germans and Portuguese, against the Catalan defences.

For 19 days he has used, without respite, all his available Italian and German artillery, aviation and tanks, hoping to secure that success which will enable Chamberlain to prepare in Rome that second Munich at the expense of the Republic.

As yet he has withdrawn no troops from this front to reinforce his hard pressed Estremadura divisions and the battle in Catalonia continues with the greatest violence.

It is pointed out that—

it will be only with the greatest reluctance that Franco and his masters will abandon their aims in Catalonia.

To do so would mean a material and political defeat, the consequence of which would be even more serious than the present enormous sacrifice of men and materials.

IN THE LAST RESORT

Franco will persist on this front and it will only be in the last desperate resort that he will withdraw any troops.

For this reason the Spanish Government and the Republican Higher Command have decided on a policy of resistance in the East and "offensive by some of the armies of the Western zone."

After stressing the necessity of increasing the reserves, speeding up the work of fortification and intensifying propaganda in the enemy's ranks, the General Staff concludes:—

"We are absolutely confident that in the vigorous and decisive application of these measures, we shall check the enemy offensive and this will be the prelude to our certain triumph."

SPAIN MOBILISES SEVEN NEW CLASSES

In addition
all men up to the age of 50 have been mobilised for work on fortifications; and
all industries connected with the production of war materials and of food have been militarised.

WITH HER TROOPS CONTINUING THEIR RESISTANCE TO THE ITALIAN-LED OFFENSIVE ON THE CATALAN FRONT AND REGISTERING FURTHER ADVANCES IN ESTREMADURA, THE SPANISH REPUBLIC YESTERDAY MOBILISED SEVEN NEW CLASSES OF HER MANHOOD.

This decision was taken at an important Cabinet meeting held in Barcelona yesterday morning, after Prime Minister Negrin, who is also Defence Minister, had reported on the military position.

Under this decree

(1) the seven classes, those from 1921 to 1915, i.e., all males up to 45 years of age, are mobilised and will be called to the Colours when necessary;

(2) the three classes, 1921, 1920 and 1919—persons of 38, 39 and 40 years—are called up immediately.

Fascists Fled In Disorder

MADRID, Thursday.

THE Republican troops made further advances in all sectors of the Estremadura front today, particularly in the Monterrubio zone, where the enemy troops, disheartened by the previous night's bitter fighting, fled in disorder. They abandoned much war material.

Icy rain is falling incessantly and this, together with the rocky ground, has made progress somewhat difficult.

VIOLENT FIGHTING

Last night the enemy launched attack after attack on the positions they lost yesterday. Violent fighting, preceded by intense artillery preparation, took place in the Penarroya zone.

The battle raged from midnight until the early hours of this morning, when the enemy were beaten back and retreated, abandoning large quantities of war material.

PENARROYA RINGED

Many soldiers in the Franco army, largely newly conscripted, took advantage of the disorder to make their way over to the Republican lines.

The Republicans now occupy the whole of the Santos heights and thus practically surround Penarroya village.

CRADLE OF THE

By AGNES SMEDLEY—

[Section of map from "An Atlas of Far Eastern Politics" (Faber and Faber).]

HOSPITAL WORK ON THE FIGHTING FRONT

South Anwhei, China.

I HAVEN'T time to say all there might be said about needs and conditions. I look right and left and do not know where to begin. I've visited so far three hospitals with Out-Patient Departments attached. Each hospital had about 150 sick and wounded. Only one hospital had wounded alone because the chief problem is sickness. Each Out-Patient Department had about 200 civilians and men of the armed forces to care for each day, but one had an average of 280. I saw them come—the " halt, the lame and the blind." This Army brought the first medical service into this region and people come carrying the sick and injured from 50 to 100 li away.

In the hospitals lie civilians, old men and little boys, wounded by the Japanese. The hospitals I have seen are in the rear—although we live under the sound of heavy artillery and squadrons of airplanes. Right at the fighting front around Nanking, Chinkiang, Wusih, are hundreds of sick and wounded Army men. They lie in the farmhouses and cannot be brought to the rear because it would take weeks and many would die.

With all this, we have the finest medical service I've seen in the Army Medical Service.

In that hospital I saw the first scientific kitchen in China. It was a joy to behold. Spotless, all things boiled, the cook and the whole business under the eye of a head nurse, a trained woman nurse of years' standing. Rules were on the wall, a committee of two wounded inspected to see about the purchase of food, etc. In the hospital I saw white-clad women nurses feeding patients with spoons—that has never happened before in the Army Medical Service.

That hospital and another are experimenting in all kinds of things: trying to make " vaseline " from the bean of the wax tree because we do not have enough vaseline to mix with sulphur for scabies.

In the rear base hospital they have a highly-organised supply department for the entire Army Medical Service. There sit men and women preparing antiseptic gauze bandages and little first-aid dressings for each soldier to carry with him when he goes to the front. The carpenters prepare small wooden boxes to contain around 15 pounds of medical supplies each ; ropes are built into the boxes, so a man can swing one on each end of a carrying pole. They send out 80 of these boxes a month. But much they cannot send because they do not have it.

We are short of nearly everything and we need a thousand and one things. Two weeks ago about 500 workers with their families came here from the refugee camps in Shanghai. Nearly all had scabies, were anaemic, and many did not even have shoes on their feet. They, with 1,400 others, are in the training camp here for the Army. It is now fearfully cold in this region, yet we do not have money to make padded winter garments. Even the army does not yet have these, and only two men in five have blankets in the army.

Slightly in the rear is Taiping. Two days ago the Japs bombed the hospital there. There were 1,100 wounded (Szechuen troops) lying in that hospital when I was there a week ago, and more were pouring in each night.

Two days ago that hospital was wiped out when the Japs dropped 100 bombs on the town and many on the hospital. We have not yet been able to learn if all the wounded were killed and what happened to the doctors and nurses.

NEW CHINESE EX-RED ARMY IS IN ACTION AGAINST JAPANESE

From Our Own Correspondent

SHANGHAI, Thursday.

HAILING mostly from the seaboard provinces of Fukien and southern Chekiang, 15,000 Communist soldiers—formerly belonging to the south-eastern Red Army, but now forming the backbone of China's new Fourth Army—are giving the Japanese garrisons on the eastern war front unending trouble with their guerilla warfare.

Led by 42-year-old General Yeh Ting, one of China's ablest officers, these experienced guerilla fighters fight on precisely the same lines as do their comrades of the great Eighth Route Army in the North—by making surprise, lightning attacks at the enemy's weakest points, by arming the people and by destroying the enemy's communications.

The Fourth Army is directly under the command of the Commander-in-Chief on the eastern front, General Ku Chu-tung.

Working closely with the peasants of the " occupied areas " and forming them into partisan bands, the Fourth Army has approximately 11,000 of its main body on the southern bank of the Yangtse and the remainder on the northern bank.

ENEMY OUSTED

During the last few days detachments of this army, operating near Nanking and along the Nanking Hangchow road, have driven out the Japanese garrison from Liyang and have destroyed a large section of the road, thus severing the Japanese communications with the former capital.

At the beginning of this month, together with peasant partisan detachments, Fourth Army troops crossed the Tsientang River, nine miles south-west of Hangchow and simultaneously with other detachments operating from the north, attacked the city.

LAUNCHES SUNK

Fierce fighting in this district is continuing, and the Japanese have sent large reinforcements to save the city.

Last week, other units operating south-west of Shanghai attacked a Japanese river convoy of 13 launches, sinking seven and killing many Japanese.

January 13 1939.

CHINA GETS PLANES FROM U.S.A.

WILMINGTON (Delaware), Thursday.—China has placed an order for fighting planes in the U.S.A. to the value of over one and a half million pounds.

According to the president of the Bellanca Aircraft Company, Mr. G. Bellanca, China has contracted to buy 200 fighting planes from the company at a cost of 8,300,000 dollars (approximately £1,600,000).

The agreement is still subject to the approval of the Chinese Government and also of its Washington Ambassador.

PRODUCTION BEGUN

But mass production of the order has already begun, says Mr. Bellanca. The company is selling 100,000 more shares. A copy of the contract has been filed as part of the registration covering the issue of common stock.

The planes can be used both as fighters and bombers. They are known as Model 28-90. The order includes fighting equipment such as machine-guns and bomb racks.

Soldiers of the 8th Route Army, elder brother of the 4th Army, move up through a pass in readiness for one of their famous lightning attacks.

NEW CHINA

and Jack Chen

25-year-old artist son of Eugene Chen, the former Chinese Foreign Minister,

tells you of a—

WONDERFUL CITY OF CAVES

I HAVE just returned from China's Special Region, the former Soviet district.

In July, 1937 at a series of meetings between General Chiang Kai-shek, representing the Central Government, and Comrade Lin Pai-Chu of the Soviets the general principles were decided by which Soviet China should be transformed into the Chinese Republic's No. 1 Special Border Region of Shensi-Kansu-Ninghsia.

It was an amazing stroke of statesmanship which shattered the Japanese hopes of stirring up a mutually ruinous civil war between Kuomintang and Communists. China, united and democratic, faced her Fascist enemy.

* * *

IN July 1938, I joined a student caravan and became a pilgrim to Yenan, capital of the Special Region. Cleaner streets, better roads, healthier people . . . many a government could get the same results. But only the Aladdin's lamp of a new democracy could have created this marvellous city of caves. Caves for government, for banks, co-operatives, trade unions. A cave where a great old Buddha sits looking at whirring presses printing text books on China's revolution.

Caves for libraries, for dormitories, lecture halls of colleges for 12,000 students. Caves of hospitals, equipped with X-ray apparatus, a kindergarten and a very special prison where the prisoners are sentenced to read books. And the caves are bombproof.

* * *

THIS is the setting for an advanced agricultural democracy in which the Chinese Communists supply the initial directive force and set the example of a spartan life dedicated to the service of the people. Is there any other community of more than a million people where the highest official wage is 8/- a month?

It is all very simple. The people elect all officials of the Government and mass organisations by universal, direct manhood suffrage. The efficiency of local administration, its freedom from nepotism and "squeeze" (for decades the twin evils of official China) show that the people are fully capable of exercising their democratic right of vote. They are thus encouraged to participate widely in all social activities and organisations.

The economic, educational and defence activities of the local government departments are realised through the mass organisations of trade unions, Women's Associations, Youth Leagues, Peasant and Merchant Associations, etc.

The Government maintains some 700 primary schools, middle schools and a normal school, but in addition these mass organisations have hundreds of literacy classes, half-day schools, and study groups, provide volunteer teachers and buildings. The local Government is responsible for the upkeep of the Eighth Route Army, but the people themselves send contributions, till the band of soldiers at the front and in their Self-Defence Corps have enlisted 60 per cent. of the able bodied population.

Thus the fabric of democratic organisation draws every man, woman and child into the work for the main collective task—the creation of an exemplary anti-Japanese democratic region as an invincible centre of anti-Japanese struggle.

Democracy brings food and culture as well as freedom. Four years of good harvests and clean administration have filled the people's bins with the first surplus in decades. Literacy has been increased from 2 per cent. to 10 per cent. of the population in three years. Four more years will raise it to 90 per cent. In Yenan's theatre, all seats in which are free, I saw the first modern Chinese opera.

This is no paradise. Venereal desease left by bandit armies of the war-lord days, is a scar on the life of the people. There are few of the conventional comforts of life, not a single arm-chair in the region, but there is a warmth of human feeling and a new spirit of comradeship that together are making the "Special Region" the base of an ever-widening movement for people's democracy in China. **The methods which have been so successful here are being applied over a huge territory in Shansi, Hopeh, Chahar and other northern provinces, where the Japanese advance has been completely isolated to the railways and a few big cities.**

* * *

MAO TSE-TUNG, world-famous Chairman of the Special Region, told me that he felt certain that the extension of the mass democratic mobilisation of the Region to all parts of China would mean the complete defeat of the Japanese invader. It was only a question of time. . . . "Thus," he continued, "we shall create a Chinese republic based on principles of equality and liberty, with an independent democratic government, a representative parliament and a constitution suited to the needs of the people. It will realise democratic principles to the full. It will be the road to the future."

REPUBLICANS NEAR FRANCO'S VITAL RAILWAY

ON THE EVE OF MR. CHAMBERLAIN'S DEPARTURE FOR ROME TODAY, REPORTS FROM SPAIN YESTERDAY SHOWED THAT SO SUCCESSFUL IS THE FOUR-DAY-OLD REPUBLICAN COUNTER OFFENSIVE IN ESTREMADURA THAT FRANCO HAS ACTUALLY BEEN FORCED TO WITHDRAW TROOPS AND AIRPLANES FROM THE CATALAN FRONT.

The position at a late hour yesterday was that:—

(1) The Republican advance troops were only 16 miles from the vital railway linking the southern and northern parts of the Fascist-held territory;

(2) Franco's S O S to Morocco for new Moorish and Phalangist reinforcements had been answered, but the detachments that have so far arrived have been unable to stem the retreat;

(3) The 17-day long Italian-led pressure on Catalonia was perceptibly weakening.

January 10 1939·

The Fascist reinforcements, several hundreds strong, began to arrive from Ceuta over the weekend. They travelled by mailboat to Algeciras and thence by train to Cordoba, which is south of the Republican point of attack.

Further detachments crossed yesterday.

So seriously do the Fascists regard the situation, that Franco has called up as conscripts boys 18 years old.

BATTLE FOR PASS

On the Catalan front there was activity only in one sector. This was near Prades where, in one of the fiercest battles yet, the Fascists, assisted by intense artillery and air bombardment, were attacking a key pass in the Sierras.

Republican troops, however, dominated the battlefield from strong positions in the foothills and on the slopes of the mountains. They beat back all the enemy attacks.

DOLORES IBARRURI
«PASIONARIA»

FURIOUS BATTLES ON THE ROAD TO BARCELONA

From SAM RUSSELL

BARCELONA, Monday.

THE ITALIAN PUSH ALONG THE LERIDA-BARCELONA ROAD WAS RENEWED WITH GREATER FEROCITY THAN EVER THIS MORNING.

AT THE SAME TIME THE BATTLE CONTINUES FURTHER SOUTH IN THE DIRECTION OF VENDELLS.

Against the avalanche of Italian war material the Republican troops are resisting magnificently. Arriving at the front after being held up and bombed for three hours on the Vendrell road, I was myself an eyewitness of the magnificent morale of the soldiers of the Army of the Ebro.

At no moment was there panic or loss of touch between General Staff and troops, as they contested every inch of the way.

I realised more than ever what it has meant for the Republic to have to defend its independence without arms, against artillery, tanks, aviation and the mobile columns thrown in by the Italians.

In a manifesto issued today, the Communist Party proclaims:—

"The country is in danger. The foreign invader is approaching the heart of Catalonia. Our soldiers are fighting with incomparable heroism.

"At the orders of the military command we shall construct around our cities invincible barriers of trenches.

"Every farm and village must be transformed into a barracks. The Fascist invader will be unable to advance a step without meeting resistance of hundreds and thousands of men and women determined not to be slaves.

"Catalonia will be the tomb of the invader."

Italian intervention becomes daily more blatant. Italian Generals were heard on the wireless sending greetings to Mussolini from Tarragona after entering the town.

From the free people of Britain there can be only one reply: "Open the Frontier"; "Arms for Republican Spain."

These are the people who get the food you collect. A delightful picture of a Spanish mother with her child. The food on that plate may have come from your town—and the child's face should be ample reward.

FOODSHIPS RACE AS BARCELONA'S MAYOR BEGS RELIEF

January 18 1939

BEFORE this month is out ten ships from Britain are expected to reach Republican Spain packed with tons of food and vital necessities.

This is the prospect opened up by the fine response to nation-wide appeals for urgent help to be hurried to democratic Spain.

Meanwhile, the Mayor of Barcelona, Senor Salvador, has wired to France and England begging for help to be sent without delay.

"If the democracies send a ton of food for every ton of munitions Germany and Italy send against our people, then we can hold them," he says.

"We have passed worse disasters and we can pass this one if we can feed our civil population."

The first foodship in the name of the people of Yorkshire will leave Hull this week. It will carry the most valuable cargo yet sent from Britain. Its 1,500 tons include cod liver oil, dried milk, condensed milk, potatoes, flour, and big quantities of oil, soap and biscuits.

And Yorkshire is working hard to equip another ship by the end of January.

Foodship Number 5 of the National Foodship Campaign for Spain will leave in a week's time.

As soon as goods can be bought and loaded, Foodship Number 6 will sail.

RACE FOR NUMBER 7

There is a keen race between Yorkshire, Tyneside, Lancashire and London to provide Foodship Number 7.

All-London Aid Spain Council has issued an appeal for the adoption of 50,000 Spanish children. Two shillings a month will help to keep a child from starving.

Left Book Club members are working to provide a foodship of their own.

IN CATALONIA'S TRENCHES THE PEOPLE'S ARMY FIGHTS STUBBORNLY, HEROICALLY . . . . FROM INVADED VILLAGES, FROM ALIEN BOMBS AND SHELLS AND SOLDIERS, REFUGEES STREAM TO BARCELONA. . . . SPAIN NEEDS HELP; SPAIN NEEDS ARMS AND FOOD!

For the attention of the Non-Intervention Committee. Italian soldiers from Franco's army captured on the Catalan front.

January 23 1939

BARCELONA'S FIGHT

DRAMATIC MOVE BY LONDON ARMS WORKERS

FOR LIFE

January 26 1939.

ITALIAN TANKS BATTERED AT BARCELONA'S LAST DEFENCES LAST NIGHT.

MASSED ITALIAN BATTERIES, FIRING IN SOME PLACES MORE THAN 100 SHELLS PER MINUTE, WERE BLASTING AT THE TRENCHES OF THE INNER CITY.

Heroically battling against enormous odds, Barcelona's defenders hung on, house by house, ridge by ridge.

On the northward roads German warplanes dived over the convoys of women and children, spraying them with bombs and machine-gun bullets, as they sought safety during the battle for the city.

From the north-west, the Italians pushed hard for Sabadell in an attempt to cut off the defenders by a flanking movement.

Meantime, aircraft workers in four of London's most important factories decided on strike action today in support of Britain's demand for arms to defend Spain and Britain.

From London, too, went out a call from the leaders of the Labour and Socialist International and the International Federation of Trade Unions to all affiliated organisations to "act with all the means in your power."

"WAR WILL GO ON"

SALSONA, north-west of Barcelona, was stated to have fallen last night.

General Molesworth, British representative on the Commission evacuating International Brigaders, declared:—

"Even if Barcelona should fall, which is by no means certain, the war will be continued in central Spain and may last another three, four, or five years."

The Chamberlain Government representative at Barcelona took the opportunity to demand from the hard-pressed Spanish Government "special measures of protection" for the Fascist prisoners in Barcelona.

Immediately after this act he fled from the city aboard a British cruiser bound for the French harbour of Port Vendres.

Telephone communication with Barcelona became more and more difficult throughout yesterday, as military calls jammed the lines.

A German bomber carrying five German Army officers to Spain crashed on French territory, and all five were killed.

In Madrid Colonel Casado was put in charge of all municipal undertakings.

Some Government offices were stated to have moved to Gerona, in northern Catalonia.

Italian warplanes bombed a vessel of the Non-Intervention Commission in Barcelona harbour.

BARCELONA DIGS IN AS ITALIANS PUSH TO CUT OFF CITY

From SAM RUSSELL

BARCELONA, Sunday.

BARCELONA IS IN DANGER. WITH ITALIAN TROOPS 32 MILES AWAY, THE HEROIC POPULATION IS FACING UP TO THE TASK OF IMMEDIATE DEFENCE AND FORTIFICATION OF THE TOWN.

January 27 1939

This morning the intense Italian attack recommenced in the direction of Manresa.

It is from this direction that the principal danger threatens. The Italian Higher Command hope to take Manresa and force the evacuation of Barcelona by menacing to town from the rear.

The spirit of Barcelona today has to be experienced in order to be understood.

I have never known such a spirit of determination and of grit, with the whole town conscious of the seriousness of the situation, conscious at the same time that they will be equal to their task.

Chancellor of Economy to the Catalonian Government, Juan Comorera, today announced measures which will ensure complete mobilisation of Barcelona.

FORTIFICATION

This decree orders closing of all shops and stores, suspension of all businesses during the coming week.

All men up to the age of 55 not mobilised or working in war industry, together with all women between the ages of 18 and 40, are to present themselves for the work of fortifying Barcelona.

Since yesterday morning the Italian aviation has come 16 times over the city.

In spite of the fact that the Junker and Savoia bombers were protected by large numbers of Messerschmidt chasers the Republican 'planes went up each time to give battle to the invaders. Time after time the bombers were attacked while below the crowds cheered the heroism of the Republican pilots.

BOMBERS DOWN

In the course of yesterday's battles over the town, three Junker bombers and two Messerschmidts were brought down, the Republicans losing two chasers.

The presence of the enemy aviation has only spurred the population to further efforts.

While the old men and women go to build fortifications, the men called to the Colours are marching to the recruiting centres. Many thousands of them have already left for the front. At 5 o'clock yesterday morning 20 volunteer battalions were complete with officers, commissars, instructors and organisation.

Every man is prepared to give his life if needs be in order to hold the Italian advance.

Yet the cruel fact is that many of them are going to the front insufficiently armed.

As the Commissar of one of the units that has put up the most heroic resistance said to me as I left the front yesterday:—

"What we need is material—aviation, artillery, tanks and machine-guns. If those people who for two and a half years have contented themselves with pious resolutions do their duty today, we shall prove worthy of our task in saving Spain, and democracy the world over."

REPUBLICAN GOVERNMENT UP NEW FIGHTING POSITIONS

BARCELONA HAS FALLEN. THE FASCIST TROOPS ENTERED THE CITY YESTERDAY.

AS THEY STORMED, WITH TANKS AND MACHINE-GUNS, THE LAST DEFENCES AT MONTJUICH, THEY FOUND THE REPUBLICAN SOLDIERS WITHOUT SHELLS FOR THEIR GUNS OR CARTRIDGES FOR THEIR RIFLES.

The great part of the Republican Army appeared, from reports reaching London last night, to have avoided the encircling pincers of the Italian attack north of the city.

One of Republican Spain's heroic women working in the factories in place of the menfolk called to the front.

THE DAILY WORKER SAYS

BARCELONA falls. The war goes on. It goes on until the people defeat Fascism.

Jose Diaz, Secretary of the Communist Party of Spain, said :—

" I do not deny that we have suffered severely. But the unfortunate Czechoslovak people lost more on one day of capitulation than we have lost in two and a half years of war."

The fall of Barcelona is a blow that must be answered by new and harder blows from us against the enemies of the people.

Every person in Britain can help strike those blows of vengeance for Barcelona.

Demand: Immediate withdrawal of all foreign troops from Spain. Immediate opening of the frontier to arms, warplanes, food, clothes, medicine, permission to old people and children to cross to safety.

London aircraft men have acted. Others can act, inside and outside the factories. Act now!

Heavy fighting is reported north-east of the city.

The Republican Government met in northern Catalonia to decide measures for the vigorous continuation of the battle against the invaders on all fronts.

Mussolini, in a violent speech from the balcony of his Palace in Rome, hailed the fall of Barcelona as a victory for the Italians.

In a passage obviously directed to France and the people of Britain he declared : " many others of our enemies at this moment bite the dust."

Blackshirts shouted "Also France" and "Tunis-Corsica."

In London, representatives of 9,000 workers at five of the biggest aircraft factories near London, stopped work, and marched to Downing Street, demanding arms for Spain.

M. Bonnet, French Foreign Minister, delivered a sinister speech to the French Chamber, suggesting a " Four-Power Conference on Spain"—a repetition of the notorious conference at Munich.

Neville Chamberlain was in consultation with the Ministers of War, Air, and Admiralty, the Minister for Co-ordination of Defence, the Chancellor of the Exchequer, and the heads of the Foreign Office.

January 27, 1939.

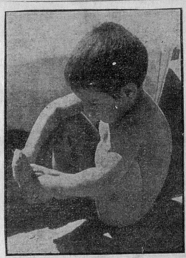

ONE OF THE SPANIARDS

Girls in Barcelona distribute leaflets calling all to the defences.

Engineers Strike And March For Republic

From PHIL BOLSOVER

KEY men in Britain's aircraft industry struck work yesterday and marched through London to the Prime Minister with the demand that the arms they are making should be sent to Spain.

This was the first political strike the aircraft industry has known.

Engineers at the aircraft factories of De Haviland, Handley Page, Witton and James, and R. and J. Beck ceased work at four o'clock in the afternoon.

The demonstration was strengthened by men from Phoenix Telephone Company, Waygood Otis, lift manufacturers, Chiswick Repair Depot of London Passenger Transport Board, and Evershed and Vignoleds, electrical engineers.

More than 9,000 men were represented by 600 to 700 demonstrators, who marched from Tottenham Court Road to Downing Street,

shouting: " We want arms for Spain."

Speaking before the march, Mr. L. Powell, one of the shop stewards, said : " In the aircraft factories we are making 'planes for the arms programme. We know some of them are going abroad, but we know they are not going to the Spanish Government.

" We feel they must go there and we are going to have a voice in this."

The letter presented at 10, Downing Street, read : " We are tormented by the cries of our fallen trade union brothers and their wives and children in Spain. We are haunted by the cries of the 14,000 children done to death by Franco's Italian and German bombers."

The men marched from Tottenham Court Road to Downing Street, shouting the slogan, " We want arms for Spain!"

TAKES
AFTER BARCELONA

THE deliberate conspiracy organised by Chamberlain and Mussolini to enable Franco to take Barcelona has succeeded.

It is natural that our hearts should be heavy. Barcelona's fall will increase the difficulties of the Spanish Government, but there are men at the head of the Government who have been facing such difficulties since July, 1936, have overcome them, and will again overcome them.

The Spanish Republic still possess 30 per cent. of the territory of Spain, ten million people still pledge their loyalty to the Government.

The word defeat has no place in their language. There should be no defeatism in Britain either.

Franco has nine pieces of heavy artillery to every one the Republicans had; he had 20 anti-tank guns to every one the Republicans had, five light machine-guns to every one in the hands of the Republicans, 50 anti-aircraft guns to every one of the Republicans.

Men And Metal

Against this tornado of men and metal, the Spanish people are still on their feet, not whining, not saying " We cannot stand against it."

What are we to do?

Do not believe that passing resolutions and attending solidarity demonstrations are of no avail. It is all helping to increase the anger against Chamberlain. It is worrying our rulers that the people refuse to be quiet about Spain. They don't like to hear " Arms for Spain " shouted in Downing Street. They don't like our aircraft workers leaving the factories at four o'clock and marching to Downing Street.

Let this cry " Arms for Spain " be raised higher and higher. Let us resort to every form of industrial and political action that we can.

The stronger our agitation here, the stronger it is felt in France, where the demand grows in volume for the opening of the Pyreneean frontier, not only to let arms go through, but to let women and children come out.

The Dawn Will Come

There have been darker nights in the history of the struggle for freedom, and the dawn has come, and the dawn will come for the Spanish Republic, but we can help it in the degree that we build up unity in the Labour movement.

We can extend that unity throughout the democratic circles of this country, and on the basis of a common pro-

MADRID, RATION REDUCED, PULLS IN BELT—AND LAUGHS

From WILLIAM FORREST

MADRID, Sunday.

MADRID'S million citizens tightened their belts today against another reduction in the bread ration and made the most of a lull in the shelling by flocking into the streets to take the sun.

" There's nourishment in sunshine," say the Madrilenos.

Young couples—mostly soldiers on leave with their sweethearts—strolled up to the first barricades of the city's war zone, children played in the squares under the eyes of their elders seated on the benches.

The cut in the bread ration was announced as follows : " Owing to transport difficulties, and in order not to exhaust the reserve stocks, we are obliged to reduce the ration to 100 grammes.

" This sacrifice, which is being imposed on the heroic people of Madrid, will be of short duration, for we are confident the Government will surmount the difficulties and that within a few days the former ration will be restored."

A hundred grammes is slightly less than a quarter of a pound.

A family of five will now receive a pound of bread a day. Until now rations have been 150 grammes. Since my arrival the fare at my hotel has not varied; for lunch and supper it has been a plate of soup and a small piece of bread.

From tomorrow the bread will be even smaller.

CITY CAN LAUGH

Madrid is not ashamed of its hunger. (Why should it be ?) It can even muster a laugh against it. Last night at a revue in one of the theatres half the comedian's jokes concerned the food and cigarette famine. There was also an act in which several couples of dancers stamped their feet and cried "Boom, boom, boom," in imitation of artillery.

At that very moment shells were falling in the square outside, for the bombardment had been resumed yesterday morning, and continued until nightfall.

SHELL HITS CROWD

One shell exploded among a crowd sheltering in one of the Metro entrances. Hours later they were still washing away the blood. When I revisited Mr. Butler's shop in the Gran Via I found the approach by the back entrance littered with the debris of a fresh explosion.

Another shell landed in the reading-room of an historic Madrid library. Today the venerable bookworms who haunt this library were to be found in their old familiar places as if nothing untoward had happened.

Scenes like these are being repeated in Madrid every day now—yes, every day. As I type the last lines of this cablegram the shelling is being resumed. It is Sunday night. Six days shalt thou labour, but the seventh . . .

CANADIAN BRIGADERS IN ENGLAND

THEY WANTED TO GO BACK TO FIGHT AGAIN

By WALTER HOLMES

SILENTLY, in darkness, without ceremony, what is left of the Canadian Battalion of the International Brigade came ashore at Newhaven at 4 o'clock yesterday morning.

Behind a barrier, overshadowed by a big policeman, only two Canadian reporters and myself silently gave them the Popular Front salute.

It met with a quick, smiling response. But I wish those thousands who crowded the London streets for the return of the British Battalion had been there to roar them such a welcome as they deserved.

They returned, 292 of them, leaving fully 600 dead on Spanish battlefields. In Spain they did a work which makes it sure that at least one Dominion of the British Empire will for ever be honoured by democrats.

Yet the welcome given them by this homeland of democracy was to segregate them as though they had been lepers, to rush them at express speed by special train across the land, pausing only to change engines at a minor London station, and to ship them forthwith

They ought to have paraded in Downing Street. I believe it was fear that they might which caused the authorities to show such remarkable efficiency in speeding their transit.

THEY CROSSED THE FRONTIER

However, I travelled on their train, and as I passed through coach after coach I received one uniform greeting:—

" DAILY WORKER! Well, you can tell us the truth about Barcelona."

When I told the grim truth I was answered by sceptical silence.

Twenty-four hours before these men had crossed the frontier into France. Rejoicing at their personal escape from Fascist bombs? If you think so, mark what Major Cecil-Smith, their commanding officer, told me when I found him in his compartment.

Stocky, spectacled, quiet-voiced, but recognisable at once as a soldier, this Shanghai-born ex-Service man talked of the men he had led.

WANTED TO FIGHT AGAIN

And this is the point I shall never forget. After four months of exasperating delay, the Canadian Battalion at last had its passports in order. Every man knew the appointed hour of departure.

Yet in those last 24 hours, as they learned that Barcelona was facing the decisive hour, 97 of these men put their signatures to a request to be allowed to return to the front.

They could form a company, they said. They could even provide a machine-gun section and experienced artillerymen. They packed their kits all ready to march. They pleaded with the officers who came up from Barcelona to explain to them that they must leave Spain at once.

" FELT LIKE DESERTERS "

" I haven't seen my wife for over two years," reflected a thrice-wounded Cecil-Smith, "but somehow we felt like deserters."

So it was a thoughtful company that glided past in the ghostly dawn as I stood on the deserted platform of Addison Road, exchanging final greetings through carriage windows with soldiers who cannot know defeat.

Salud, Canadians.

WILLIAM FORREST

has for long periods during the last three years reported the War in Spain. As News Chronicle Special Correspondent he has established a brilliant reputation for his vivid, accurate and human dispatches. Wherever pressure is hardest and danger greatest, Forrest is there. Now back again in Spain's long-besieged capital, he writes the story of his latest—

JOURNEY TO MADRID

MADRID, Sunday.

IN London and Paris they raised their eyebrows and exclaimed: "Madrid? Impossible!" Madrid was . . . well, for the *nth* time Madrid had been given up as doomed.

Destruction hangs o'er you devoted wall
And nodding Ilium waits the impending fall.

The journey was difficult, but manifestly not impossible, otherwise I should not be sending this article from Madrid.

On the way I had my first glimpse of conquered Barcelona—a distant one from the air: I passed over the Fascist-held island of Ibiza, was carried all the way to North Africa and finally touched Republican soil at Alicante. Five days from London to Madrid. In normal times the trip could be done in one day.

In Alicante one of the first things I saw was an announcement chalked on the wall: "We prefer Spanish lentils to Italian macaroni." Happily, they still have lentils in Alicante, as well as fish, bread, wine and coffee. That was the menu at the hotel where I had lunch and supper. All the rooms at this hotel were already taken, but I had no difficulty in finding accommodation for the night at another hotel in the devastated and deserted harbour district.

★

THE proprietor warned me not to expect a comfortable lodging. Pointing to a bomb crater in the street outside, he said: "That one fell yesterday. Half the furniture in the hotel is wrecked and there is not a pane of glass left. It will be rather cold for you, I am afraid. By the way," he added, "you'll find the —— " I thought he was going to say "toilet," but it wasn't that—" you'll find the refugio up the street, and first turning to the left. It's best to know where it is in case there's a raid during the night."

It *was* rather cold in my windowless bedroom, but there was no raid. The only disturbance of the night was produced by a lean and hungry-looking rat which made repeated attacks on my package of iron rations.

In the morning I met a man who was a walking compendium of air-raid information—a man that Finsbury would be proud of. He had at his finger-tips all the facts and figures of Alicante's I forget how many raids —the number of planes, the direction of flight, the bombs dropped, the dead and injured, the houses destroyed, and all the rest. Such was his devotion to his self-imposed task that he never—so he assured me—went below ground during a raid, lest he should miss anything that was to be seen.

★

"COME with me," he said, when he learned that I was a British journalist, "and I'll show you enough to fill half a dozen newspapers. See that wrecked ship there? That was July 25, 1938. Five Savoias, escorted by 28 chasers, came in from the north-east. Flying at a height of 2,000 metres, they circled above the castle and then passed over the city and out to the sea. They dropped 20 bombs of 100 kiloweight. One bomb fell right down the funnel of that ship.

"Now, look at this house (pointing to a building that appeared to be quite intact); you wouldn't think that had been hit, would you? Well, on September 13, 1938 . . one of the bombs landed on the roof of this house. But it didn't explode. When the family came up from the refugio after the raid they found the bomb lying on the bed, just as if it were an infant asleep.

"But on May 25, 1938 . . ." I let him chatter on to his heart's content. It would have been cruel to tell this enthusiast that the systematic, relentless destruction of his beautiful city no longer made news. Why, hadn't I just come from London, where I had failed to hear of a single protest being raised against the inhuman bombing and machine-gunning of the Catalonian refugees during the retreat from Barcelona? To me the silence of the civilised world after the Catalonian horror had been more appalling and more disquieting than the perpetuation of the horror itself.

★

AFTER a parting coffee with my Alicante air-raid guide I took the road to Madrid.

There were four of us in the car—a French Press photographer, a member of the Government's counter - espionage service, the chauffeur and myself. The first stop was Albacete, which used to be the base for the International Brigade.

Here the problem—the perennial problem—of food presented itself. How, you may wonder, are travellers catered for in a country where almost everything is rationed and where you cannot just walk into the first restaurant and order a meal? Well, in Albacete we sought out and found the office of Abastos (food).

There we joined a queue of people, all non-residents, and all provided with papers showing what their business was. I, for example, had my War Ministry pass, certifying that I was a war correspondent. This I showed to the official who was dealing with the queue, and from him I received a note instructing the Grand Hotel of Albacete to provide me with one meal.

On presenting this note at the hotel, and paying seven pesetas (about a shilling at internal rates), I was given in return a ticket for the hotel restaurant. There I had a plateful of beans and lentils, three mouthfuls of oil-soaked pancakes and an orange, and, thus fortified, I resumed my journey across the broad plain of La Mancha, which Cervantes chose as the theatre for the immortal exploits of Don Quixote.

★

IT was dark when we came to royal Aranjuez (where Schiller's "Schöne Tage" are now, indeed, all ended), and, leaving the main road, we began the long detour to Madrid. The chauffeur was no longer sure of his way, but there was no danger of running into enemy territory, for between the lines flowed the Jarama River.

Here in February two years ago today fell four hundred British members of the International Brigade in one of the decisive battles of the war. I wondered what was now being meditated and prepared on the other side of the Jarama. Flushed with their triumph in Catalonia, would the enemy make another attempt to get across the Valencia road and close the circle round Madrid? Now there is no International Brigade to help the Republican Army, but the Italian divisions are still with Franco and the Non-Intervention Committee still stands adjourned in London.

★

WE reached the Valencia road, but after a few miles beyond the village of Perales all was dark and silent. We left it again to begin the second lap of the detour.

At last we were on the Guadalajara road. A left turn and we had a straight run of twelve miles to our journey's end. Perhaps the enemy attack will be made along this road. There is little doubt that the Duce would dearly love to wipe out the stain of the crushing defeat which his legionaries suffered here two years ago.

All day we have been driving towards Madrid from the southeast. Now we are entering it from the north-east. The headlights fall on the inevitable roadside advertisements which herald the approach to a metropolis. "Madrid, Hotel Florida. Every Comfort. Twelve Kilometres." Another, which only this indomitable capital can show: "Army and people united under the banner of solidarity." And, finally, just where the first houses begin, a hoarding with the single word, "Shell."

Thank you, Royal Dutch, for the reminder. But we really didn't need it. We could hear already the booming of the guns.

January 20. 1939.

FASCISTS MACHINE-GUN FLEEING REFUGEES

January 28. 1939.

MADRID HURLS DEFIANCE AT FRANCO

BOMBED AND MACHINE-GUNNED BY FRANCO'S FOREIGN WAR PLANES, THREATENED BY ITALIAN AND MOORISH TROOPS IN THEIR REAR, REFUGEES FROM BARCELONA AND OTHER SPANISH TOWNS WERE YESTERDAY BEING MASSACRED IN HUNDREDS.

YESTERDAY IT WAS ANNOUNCED THAT

"GRANOLLERS, WHICH IS JAMMED TO OVERFLOWING WITH REFUGEES AND IS NOW CLOSE TO THE FRONT LINE, WAS BOMBED INCESSANTLY YESTERDAY (THURSDAY) AND HUNDREDS ARE BELIEVED TO HAVE PERISHED."

In nearly every town and village between Barcelona and the French frontier the same story is told . . . bombing planes unloading high explosives to blow into fragments the bodies of men, women and children who are struggling with a few hastily collected belonging towards the frontier . . . plains diving to spray crowded streets with lead . . . civilians dying of wounds. . . .

Madrid remained defiant. "The war is now beginning," says the "Socialista." Other papers tell the people to prepare for a long resistance. "The last battle is the one that counts," they say.

"The invaders are proclaiming to the world that the war is nearing its end — nothing could be further from the truth," said Colonel Casado. "The war will last as long as it is necessary to drive out the invaders and make Spain for the Spaniards."

The vengeful attack on Catalonian towns recalls the terror of Guernica, the Basque town that was wiped out by bombers, the massacre on the coast road from Malaga, and other episodes of Franco horror.

Even while the attack was taking place, Mussolini sent from Rome (reports Exchange Telegraph) a personal telegram to General Gambara, commander-in-chief of the Italian divisions in Spain, promoting him "for merit in war.

The Republican Army in Catalonia has re-formed on a new line north of Barcelona, says a message from Gerona, adding that "the rapid evacuation of a civilian population of more than 2,000,000 was made impossible by the Italian and German planes, which incessantly machine-gunned the coast road, causing hundreds of victims among the refugees attempting to escape northwards."

ON THURSDAY

London newspapers said the British Government had asked Franco not to commit acts of vengeance if his troops entered Barcelona. The reply was that "such acts would be completely out of keeping with the character of General Franco."

Representatives of the two aircraft and two engineering works in London, that struck for arms for Spain on Thursday, at the Premier's door. At 3 p.m. this afternoon in the Conway Hall, London, engineering shop stewards meet to discuss what further can be done. They also invite to the meeting elected representatives of factories, shop or ticket stewards from any other trade. The Hawker Aircraft factory also took strike action on Thursday in support of arms for Spain.

January 30. 1939.

LADY WINTERTON AGAIN

From Our Own Correspondent

BRIGHTON, Sunday.

LADY WINTERTON was attacked by Professor Haldane at a Brighton memorial meeting tonight to local members of the International Brigade who were killed in Spain.

The attack followed the reading of a letter from Lady Winterton to the mother of one of the Brighton men who returned safely.

The letter read :

"I imagine your son, who fought in the International Brigade, shares all my feelings about the two men in it who on their return from Spain are now trying to exploit the London men out of work.

"Certainly the London unemployed do and have publicly repudiated their activities. It is a great service to the Nazi leaders like Herr von Ribbentrop, who are trying to persuade Germany we are a weak and degenerate people who allow street rioting in our capital.

"English boys should join the fighting forces of our own country.

"The German pay to people who cannot work is about a quarter of what they get here. But perhaps you prefer German rule."

Professor Haldane said : "The party to which she belongs and supports has systematically broken international law in the interests of Hitler and Mussolini.

"I have seen women and children smashed to pieces because the present British Government has broken solemn pledges made at the last General Election to keep the Covenant of the League of Nations."

[Lady Winterton, in a speech last week said she regretted that "these people who have come back from fighting in Spain and are making a nuisance of themselves with coffins and chaining themselves to railings did not get shot in Spain."]

FOOD FOR SPAIN MORE URGENT NOW

From Our Own Correspondent

BIRMINGHAM, Sunday.

SPEAKING at a Birmingham meeting yesterday in connection with the South Midlands food ship for Spain, Mr. George Cadbury revealed that the Bournville Works Council had already voted £200 to the fund.

A collection in the works had raised a further £20.

Mr. Cadbury added that the need for food in Spain was greater than ever now after the fall of Barcelona, which meant that more refugees would require help in all parts of the Government territory.

The civilian population was on the verge of starvation.

At a second meeting Commander Fletcher, M.P. for Nuneaton, appealed for action which would show the Spanish people that despite officialdom the British people were good-hearted and anxious to help them.

Barcelona women and children snatch some troubled hours of sleep on their great trek from Saviour Franco. And wherever Franco's Italian airmen find them, hundreds are killed

SINCE yesterday about 16,000 Spanish refugees have passed the frontier at Cerbere, Le Perthus, Prats del Mollo and Bourg-Madame.

In the course of a 220-mile motor run along the Pyrenees, part of which was in the snow-covered mountains, I visited all the frontier posts today. I passed thousands of refugees on foot, as well as squadrons of French cavalry, Senegalese troops, army kitchens and ambulances on the way to the points where the flow of refugees is the biggest.

At Cerbere, on the extreme east of the Pyrenees, 3,000 militiamen are sheltered in the railway tunnel waiting permission to enter France. They are provided with food and are expected to be disarmed and allowed in to-morrow.

A woman refugee gave birth to a child today in the railway tunnel between Port-Bou and Cerbere. She had no medical attention and was cared for only by one or two women refugees and some French soldiers with a first-aid outfit.

While this was happening a young mother sat on the railway-track a few yards away wailing hysterically and nursing the body of her baby shot dead in her arms two days ago by a machine-gun bullet from one of Franco's neroplanes. She would not let the soldiers take away the baby.

Since yesterday afternoon the flow of refugees at Le Perthus has been so great that the Spanish carabiniers and officials at the barrier lost all hope of controlling the entry. Great confusion prevailed all day.

CARRIED LIVE SHEEP

Thousands of men, women and children and wounded soldiers, and other men in uniform, carried suitcases, parcels and bundles of all kinds. Some carried live rabbits. One had a live sheep round his neck. They filled the road going up the hill for over a mile.

They were in such numbers that motor transport was totally insufficient to take them to the camp established in the neighbourhood. They had to park in the roads.

They filled the streets waiting in the muddy roads with their parcels for motor coaches and lorries to take them to various neighbouring centres. Wounded soldiers—some carried on stretchers with filthy dressings on their wounds—arrived by the hundreds.

I have never seen such an exhibition of misery, and Victor Hugo's description of poverty in "Les Miserables" is nothing compared with the scene at Le Perthus.

At Prats del Mollo, where a few thousand woman and children arrived during the last two or three days, 6,000 soldiers are reported to be advancing towards the frontier.

On the narrow wooden bridge over the river which connects Bourg-Madame with Puigcerda there was an interminable line of people exhibiting their papers to the authorities on both sides. Fifteen thousand militiamen are in the district ready to pass the frontier when they get permission from the Spanish authorities.

Last night a colonel in command of the district deserted as he was on his way to the frontier through the mountain passes. He was stopped by two carabiniers. The officer beat one with a stick, whereupon the carabinier struck him. The colonel drew his revolver and injured the two men. He then ran down to the river and swam across into France, where he surrendered to the French authorities.

Le Perthus yesterday have been described by correspondents on the French side of the frontier. Let me show you something of the picture on the other side as I saw it when with my colleague I went forward on foot as far as La Junquera to see what the chances were of our food lorries getting through

ROAD JAMMED

For more than a mile the road was jammed with vehicles of every description. There were vans so tightly packed with children that we could see only a tangled mass of legs, arms, heads There were ambulances filled with wounded.

There were lorries and cars and carts and barrows and prams—all the traffic I had seen every day for five weeks thronging the highways and byways of Catalonia seemed to have been drawn as by a magnet towards the Pass of Perthus.

At La Junquera there was another barrier, this time of carabineers Behind the barriers was another mob of refugees, more frantic than the first because more distant from their goal.

We walked back to La Junquera to report that there was no passing because of the food lorries.

Towards midnight it began to rain, and with that the refugees must have touched the uttermost of their misery.

There was nothing for us to do but to spend the night in the lorries and see what the morning might bring.

It brought an early surprise. First we became aware of a commotion among the refugees. Someone was trying to come through We saw only his black hat bobbing above the sea of faces, as he pushed and squeezed his way forward.

At last he was through and we rubbed our sleepy eyes when we saw it was Alvarez del Vayo. He had come from Figueras, the new seat of Government, and was making for Perpignan, where he hoped to persuade the French to speed up the admission of refugees.

MORE HELP NEEDED

"Up to the present," he said, "France has been admitting between two and three thousand a day. That is not enough. We have 160,000 who are in need of help."

A car was waiting for him in Le Perthus to take him on. In a few hours he was back, looking rather grim but able to report that he hoped his mission had been a success.

Apart from the carabineer, Del Vayo's only bodyguard was his chauffeur. The car in which they had driven up from Figueras in the morning was waiting at the end of the refugee line. We reached it at last and on the way down to La Junquera I heard from the Foreign Minister the latest news from the front.

The enemy, he said, had advanced along the coast from Barcelona as far as Arenys del Mar. "There," he said, "we hope to be able to hold him."

"Order is being re-established," said Del Vayo. "See how the carabineers are getting a grip of the situation. No men of military age are being allowed out. Arms are being recovered. We are taking back some ourselves"—and he pointed to four automatic rifles packed in the back of the car

One can say in truth that the Republic's leaders, faced with a situation as critical as any with which a State has ever been confronted, have not lost their heads.

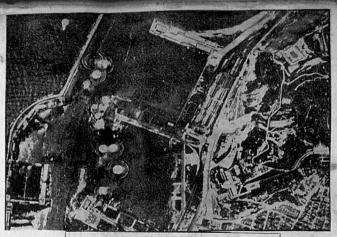

Through the Raider's Eyes

White patches in air picture of Barcelona Harbour (below) are exploding bombs dropped by rebel planes during one of the last raids on the city before its capture. British ships were among those hit

Last Look At Her Homeland

Still wearing an apron, an elderly woman sits among her bundles and looks back to her native land. She weeps—and in her face is all the tragedy of Spain.

January 30 1939.

Hundreds of refugees wedged in the roadway at the frontier

Gendarmes with linked arms kept them back until the barriers could be raised. Then they were shepherded to encampments and given food.

RETREAT TO SAFETY: Spanish Republicans enjoy soldierly hospitality on the French frontier

CATALONIA HITS BACK

FASCISTS SUFFER HUGE LOSSES

FASCISTS SUFFERED HUGE LOSSES YESTERDAY IN FURIOUS FIGHTING NEAR MANRESA, NORTH-WEST OF BARCELONA, EXCHANGE TELEGRAPH REPORTS.

ALL ALONG THE CATALONIAN FRONT THE REPUBLICAN LINES WERE RE-FORMING AND HOLDING UP THE ATTEMPTED FASCIST ADVANCE NORTHWARDS.

Fierce battles were reported near Mataro on the coast 20 miles north-east of Barcelona.

Garcia Morato, " ace " Fascist flyer, was shot down by Republican planes as he was taking part in an attack upon the women and children refugees trying to escape from the battle zone.

Fascist bombing and machine-gunning of helpless refugees jammed on the roads or packed into makeshift camps near the frontier, continued violently.

Scenes of extreme pathos are being enacted along the Franco-Catalan frontier as thousands of refugees besiege the gateways of France, Exchange Telegraph reports from Cerbere.

Hundreds of refugees packed the 1,000 yards long international tunnel at the frontier at Cerbere, and huddled together, hungry, helpless, and soaked with rain, passed a night of tragedy.

A woman gave birth to a baby in the early hours and near her stood a distraught mother cradling in her arms her child killed two days ago by machine gun bullets.

Milk and bread were distributed this morning.

In an interview at Figueras with the Paris evening newspaper, Ce Soir, Dr. Negrin, Prime Minister of the Republic, declared : " The war is not over. We are firm and determined."

In London on Saturday, shop stewards from 26 engineering and aircraft factories in the London area, meeting in emergency conference at the Conway Hall, Holborn,

decided on a deputation to the Premier next Thursday afternoon, backed by a great mass demonstration of London engineering workers, with maximum possible industrial action on that day, to demand arms for Spain.

Forty thousand workers were represented at the meeting, with 150 shop stewards present, and—in addition to the representatives of 26 engineering works—delegates from the Printers' Anti-Fascist movement, and from Lambert and Butler's tobacco factory.

So deep had the feeling on Spain become since the fall of Barcelona, it was stated, that several factories would be ready for a whole day's stoppage o work.

It was decided to send a letter to the Prime Minister telling him to expect the deputation on Thursday.

Tomorrow, engineers will meet at Temple Station at 8 p.m. and then take part in a mass lobbying of M.P.s. Factory deputations to local M.P.s are being organised.

DEPUTATIONS

The factory deputations will also visit local Labour and Trade Council offices to urge unity of all progressive forces in the campaign to aid Spain.

Executives and District Committees of the engineering union are being asked to give official leadership to the campaign, and to call an all-London engineers' demonstration.

The four points adopted by the *(Continued on Page 8 Col. 3)*

conference on Saturday are the demand for:—

lifting of the embargo on arms for Spain,

convoys for British ships trading to Spain,

withdrawal of foreign troops from Spain,

shipments of food to Republican Spain.

Arms for Spain and freedom for India were the twin demands of the mass rally in Trafalgar Square yesterday in celebration of Indian Independence Day.

Earlier in the afternoon there had been a big march to the Square from Mornington Crescent.

FLAGS CARRIED ON MARCH

The demonstrators included Indians, Arabs and Irishmen, who marched with Londoners bearing flags of India, Spain, China and Ireland—the countries fighting for their national freedom.

The meeting received messages from British and Indian leaders.

A resolution, which called for unity of the British people, for Indian freedom, demanding that the Government grant arms for Spain, and congratulating the Indian Congress on the boycott of Japanese goods, was unanimously adopted.

Next Tuesday, January 31, the Foreign Office and the houses of certain Cabinet Ministers will be picketed for eight hours between 12 noon and 8 p.m. by men and women carrying posters urging arms for Spain.

At 8 o'clock the pickets will join in a mass lobbying of M.P.s.

The Spain Emergency Committee is calling upon all who have been associated with its work to take part in this lobbying on Tuesday, the date of Parliament's re-assembling.

Hammersmith Building Workers yesterday decided to assemble at Hammersmith Broadway, at 7 p.m. Tuesday, to support the mass lobby.

OFF TO THE FRONT AGAIN

A Spanish soldier says goodbye to his wife and child.

The Duce's Victory

SIGNOR MUSSOLINI exuberantly hails the surrender of Barcelona as an Italian triumph.

Well he may. For it is precisely that.

A triumph, he says, not merely over the Government of Spain, but over those whose interests be with it. True, also.

It has been said that at no European statesman has been taken so much trouble as Herr Hitler to tell other nations well in advance exactly what he meant to do to them.

But Signor Mussolini in his repeated statements on the Spanish conflict has been no less frank than Herr Hitler in " Mein Kampf."

☆ ☆

He has from the beginning declared that he would tolerate no outcome to the civil war save a rebel victory. And though it has taken longer than he first imagined, he has never swerved from the policy of supplying Franco with the men and the arms necessary to carry him forward.

Without him, the rebellion would never, in all probability, have broken out. Without him, it would with complete certainty have been long ago suppressed.

Without him, Spain to-day would be a peaceful and happy democracy. Instead, it is a nation of war cemeteries, of ruined towns, of bitterness, hate and sorrow. That is his triumph.

☆ ☆

There are two things—it seems to us there are only two things—to say now.

One is to salute the moral heroism of the Spanish democrats. Their men have given their lives, their women have endured hunger and terror, in a superbly brave effort to save themselves and Europe from a brutal and evil thing.

The other is bluntly to say that the democratic Governments of the Western world will not avoid the fate of Spain if they cannot now show a spirit very different from that which has enfeebled their Spanish policy for two and a half years.

FRANCO MACHINE-GUNNED THEM

January 30. 1939.

Spanish women and children refugees—footsore, weary and starving from their long trek in front of the Fascist sub-human machine-gunning aviators—queue at Perpignan on the French Border. Meanwhile, the Spanish men form a new line of defence North-West of Barcelona and are holding the Fascist armies.

Safe on foreign soil, refugees

So great is the rush at Le Perthus that refugees must wait for hours bef
don't mind waiting—they're safe. Some carry a bu

January 30. 1939.

TRUDGING ALONG THE ROAD TO SAFETY

Refugee children in the picture above had each lost a limb.

Right : Looking down the rugged mountain path along which the refugees trudged to Le Perthus, seen in the valley on right of the picture.

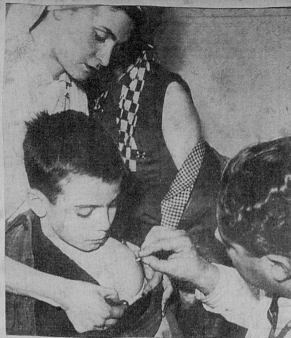

wait—and wonder 'What now?'

going on to the camps. Mobile Guards keep them in line. The refugees
... They're the lucky ones—others have only their clothes.

Every refugee is vac-
cinated before being
allowed to go farther into
France.

The boy patient looks
on curiously. He has known
air-raids—so why should he
worry about a little thing
like this?

The refugees arrive at
the frontier in thousands,
faster than the French
authorities can deal with
them. Already there are
more than 150,000—and
there are many more on the
way.

Observers tell of roads
blocked for miles on the
Spanish side, of hundreds
collapsing before they can
reach the sanctuary of the
frontier.

Not yet is Spain's story
ended.

January 30. 1939

Food for the hungry—and rest for the weary

Every mother, every
father will understand
this smile. It is the smile
of a refugee who sees her
children receiving their first
hot meal for days.

They have known hun-
ger, the nightmare journey
to the frontier, the threat
of death from the air.

But now, at Boulou, they
are safe. They eat. And
so their mother is happier
than she has been for many
days.

Meanwhile thousands trudge the roads to seek refuge in France.

Safe across the French frontier, a woman refugee is carried to shelter by two Mobile Guards. By their side an old woman, her face lined with exhaustion, plods grimly forward. And behind them for mile on mile stretches the line of refugees. This is the other side of Franco's victory. As his troops march into Barcelona, thousands flee before them into France.
—(Daily Sketch picture.)

January 31 1939.

GENERAL SAYS, WE WILL STICK

" The army of the Republic is fighting on—to the death," declares General Miaja, Spanish Government military leader, in a statement reported in the London Evening Standard.

If not out of affection for Spain at least for their own advantage, the democracies should help the Republic, says General Miaja.

General Miaja's message goes on:—

I have just been round my five armies in Central Spain. My men have told me that they will stick with me to the end.

Madrid and the territory under my control will never yield until the last man has fallen. Tell that to Franco, to Mussolini, and to the world.

WAR GOES ON

Let nobody suffer from delusions that the war will soon be over because Barcelona has fallen. Oh no! The war goes on. Even if the whole of Catalonia falls our battle is not lost.

We will only hope, as we fight, that justice and international right will be reinstated and that those who now lead democratic countries will discover their own error.

From Retirement To Defence Of Republic

By W. RUST

CORDON is a lifelong soldier, an officer who knows his job throughout. Living in voluntary retirement at the time of the rebellion he at once hurried to the defence of the Republic and headed some of the early groups of militia.

Today he is Under-Secretary for the Army and works alongside Negrin, the Premier and Minister of National Defence.

I first met him in the early hours of an April morning in a small house not far from Lerida, where Campesino was holding out against the enemy. Those were dark days, but Cordon, then in command of the Southern Sector of that front, was coolly confident about everything.

GREAT CONFIDENCE

He plunged into a discussion about modern military tactics just as he did when I saw him for the second time when I talked with him in his Ministry office just before I left Barcelona. He has great confidence in the new system of fortifications which he has worked out with his General Staff.

During these two years, Cordon has accumulated great experience both in fighting and in administration. In addition to various

Ministry posts he was Chief of Staff of the Eastern Army in the successful offensives against Belchite and Quinto last year. He also directed operations in the mountains of Northern Aragon.

Cordon also possesses a keen political mind and his co-operation with Negrin is the guarantee of political unity in the Ministry of National Defence.

SPAIN FIGHTERS HOME WITHIN THREE DAYS

AT SOME TIME BETWEEN TUESDAY AND THURSDAY EVENING THE MAIN BATCH OF THE BRITISH BATTALION OF THE INTERNATIONAL BRIGADE WILL ARRIVE IN LONDON. THEY WILL NUMBER OVER 300. ON THEIR JOURNEY FROM THE FRENCH FRONTIER THEY WILL BE ACCOMPANIED BY FRANK PITCAIRN, FIRST DAILY WORKER CORRESPONDENT IN SPAIN.

Yesterday they received their passports. All have been vaccinated. Arrangements for their transport through France and across the Channel have been completed. The men whose valour in the trenches saved Britain's blackened name are coming home.

It is hoped to be possible to give more definite information tomorrow about the exact time of arrival.

There are still a few small groups of the British Battalion left in the southern part of Spain. These are expected back shortly.

NINETY IN FRANCO JAILS

In addition, there are still 90 British subjects in Franco's prisons. As they are now no longer combatants the Foreign Office is being asked to secure their release before Christmas.

LOCOMEN MAY SEND SPAIN FOODSHIP

BRITISH locomotive men may send their own foodship to Spain if the special effort they are running this week brings in enough to load a ship.

In any case all the money being raised will go to help the fight of the Spanish people.

Mr. W. J. R. Squance, general secretary of the Associated Society of Locomotive Engineers and Firemen, told the DAILY WORKER yesterday that the decision to run a special Spain week among their members was taken by the Executive in October.

The branches were immediately informed of the decision and asked to make preparations for special collections beginning today and continuing all this week.

The magnificent work of the miners and engineers was quoted as an example of what could be done.

Later the Society sent out small posters to be put up in the branch rooms, depots, canteens and so on. Special "Spain Week" collecting sheets have been circulated.

"We are hopeful of raising a substantial sum during the week," said Mr. Squance. "Our members have on many occasions shown themselves ready to fight for justice. This time will be no exception.

"When the money is in hand, the executive will decide how to dispose of it."

LEVY PLAN

In one Scottish depot the men have decided on a grading scheme for contributions. Drivers will give a minimum of 1s. 6d., firemen 1s. and cleaners 6d. Although the scheme is voluntary, no one is going to be left out.

Similar schemes will be organised in other depots.

J. R. SQUANCE

600 Visitors Will Give Chamberlain Message For Rome

MR. CHAMBERLAIN is to have a lot of visitors on January 7. From all parts of Britain delegates will travel to London to see him—600 of them. They will ask that the British Government does not grant belligerent rights to Franco in Spain.

This follows the success of the campaign opened by the Spanish Emergency Committee of the International Peace Campaign against these rights for Franco.

Organisation in all parts of the country, particularly those which were most active in distributing the Committee's ten million leaflets on the question, are being asked to elect representatives in every Parliamentary constituency.

BEFORE ROME

These delegates will call on Mr. Chamberlain on January 7, a day or two before he leaves for his visit to Rome, and will present credentials from the organisations and prominent individuals they represent.

Members of Hull Students' Union have passed a resolution condemning the Anglo-Italian Pact and urging students to oppose this surrender to Fascist aggression.

A similar decision was taken by the general meeting of Manchester University Socialist Society, which declared the Pact would give further encouragement to Fascism.

LABOUR MOVES

Grantham Labour Party has unanimously declared its opposition to the Pact, and the Labour Party at Weston-super-Mare adopted a resolution demanding that no belligerent rights be given to the Fascists in Spain.

"No rights for Franco until every foreign soldier and piece of war material has been withdrawn from Spain," declares a resolution of Swindon No. 2 Branch of the National Union of Railwaymen, a demand also pressed by Eastleigh.

Workers at the clothing works of Messrs. Godfrey are seen here with some of the food they are collecting for Spain during Stepney's campaign for a Christmas foodship.

FRANCO ORDERS AERIAL TERROR

From SAM RUSSELL

BARCELONA, Sunday.

UNABLE, after two and a half years' war, to defeat the Spanish people at the front, the Italian and German invaders who are laying waste to Spain, yesterday declared their intention to pursue a calculated policy of destroying the towns and villages of the Republican rearguard.

The announcement was made from Radio Salamanca.

It declared that it had been decided to bomb over 200 small towns and villages in Republican territory. Then followed a list of 137 places scheduled as targets for the German and Italian aircraft. Sixty-three are in Catalonia, 29 in the Levante region, 30 in Central Spain and four in the South. The rest are still to come.

These towns and villages will be attacked by the fleet of over 800 planes, which for four months was used with such little effect against the Army of the Ebro.

During that battle 214 foreign planes were brought down by the Republican air force and anti-aircraft defence. So presumably

Mussolini's pilots have though twice and believe they will get a better chance to demonstrate their valour by leaving the front severely alone and concentrating instead on the massacre of women and children.

They have not waited long.

All day yesterday and again today, hour after hour, came in to Barcelona news of attacks on small villages in all parts of Spain. Fifteen villages on the radioed list have already been attacked, while the attack on the large towns have been intensified.

BARCELONA BOMBED

Barcelona was bombed eight times on Friday. Yesterday it was bombed three times. Today we have already been raided once.

Valencia has also been subjected to continuous air attacks.

But, whereas in Barcelona and Valencia, the anti-aircraft defences give a certain amount of protection, in the small villages there are often not even air-raid shelters.

The worst raid yesterday was that on Cervera. Five heavy bombers flew over and dropped 100 bombs in the very centre of the town. Their objective was the local food distributing centre. The hour chosen was one o'clock, when the building was surrounded by women collecting the daily rations for their families.

The queuing woman did not have time to take shelter before the bombs fell. Those bombs killed 25 women. They seriously injured 48 women and children. They destroyed 30 houses.

Then, after the bombs had done their work, the Fascist airplanes swooped low and machine-gunned the women and children who were fleeing to the fields in the hope of finding safety there. Camprodon, an even smaller town, was bombed by five planes, which dropped 12 bombs each, killing and wounding some 60 people.

THE SAME STORY

Gerona, Puigera, Palamos, Baddalona, Borjas, Blancas, Artesa, Tarraga, Bayas—they were all the same.

In not one of these villages is there anything that can be considered as a military objective. The truth is that no military objectives are being sought. This is a deliberate attempt to terrorise the people of Spain by bombing every tiny village and hamlet, an attempt to force a decision which the Fascists have not been able to obtain on the field of battle.

Hampshire, Section of the National Clarion Cycling Club.

Cinema Fans Give To Spain

The proposal to send a Christmas Foodship from London to Barcelona is winning wide support from the anti-Fascist people of the Metropolis.

Typical of the activity is that now under way in Stepney. Here in those cinemas where the film "Blockade" is showing, excellent collections are being taken, while in many of the factories food collections have been organised.

FOOD WEEK

Yesterday Stepney's special Spain Food Week started, and from today on house-to-house and factory-to-factory collections will be held.

Three depots have been open for the receipt of food and money. These are: Dew Drop Inn, 71, Vallance Road, E.1; Carter's Bookshop, 19, Church Lane, E.1, and the National Union of Tailors and Garment Workers, 48, New Road, E.1.

ISLINGTON

Meantime, Islington Spain Aid Committee supporters were active last week taking collections at those local cinemas showing "Blockade."

Collections averaging 30s. a night have been taken at the Astoria, the Odeon, the Marlborough, and the Angel.

FIGHTERS TELL THEIR STORY

Two Letters From Spain

THE two letters printed here were written by members of the British Battalion of the International Brigade in September.

They describe experiences which were not unusual in the two years' active service of the Battalion; and they reflect a spirit which was general.

The first is from Alec Cummings, well known in Liverpool and Cardiff, and, when t' s letter was written, had been in Spain for more than 18 months, having returned to the front line after being wounded. He was later reported missing.

JUST left the hottest spot I have ever been in. Impossible to dig trenches or build anything like comparatively safe refugios. And the stuff that came over from the enemy!!

In that position for ten days and nights. You have to count nights separately under such conditions. Hardly any difference in activity. No sleep, plenty of lice, little food and practically nothing to drink—too difficult and dangerous for the muleteers to bring rations.

EVERYTHING UNDER FIRE

Away up on the Aragonese heights, rock and rubble, rubble and rock, deep winding canyons, or, as they are called here, "Barrancos," where explosions echo thunderously the whole night and day. Everything and everywhere under shell fire.

Here a bunch of dead mules, stinking like nothing on earth; there a dead comrade, buried under a thin layer of earth, not sufficient to conceal the tell-tale smell. You simply can't dig deep.

The lads on the very front line have, painfully and under cover of darkness when things are a little more quiet, built parapets of stone and sandbags. But these are under direct anti-tank fire from the enemy, and frequently those hard won parapets are shattered to bits in different places.

BURIED BUT ALIVE

Several times comrades extricate themselves from underneath a heap of debris to everyone's surprise, alive!

Our last night on this position, just before we went into reserve, was terrific. Someone got scared, I don't know on which side, and threw a hand grenade into the barranco. That started it! The Fascists, who must have been more scared than anyone, hurled every bloody thing at us. Trench mortars galore. The place was

plastered with them, and they are hellish things. You can't hear them coming—they come down almost perpendicularly.

I thought Armageddon had been ushered in—ushered in is perhaps too euphemistic—was bludgeoned in. It lasted twenty minutes Greenwich time. In human emotional time—an age. We've come through that not without our wounded and killed. Now we occupy an immediate reserve position. Our only trouble for the time being is the Fascist aviation—huge black bombers.

This letter is from John Richardson, 17-year-old member of the Young Communist League, to a friend in Luton He wrote from a Spanish hospital where he was recovering from the effects of wounds caused by a hand grenade.

WE were told to attack and take a heavily-fortified hill, just outside Gandessa.

At dawn we went over the top. And the world went mad. Machine-guns sent a hail of bullets at us, snipers shot at us, shells and trench mortars burst all around.

But we came through and reached cover at the bottom of the valley, where we lay all day unable to move because of the snipers. The heat of the sun became unbearable. The ground scorched and our clothes stuck to our backs. We had no water. My mouth and throat were swollen and hard with thirst. Still we lay there all day. Then at last came the night and we were able to stretch our cramped and aching limbs.

REAL BUSINESS

At 10 p.m. we got the order to attack. In a long line, stretching along the side of the hill we crept up, carefully avoiding the mines tied to the bushes, which all you had to do was to touch to get blown to pieces.

We reached the very summit without a mishap. A little later came the signal for the real business. We rose with a yell and rushed forward, throwing hand-grenades as we ran.

But machine-guns rained death at us. Red-hot lead. Hand-grenades burst all around. Time and time again we attacked, only to be driven back. The fortifications were too strong. Solid concrete pill-boxes lined the hill-top.

And we were only flesh and blood.

It was at this action that I got a hand-grenade all to myself, and so I am writing this letter in hospital.

Our company suffered terrible punishment on the hills around Gandesa. Our officers were either killed or wounded without exception, and many other comrades were wounded, yet the company's morale was never shaken. They swore to take that hill if they had to carry it away in sacks.

So I say, hurrah for Company No. 2, the best in the Battalion, of which I am very proud to be a member.

And I say it was worth while coming to Spain. For to see the way the International Brigade and our Spanish comrades went into action was a revelation, a sight I will never forget. . . . .

Thanks again for the fags. Don't use the Y.C.L. as a club for amusements only. Remember it is a democratic organisation fighting for the working-class. Salud!

BACK from war-torn Spain to peaceful England are coming 300 men of the British Battalion of the International Brigade.

They are the last of the 2,000 who went from Britain to fight side by side for freedom and democracy with Frenchmen, Americans, Canadians, Germans, Italians, Czechs, men from 52 countries, in an international army the like of which the world had never seen before.

by Bob Cooney
Political Commissar of the British Battalion

THE first British volunteers arrived in Spain in October, 1936. They came singly at first, then in small groups. By December they were coming in hundreds and early in January they were able to form a complete Battalion, becoming the foundation Battalion of the XV Brigade.

When the Battalion went into action in February at Jarama, it was fortunate to have within its ranks a company which had already gone through the baptism of fire.

The first English-speaking company—now the Major Attlee Company—composed of British and Irish volunteers, did valiant work during December and January on the Cordova and Madrid fronts. It joined the British Battalion on the eve of its departure in February.

FROM that day to this, the British Battalion, now the oldest Battalion in the XV Brigade, has taken part in every action in which the Brigade has fought. Its history is one of sacrifice, heroism and endurance, that could only be found in a Battalion of high morale and deep political conviction.

From every one of its actions the Battalion has been able to draw some lesson. In every succeeding battle it has gone in more highly trained, able to deliver more powerful blows to the enemy. Today it is at the height of its glory and is the pride of the British Labour movement.

At Jarama the volunteers had practically no knowledge of the peculiarities of the type of fighting in Spain. Lack of arms and pressure of time had robbed them of the opportunity for adequate training. The Jarama campaign was a baptism of such a fierce and sudden character, fought under the worst possible conditions, that even if no other action had been fought, the record of the Battalion would still be an epic.

IN subsequent actions the high traditions of Jarama were well maintained.

There is not sufficient space available for me to detail the various campaigns, but in every one of them the British volunteers have brought honour to their country.

Who can mention Teruel without remembering the British Battalion which for nearly a month held and improved its

positions in face of the most cruel artillery barrage which the war had up to then produced?

In the tragic days of March and April, 1938, when the defeatists and pessimists were at their loudest, the Battalion fought to the last ditch for every position.

At Belchite it fought its way out of the town when its flanks had gone and disaster seemed inevitable.

AT Caspe, surrounded by machine-guns and tanks, the Battalion again fought its way out.

When Sam Wild, Battalion Commander, and a number of others were captured they used their fists in good old British style and got away.

Three times the Battalion was driven back by the withering artillery and machine-gun fire. Three times it went forward again at tremendous cost until ordered to withdraw by the Brigade.

At Gandesa, reduced to 70 men —with the other Battalions to 200 —it held the road all day in that vital April 2. It repulsed six attacks by tanks and did not budge an inch in face of the continuous artillery fire. By its stand that day the Battalion gave the main army time to cross the Ebro and blow up the bridges, thus bringing to an end the Fascist advance.

NOW the Battalion has fought its last action as an International Battalion.

In the first Ebro offensive the Battalion has fought in the glorious traditions of Jarama. The epic of Hill 481 is too fresh in the memory, the thoughts of comrades who fell too painful to allow of an adequate description.

It is a story that will thrill generations to come—the story of action that won for the British Battalion the title "Shock Battalion of the XV Brigade."

And those who return—they return with the pride of men who have made history. They have saved the honour of their country. They have proved to the brave people of Spain that the real Britain is their friend and has nothing in common with Chamberlain.

They go home to launch such a campaign as will rouse the entire country and drive this Government of Chamberlain into the oblivion it deserves.

Reprinted from The Volunteer for Liberty, newspaper of the British Battalion in Spain.

December 6 1938

POET AND DEMOCRAT: *Letters Reveal Conflict in Mind of Poet Killed in Spain's Civil War*

Julian Bell, Essays, Poems, and Letters. (The Hogarth Press, 12s. 6d.)

THIS, a collection of Essays, Poems, and Letters of the late Julian Bell, is of particular interest at the present time, since in all his writings he reflected the struggle that is uppermost in the minds of many of the world's foremost artists, poets, writers, etc., a struggle between realisation of the need for some form of socialism to alleviate the misery and suffering of the masses, and a natural desire (born of their bourgeois traditions and up-bringing) to avoid the horror and personal discomfort which a proletarian revolution would, they believe, bring them.

JULIAN BELL
—a Franco bomb killed him

Julian Bell was born in 1908, son of Clive and Vanessa Bell, grandson of Leslie Stephen, nephew of Virginia Woolf, and first-cousin once removed of H. A. L. Fisher.

He summed up his ancestry thus:—

I stay myself—the product made
By several hundred English years,
Of harried labourers underpaid,
Of Venns who plied the Parson's trade,
Of regicides, of Clapham sects,
Of high Victorian intellects,
  Leslie, Fitzjames.

He was educated at a public school and at Cambridge. Through the years he gradually developed a "political consciousness," though he frequently diverged from accepted Communist doctrinaire.

Professor

In 1935 he was appointed Professor of English in the Chinese University of Hankow. All the time he was in China the news from Spain made him long to return to Europe, to assist in any way that he was able the struggle of the Spanish people against the Fascist invasion.

In 1937 he returned to England, and, in spite of efforts to dissuade him, joined the British Medical Unit in Spain as a lorry driver.

On July 18, 1937, twenty-nine-year-old Julian Bell was slaughtered by a bomb from an insurgent aeroplane as he drove his ambulance on the Brunete front.

Of his poems, the one titled "Nonsense" is of especial interest:

Sing a song of sixpence
A pocketful of rye,
The lover's in the garden,
And battle's in the sky.
The banker's in the city
Getting off his gold;
Oh isn't it a pity
The rye can't be sold.

The queen is drinking sherry
And dancing to a band;
A crowd may well feel merry
That doesn't understand.

The banker turns his gold about
But that won't sell the rye,
Starve and grow cold without,
And ask the reason why
The guns are in the garden,
And battle's in the sky.

Of interest also is his letter to C. Day Lewis, in which he scorns what he calls Lewis's tendency to make a "saviour" out of the worker.

Saviours

He wrote ". . . . Saviours are what you . . . . and your minor followers are trying to make of them. The Idealised Hero; the Proletarian, the Worker, of the cartoons and posters, stripped to the waist, muscular, with hammer or axe in hand; lean and brawny, smashing, kicking, humiliating the round fat capitalist in top-hat and striped trousers. Quite apart from the mischief this romantic fiction causes, does it not strike you as a little absurd? And so very like its dialectically interpenetrated opposite, the fascist youth, just as muscular and arrogant and full of kicks and clouts. Tough for tough, I like your worker better, but, alas, in reality he kicks so seldom and is so often kicked."

His Difficulties

In a letter to E. M. Forster, he very clearly states his difficulties in accepting the communist doctrine.

". . . . For my own part, my position is that of a social-democrat of the right, but a social-democrat who is not a Liberal. I am all for compromise and moderation, and for avoiding civil war at any cost. But I do not think you can have any compromise that will avoid civil war and yet does not settle the question of power in favour of some body of convinced and organised socialists.

". . . . Many revolutionaries of the vaguer kind ignore the question of power, and almost all, including the Communist party, ignore the prospect of civil war and speak instead of 'revolution.' Now revolution suggests . . . . a very easy victory, a walk-over, for the insurgent proletariat."

Included also in this volume are the replies to many of the points raised in Julian Bell's letters, and many of these replies succeeded, before his tragic death, in convincing him that his views were, in a great many cases, wrong.

"Cavalcade" December 3 1938

A SMILE WILL GO A LONG, LONG WAY (LONDON TO MADRID)

"SMILE comrades, smile. Pull yourselves together. Never mind the fog, don't stand bewailing the fact that you've missed your usual Sunday morning lie in. Get ready to do your good deed for the day."

Such was the greeting given to a small group of London workers, equipped with rucksacks and shopping baskets, who had assembled to collect food for Spain.

The forced smiles turned to expressions of real pleasure when parcels of groceries already packed were handed out as a result of a previous leaflet distributed announcing the collection.

Three out of every five householders in one particular block of flats contributed.

Rucksacks were so heavily laden that runners were busy taking the goods back to th local headquarters, whilst collecting still continued.

Most encouraging was one particular woman tenant, who, after piling tins of food into the basket, putting a shilling into the box, asked the collector to call again, saying: "Call every week."

STROUD JOINS IN

The renewed enthusiasm of this group of London workers is equalled if not exceeded by the Stroud, Gloucestershire, friends of Spain, who from an adult population of just over 10,000, collected the magnificent sum of £70. 8s. 6½. by means of a Flag Day last week-end.

FACTORIES COMPETE

A friendly rivalry as to who can send the most assistance to Spanish democrats has developed between two sections of members of No. 2 London Branch of the Tailors and Garment Workers' Union.

The employees at Godfrey's workshop, have challenged those at Wallis' to a competition.

Godfrey's shop committee has pledged itself to collect at least 1 lb. of sugar and 1 tin of food per head and in addition to raise the transport costs.

Speaking of clothing, workers brings to mind another good record, this time from Zurich.

Twenty tons of woollen clothing and dried fruits and vegetables left here for Spain last week-end, and another similar consignment will go before Christmas.

The workers of the Maggi factory, who have already sent several scores of tons of food, are making another gift of 600lbs. of food, and the directorate of the factory are to send 300lbs. of oatmeal.

At the Knorr factory, 100lbs. of oatmeal have been collected. The staff of the Zurich tramways are making weekly collections of 200 Swiss francs.

WAGES SACRIFICED

In one of the metal foundries the staff and workers are to give two hours' wages for Spanish children.

From Stockholm, Sweden, comes an announcement that the l cal Spain Aid Committee has collected about £5,265, which with a further collection of nearly £2,630 from Gothenburg is to be sent to Barcelona.

The latter city is also pleased to receive a gift of 600,000 antidiphtheria vaccines from Dr. Junod, delegate of the International Red Cross Committee.

The North American Society of Friends combines the fight against starvation and disease with a gift of flour, enough to ensure 3,400 daily rations of bread to the children of Alicante.

December 7 1938

FRANCO PLANS NEW OFFENSIVE

ACCORDING to information in the possession of the Spanish Republican General Staff, General Franco is preparing for a new offensive in the district between the French frontier and the middle course of the River Ebro.

In this area about 25,000 Italian troops are now massing, while during the past few days attacks on the civilian population have been concentrated on the district between Barcelona and the French frontier.

(Incidentally, it is estimated that not more than seven per cent. of the bombs have been aimed at military objectives.)

During the past fortnight, fighting has been practically at a standstill on all fronts, except for an unsuccessful Fascist attack in the Sierra Guadarrama.

POSITIONS CONSOLIDATED

No attacks have been made on the recently won Republican positions on the west bank of the River Serge, which the Government forces have been steadily consolidating These positions threaten the communications between Lerida and the Fascist base and the worsening of the weather should make things increasingly difficult for the Franco forces isolated here.

The Republican General Staff is confident that the People's Army will be able successfully to hold the threatened offensive.

SPAIN ASKS BRITAIN

The Spanish Ambassador in London has informed the British Government that, according to information received by his Government, German and Italian aviation intend to intensify their aerial terror against the civilian population of the Republic.

He has asked the Under-Secretary for Foreign Affairs, Mr. Butler, what the British Government is prepared to do in face of these new crimes against humanity?

305 BRITISH MEN CROSS SPAIN'S FRONTIER FOR HOME

From FRANK PITCAIRN

LA TOUR DE CAROL, Tuesday.

THEY HAVE CROSSED THE FRONTIER AT LAST! THREE HUNDRED AND FIVE BRITISH MEMBERS OF THE INTERNATIONAL BRIGADE —SOME OF THEM MEN WHO HAVE SEEN TWO YEARS OF SERVICE IN SPAIN—REACHED THIS LITTLE FRENCH FRONTIER STATION THIS MORNING.

December 7 1938

They will not detrain at Paris, but according to present official arrangements will be routed round Paris and their carriages attached to the train leaving Paris for Dieppe at 10.19 tomorrow morning. They are expected to arrive at Victoria Station, London, at 6.45 p.m. tomorrow.

It was an extraordinary moment as these men, who have played such an enormous part in the history of our times, arrived in France at last on their way home. It was almost exactly the anniversary of the first naming of the Attlee Company.

On the platform were representatives of the local People's Front organisations, representatives of the Dependants' Aid Committee from Paris, and an efficient squad of nurses and doctors to take care of the wounded.

In the background local helpers worked strenuously preparing food and drinks.

HEAVY AERIAL BOMBARDMENT

For an hour before the train came, could be heard from beyond the mountains on the Spanish side the sound of heavy intermittent aerial bombardment.

It was feared that the Fascist planes were attacking the convoy of the British as they did that of the Americans a few days ago.

For the British Government's delay in bringing the men out has of course added immensely to the risk of the voyage.

However, this time they came through without danger.

Just after ten o'clock the little electric train crawled in, its sides decorated for the occasion with branches of fir, and every door and window packed with eager faces.

Major Sam Wild, very quiet and smart in a new civilian outfit, was first out of the train and took command of the detraining.

Looking from the train you saw the faces of men who were in Spain as long ago as December, 1936, men who were there at the birth of the British Battalion, amid the cold and mud of Madrigueras in January, 1937, men who fought in the incredible defence of Arganda Bridge, men who spent the summer of 1937 in those trenches on the Jarama, from which it seemed sometimes nobody was ever going to get out, and almost all of them who took part in that greatest military defence in the whole of the Spanish war, the battle of the Ebro.

They are carrying with them a new British Battalion banner just made in Barcelona, whereon, on a background of red silk, are inscribed the names of all the battles in which the Battalion has taken part.

TODAY AT
6.45 p.m.

the men of the British Battalion will arrive at Victoria Station, London. The Daily Worker calls on all London readers to rally to the station to give them a great welcome.

December 9 1938

Greetings and salute for a British Battalion standard-bearer as he stepped off the train at Victoria on Wednesday night.

December 13 1938

Dalston (London) Bus Garage hold a Food Day for Spain. Here are some of them busy loading up the food.

THEY ARE BACK!

British Men Reach London From Spain's Front Line

THE 305 MEMBERS OF THE BRITISH BATTALION OF THE INTERNATIONAL BRIGADE ARE HOME AGAIN. BACK TO A GREAT LONDON WELCOME THEY CAME YESTERDAY—BACK FROM THEIR FRONT-LINE FIGHT FOR LIBERTY AND DEMOCRACY ON SPAIN'S BATTLEFIELDS.

Thousands of people waited to cheer admiration of the bravery and self-sacrifice that had sent them from secure homes in Britain to risk death or wounds in defence of freedom for Spain and all the civilised world.

On the platform at Victoria Station waited representatives of the Labour Party, Communist Party, Liberal Party, trade unions and many other organisations as well as the mayors of a number of London boroughs.

December 8 1938

SAM WILD
who headed the returned fighters.

DOCKERS GIVE RED FLOWERS

From WALTER HOLMES
NEWHAVEN HARBOUR, Wednesday.

THE British Battalion of the International Brigade landed in England this evening. As the little steamer Versailles came slowly up the harbour in the twilight, the sounds of poderful voices singing was heard ringing over the water.

As the ship neared the keyside we could see the singers massed on the boat-deck and above them floating the colours of Republican Spain. Proudly held aloft was the Battalion banner presented in Barcelona, inscribed with the names of all the places in which the Battalion has been in action.

INTERNATIONAL

As the ship tied up, the International rang out until the surrounding hills seemed to echo. Never has the quiet of a December afternoon in Newhaven Harbour been dispelled by such a greeting.

When they began to file ashore. All looked tanned and fit. Last, a striking company, came the score of wounded moving slowly on crutches and sticks. Quickly and in orderly manner the Battalion was assembled on the special train which conveyed them to London.

The Battalion was divided into sections according to districts from which the men had come.

At the rear were the wounded under the guard of Dr. Tudor Hart, who returns with the Battalion to England after a long period of distinguished service in Spanish Government hospitals.

In a compartment forward I found Battalion Commander Sam Wild, Political Commissar Bob Cooney, Quarter-Master Hookey Walker, famous for his achievements in finding food for the Battalion in apparently impossible circumstances, Corporal Hugh Barker, of Manchester, longest serving member of the Battalion, having been in active service since November, 1936, without a break, and Ernie Woolley.

GREETINGS TO THE FIGHTERS

ALL over the country yesterday people were making preparations to welcome the returning members of the British Battalion. Below are printed greetings from well-known people.

WILLIAM GALLACHER (Communist M.P. for West Fife): The men of the British Battalion of the International Brigade now returning have written a page in history that will never fade, and those who have been carrying on the work at home will welcome back with all the great honour and admiration that is their due to take part in the fight here for food and aid to achieve the victory of the Spanish people.

WILL LAWTHER, Acting President of the Miners' Federation of Great Britain and member of the General Council of the Trades Union Congress: Heartiest greetings to lads who have returned from Spain. We in this country appreciate the services they have given to the cause of freedom and democracy.

TOM MANN: I rejoice that you have set the example you have by the work you have done, the courage you have shown, and the great things you have achieved.

We will continue that work now for Spain, and for all other similar workers throughout the world, we will go on, confident that we shall win ere long.

VERNON BARTLETT, Independent M.P. for Bridgwater: I am proud to join in welcoming men who, with none of the usual hysterical encouragements that accompany war have had the courage to fight under terribly hard and harsh conditions for an ideal.

I hope that they will put the same courage and energy into the job of giving us a better Britain.

MAURICE HANN, secretary Shop Assistants' Union: I gladly send a word of welcome to the members of the International Brigade. They at least had the courage of their convictions and took part in the actual fighting.

G. R. STRAUSS (Labour M.P. for North Lambeth): Welcome back to the country whose finest traditions you have so gloriously sustained. Your courage has inspired all those throughout the world who are struggling for peace and liberty and social justice. May your fellow citizens never forget the debt of honour they owe you.

The Standard and Wreath Bearers at the head of the British Battalion march to the Cenotaph to pay tribute to their comrades who died fighting for democracy in Spain.

Fighters At Cenotaph Take Pledge

TRAFFIC was held up and taxi drivers from a near-by rank left their cabs to join the ceremony when the returned members of the British Battalion of the International Brigade yesterday laid wreaths on the Cenotaph.

The wreaths were inscribed:—

"In memory of those of our members who gave their lives in Spain so that Peace and Democracy may live, we salute you."

A spray of white lilies, sent from Wales in memory of Harry Dobson, was laid with the red wreaths of the Brigade.

Major Sam Wild then made a short speech pledging the Brigaders to continue the struggle for peace and freedom at home.

December 10 1938

NEWCASTLE WELCOME

Prominent members of the Newcastle Labour movement met the members of the British Battalion from the North-East when they returned to Newcastle last night. They included the President of the Northumberland Miners' Association, the Labour candidates for East Newcastle and Central Newcastle, and representatives of the District Committee of the Amalgamated Engineering Union, the Council of Action, the Communist Party and the Spanish Medical Aid Committee.

"WE HAVE ONLY CHANGED FRONTS," said the men of the British Battalion to Leaders of every section of the Labour and Progressive Movement in Britain when they stepped from a train at Victoria Station.

"We want," they said, "to use all the experience we have gained in Spain for the purpose of leading a great campaign to obtain aid for Spain and to give the Spanish Government the rights that are its due.

"We want to help in overthrowing the British Government, which has done nothing but hinder the Spanish Government and bring distress and unhappiness to the Spanish people. We want everyone to help us."

Cheers rolled around the echoing cavern of the station; the banner of the British Battalion that had seen gallantry and sacrifice on every great battlefield of the Spanish war moved slowly down the long platform at the head of the flags of the 52 nations represented in the International Brigade; the crowd outside roared its greetings and so that's . . .

IN VICTORIA STATION—FLAGS OF ALL NATIONS

Flags of all the nationalities which made up the International Brigade, carried by men who are an honour to the very best spirit of their country are greeted by wave after wave of cheers from the waiting throng.

THE pictures on this page, vivid though they are, give little idea of the tremendous welcome accorded to the British Battalion of the International Brigade and its return to England.

Accompanying the scenes at Victoria Station shown here was the roar and thunder of cheering that went on and on as though it would never stop.

All round these scenes was a packed crowd of Londoners, numbering scores of thousands, the warmest and most tumultuous crowd seen in London for years.

The returned men have come back with an objective in view as urgent and important as the task they undertook in Spain. That object is best expressed in the farewell message sent to Dr. Negrin, Prime Minister of Spain, by the Battalion just before its departure. The message said:—

"We will never forget Spain or the Spanish people. We will work with all our might for the triumph of the Republic. We realise our responsibility. We know that the foreign invasion of Spain is only made possible by the reactionary policy of Chamberlain. Chamberlain will go. All the efforts of our Battalion will be concentrated towards this end.

"We have faith in you and in the people of Spain. You are fighting the battle of world democracy. Your splendid army and equally splendid rearguard have demonstrated their capacity for the battle.

"You will win the battle. Of that we have no doubt. It will be our task to see that the victory is a speedy one, by supplying you with arms and food, and securing the withdrawal of all supplies from the Fascist aggressors."

All those who admire the work done by the Battalion in Spain have, with the return of these men, an opportunity to indicate that admiration in a practical form. The best friend in Britain of every member of the British Battalion is and has been for two years the Wounded and Dependants' Aid Committee.

That Committee was never so sorely in need of funds as it is now, for the return of the 300 men of the Battalion has put a tremendous strain on its financial resources. The men have had to have clothes, food, railway tickets and many other things provided for them. Many need work, they all need help in some form or other. Will you help?

HOW THE BOYS CAME

December

THE NEW BANNER

In this banner on a background of red silk are inscribed the names of all the battles in which the Battalion took part. It was presented to the British Battalion, in the name of the people of Spain, when they were leaving Barcelona—from a free people to fighters for freedom.

LONDON TURNS OUT

Three hundred and five Members of the Battalion came back. Twenty thousand people turned out to welcome them. Leaders of all political parties waited on the platform with trade union leaders. It was a United Front of admiration for bravery and self-sacrifice.

As the steamer Versailles neared the quayside at Newhaven, powerful voices were heard over the waters, the singers massed on the boat deck and proudly held aloft the Battalion banner. The Internationale rang out. . . . The boys were back!

HOME!

10 1938

"TO STRUGGLE HARDER THAN EVER BEFORE"

The brigaders know, as William Gallacher, M.P., said, that they have a welcome home, "Not to rest, but to struggle harder than ever before to carry through to a conclusion the cause for which you have suffered so much."

"ENGLISH CIGARETTES—AH!"

Some of the boys came back wounded. They knew the risks before them when they went out, and they counted the cause worth it. Now they are back—to English cigarettes and perhaps a more comfortable mode of living—but they will carry on their fight for freedom in memory of those who did not come back.

TOM MANN AND THE BOYS

The cheeriest, youngest-looking fighter of the Labour Movement welcomes the other fighters back. Men after each other's hearts, and they showed it as they met on the platform.

Spain Ready For Franco's New Attack

From SAM RUSSELL

BARCELONA, Wednesday.

WHENEVER Franco decides to launch his expected new offensive on the Ebro front, he will find the Government ready with all its forces to break the attack.

During the month since the People's Army successfully withdrew across the Ebro, the entire forces of the country have been concentrated on preparations to meet a new enemy offensive.

All political parties and organisations have been in close collaboration with the Government. The Political Bureau of the Communist Party met and reviewed the situation in the whole Republican territory, on the basis of reports by Antonio Mije, recently in Madrid, and Francisco Anton, Secretary of the Party's Military Commission in Catalonia.

Summing up its conclusions, the Political Bureau confirms that the enemy, with foreign aid, is preparing a new offensive which may begin any day.

It also reports that the Republic can count on forces with which to face new attacks, but it issues the warning that **this time the enemy will redouble his efforts in order to achieve more decisive results than hitherto.**

"For this reason," the Communist Party concludes, "our activities and efforts must also be greater than ever before."

PREMIER REPORTS

The Prime Minister, Dr. Negrin, began the campaign of political preparation by calling together the National and Catalan Committees of the Popular Front.

After hearing the Premier's report these bodies expressed their firm support of the Government. The Governments of the Basque country and Catalonia did likewise.

The Co-ordinating Committee of the Socialist and Communist Parties met and gave added stimulus to the working-class unity, which is so vital to successful resistance.

One after another the executive organs of political parties and of trade unions have met and endorsed plans to meet the attack.

IMPATIENT FOR ACTION

The spirit of the people of Barcelona is expressed in the impatience for the latest news from the front. When the morning newspapers are read, and it is seen that one more day has passed without an enemy attack, there is almost a sigh of disappointment.

The news that the rearguard forces of Carabineers and Assault Guards have been mobilised for front line service was received with the greatest approval, especially by the units concerned.

Perhaps the spirit of those who await the enemy offensive is best expressed by an incident which occurred yesterday.

WANTS TO GO BACK

A Corporal of Infantry, Armando Diaz, who is recovering from wounds in a Barcelona hospital, presented himself at the War Office and asked to be taken to rejoin his unit at the front.

The Corporal has lost his three brothers in the war, and is the only son left in his family. His request was so insistent that it was granted by the Minister of National Defence, providing he is certified as fit for service by the medical authorities.

December 15 1938.

Dr. NEGRIN

Fascist Planes Active

From Our Own Correspondent

BARCELONA, Monday.

FASCIST patrols and reconnaissance planes have been very active on the Segre front during the past few days, where a new enemy offensive is expected.

The two forces in this sector are in the main separated by the River Segre itself. In the region of Balaguer to the north, the Fascists occupy a strongly fortified bridgehead.

December 18 1938.

HINDER ENEMY

To the north and south of Lerida the Republican troops who crossed the river during the Ebro fighting still hold their positions on the west bank of the river and hinder the enemy communications with Lerida itself.

Meantime the new Republican line on the Ebro has been very heavily fortified and the river is rising rapidly. Snow has already fallen in the Pyrenees and the enormous difficulties of an offensive against the Government line stretching from the mountain peaks down to Camarasa on the Segre are increased by the worsening weather conditions.

PREMIER'S APPEAL

Prime Minister Negrin yesterday appealed to the Army "to resist as never before."

"You will have to fight," he stated, "even more courageously and brilliantly than in the days of the Ebro. The foreigners must be beaten as never before and the enslaved Spaniards must be given the opportunity for which they have been waiting to free themselves of the foreign yoke and to co-operate with the patriots in the extermination of the invaders. Spaniards, fight without rest for the independence of Spain."

'ON LEAVE'

A homely street scene from the brave city of Barcelona. The Militia man, home on leave from the front, poses with his mother for the street photographer's camera.

Orphans To Run Own Village

A CHILDREN'S village in the hills of Catalonia is nearly ready to receive its population—one thousand war orphans.

These children, aged eight to fourteen years, will set up their own administration and grow their own food. The older children will be given professional education, and will in turn help to teach their juniors.

FOWLS ARRIVE

Fowls for the farmyard arrived on Tuesday. Spanish Children's Committees in 15 countries are responsible for this scheme to help children who are stated to be "much older than their years" because of their wartime experiences.

The village was planned by eminent French architects. It will have a library, farm, hospital, school, gymnasium, houses and playing fields.

MERSEY XMAS BOX TO SPAIN SAILS SOON

IN a few days time there will steam from the Mersey a foodship for the hard-pressed Spanish people.

By their own efforts the portworkers and other folk of the Merseyside have raised over £5,000 to stock the ship. £1,000 was raised in door to door collections.

Two tons of biscuits from the Crawford factory will be included among the cargo. In addition there will be four cases of women's and children's footwear from Dunlops.

Among individual towns Chester has collected £300, Wallasey £120, and Burnley £75. The warehouse in Hanover Street, Liverpool, is almost full of goods collected.

To safeguard the ship from attack by Franco pirates the identity of the ship is being kept secret.

December 10 1938.

GOVERNMENT SILENT

No reply beyond a formal acknowledgment has been received from Lord Halifax, who was asked to provide naval protection until the ship reached Spanish waters.

Already between 200 and 300 people, including seamen, clerks and accountants, have volunteered to serve on the ship.

VATICAN PROTEST TO FRANCO

SAN JEAN DE LUZ, Tuesday.

THE Papal Nuncio at Burgos has, during the past few days, visited the Fascist Minister of Justice, Count Rodezno, to protest, in the name of the Vatican, against the torture and execution of prisoners and hostages held by Franco.

He warned Count Rodezno that if any further protest were necessary, it would be made publicly. It is reported here that the Nuncio refused to attend a luncheon given by Count Rodezno, after he had entered a second protest against the pressure brought to bear on Cardinals Goma and Segura to force them to condemn attempts at mediation in Spain.

The Fascist Press has for several days been featuring stories alleging "religious persecution" and outrages against religious bodies in Republican territory.—(Spanish Press Agency.)

RAIN HOLDS UP FASCIST ATTACK ON CATALONIA

From SAM RUSSELL

BARCELONA, Sunday.

ALMOST exactly one year after the beginning of their victorious offensive at Teruel, the soldiers of the Spanish Republic are today waiting with equanimity for the long-heralded enemy offensive against Catalonia.

The enemy have been ready for more than a week now, but the attack has still not begun. The bad weather is certainly one of the reasons for the hold-up. But, judging from the reports received from the enemy rear, unrest behind the invaders' lines seems to be another.

The rain is slowly making the country over which the attack is planned impossible for the foreign Fascist tanks and heavy artillery, and each day they rely more and more on the five hundred German and Italian warplanes they have massed.

There is no doubt that this battle which is preparing will be one of the most difficult and, at the same time, one of the most decisive, but every day of rain is a day gained by the Republican command.

VISIT TO THE FRONT

Today I returned to Barcelona after a visit to the headquarters of the Republican army of the Ebro, where I discussed the coming battle with commander Colonel Modesto, with Political Commissar Delarge and with other officers and men.

I can now understand very clearly the extent of and reasons for their great confidence that the invaders are going to experience one of the most decisive defeats the People's Army has ever inflicted on them.

Six days of unending air raids by the German and Italian airplanes have only increased that confidence and that desire for battle—a measure of the military, moral and material improvements which this army has undergone since they recrossed the Ebro a month ago.

ENEMY TROOPS ARE MASSED

The enemy have concentrated their best soldiers and material along the whole line of the river Segre at the bridge-heads of Seros and Balaguer, right up to the north of Tremp. All the troops and guns that have poured into Spain since the Anglo-Italian Pact have been massed here.

Five Italian divisions, comprising some 75,000 men—"Arrows of all colours of the rainbow," as Modesto put it—are ready to push into action.

The enemy are risking more than ever before on this offensive. They have been forced to do so. Since July 25 they have suffered constant defeat. Simultaneously the pressure of the unrest in their rear is increasing.

BEHIND FRANCO'S LINES

Commissar Delarge told me of the activities of the "guerilleros" working for the Republic behind Franco's lines, with the assistance of the Aragon peasants and the people in the enemy-held territory of Catalonia.

He told me of two "guerilleros" who had just returned after 18 days

in Saragossa. These two men had organised

the blowing up of one enemy troop train and two bridges; they had distributed much literature especially the Thirteen Point Programme of the Negrin Government.

The anti-Franco feeling grows as the Thirteen Points are read by wider and wider circles in the enemy rearguard and is effectively encouraged by the nightly talks from the Republican radio station.

SPEECHES DISTRIBUTED

So great has been the effect of recent speeches by La Pasionaria and Modesto himself that the Franco stations have been forced to try to answer them directly.

The most recent speech by Pasionaria was, I was told, taken down in shorthand by nuns in a convent in Franco territory, reproduced in cyclostyle and distributed secretly in thousands of copies by the nuns themselves.

No Republican, however, attempts to minimise the seriousness of the enemy plans and everything has been prepared. Commander Modesto has himself supervised every preparation. He has toured the whole front more than once, he has visited every unit and discussed the position with officers and men.

"The traitor, General Garcia Velino, may have wept when he reviewed his troops that returned from the Ebro," Modesto said to me. "But before this battle is finished he will have cause to weep buckets full."

December 19 1938

Pictures show the exterior and interior of one of Spain's new hospital trains.

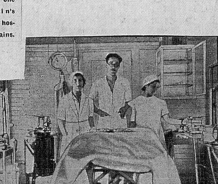

The Wounded Return To New Battles

By WALTER HOLMES

I WAITED on Newhaven quay on Monday evening for the homecoming wounded of the International Brigade, and wondered what they would talk about.

The Dieppe boat was late. It was almost dark when she appeared, rolling and pitching, her rigging sheathed in ice, slowly approaching the entrance to the harbour.

After the hasty rush of the ordinary passengers there was a pause. Then there appeared under the lights of the quay the figures of men bowed against the bitter wind, limping arm in arm, hobbling on sticks and crutches, moving painfully towards the Customs shed.

A Scottish voice reached me through the wind—"Give me sunny Spain."

"Ay, let's go back," came another.

Jesting their way in this fashion, the battered little column passed through to their reserved coaches on the train. The stretcher cases were carried in wi the kindly help of the station staff.

RUSH FOR "DAILIES"

I stepped into a saloon coach and cut the string of a parcel I was carrying.

"Anyone like a DAILY WORKER?" I asked.

There was a shout of surprise, and in a matter of seconds m 50 copies had scattered like snowflakes in the wind.

After that, talking was easy Straight out came matters that were uppermost in their minds. They were not the weather, nor the prospects for Christmas.

ORDERS FOR TEA

It came out as Pullman car attendants appeared to take orders for tea.

"Tea with sugar," was the chorus. And then one turned to me.

"When we crossed the Spanish frontier," he said, "we got a shock.

"We had forgotten that you could see food lying about, being wasted," he explained.

"And there, only a few minutes away, through that tunnel from Port Bou, there were villages all bombed to bits and people wanting food.

NONE FOR SPAIN

"It was a bit too much for some of our lads. And I don't mind admitting we all felt pretty near

weeping at the thought that not a scrap of that food is being got through to Spain."

Then the story turned to the send-off the Spanish people had given them. Such an ambulance-train, they declared, had never before been seen in Cerbere.

"And at Gerona," said one, "they gave us all coffee with milk. I expect you can guess what that means to them in Spain."

Admiration for the Spanish people, their generosity, courage, spirit, was an inexhaustible theme.

GIRLS SING ON

They told how, in hospital near Barcelona, they had been entertained with songs and dances by the local girls

One night, while an entertainment was in progress, the approach of bombers was signalled. The lights went out.

"Some of our chaps," one explained, "made for the trenches. You see they had been bombed so often some were a bit shell-shocked and nerves were a bit rattled

"But the girls just sat down in a circle on the floor and began singing Popular Front songs. That brought our chaps back, and soon we were all sitting round singing

"That's the sort of spirit they have in Spain."

COMING BATTLES

No one spoke much of himself. Most had received their wounds on the Ebro. But they were thinking now of coming battles

One, with a shattered foot and hand, summed up the general feeling when he answered my question as to what he would do now.

"I am going," he said, "to continue the fight for democracy here in Britain and to rouse the people of this country to drive out the Chamberlain Government."

December 21 1938

Foodship Rush In London

LAST-MINUTE efforts in London are likely to achieve the object of filling London's Christmas Goodwill Foodship for Spain.

The staff at Victor Gollancz, the publishers, have been making weekly collections of food and money, and girl members of the staff are selling vouchers among their friends to raise money

A number of South London sympathisers have forwarded £20 to the Committee at 4, Great James Street, W.C.1.

During a three-week campaign, Woolwich has collected £21 and 7 cwt. of food. Collections at a cinema showing "Blockade" raised £7.

GARAGE'S GOOD COLLECTION

A collection at Barking bus garage organised by the local branch of the Transport and General Workers' Union was well supported both by members of the Union and by non-unionists. The result was £3 10s. in money, 36 lbs. of food, tinned goods, and bundles of clothing.

The Goodwill Foodship will be given a send-off at a big meeting at St. Pancras Town Hall to-morrow evening.

Speakers will include the Dean of Canterbury, Professor J. B. S. Haldane, Lord Listowel, Rev. A. D. Belden, Mrs. Isobel Brown, Mr. Fred Copeman (former Commander of the British Battalion of the International Brigade), and Mr. G. R. Strauss, M.P.

EDINBURGH RAISES £1,000

In two days Edinburgh people have raised £1,000 for Spain.

This result was announced at the end of the Spanish Fair held at the Central Halls, which was attended by thousands of people.

Dr. Albert Einstein, the mathematician, is one of 39 prominent scientists who have sent from the United States to Barcelona a quantity of nicotine acid for the treatment of pellagra, a disease brought about by malnutrition.

COSTS LESS THAN A BOMB

"This gift costs hundreds of dollars less than a bomb that falls on Madrid," states a message from the donors.

"Men of science will always be grateful to the Spanish people for their brave fight against the invaders of their country in defence of free democracy," they add.

The gift is part of a cargo of food and medicine on its way to Spain on board the Erika Reed—the ship that armed Fascist trawlers tried to intercept off the coast of Spain last month.

When You Are By Your Fireside REMEMBER

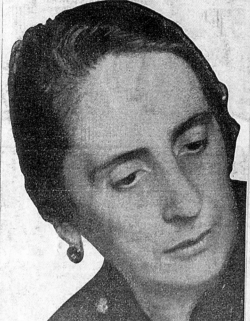

From Our Own Correspondent

BARCELONA, Thursday.

ON the occasion of the celebration of Christmas, Pasionaria, Republican Spain's foremost woman leader, has addressed the following appeal to the English-speaking people the world over:—

"Once more we are about to celebrate a universal holiday, that of Christmas. It causes further sorrow for our children and our womenfolk, who at this time recall days gone by spent in the warmth of their humble but happy homes.

"Thousands of women and children have been forced to flee before the advance of the invading hordes, in tragic exodus, along the roads and paths of Spain.

"Today they live, sad but determined, in refugee homes, where they are cared for by the Government of the Republic and that of Catalonia. They long for their homes and their native towns, which Fascism has destroyed and laid waste.

"All of you who, during these days of family gatherings and festivity, are enjoying the affection of your loved ones, remember the women and children of Spain who are suffering while they await a tomorrow of peace and well-being, which will be assured by the victory of the Republic.

"Help our children. Help our mothers. Make their lives less hard and less sad."

Two British women—a nurse and a radiologist—have saved hundreds of lives in Spain by their medical work. The nurse, Ann Organ, and the radiologist, Mavis King, working with two drivers, have in their charge a travelling operating theatre and a portable X-ray apparatus, sent from Britain.

One of the pictures here shows Mavis King attending a wounded man. The other picture shows the two travelling vans: on the left, Ann Organ in her operating theatre, and on the right, Mavis King with the radio apparatus.

X-RAYS in action. The Spanish soldier has been seriously wounded, and X-ray apparatus is being placed in position for an examination. Operators and apparatus were sent from Britain by the Spanish Medical Aid Committee.

Catholics Are For Republic

From SAM RUSSELL

BARCELONA, Friday.

THE growing feeling of free Catholics the world over in support of Republican Spain is reflected by the visit which the General Secretary of the French Catholic Committee, Madame Malaterre-Sellier, is paying here.

This Committee is one of the leading French Catholic organisations, and its honorary president is Cardinal Verdier.

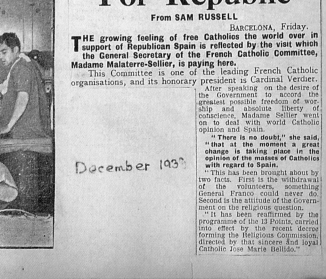

After speaking on the desire of the Government to accord the greatest possible freedom of worship and absolute liberty of conscience, Madame Sellier went on to deal with world Catholic opinion and Spain.

"There is no doubt," she said, "that at the moment a great change is taking place in the opinion of the masses of Catholics with regard to Spain.

"This has been brought about by two facts. First is the withdrawal of the volunteers, something General Franco could never do. Second is the attitude of the Government on the religious question.

"It has been reaffirmed by the programme of the 13 Points, carried into effect by the recent decree forming the Religious Commission, directed by that sincere and loyal Catholic Jose Marie Bellido."

December 1938

It's Different Over There
—IN SPAIN

BARCELONA, Friday.

AFTER five weeks' calm at the front, and in the coldest weather known for many years, Barcelona, together with the whole of Spain, prepares to celebrate its third war Christmas and New Year.

Spain prepares for Christmas, more confident than ever in victory, but at the outset it must be said quite frankly that because of the insufficient response by the democratic people, Spain prepares to celebrate the season of good cheer with the grim spectre of starvation looming over the whole country.

Spain has yet to face the two most rigorous months of the Spanish winter—January and February. Through all the Christmas and New Year preparations this problem presents itself with ever-greater urgency.

Spain needs food.

WITH the men at the front, it has fallen to the women of Spain, this year more than ever, to make the

◆◆━━━━━━━━◆◆

**FOOD RATION IN
MADRID IS . . .**

4½ ounces of bread

¾ ounce of rice

1-5 ounce of beans

1-7 ounce of chocolate

1-5 ounce of codfish

½ ounce of onions

1½ ounces of oranges

That's for Christmas dinner and all the other meals of the day—and it will be less on New Year's Day if we do not help.

◆◆━━━━━━━━◆◆

necessary preparations. The Women's Aid Committee, with the support of all the women's organisations, political parties and bodies, is certainly facing up to the task.

I have spent this morning speaking with women who have been working day and night during the past month. With them I visited the various institutions where their work lies. Quite naturally, the first care in Christmas preparations has been for the children, half a million being refugees in Catalonia alone.

The Women's Aid aims to give every child a New Year parcel. This will contain a toy or a book, a tin of milk, packet of chocolate, a cake, some soap, and a pair of gloves or socks.

The women have been working feverishly to prepare these parcels, and at the same time, after their working hours in factories and offices, have visited the children's colonies and restaurants, the refugee homes and hospitals, decorating them with streamers, flowers and bunting, creating a festive atmosphere.

This work is not limited to Barcelona or to the children. Groups of women and young girls have visited hospitals and refugee homes outside Barcelona, distributing special gifts of food and clothing.

THE Women's Aid is making an even greater effort to provide extra delicacies for the soldiers who lie wounded in the hospitals.

An extensive plan has also been

━━━━━━ *by* ━━━━━━

Sam Russell

*Our Correspondent In
Spain*

prepared to send personal parcels to the soldiers at the front.

As I could see, everything is prepared, and the organisation is ready, which can give Spain's children and sick a really happy Christmas.

All that is necessary is the food and clothing with which to make the parcels. Half a crown can buy one of these New Year packets, which will make happy some child whose father is at the front.

Half a million are needed. If you send food from abroad you will help a Spanish mother to prepare a meal for her child, and a parcel for her husband at the front.

IN this work of preparation for Christmas, Spain's leading woman, Pasionaria, has played a prominent part. I visited her after my tour of the refugee homes.

Pasionaria spoke with gratitude of the assistance from the North American Committee, from the Medical Bureau at New Zealand, the Women's Club in Johannesburg, from Canada and Australia. She spoke with gratitude of the foodships which the British people are preparing.

Yet not nearly enough food has come in for the Christmas campaign. Not only that, but not enough has come to meet the elementary needs of the civil population of Madrid.

PASIONARIA handed me a telegram which she had received this morning from Madrid, begging her to send food. It contained particulars of the daily ration on which the people of Madrid have had to exist for the past week.

It consists of ¾ ounce of rice, one-fifth ounce of codfish, just over half an ounce of onions, just over one-fifth of an ounce of beans, one and a half ounces of orange, four and a half ounces of bread, and one-seventh of an ounce of chocolate.

If help does not come next week, the ration will be even smaller.

The democratic peoples of the world, and, above all, the English-speaking people, can

(Above) A Spanish family being evacuated from a wrecked house in the icy cold of a Madrid December and (right) food queues in Barcelona last month, this month the people still queue up, but food is scarcer.

and must remedy this state of affairs. Spain's mothers and children are threatened with starvation if you do not come to their aid.

In Madrid, together with the shells of the invader, snow is falling. Throughout Spain the cold is intense. Spain's civil population needs clothes. It needs food, meat, fats.

At this season of good cheer, Spain appeals to the world; her call must not pass unanswered.

XMAS AMNESTY IS ANSWER TO MASSACRES

From SAM RUSSELL

BARCELONA, Monday.

IN his Christmas speech addressed to all Spaniards, the Prime Minister, Dr. Negrin, once more made an appeal for the humanisation of the war.

"Speaking to all my fellow-countrymen," he said, "I wish to take advantage of the significance of this day to appeal to our Spanish adversaries and to those who consider themselves as the Knights of the Catholic faith. I call upon them as Spaniards and as Christians to eliminate from this war, so far as possible, all unnecessary cruelty."

Dr. Negrin told how four months ago the Government proposed the suspension of all death sentences and proceeded to do so at once, although the rebels continued their mass executions.

"The Spanish Government," he continued, "wishes this measure to be extended to all those possible, and to this end proposes the suspension of the execution of all those who have been sentenced to death up to and including December 24, 1938; as well as all those who have committed crimes punishable by death, except those committed on the field of battle, always providing that the enemy undertakes and observes the strictest reciprocity.

"This proposal is in accordance with the continued desire of the Spanish Government to humanise the war.

NO REPRISALS POLICY

"We have considered as prisoners of war all those professional soldiers that we have captured. We have not inflicted the death penalty for merely political crimes. We have denounced the unjustifiable bombing of civilian population. We have discarded all measures of reprisal.

"The Government will continue in this line of conduct, ever reaffirming the tolerance which is the essential of our law.

Dr. Negrin also announced the suspension of all legal proceedings against those State officials and civil servants who for various reasons have been deprived of their posts—except in cases of high treason, rebellion, espionage, or flight of capital.

WAR OF INDEPENDENCE

Concluding his appeal, Dr. Negrin said:—

"At this moment, when you are hurling Italian divisions against a front of Spanish hearts, we are more confident than ever in our success and triumph. Here only Spaniards fight. We are fighting alone not in a civil war against compatriots, but in a war of independence against Moors, Germans and Italians. They came as lackeys and have made themselves the masters. We are fighting to free ourselves and to free you from this invasion. We shall conquer."

Mac-Paps Made Kiddies Merry

From SAM RUSSELL

BARCELONA, Wednesday.

WHILE Ottawa's official, specially sent to repatriate Canada's volunteers, tarried in Paris, the 300 volunteers of the Mac-Pap Battalion, still awaiting the signal to leave Spain, celebrated Christmas Day in the best tradition of the home country.

On Christmas Eve a dance was organised, in aid of the Fund for the Winter Campaign. Although it is three months now since the volunteers left the front they have not forgotten that the fight still continues, and their first thought was to provide warm clothing for the soldiers who have the winter campaign before them.

On Christmas Day 500 refugee children were entertained by the camp. In the morning sports were organised for the children, with prizes for the winners of the various events.

They then did justice to the magnificent meal which the battalion cook had prepared, with the help of the girls from the village.

In order to make this meal possible, every man had given up one-third of his ration for two days.

Although the turkey and Christmas pudding were absent, quantities of potatoes, rice, meat and chocolates made up for the deficiency. At the end of the meal each child was given a toy.

DANCE AND CONCERT

In the evening, while one hall was devoted to a concert for the children, another was given over to a concert and dance for the grown-ups.

Dancing ended the day, which will live long in the memory of the Canadian volunteers as one of the best Christmases they have ever spent.

Canada's volunteers asked me to send the season's greetings and their very best wishes to the comrades of the British Battalion and the British people, whom they hope to be seeing in the very near future.

Heavy Italian Losses

From SAM RUSSELL

BARCELONA, Thursday.

AFTER one week of intense fighting, in which the Italian army of invasion has thrown everything it has—troops, tanks, artillery and aviation—the enemy has been definitely held in the Lower Segre sector by the heroic resistance of the veterans of the Army of the Ebro.

Yesterday the material thrown against the Republican positions was even greater than before. After the artillery barrage had lifted, and with clear skies favouring, Italian aviation and tanks attempted to open the way through the Republican lines for the Italian March 23rd, the Vittorio, and the Arrow Divisions of All Colours. But it was in vain.

Mussolini's "warriors" soon discovered, however, that the army of the Ebro has not been idle during the past month. There is not a hundred yards of territory without its trenches, machine-gun nests, and bomb-proof shelters, from which the Republican infantry cut down the Italians when they attempted to advance.

In the Lower Segre sector alone, the Italians have lost between five and eight thousand casualties, killed, wounded and prisoner.

The desperation of the enemy can be judged from the fact that yesterday's offensive has been re-opened in the Balaguer sector, where the enemy had the advantage of an extensive bridge-head on the left bank of the Segre.

In all the sectors of the Catalan attacks, German and Italian planes have been forced down by our chasers and anti-aircraft batteries.

£5,300 OF CARGO FOR BARCELONA

AFTER three week's intensive effort, the plan to send a goodwill foodship from the people of London to the city of Barcelona has been realised.

In a few days time, the ship will sail with £5,300 worth of cargo—a magnificent demonstration of British aid to the Spanish democracy.

In addition to the 50 tons of assorted foodstuffs collected by the Borough Committees, the ship will carry 300 tons of dried milk, 25 tons of soap, 20 cases of beef extract, 2½ tons of coffee, 5 tons of cocoa, and 15 tons of dried fish.

This splendid result has been to a large extent due to the well-organised campaign in the Boroughs and the efforts of working class organisations.

For instance Dalston Bus Garage gave £15 and quarter of a ton of food, the De Havilland workers, half a ton of food, L.C.C. staff £30, Chelsea Spanish Aid Committee £45, a "group of business men £500, Finchley Spanish Aid Committee £107.

"ONE A MONTH"

At the send-off meeting representatives of many democratic organisations, including Ted Willis of the Labour League of Youth, Lord Listowel and Dr. Betty Morgan of the National Joint Committee, and the Dean of Canterbury, were present to send their messages of goodwill.

More than £600 additional money was collected at the meeting itself.

The Committee, well satisfied with the result, declares that the decks are now cleared for Foodship No. 2, and calls upon all Committees to continue the work on such a scale and with such energy that every month a foodship will leave the Thames with its life-saving cargo for Spain.

No Stopping This Horse

MANCHESTER, Wednesday.—The horse refused to stop at the traffic lights, the boys shouted in chorus, "Whoa Chamberlain," the man in charge of the reins tugged hard, and the packages of food on the lorry wobbled dangerously.

The Manchester traffic policeman started to argue, but the blizzard overhead and the ice underfoot were goading that horse to take the quickest course back home to the stable.

The boys were feeling the cold, too, especially as they had just returned from "Sunny Spain," but under the leadership of Major Sam Wild, these returned International Brigaders were determined to carry on with their good work.

STILL FIGHTING

The lorry was inscribed "The British Battalion continues to fight for Spain," and had already collected 200 tins of milk and scores of tins of beans, and there was 30s cash in hand, as the result of 1½ hours' collecting, door-to-door.

"We're going to canvass every district in this city," said Sam Wild. "Of course we would have liked a Christmas Party of our own, but we prefer to celebrate Christmas by getting food for Spain."

---

33 Dead And 100 Wounded

BARCELONA experienced the unhappiest New Year's Eve of all of Europe's capitals, when in three raids by Franco's Italian planes,

33 people were killed and 100 more, including eight women, were wounded.

The death-roll was, to a late hour yesterday, still incomplete and it was expected that further bodies would be recovered from the debris of destroyed buildings.

The majority of the bombs fell in the areas of the University and the Ritz Hotel and in the densely populated central section of the city.

"DELIBERATE"

The raids, said the Exchange Telegraph Barcelona correspondent yesterday,

bore the appearance of a deliberate attack on the civilian population of the city.

Five bombs fell within the space of 100 yards at one street corner. Five waiting cars were smashed to scrap.

A room in a hotel—used as a refuge for women and children—was narrowly missed when a bomb fell nearby smashing all the windows.

One of the raiders was forced down in flames by a Republican fighter.

NEW RAIN OF SHELLS ON MADRID

MADRID, Friday.—The deafening thunder of heavy artillery could be heard all over Madrid in the early hours of this morning, when the insurgents began shelling the Valescas district. Two hundred shells fell in the city.

Five persons were reported killed and 30 injured.

During a raid on Valencia today the British steamer Mirupanu was bombed and badly damaged.

The Mirupanu was holed in her side and on deck. Nobody on board was hurt, as the crew rushed to shelters when the ten Savoia machines which carried out the raid appeared overhead. Five barges were sunk.

The Mirupanu, a vessel of 2,539 tons, is owned by Wood, Skinner and Co., Ltd., of Newcastle, and her port of registry is Glasgow.

ART SHOW TO BRING FOOD TO SPAIN

EAST LONDON people have opened a fund for 1,000,000 pennies, to be used to send their own foodship to Spain to help prevent starvation from robbing the Republic of victory.

Central feature of this campaign is a splendidly illustrated eight-page paper called "The Voice of East London." This contains a full-length article from Mr. Attlee, and messages from Sir Stafford Cripps, the Mayor of Stepney, the Archbishop of York, and other political and religious leaders.

An exhibition will be opened by Major Attlee, with the Mayor of Stepney, at Whitechapel Art Gallery next Saturday at 4.0 p.m. The Exhibition will continue till January 15.

"Guernica," the famous Spanish artist Picasso's painting, will be on view.

During the same period film shows and other activities will take place nightly at the Art Gallery. Door-to-door collections will be taken.

The work is being organised by the East London Aid Committee, under the auspices of the Stepney Borough Trades Council and Labour Party. Offices of the Committee are open at 25, Leman Street, E.1, and volunteers for work will be welcome.

ABERTILLERY GIVES FREELY

Abertillery Trades Council and Labour Party have collected over £40 worth of foodstuff and £18 in cash. Almost every house in the town gave something. Women said: "I am sorry it is not more," or "Why don't you come more often?"

Counter-Attack By Republic Against Tanks

HEAVY fighting is reported on all three sectors of Catalan front, where Franco is carrying on his great offensive. Republican troops are maintaining resistance, counter-attacking in face of tremendous masses of material equipment used by the Fascists, says a Spanish Press Agency message from Barcelona.

In the Tremp zone, fighting was more violent than on previous days, and south of Montsech, the insurgents occupied hills of little importance after a number of fruitless attacks caused them extremely severe losses.

In the Balaguer sector, after intense artillery preparations, the insurgents resumed their attack in the Camarasa road. The first and most violent of several attacks in this sector was made at nine in the morning on a very narrow front.

Thirty tanks preceded the infantry in the assault, but the attack was broken and the insurgents were forced to retire.

After receiving reinforcements, the insurgents again attacked and succeeded in occupying positions at Montero, which were evacuated in orderly fashion by the Republican troops.

Two insurgent tanks were destroyed in these operations, and the insurgent losses were very high.

An Exchange Telegraph message from Madrid says that a Government communiqué issued there reports the Fascist capture of Granadella, 20 miles south of Lerida.

The main Lerida-Tarragona road is not immediately menaced.

In the Seres sector, Vertice Sabates was retaken in a Republican counter-attack.

Mr. C. R. ATTLEE, M.P., Leader of the Labour Party, welcomed by Mr. S. FRANKEL, wounded International Brigader, when he opened an Exhibition of Spanish Art at the Whitechapel Art Galleries, London. On right is Mr. Christmas, another returned fighter.

Profits from the Exhibition will go to the East London Food Ship which is to be sent to Spain.

KEEP HIM AWAY FROM ROME

P ACE out nine yards on the roadway. Picture a field gun where you began and a field gun at the end. Almost touching.

That is how thick Mussolini has placed his guns along whole stretches of the Spanish front.

One gun every nine yards is the density of his artillery there according to the Daily Telegraph correspondent on the spot.

That is a measure of what Mussolini thinks of the importance for him and Hitler of the offensive he is leading against Spain.

Pace the nine yards, and think what one gun every nine yards means in terms of Mussolini's wealth, in terms of the weight of fire the Spanish Republican Army is resisting.

Then read, if you can stomach so much cynicism, this remark from The Times yesterday. The Times says that Fascism does not profess "any desire to impose its ideas or its system" upon other people. Not at one gun per nine yards?

A DIFFERENT STORY

But The Times Rome correspondent had a rather different story to tell. Speaking of the Fascist Government he wrote: "There is little doubt that the Government are becoming anxious about the continued draining of Italian resources by the war in Spain, which threatens to cost as much in money and material as did the Abyssinian war. It has already cost far more in men."

In other words: the Duce has the wind up. And the medicine he wants to make him well again can be described in one word: Chamberlain. It is a physic that has been tried before. In May, Hitler had the wind up. He was faced with the powerful armed force and determination of the Czechoslovak people. He dared not go on. He could not go back. He was cracking.

He sent for the healing medicine of Fascist dictators—Chamberlain. And Chamberlain sent Runciman, and Runciman and Chamberlain together worked away undermining the defences of Czechoslovakia, and the end of it was Munich, and Hitler on his feet again.

Chamberlain is going to Rome to try to repeat Munich. But this is a tougher job. Spain is fighting. Diplomacy and threats alone will not do this time.

MILITARY ASSISTANCE

Chamberlain has got to bring to Mussolini something that will give the Duce some real military assistance. Something to help him beat the great army of the Republic that stands between the western world and the Fascist advance.

To find some arrangement—by belligerent rights or some other means—of giving Mussolini the military advantage he needs, is the central purpose of the Rome visit Chamberlain plans. It is the essential purpose. It is a cold-blooded attempt to find some way or another a means of beating by foul means the unbeaten arm of the Republic.

That is what the visit is for. That is why it ought to be stopped. Make no doubt about it: it can be stopped.

Within the Conservative Party itself is raised a growing volume of voices crying: "Don't go to Rome."

Millions of others join in that demand. Even the Sunday Times admits that the revolt against the visit forced the Cabinet to consider calling it off.

TIME WE WENT FORWARD

It is time we went forward in this country with the same assurance of victory that the Spaniards have: the same certainty of dealing confusion to our enemies as shines from the words of Premier Negrin broadcast a few days ago to the Fascist Generals, when he told them:—

"You are now making a supreme effort. Or rather you are forced to make it. You will not reach your goal. You will be broken by our unshakeable resistance, and we shall fight back with the same stubbornness with which we now parry the blow. We are fighting for Spain, and **WE SHALL BE VICTORIOUS.**"

HOMELESS Chinese refugee fleeing with all her belongings from the Japanese invaders halts for the night and takes the opportunity to give her small child a homely bath by the roadside.

January 3 1939

SHOULDER-HIGH

The youngest International Brigade officer, Major Milton Wolff, 23-year-old New Yorker, was lifted to the shoulders of his comrades in the disbanded Abraham Lincoln Brigade, when the 149 U.S. Volunteers on the side of the Spanish Government forces returned to the United States.

BRITISH SOLDIERS WHO DIVED INTO THE MEDITER-RANEAN IN THE DARK TO SAVE THE LIVES OF DROWNING SPANISH REPUBLICAN SAILORS WERE AMONG THE LAST HEROES OF A GALLANT, THRILLING AND DESPERATELY UNEQUAL NAVAL BATTLE BETWEEN DEMOCRATS AND FASCISTS, FOUGHT OFF THE ROCK OF GIBRALTAR YESTERDAY.

The Spanish cruiser Jose Luis Diez was last night aground in British territory at Catalan Bay, just east of Gibraltar, after being ordered out of Gibraltar harbour by the British Government authorities into the teeth of four vessels of Mussolini's Navy flying the Franco flag for the occasion.

Several weeks ago the Jose Luis Diez limped into Gibraltar damaged on its way from Falmouth.

A few days ago the British Government authorities suddenly gave orders that the Jose Luis Diez, now fully repaired, had got to be out of Gibraltar harbour by Saturday, December 31 (today).

The order was described by people in Gibraltar as "sheer murder." A big Franco cruiser was permitted to patrol just outside the entrance to Gibraltar harbour.

December 30 1938

ELUDED THE PATROL

Very early in the darkness of yesterday morning she nosed her way out of the harbour, and eluding the patrol in the darkness, looked like making a clean break-away south round Europa point.

But British-controlled Gibraltar is full of spies tolerated and even encouraged by the British authorities there.

From a window in dark Gibraltar a light signalled to the waiting patrol told the news of the leaving of the Jose Luis Diez.

Four Italian cruisers, which on the previous day had appeared flying the Franco flag, rushed off in pursuit.

The wolves found their small quarry.

The Jose Luis Diez was game. She fought back with everything she had—fired torpedoes at the Italian cruisers, blazed away with her small guns at the big vessels against her, and finally rammed and sank a Franco sloop before she herself went aground in Catalan Bay.

A number of the crew were dead and many others wounded. As the victims of this brutal agreement between the British and Italian Governments swam in the dark waters, British artillerymen heard their cries for help, and at risk to their own lives saved several of the men like themselves who were struggling in the Bay.

The four Italian cruisers were yesterday still cruising proudly within British territorial waters off Gibraltar.

The Jose Luis Diez has now been interned by the British authorities.

ITALIAN PLANES
USE NAZI BOMBS
From SAM RUSSELL

BARCELONA, Sunday.

EIGHTY-THREE persons were killed and one hundred and twenty-two were wounded when Italian warplanes, taking revenge for the frustration of Franco's plans at the front, bombed twice Barcelona last night.

It was the first time since the March days that bombs have been dropped on the Plaza Catalunya, Barcelona's Trafalgar Square.

On one occasion 25 bombs fell in rapid succession—all in the city's main thoroughfares. As they hit the pavement and exploded, the whole town was lit up by the lurid light.

I picked up some of the fragments of the bombs. Putting two of these together, I read— Rheinische Stahwerke, 1937. Mussolini's planes, Hitler's bombs!

One hour later, in his New Year's Speech to the United States, Spain's Prime Minister, Dr. Negrin, conveyed to the world the protest of the Spanish people against this new act of horror.

"I denounce," he said, "the crime that has been enacted here an hour ago." The ferocious bombardment of Barcelona, the most terrible that the city has suffered, has spread sorrow and mourning among our civilian population on this New Year's Eve.

"In the face of this new aggression we declare anew that in spite of the horrors and sufferings, we are certain that we shall triumph, not only in the struggle for our independence, but for the liberty of all men of liberal and democratic opinion."

Since Dr. Negrin's statement, more killed and wounded have been brought in to Barcelona's hospitals and mortuaries.

ITALY GAMBLING ON SPAIN PUSH

BOTH the British and the French Press yesterday stressed the enormous part being played in Franco's new offensive by the Italian troops; and the importance for Mussolini of a military success against the Spanish Republic before Chamberlain arrives in Rome.

Here are some typical comments:—

DAILY TELEGRAPH

"It is believed in Barcelona that the Italian troops have received drastic orders to secure success before Mr. Chamberlain's visit to Rome next week. Not since Guadalajara has Italian infantry been used in Spain on the present scale.

"For this push alone General Franco must have contracted huge debts of many millions of pounds to Italy. It is believed here that his debts to Italy totalled £100,000,000 before the present offensive. (Barcelona Correspondent.)

"Signor Mussolini personally desired that the Italian divisions should be given a place in the forefront of the battle, and he will urge that the heaviest support should be given to their attack in the hope that it can be represented to the Italian people as a big triumph.

"This knowledge lends some support to the view that the Duce was anxious to record such a success before the visit to Rome of Mr. Chamberlain. . . . It is therefore significant that Saragossa admits that the Italian divisions have been badly held up in their offensive." (Diplomatic Correspondent.)

NEWS CHRONICLE

"What good can come of talking with the Duce about Spain in the present circumstances? At this moment Italian legionaires, including veterans who were supposed to have been permanently withdrawn, are making a desperate effort to end the war in Franco's favour.

"If this is not an attempt to present Mr. Chamberlain with an accomplished fact in Rome or an attempt to blackmail him into the grant of belligerent rights to Franco, it is difficult to put any other interpretation on it.

"We think Mr. Chamberlain should call off his visit in which there is no possibility of good and much of evil." (Leading article.)

MANCHESTER GUARDIAN

"General Franco and Signor Mussolini both remember the influence the Aragon offensive in the spring had on the signing of the Anglo-Italian agreement. The desire now is for another victory before Mr. Chamberlain arrives in Rome.

"The Italian 'veterans,' whom all supposed had gone home with the 10,000 in October, have suddenly reappeared. . . . A failure to force his offensive home, let alone a defeat, might be disastrous for General Franco."

L'OEUVRE

Madame Tabouis writes:—

"Mussolini personally wanted this operation in spite of the opinion of military technicians and even Franco's General Staff. The Duce was determined and for months there has been considerable transport of men and materials to Spain.

"Mussolini hoped for a speedy and complete liquidation of the Spanish Republic. He based all his plans on this hypothesis."

January 4 1939

Italians Again Held In Night Attack

From SAM RUSSELL

BARCELONA, Tuesday.

ITALIAN attempt to batter down Republican resistance yesterday reached new records, but the enemy was again successfully held.

After a day of comparative quiet in the Tremp and Balaguer sectors, the battle raged yesterday along the whole front.

As on previous days, the fiercest fighting was in the lower Segre sector, where all the forces of the Italian command in men and material were employed.

From 9 a.m. till nightfall the Italian artillery battered away at the Republican lines in the sector of Pobla de Granadella.

As night fell, the shelling slackened off and, while the enemy guns were being trained on the Republican rear, Italian tanks loomed out of the uncertain light, in another attempt to open a passage for Mussolini's "Black and Blue" Arrow.

This time, in the direction of the road from Pobla de Granadella to Ulldemolins, the Republican troops fought every inch of the way, and the total result of the enemy advance, after the whole day's fighting, was the occupation of three hills of no importance.

In the adjoining sectors of Albajes and Bisbal de Falset, the fighting continued far into the night, with no result except the loss of hundreds more crack Italian troops.

"HAS GOD TURNED HIS HEAD AWAY FOR A LITTLE WHILE?"

HEARTBREAK pictures in their thousands have been collected in the last few years by the News Chronicle from China, Abyssinia, Spain and Czecho - Slovakia, but photographs that came from the French frontier last night were as harrowing as any.

They tell, more eloquently t h a n words, what the people fleeing from Catalonia are suffering.

Heading on this page is quoted from an article by Captain G. E. Lennox-Boyd, which appeared in the London "Star" on January 19. He told of the horrible things he had seen in Spain and ended with that dreadful question.

Children on right are enjoying their first meal after reaching the sanctuary of French territory.

First Message From Spain

People of Britain, as you know that at the frontier and with the connivance of your Government, troops are beating back refugees?

Do you know that women and children, who have treked by foot miles from Barcelona, starving and fainting, are being treated worse than animals?

Do you know that women and children have had to spend nights in the pouring rain, with no shelter, and not even the slightest medical attention?

Women are giving birth to children on the roadside. Tiny tots, who can scarcely walk, struggle along with bundles. Crazy with fear, they have fled before Moors and Italians, and when they arrived at the frontier, they are faced with a double line of French troops, with rifles at the ready—the frontier is closed till seven o'clock tomorrow.

GHASTLY PLIGHT OF REFUGEES

That is the order, and in the meantime, women faint.

Here a soldier, with two legs off, bleeds slowly, while near him another, blind and his head swathed in a dirty, blood-soaked bandage, falls in a dead faint.

All around me more than 20,000 women and children clamour for food. There is no food. There is no warmth. There is no shelter.

Before I left Figueras I had a few words with Rodriquez Vega, General Secretary of the Spanish Trade Unions.

"In these moments," he said, "there is one thing which I wish to tell the British people in general, and the British working class in particular. The roads to Catalonia are the witnesses of the results of the criminal policy of Chamberlain.

"All your efforts must be directed, in the first place, to the salvaging of the victims of this policy. Every woman or child that dies of hunger or cold is one more blot on Britain's name.

CATALANS NOW HITTING BACK

From GEORGES SORIA
(Special Correspondent of the Paris News Agency "France Monde")

PERPIGNAN, Tuesday.

IN the last 48 hours there has been a complete transformation in the position in Catalonia. Order has been restored, and confidence remains. In spite of all the weight of artillery, tanks and airplanes, the Italian forces have not been able to advance more than a few hundred yards.

The armies of the Ebro and the East, commanded by Colonels Modesto and Perea, which make up the Catalonian Army, are resisting fiercely on lines established to the west of Vich and Arenys de Mar.

General command of the army, up to now in the hands of General Sarabia, has been taken over by General Jerudo, ex-inspector of artillery in the central army, while Colonel Gordon is acting as chief of the General Staff.

BETTER THAN EVER

Not only is the Catalonian army not beaten: it is in a better position than before Barcelona was taken. The main reason for this is the remarkable change there has been in the situation in the rear.

Today in Figueras—where yesterday all was disorder—there is calm, discipline and determination.

As we walked through the streets this morning we heard the sound of drums. It was a newly-formed battalion of three companies marching by. Composed of volunteers of all ages, the battalion marched in perfect order.

Many such battalions are being formed. Their aim is the defence of Catalonia from Italy. They will carry it out if provided with enough ammunition.

These men are joining up in response to appeals made yesterday by the National Committee of the U.G.T., the Spanish Communist Party and the United Socialist Party of Catalonia.

From GEORGES SORIA (Correspondent of the French news-agency, France Monde, one of the last journalists to leave Barcelona)

AT mid-day on January 24 Barcelona was subjected to its 44th bombardment in four days.

A few minutes later I finished telephoning a story—and then telephonic communication with the outside world was finally broken off.

Isolated, the Catalan capital was to live two unforgettable days. I went to the station. There were the trains full of refugees, as I had seen them many times before.

But there was not a living soul in the whole station except the old men, women and children, who were waiting for the refugee train to move out.

There were vast craters, 12 feet across. They were red with blood. Mangled bodies of children lay across the railway lines.

In the afternoon there were aerial battles over the city. Fifth column men took advantage of this to fire from windows, attempting to create disorder. On the front, a short distance away, guns fired without cease. Air raids followed in quick succession.

It was an inferno, a continual rain of steel and fire.

"WE HAD NO ARMS"

The Italians I saw, had crossed the Llobregat. I spoke to Colonel Modesto. "After the battle around Martorell," he said, "we had only 200 men of a brigade left. We had no arms. If we had had machine-guns, artillery, all this could be changed. We have the men, but they cannot fight without weapons."

The wall of steel advanced towards the city. The workers' organisations made a supreme effort. Thousands manned the barricades, hundreds of young girls braved the fire of Italian machine-guns to dig trenches.

But step by step the Government forces were compelled to retreat under Italian artillery fire. Moorish troops rushed the barricades; then, shooting men and women as they passed, rushed to the centre of the city shouting their war-cries.

The massacre was about to begin.

MACHINE-GUNS FOR REFUGEES

From young Socialists who escaped at the last minute I heard how machine guns had been turned on those who had not been able to flee... One cannot even guess how many are dead.

On the road from Barcelona we passed some of the two hundred thousand people who were escaping. Bombarded without cease, their condition was indescribable. On their faces, fearful distress, but fierce determination. Only one thought, abandon everything, but flee, flee from Franco.

Resistance is being organised Catalonia is not Barcelona. New lines are being constructed. The Catalan people will resist. If they are armed, they will yet conquer.

February 1 1939.

SPAIN RE-FORMS
ITS FRONT

Thousands Rush To Fighting Line

FIRST MESSAGE FROM FIGUERAS

From SAM RUSSELL

PERPIGNAN, Monday.

IN THE PAST THREE DAYS I HAVE BEEN THE ONLY BRITISH CORRESPONDENT IN FIGUERAS AND GERONA.

With communication by telephone still impossible from Figueras, I have been forced to leave Spain to transmit the message of the Spanish people to the people of Britain in these critical moments.

The message is that of over 15,000 people in Figueras last night, and over 30,000 in Gerona the day before.

"Spain is not beaten. Neither is Catalonia."

In the failing light and in a tremendous downpour of rain, 10,000 men marched last night from Figueras to the front.

Their wives and families, refugees from Fascist terror, accompanied them, while the entire population gave them a send-off never before seen in the history of this little frontier town.

It was a demonstration of confidence in the measures taken by the Government

As in many difficult situations in the past, Spain is already showing that, in spite of the fall of Barcelona, and the advance of the invading troops, the front will be reformed, and the Fascist advance held.

Whatever the rest of the press may say Daily Worker readers can be assured that Spain still has the possibility of triumphing over the Italians and Moors.

This truth, which represents Spain's iron will and determination can and must be made into a reality by the action of the British people.

In spite of the terrible losses that the Republican troops have sustained, due to their lack of arms, the morale is still high; in spite of the fact that one brigade, for instance, was reduced to 200 men, they still fight on.

As Colonel Modesto said, "If we only had a certain minimum number of machine-guns, mortars and artillery, the situation could be changed immediately."

While the enemy is attempting to create further disorder, bombing ferociously all the towns and villages along the Catalan coast, the Government was in session, planning the re-establishing of the situation.

Already results can be seen.

SPAIN AND THE WORLD

The situation can be changed. The democratic people can count upon Spain now as never before

The question now is: Can Spain count upon the people of Britain, and decent-minded people the world over?

From all organisations, from all decent minded people, the cry must go up to open the frontier; to send arms for Spain's fighters; food for Spain's mothers; to receive those women and children, who, by the thousand, are streaming along the roads, seeking a haven where to rest.

Passing through the frontier at Le Perthus, I was appalled at the treatment being suffered by the refugees.

Feb 2 1939.

3,000 Shot, Food Riots In Barcelona

THREE thousand Republican supporters, down for execution on Franco's notorious " death-lists," have been shot without trial in Barcelona.

Food riots, led by the women who stood for hours without murmur in the long food queues before the city fell, are taking place daily and have been admitted both in Barcelona and in London.

So serious, from the Fascist point of view, is the situation that **General Franco's " triumphant entry " into the former Republican capital—scheduled for last week—has still not taken place.**

In an attempt to " establish order," Suner, the Franco "Minister of the Interior," is rushing through preparations for the establishment of permanent military tribunals.

So far there has been no order to the terrorised population to come forward and denounce Republican supporters. But such an order will, it is learned, be made soon in the Fascist Press.

The machinery for military terror is also being established in all the other towns and villages in Catalonia occupied by the invaders.

Permanent military tribunals are to be set up, and these, according to announcements made on Monday night by the Salamanca and Saragossa radios, will deal "summarily" with " enemies of the new Spain."

BARCELONA RIOTS

This information received in London yesterday from impartial observers who have been in Barcelona since its occupation by Franco also confirms reports that **The population that remains is hungrier today than it was before the Republican withdrawal.**

One of these reports from the Daily Telegraph and Morning Post Barcelona correspondent, gives the following description of one of the food riots:—

" Hundreds of hungry women, many carrying babies in their arms, tried to force their way into a bread distributing centre an were driven back by police, Civil Guards and soldiers. . . . Those at the head of the queue were admitted only one at a time and at long intervals, murmurs arose, the queue was finally broken and the women thronged around the entrance.

"Iron grilles were hastily dropped in front of the door. The crush grew terrific as the women, now frantic, dashed forward crying: 'Bread! Bread! Give us bread.' Many were holding tiny children high in the air.

"Then the police began to lift people bodily and hurl them back, but the hysterical women took no notice. Soldiers appeared, entered the melee and cleared the pavements.

" At the height of the confusion—with women screaming, children crying and men cursing—a notice was posted at the door: ' All stocks exhausted for the day. Try again tomorrow.'"

It appears that 100,000 rations of chocolate and some other food—although in very small quantities—is all that has so far been distributed.

REPUBLIC GAINS GROUND IN HEAVY FIGHTING

From Our Own Correspondent

GERONA, Tuesday.

VIOLENT fighting yesterday just north of Mataro, on the line of Franco's advance along the coast, resulted in the Republican troops throwing back the enemy at least two miles.

On other sectors of the front there was also heavy fighting in which the Republican forces held off repeated attacks by Italian divisions.

The loss of Barcelona does not mean the loss of Catalonia, said President Companys, speaking at Figueras yesterday.

" Much territory yet remains to us " he added. " We will resist the invader inch by inch. We will summon all our forces and all our resources against the enemies of our country."

MORE ARMS

The attitude of President Companys bears out the statement of Premier Negrin at the week-end.

" As for war materials," he said, " overcoming the difficulties put in our way by non-intervention and the sea blockade, the Government has succeeded in assuring abundance of material, which—well utilised—will present the enemy with an unconquerable barrier. These fresh reserve troops, this new material of war, has now been put into operation.

" This material arrives late," said the Prime Minister, " as it arrived late at Madrid, but it has arrived in time, as it arrived in time in 1936."

WOMEN APPEAL

Margarita Nelkin, a deputy of the Cortes has addressed the following telegram to the Duchess of Atholl, Mrs Roosevelt, Madame Cardenas, wife of the president of Mexico, Isabel Blum, a Belgian deputy, and Senator Branting of Sweden:—

"In the name of Spanish women, whose sons and husbands are determined to fight to the end against the Italian and German invaders, I ask you to use your influence to see that milk and food are sent via France for the thousands of women and children fleeing from the Fascists. We also need most urgently large cars to assist evacuation

"We are sure of final victory. We ask only for solidarity from the democratic nations."

SPORTSMEN WHO WENT TO SPAIN

By George Sinfield

(Daily Worker Sports Editor)

IN these days of bitter back-to-the-wall fighting by Republican Spain, when all available forces are marshalled to meet the hordes of Fascism, when the terrible inner enemy of hunger is ravaging the country, every true democrat must be filled with burning anger.

When we reflect a little on those glorious British lads who risked all, gave all, in the cause of liberty in Spain, we must hang our heads in shame that this rape of a proud people should be allowed to continue.

MANY were sportsmen; grand sportsmen with a mission and ideal. I want to tell you about some of them.

Tom Picton, of Treherbert, South Wales, was killed by one of Franco's mob when a prisoner. Tom was once the amateur middle-weight boxing champion of Wales, and later, during the 1914-1918 war, became light-heavyweight champion of the Navy.

Twice Tom's ship was torpedoed, and twice he received decorations for bravery.

So, you see, he was a man, a very brave man; and human. So full of feeling.

FROM the front line trenches he wrote many letters to George Thomas, a pal. Here's a sentence or two from one of them:—

"George, I would be pleased if you would see about my girl (his daughter); I mean that she's in a good place. Tell her I am A1, and to look after herself, not to worry about me, and explain what we are fighting for, or she won't understand."

"TAPPY," or Walter Tapsell, was killed at Calaceite. A magnificent fighter if ever there was one.

He joined the Workers' Sport Movement about 1926, and two years later toured the Soviet Union with a football team. He was a half-back, not outstandingly clever, but with a big heart, and foraged with the best.

I can see him now among my mental impressions. We played a superior side in Moscow. The end of the match found him spent to the wide. He gave everything. That was Tappy.

WHEN Speedway roared its way into popularity in this country, the crowds loved the name of Clem Beckett, another of the older school of worker sportsmen.

Clem met his death at Jarama. He had a vivid life as a speedway rider. Fighting for his colleagues' interests, Clem was expelled from the controlling organisation.

Particularly daring, he hurtled round and round the "Wall of Death" in several continental countries and introduced the thrill of speedway to the Russians in 1931.

Soviet workers raved about Clem. His deeds on the track sent them crazy with excitement.

LEWIS CLIVE was another outstanding sportsman whose brilliance was cut short when he gave his life in Spain.

An Oxford Blue, Clive rowed Number Six in the Boat Race in 1930 and 1931. In the next year he successfully competed in the double sculls for England in the Los Angeles Olympic Games.

Then there was Phil Richards, of St. George's, now immortalised in Spain's Roll of Honour, who won fame as a professional boxer.

Tommy Flynn, of Glasgow, George Hardy, of London, were cyclists of exceptional ability. Both competed in the Soviet Union, while Hardy also earned tremendous popularity in Paris through his skill on the track.

EAST LONDON sportsmen will always remember Sam Masters as an athlete in the true sense of the term.

Bill Tattam, of Newcastle, could use his mitts. In a bout in Spain he defeated Danny Shugrue, an American, later wounded at Brunete, who once fought Benny Leonard, former light-weight champion of the world.

Bill Meredith, killed by a Fascist at Brunete when attempting to save the life of a woman, also revelled in boxing.

JOE NORMAN—they called him Norman The Butcher in his ring days—wrote the other day telling me of his experiences in Spain. Joe once pleased Soviet fans by his skilful boxing.

A name which brings to mind the one and only Bobby Walker, famous Scottish international footballer, the man who received nearly 30 international caps, is Bobby Walker, the son.

Son Bobby carried the tradition of Scots football into Spain. He can tell of many enthralling games with Spaniards.

THESE men have proved that British sportsmen have very close to their hearts the cause of liberty. That they are fighters for fair play; strugglers for all that is decent in humanity.

Remember that just as the General Purposes Committee of the Amateur Athletic Association threw into the waste paper basket the invitation to take part in the Olympic Games, when the Games were scheduled for Tokyo in 1940, so, too, can the members be moved for progressive action on behalf of Spain.

THESE British sportsmen and women saw only too clearly that the mere suggestion of holding this athletic festival in a country waging war on an innocent people, prostituted the very ideals upon which that festival is founded.

How far, then, are the majority of British athletes away from the cause for which Republican Spain is fighting day in and day out?

They are just round the corner.

We all know that British sportsmen are lovers of fair play. The war of Chamberlain, Hitler, Mussolini and Franco is a degrading alien invasion against a noble people.

On these grounds alone British sportsmen can be won in support of Republican Spain.

Never have lovers of fair play and sportsmanship a more urgent duty to perform. This is the hour of Spain's greatest need.

February 2 1939.

Picture on left is of refugees building a temporary encampment at Argeles-sur-Mer under the supervision of French soldiers.

NURSES PUT SYMBOL OF BLOOD ON DOOR OF NO. 10

WHILE NURSES FROM SPAIN DISTRIBUTED LEAFLETS AT THE ENTRANCE TO DOWNING STREET YESTERDAY DECLARING THAT NEVILLE CHAMBERLAIN WAS RESPONSIBLE FOR THE DEATHS OF MEN, WOMEN AND CHILDREN IN SPAIN, TWO GIRLS WALKED UP TO No. 10 AND THREW RED PAINT OVER THE DORWAY.

The paint was intended to be symbolical of the blood spilt in Spain. The girls were nurses who recently returned from service with the Spanish Republican forces, one of them being Angela Guest, particularly well known for her work, and the other Eileen Palmer. Both were arrested.

The leaflets said: " Chamberlain is guilty of blood that has flown in Spain for two and a half years, because the legal Spanish Government has been deprived of the right to buy arms to defend itself against foreign invaders.

" We British nurses who have served in Spain demand that Spain be given back her right to defend herself. Open the frontier! Send arms to Spain! Save Spain, save Britain, save peace!"

The girls, who had shouted " Arms for Spain " as they threw the paint, later appeared at Bow Street Police Court charged with " insulting behaviour " and with damaging property. The charge of insulting behaviour was withdrawn, but they were bound over for six months and ordered to pay 5s. damages for damage to property.

A young Spanish refugee, just arrived in the safety of a French police post on the frontier, uses a trunk on which to write to some loved one still in the firing line.

February 1, 1939.

The Dependants' Aid Committee of the International Brigade has just issued a financial statement covering the activities for two and a half years preceding last November.

About £48,000 has passed through its hands, the money being contributed from all parties, including Conservatives.

Miners have sent it more than most people. For some time now the South Wales miners have sent about £12 per week.

Jobs For Brigade

As I mentioned some time ago, the Committee is running an employment bureau for ex-fighters and 56 have been found jobs.

Off on the high seas are Jack McNalty, sailing in a food ship for Spain, and young Jack Dempsey, who has found a job as a galley boy.

John Penrose has started as orderly in a London hospital, and teacher John Angus has been found another teaching job.

February 3 1939.

Rigours of the Spanish refugees' flight into France are intensified by snow. Pictured are two refugees, one with a baby, trudging through a blizzard.

REPUBLICAN SPAIN FIGHTS ON "TO THE BITTER END"

From WILLIAM FORREST
News Chronicle Special Correspondent

FIGUERAS, Thursday.

AT two o'clock this morning, in the bomb-proof vaults of the fortress of Figueras, Dr. Negrin and his Government received a mandate from the Spanish Cortes to carry on to the bitter end the fight "for the defence of the Republic and the independence of Spain."

After speeches from the party leaders pledging support for the Government, the Speaker, Don Diego Martinez Barrio, called upon each of the deputies in turn to rise and answer "Yes" or "No" to a declaration of "no compromise."

Negrin : "Si," said the Prime Minister.

Del Vayo: "Si," said the Foreign Minister.

Gonzales Pena : "Si," said the Minister of Justice.

And so on down the Government Bench draped in the traditional blue, and along the rows of deputies, with not a single negative response.

LONG LIVE SPAIN

When the vote was over someone cried : "Long live the Republic ! Long live Spain !" and the vaults rang with the answering "Viva."

Even the carabineers standing guard at the stairway joined in the cry. I wonder if there has ever been a more dramatic moment in the long history of Europe's oldest Parliament.

Sixty-two deputies were present, and among them one woman, Margarita Nelken. Many deputies, including La Pasionaria, are over in the Madrid zone.

The reasons why the Republic is determined to fight on were stated briefly by Dr. Negrin in an eloquent speech to the Cortes. It was not, he said, a civil war they were fighting, and it was something more than a war of independence. Spain was fighting for her very existence as a nation.

THREE DEMANDS

He reduced his famous 13 points to three essential demands :

1. Guarantees for Spain of her independence and her territorial integrity.
2. Guarantee of the liberty of the Spanish people to decide their own destiny.
3. Guarantee that after the war there shall be an end to all persecution and repression.

Dr. Negrin analysed the causes of the Republic's present difficulties, among which he stressed the "organised panic" in the rearguard.

"The provocateur and the rumour-monger have been our worst enemy," he said. "Within three days, however, order and discipline had been established without recourse to bloodshed."

The military situation he summed up in the statement that although the Government had lost territory the enemy had not succeeded in his prime aim—the destruction of the Republican Army.

The Government would defend this corner of Catalonia, and if that went there remained a central zone, where the struggle for their existence would be carried on.

[According to a Reuter message, Dr. Negrin in his speech said : "We have been forced to deal in contraband arms. We have even bought them—why not say so ?—in Italy and Germany.]

POT-AU-FEU
—young Spain refugee at Argeles adds the condiments

HOW LONG ?

Denouncing the strangulation of arms for Spain yesterday, Dr. Negrin is reported to have said:—

"Our friends have forced us to buy arms here, there, everywhere, where we could Even—why not say it?—in Italy and Germany."

The statement, if correctly reported, is at the same time a hideous condemnation of the democratic "friends" of the Republic, and a tribute to the hard-boiled ingenuity and realism of the men who work for the Republic.

Even to the corrupt and corruptible arms-sellers of Germany and Italy they had to go, offering them high prices for the arms Chamberlain would not let them buy in Britain. How long, British people?

Spain's Fighting Cabinet Meets In Secret

February 3 1939.

YESTERDAY, one week after the fall of Barcelona, the Government of the Spanish Republic met in the noblest session in Spain's history.

Sam Russell, correspondent of the Daily Worker, was present at this historic occasion. In the despatch below he tells you about it.

This heroic story of order brought out of chaos, of sheer, unbeatable, human effort in the face of odds that might seem overwhelming, is the answer to the feeble-hearted, feeble-headed defeatists who thought " Barcelona lost . . . all lost."

It is more than an answer—it is a challenge. Spain fights on. Spain calls for arms. Britain can act. Must act. NOW.

CAMPAIGN PLANNED IN CASTLE CELLARS

From SAM RUSSELL

FIGUERAS, Thursday.

"THE safety of the world is being decided here in the foothills of the Pyrenees."

Voicing the grim determination of the Spanish people to fight on to victory, Dr. Negrin, in his speech to the Cortes, thus placed the war in Spain in its proper perspective in the world today.

This was the fourth meeting of the Cortes which I have attended : it was the most dramatic, the most historically significant meeting of the people's representatives that Spain has ever seen.

Up to the last moment no one knew where it was to be held

At the last minute, shortly after 11 o'clock, members of the foreign Press, together with the deputies were taken to a castle at Figueras

Passing through one gateway after another we finally came to the centre of the castle, and going down into one of the dungeons beneath, we found the hall prepared for this meeting of the Cortes.

SIXTY-TWO

SIXTY-TWO DEPUTIES

Sixty-two deputies had met to hear the Prime Minister outline the course of events since the last meeting, and review the actions of the Government.

Dr Negrin's speech constituted the most damning indictment of the action of the democracies and above all of Britain.

As I looked at the faces of the Ministers on the Government Bench I could see the strain which each and everyone of them has undergone during the past few days. All were there. At Dr. Negrin's side was Spain's Foreign Minister, Alvarez del Vayo, and then the rest of the Cabinet, including the two Ministers without portfolios, Signors Giral and Bilbao.

SITUATION AT THE FRONT

Dr. Negrin spoke of the situation at the front, of the heroism of the Republican Army.

"Never has there been such heroism as that shown by our soldiers who have gone back time and again to continue the fight. I have seen them this morning. I have seen how many of them have had to fight without arms, have had to wait till one of their comrades fell before taking up a rifle."

On my way into Spain from the French border I passed some

thousands of soldiers returning to the front. The measures taken by the Government had inspired them with new confidence and overcome the temporary panic and fear which overtook some of them. They return to the front of their own free will, to take up the fight again, no matter how great the odds.

ARMS GOT ILLEGALLY

Speaking with them, I discovered that they know that they are returning to a front which has been deprived of arms by the action of democratic Governments, because of the inaction of the British people.

The Spanish people and its Government know that Catalonia can be saved if the democracies do their duty.

Dr. Negrin pointed out how the Government had been forced to obtain its arms illegally, that it had met with difficulties on every side.

"That control which forced us to buy arms contraband was formed not only by our enemies, but by our so-called friends who talked of a blockade at our ports."

Despite all these difficulties, arms have been obtained. They have arrived by road and in very small quantities.

Yet, as Dr Negrin said: " They will assist us in establishing a line and to smash the enemy even now. Our front is made up of men who still maintain their high morale and their determination to fight on for they know they are fighting for their very existence."

One after another the representatives of the various parties rose to voice the confidence of the nation in the Government, presided over by Dr. Negrin Republicans, Socialists, Communists, representa-

SPAIN: *Barcelona Falls, Refugees Surge Into France; Premier Negrin Still Confident of Republican Victory; General Franco Prepares Decisive Battle for Valencia*

THIRTY - FOUR days after launching his offensive across the Segre River, General Francisco Franco, Thursday, stood on Montjuich fortress overlooking his objective, watched his Navarrese, Moorish, Italian divisions enter Barcelona.

Overhead flew Italian aviation squadrons, observing in brilliant sunshine the progress of Insurgent occupation as a forest of flags grew above the houses all the way from fortress to harbour.

By noon the whole magnificent city, richest in the Peninsula, reputed centre of every progressive movement in Spanish history, was in the hands of the invaders. That night, forgetting with mixed feelings the previous six days' bombardment, its two million inhabitants enjoyed their first unbroken sleep since Franco's bombers took charge of the sky in 1937.

Declared General Franco, setting the radio sizzling with jubilations not yet ceased: "You are free. Barcelona again belongs to Spain."

As Don Miguel Mateu Pla, Insurgent mayor, took over the offices of Catalonia's numerous political parties, set up the totalitarian machine in all public establishments, thousands of Catalonians, streaming north-eastwards, manifested their doubts.

They were following the Republican Government to its fourth capital, Figueras: fleeing beyond to the Pyrenees border, seeking safety in France, traditional sanctuary of Europe's refugees.

By evening the roads were a jam of men and vehicles, women and children, bales and crates of household effects. Continuing over the week-end, the mass exodus gathered tributaries from all directions as Insurgent forces pushed northwards and along the coast from Barcelona.

Republican organisation swamped in the chaos, here French authorities took charge. Ten thousand women and children passed into security, followed in subsequent days by thirty thousand more. Able-bodied men, remnants of the broken Republican army, found no sanctuary, were turned back by reinforced guards to make what stand they might as Franco's pincers close on the last corner of Catalonia.

Meanwhile, in the new Government centres of Figueras and Gerona fifteen thousand hungry, shivering outcasts crammed the narrow streets, found instead of food a rain of death from Insurgent bombers.

Lacking other substance, Premier Negrin, fresh from a row with Catalan President Luis Companys over the military debacle,

issued hope of further resistance, said: "Barcelona is not the end. The enemies of Spain who staked everything on this offensive will again be disappointed. We have lived through many disasters, will live through this one, too."

Denouncing the "non-intervention" blockade, he assured "abundant material" on hand to "present the enemy with an unconquerable barrier" in the new lines now manned by Republicans twenty miles north-east of the fallen capital.

From General Segismundo Casado, commanding in beleaguered Madrid, came the same defiance: "The war will go on till Spain belongs to Spaniards."

But the tragic exodus continued. Reports an eyewitness:

"I watched an old man and woman lead a blind soldier into the town. His face was partly torn away by a hand-grenade. They had walked from Tarrasa, guiding him along the road. He was their son.

"They, too, had no bread. Their tragedy can be multiplied a hundredfold."

There were other dramas, too. One Spanish woman met for the first time in two years her husband, who had been torn away by military duties. More often the great trek involved separation, leaving parents, children frantically seeking each other by the score.

Against this sad outward flow on Monday began a happier trek, a thin stream of Spaniards, all Insurgent sympathisers, trickling back to secure the possessions abandoned at the outbreak of hostilities in July, 1936.

Proposing no halt in his advance, General Franco asserts his forces will be on the Pyrenees within a month. In the meantime he is preparing a second onslaught on Valencia where, he says, will be fought the last decisive battle of the war.

February 4 1939

Refugees Lost in the Snow

THESE Spanish women had trudged for miles through deep snow over a mountain pass in the Pyrenees.

They had left their homes in Catalonia to seek safety in France. Nearing the frontier they were lost in a blizzard.

French soldiers found them sitting exhausted on their pitiful bundles which contained all they possessed.

FASCIST RETORT: A last-minute inspiration of the Spanish Aid Committee, this poster was painted in the centre of London's newsdom by members of the Artists International. On Monday it was defaced by "Mosley" slogans.

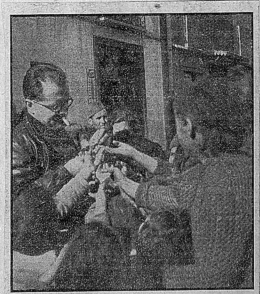

Hungry hands are those of Spanish refugee children at Le Perthus, on the French frontier. They are clutching for bits of chocolate handed round by Mr. Eddie Williams. With two companions Mr. Williams arrived in London yesterday after driving a printers' food lorry to Spain.

PASIONARIA SPEAKS

By Malcolm Dunbar

Malcolm Dunbar

son of Lady Dunbar, was among the first to go to Spain from Britain after the outbreak of the Fascist attack, reaching Madrid in December, 1936.

In June, 1937, after recovering from a wound, he was appointed commander of the first anti-tank battery in Spain. Went through the very heavy Brunete offensive with the anti-tank corps, but was again wounded, this time in the neck.

Coming out of hospital, he was appointed as a staff officer to the 15th Brigade of the International Battalion (the Brigade included British, American and Canadian battalions). Before the battle of Ebro he was made Chief of Operations and during the offensive became Chief of Staff. Was promoted to the rank of major just before the International Brigade was disbanded.

Pasionaria

daughter of miner, born December, 1895, at Gallerta, mining village in the Basque country. Turned out with mother and father as child in miners' strike against strike breakers. Married a miner at 20, took part in Spanish movement against the monarchy in 1917, distributed arms and dynamite, joined the Socialist Party in that year. Wrote under the pen name "Pasionaria," becoming very popular.

Joined the Communist Party when it was formed in 1920, was a delegate to the first congress. Under Primo de Riviera dictatorship suffered years of hunger and hardship, saw four of her children die. Became a member of the Central Committee of the Communist Party in 1930. Did magnificent work helping victims of the terror in 1934 after the October revolutionary movement, was imprisoned for this and released again by great protest movement.

In 1936, when the Fascist attack broke out, she was the first to give the now historic slogan : "They Shall Not Pass !" Her whole life has been an expression of that slogan.

OF ALL THE personalities which have emerged as figures of International importance in the course of the Spanish war, none has impressed itself more vividly on the imagination of the world than Dolores Ibarruri—"La Pasionaria."

Until now, however, it has not been possible for the English reader to acquaint himself at first-hand with the work and personality of this outstanding working-class leader. The publication to-day of "Dolores Ibarruri. Speeches and Articles, 1936-38." (Lawrence and Wishart, Ltd. 2s. 6d.) remedies this omission.

It is difficult for the average Englishman to realise just how much "La Pasionaria" means to the Spanish people. The picture that has been most fostered in the foreign Press has been of the great and fiery orator laying bare the sorrows of her martyred country to the outside world. This is true as far as it goes, for there is perhaps no greater orator in the world today.

BUT PASIONARIA IS more than a great orator.

To the people of Spain she represents the vanguard of the Popular Front, fearless critic of inefficiency and slackness, the enemy of all compromise and defeatism, the soul of victory itself.

It is impossible fully to understand the course of the war in Spain without insight into the role played by the P.C.E. and the P.S.U.C. (the Communist Party of Spain and the United Socialist Party of Catalonia).

Leaders in the struggle for the militarisation of army, leaders in the fight for unity against the disruptive tactics of Caballerists and Trotskyites, leaders of the demand for the mobilisation of industry, for a forward agricultural policy, and leaders in the fight against petty - bourgeois defeatism and compromise, these parties of the Third International can truly be said to be the forgers, the activisers and the main strength of the Popular Front.

RUNNING THROUGH these pages we can see how Pasionaria, chief spokesman, with Jose Diaz, of the Communist Party of Spain, gave a lead, time and again, to the people and to the Government on questions of vital importance. How, again and again, that lead proved vital in the saving of Spanish freedom.

In speeches to mass audiences in Spain and in France, speeches to the Central Committee of the Communist Party of Spain, in radio addresses, in newspaper articles, and in letters to her children, Pasionaria reveals to the world the true greatness of the Spanish people.

It is in her recognition of essential tasks of the moment and in the manner, forcible and eloquent, of their presentation that gives her a unique place in the consciousness of her people.

IN THESE SPEECHES and articles, ranging over a period from the first day of Fascism's cowardly attack on Spanish liberty up till July, 1938, we have a commentary on all phases of the struggle.

Sometimes it is an ironic commentary, as when we compare the policy which the P.C.E. urged repeatedly on the Caballero government throughout the winter and spring of 1936-37 as exemplified in Pasionaria's article in Frente Rojo of February 4. If that policy had been followed, the tragic events of May, 1937, caused by the P.O.U.M. (the Spanish Trotskyist group) would never have occurred.

In this way, by comparing these speeches and articles with the actual course of the Spanish conflict we can see how correct has been the role of the P.C.E. in determining the direction of the policy of the Popular Front. By its realism and correct analysis of the situation, the party has time and again saved the republic from policies which would have spelt inevitable defeat.

THE SITUATION IN Spain today is serious, more serious, it must be admitted, than at any time since the start of the war.

We cannot blind ourselves to the fact that the loss of Barcelona is a disaster for European democracy. This is, however, no time for despair and defeatism. The Spanish Government still retains more territory than it did at the highest peak of the Napoleonic invasion over a century ago. Then as now Spain fought on to give the lie to pessimism and defeatism.

In these pages the reader will find much of the soul of Spain; he will see how Spain has grappled with her difficulties in the past and has surmounted them.

THE WORDS OF Pasionaria herself, spoke in Paris last July, hold good today :—

"We Spaniards will not surrender; we will fight on until we have expelled the invader from our soil.

"From the trenches of Spain, where the cause of world peace is being defended, thousands of eyes turn towards you in insistent interrogation and await an answer.

"I know that you will hearken to the appeal of our people. And meanwhile, echoing the sentiments of our soldiers, our workers, our women and our children, today, as on July 18, 1936, putting into my words all the strength of my soul, all the conviction of my enthusiasm, I declare to you that Spain will never be Fascist."

About turn (if Franco has his way). Refugees queuing up to get into France.

February 8 1939.

Two forms of activity for Spain, and both of them effective. Above, two spectators run across Nottingham Forest football ground with their striking banner. Top picture shows three lorries loaded with medical supplies. They were provided by the Voluntary Industrial Aid Committee, and left London this week.

FRANCE THROWS OPEN FRONTIER TO 200,000 TROOPS

THE SPANISH GOVERNMENT HAS ABANDONED CATA-LONIA; FRANCE LAST NIGHT OPENED THE FRONTIER TO MILITARY REFUGEES, AND THE 200,000 LOYAL TROOPS RETREATING BEFORE THE REBEL ADVANCE HAVE BEEN SAVED FROM ANNIHILATION BY FRANCO'S WARPLANES.

The decision to open the frontier was taken at a joint French-Spanish Conference at Le Perthus. The shattered remnants of the Republican Army will lay down their arms at the border and will be taken to a vast concentration camp at Argeles-sur-Mer, near Port Vendres.

Already 4,500 carabineers have crossed over; 5,000 foreign volunteers are waiting near the border.

As soon as the carabineers entered France they were disarmed and sent to Argeles.

February 6. 1939.

The greater part of the Republican army is expected today and tomorrow.

France has begun preparations for the influx of troops. Field guns, machine-guns and anti-aircraft batteries have been placed along the border road outside Le Perthus lest the cordon of troops be overwhelmed.

Further large detachments of police and soldiers are being sent to the border. The entire region between Perpignan and Spain has been declared a military area through which no civilian may pass unless he has a special permit.

Twenty-two Government planes from the Figueras area landed in France, near Carcassone, yesterday. Sixty others have left the same district and are believed to be seeking refuge in France.

Two Government armed coastal torpedo boats and two feluccas (speedy sailing boats) with 16 Republican Army officers on board arrived last night at Port Vendres. A quantity of arms of German origin in the feluccas was unloaded.

Del Vayo's
Peace Terms

Early this morning the News Chronicle special correspondent in Perpignan telephoned that in the course of long talks between Senor del Vayo, Mr. Stevenson (British Minister to Spain) and M. Jules Henry (French Ambassador) the Spanish Foreign Minister stated the terms on which the Government of Spain would be ready to conclude peace.

Miaja To 'Daily Sketch'

I STAY AT MY POST

General Miaja, defender of Madrid, in a special message to the "Daily Sketch" yesterday, said:

"I shall remain on my post until the last moment. I am a soldier and my only code of conduct is the glorious tradition of the Spanish Army: Stay on your post and die with a smile if need be.

"I am not concerned with the latest international developments. My allotted task is to defend Madrid, Valencia and Central Spain. And defended they will be."

February 9 1939.

February 8. 1939.

Refugee Column Reaches Safety

Ambulances, buses, lorries, in the long line of vehicles which carried refugees on the flight into France.

And, reaching France, they go straight to a temporary camp (left). Men and women, soldiers and civilians, stand watching new arrivals.

THE TREK ACROSS THE FRONTIER.

A British volunteer embraced at Victoria yesterday on his return from Spain. He was one of 67 British prisoners released by Franco in exchange for Italians captured by the Spanish Government troops. They had been imprisoned at San Sebastian.

THE streams of refugees across the Pyrenees from Catalonia to France are now being swelled by the members of the Republican Army. Over 100,000 refugees have tramped wearily along the road to Le Perthus, where pictures above were taken. Party on left were able to take their belongings with them in waggons. Others, not so fortunate, had to leave all behind. A few of the soldiers (top right) carried suitcases.

February 9 1939.

'NO RETREAT' VOW BY A THOUSAND SPANISH TROOPS

From Our Special Correspondent

PERPIGNAN, Tuesday.

THE main body of the Spanish Republican Army is still engaged in confused fighting with Franco's forces near Figueras, and the advance of the rebels towards the French frontier, though steady, is slow.

The few roads on the Spanish side of the Pyrenees are in such a bad state and the snow is so deep on the open ground that even if they keep up their present rate of progress Franco's troops will not reach the Eastern end of the frontier for several days.

Further west, around Puigcerda and along the borders of Andorra, Spanish volunteers of the Republican Army are preparing a desperate stand. About 1,000 of them have sworn to die fighting rather than retreat into France.

They have collected enough light artillery, machine-guns and ammunition to hold out for some time at the head of the pass leading to Puigcerda.

Senor del Vayo, Spanish Foreign Minister, again came to the frontier this afternoon. He spent about two hours at Le Perthus, talking with French officials and making arrangements for the reception of refugees.

800 LOST

The first organised infantry units of the Republican Army marched across the frontier at Le Perthus today. They were men of the International Brigade, about 1,000 strong — Americans, Italians, Canadians and Czechs.

All these men, except those who lived in France, are now in the concentration camp for Spanish soldiers at Argeles.

André Marty, French Communist deputy, who was with the volunteers, said there were not more than 5,000 men of the former International Brigade left in Spain. About 800 of them, he added, were lost in the Pyrenees, trying to find their way over the frontier.

The column arriving at Le Perthus was headed by the famous Garibaldi battalion of Italian anti-Fascists. The men carried no arms. They wore civilian clothes with a red scarf round the neck and after marching smartly across the border line they halted at the roadside for inspection by members of the International Control Commission, who will certify that they have left Spain.

After the Italians came 400 American troops of the Lincoln battalion, also unarmed.

The foreign volunteers on the Republican side were disarmed after the Spanish Government decided to send them home, but those who were caught in Franco's offensive did useful service in policing the roads and organising the retreat.

TATTERED EQUIPMENT

About 400 wounded men belonging to the International Brigade have been refused admission by the French authorities and are lying at La Junquera.

Four batteries of light and medium artillery, with 30 guns of various types, all hauled by motor-lorries, and about 600 men, entered France today by the "neutral road" from Puigcerda to Llivia.

I saw these Republican artillerymen resting and cleaning up their tattered equipment. They and their guns had been parked in two fields near a stream far from the nearest village. Luckily the weather is fine for these men had to sleep in the open.

BUT NO AMMUNITION

Their guns consisted of 17 French and British howitzers (some of them 1916 models) in good condition, French, Russian and German field guns and one mountain gun. All the motor-lorries and two travelling workshops were American.

But for all this artillery not a round of ammunition could be seen.

Special trains which took refugee children from the frontier into the interior of France stopped at Juvisy, where food (right) was distributed. Soup, too, was served from a mobile kitchen in the station (below)

NEGRIN READY TO GOVERN FROM VALENCIA

IN ORDERLY RETREAT BEFORE THE OVERWHELMING WEIGHT OF ITALIAN AND GERMAN ARMAMENTS, THE MAIN BODY OF THE REPUBLICAN ARMY IN CATALONIA BEGAN TO CROSS THE FRONTIER INTO FRANCE EARLY YESTERDAY MORNING.

Headed by cavalry contingents, the infantry marched across the frontier bridges and valleys, and were forced by the French there to give up their arms.

They were led to huge concentration camps constructed by the French.

February 7, 1939.

Dr. Negrin also entered France unexpectedly yesterday, together with the majority of his Cabinet.

Fascist fighter planes who had been sent up to intercept their reported direct move from Figueras to the Central Front, were baffled by this sudden change of plan.

Dr. Negrin was understood yesterday to be flying to Valencia and the Central Front within the next 48 hours.

He and his Ministers arrived in France in cars, of which several had been badly damaged by shrapnel and machine-gunning from the air.

Meantime, Fascist bombers killed one more British seaman by bombing raids on the port of Cartagena.

There was other evidence, too, yesterday, that the starvation blockade of the Republic is to be intensified by Mussolini.

The need for food on the central front, and for the refugees, was regarded yesterday as being one of crucial importance for the whole next phase of the war.

Authorities on the Central Fronts yesterday, despite grave food shortage and the defeat in Catalonia, proclaimed their absolute determination to fight on in defence of the Spanish Democracy.

One of the pictures brought back to England by three anti-Fascist printers who drove motor lorries full of supplies to Spain.

The lorry is full of child refugees who escaped from Barcelona and other bombed towns. Notice the women with only a suitcase each to carry their possessions.

ARMS, DEFEAT AND VICTORY

AFTER forty-five days of dogged resistance the Republic troops in Catalonia have been driven back to the frontiers of France. These brave soldiers have disputed every inch of the way, whole brigades have perished rather than surrender and bitter fighting still continues in some sectors. It has been an orderly retreat, not a rout.

The frontiers of France have been opened to receive the soldiers of Spain, the same frontiers which have been closed so long against the transport of the arms which the soldiers so desperately needed. These soldiers are driven to these frontiers only because Britain and France deprived them of the weapons necessary for their defence.

When the full story of these last days comes to be written, all democrats will glow with pride and admiration. Barcelona taken, the roads swarming with hungry women and children and hundreds of victims claimed every day by Mussolini's aviators: yet the army fought on and the Government calmly continued its functions.

History knows no parallel except the mighty stories of the Russian Revolution. In all other wars defeat has come because military disaster has been followed by the collapse of morale and political upheaval.

But not so in Spain. The Spanish people are greatest in their hour of adversity. Franco has conquered Catalonia, but eyes full of hatred glare at him in every village and every street in Barcelona. Hundreds of thousands have sought the hardships of a foreign land rather than suffer the living death of Fascism. The soldiers who have crossed the frontier are ready for the fight on other fronts if the arms they need are made available.

No wonder Mussolini now proclaims that his troops will remain in Spain until the " political victory " has been won. But you have spoken too quickly this time, Mussolini. You have yet to win your military victory over Spain.

FREE AND DEFIANT

Spain fights on. Brave old Miaja is in Madrid and in southern and central Spain he has half a million troops. Proud, heroic Madrid, which crushed Fascism with its bare fist in July, 1936, will not surrender. Nearly one-third of Spain is still free and defiant.

Democracy is stronger than Fascism in the world today. Stronger in resources, stronger in spirit and courage. Fascism can be defeated if in this fateful hour the people unite to remove the stranglehold on democracy maintained by the millionaires of Britain and France.

Arms and food for Spain! At this moment gallant British sailors, risking Franco's bombers, are in the port of Valencia with the food collected in the towns and villages of Britain. Keep on sending the food, this message of human solidarity, and demand protection by the British Navy for the foodship.

Rally now as never before with the demand that the crime of non-intervention be ended. Heroic Spain must be allowed to obtain the arms she so sorely needs.

We make this appeal in the name of a gallant nation, in the name of peace, humanity and justice. We make it in the name of Britain's security. An army which would have fought alongside Britain if needs be has crossed the frontiers of France and deprived of what arms it possessed. The day may come when another army armed to the teeth, the army which Mussolini refuses to withdraw, may also attempt to cross that frontier in the name of Fascism.

The day may come when the coasts of Spain will conceal the cruisers and submarines which will strike at British shipping and naval supremacy.

Let those in this country who have been indifferent so long think of this in these days when Spain continues her great struggle which is for our cause as well as her own.

Just as they travelled home from Franco's jails, British International Brigaders in London yesterday before being fitted out with new clothes by the Dependants' Aid Committee.

Front row: (left to right) Edward Hughes, Glasgow; Morgan Havard, Willesden. On Page Four Walter Holmes tells how Havard lost his arm.

Back row: Patrick Brady, Co. Cavan; Louis Shine, Whitechapel; Joseph Farrell, Dublin.

Negrin At The Front: Franco's 30-Year Sentence On Irishman

IN A SENSATIONAL AND STIRRING MESSAGE DIRECT FROM THE CATALAN FRONT TODAY, SAM RUSSELL, DAILY WORKER SPECIAL CORRESPONDENT, TELLS THE TRUTH ABOUT THE EPIC REARGUARD ACTION OF THE ARMY OF CATALONIA, STILL FIGHTING HEROICALLY AND VIGOROUSLY SOUTH OF FIGUERAS.

Newsagency reports from the frontier (given in the Daily Worker yesterday) stated that the Army of Catalonia was crossing into France. These reports now prove to be baseless. On the Catalonian front the Army of Catalonia fights on.

Premier Negrin was himself at the front yesterday. With half a million first line troops and four hundred thousand trained reserves on the central fronts, the Spanish Government has no thought of surrender.

The Spanish Embassy in London yesterday informed the DAILY WORKER that the Republican Government will be established either at Valencia or Madrid.

The Spanish Government, following grossly unconstitutional and treacherous pleas for "mediation" by President Azana—who was due in Paris last night, is demanding that Martinez Barrio, Vice-President, take over Azana's duties.

British members of the International Brigade released from Franco's prisons, reached London yesterday with the news that

Frank Ryan, famous Irish leader, after first being condemned to death, has been sentenced to 30 years' imprisonment, and is now in the Central Prison at Burgos.

Government Leaders At The Front

From SAM RUSSELL

PERPIGNAN, Tuesday.

IN spite of all reports, the Republican Army in Catalonia is not yet entering France.

Yesterday afternoon I was assured at the frontier that the army was coming into France and that all was up. I looked in vain for Modesto and Lister, for I knew that where the army was, I would be certain to find them.

They were not at the frontier, for the simple reason that their armies were fighting seven-and-a-half miles to the south of Figueras, on the main Figueras-Gerona road.

GALLANT BAND

That gallant band of fighters held out despite the activities of the Fifth Column and Trotskyists, who caused the retreats of the rearguard in Catalonia, and thus forced the army at the front to retreat too.

With that gallant band are all the leaders of the army, General Rojo, General Cisneros, Commander-in-Chief of the Air Force, Colonel Cordon, Under-Secretary for War, and with them, Dr. Negrin, Alvarez del Vayo, and the Communist Minister for Agriculture, Uribe.

It is true that between 15,000 and 20,000 men have crossed into France at Le Perthus. They were not the Army of Catalonia.

Those men who came into France were men from the rearguard forces and services, Caribinieros, Assault Guards, Police, and medical services, who had been demoralised by the fall of Barcelona, and who had been in the process of reorganising in villages away from the front, when they were overtaken by the second great wave of panic, stimulated by the enemy agents who stabbed the Republican Army in the back.

Although it was getting late, I decided to go through to Spain. With one French journalist I went through on foot towards Junquera until we encountered that veteran of the struggle against Fascism, André Marty.

TRUE TO HIS POST

With Luigi Gallo I found him true to his post, with those of the International Brigade who, because of the criminal policy of the French Government had not been able to get out of Spain.

Germans, Austrians, Czechs, Poles, Italians and Bulgars, had been refused free entry into France and this, in spite of the efforts of the International Commission, whose president, General Molesworth, had been refused permission by the French authorities to visit the volunteers in the concentration camp in France.

The epic of the magnificent rearguard action since the fall of Barcelona is perhaps the most tremendous of this war.

In his final words André Marty summed up the situation. "The armies of Catalona are fighting to the last ditch.

"Their heroism is an example to the world and the undying shame of the inaction of the leaders of the international working-class movement.

"If Chamberlain is to blame, it is because the British Labour Party and trade union movement have allowed Chamberlain to throttle the Spanish people."

From La Junquera, right along the road to Ponts de Molins, and on to Figueras, the road was deserted.

WHY CATALONIA WAS LOST

LA JUNQUERA, Tuesday.

"THE Republican Army of Catalonia, after fighting without rest since December 23, has been defeated. But not one of the many reasons for this defeat is dishonourable," said a high military official here today.

The Catalan Army, divided into the two groups, was commanded in the east by Colonel Perea and on the Ebro front by Colonel Modesto, whose troops so daringly crossed the river on July 25 last year.

The two groups, comprising about 120,000 men, defended a front of more than 125 miles, stretching from the Pyrenees to Tortosa. They had no reserves, and they were insufficiently armed. Despite this, they succeeded in resisting effectively, and in counter-attacking.

On December 21, the official said, the comparative strengths of the opposing armies were as follows:—

REPUBLICAN ARMY: Men, 120,000; Cannon, 300; Tanks, 50; Planes 50 (including bombers and pursuit planes); Shells for approximately two weeks of fighting.

FRANCO ARMY: Men, 250,000; Cannon, 3,000; Tanks, 500 (both light and heavy); Planes, 800; Unlimited supplies of ammunition and technical equipment.

On the Republican side, Spanish troops only were fighting. Against them were a mechanised Italian division, the Littorio; four Italian "mixed" divisions, of which the command were exclusively Italian, and in which there was a small percentage of Spaniards; one Army Corps and several divisions (at least four) of Moroccans; the German Condor Legion; the Foreign Legion, including White Russians, Portuguese, French, Rumanians and others, totalling several thousands, in which had been incorporated prisoners of war; and Spanish troops recruited in Navarre and Galicia.

On the eleventh day of the offensive, the Republican artillery began to feel the lack of ammunition. They were able to fire only one shell every five minutes.

Republican aviation, somewhat strengthened, made daring efforts to overcome the Italian and German planes ten times their number. It was this lack of ammunition and overwhelming numerical inferiority in the air which caused the los of Artesa de Segre and Borjas Blancas.

NEW STAGE

From this point the battle entered a new stage. Positional warfare became one of movement. Had it been possible to obtain reinforcements from the Centre and the South; had it been possible to withdraw the exhausted Republican divisions from the fronts and replace them with fresh troops, the enemy, in spite of their material superiority, would never have obtained the results they did.

NOT DEMORALISED

It was necessary to demand from the Republican troops, exhausted by lack of sleep and food, and dazed by terrific bombardment, continuous effort. They were discouraged by news from the rear which told them of the massacre of the civilian population by Italian and German planes. Though this discouragement sapped their morale, they were at no time demoralised. Discipline was maintained and respected, even when hope had been lost.

On the other hand, the Fascists, fighting with the support of thousands of heavy guns and hundreds of planes and tanks, were able to replace their shock troops every three or four days.

February 9. 1939.

3 Ships Relieve Hunger

FOODSHIPS, giving welcome relief to the hungry inhabitants of Republican Spain are now being unloaded at Valencia.

The three ships now being unloaded include the First Yorkshire Foodship discharging £5,000 of potatoes, cod liver oil, dried milk and clothing.

The other two ships carried cargoes of milk shipped by the National Joint Committee for Spanish Relief.

London's second foodship left Iberia Wharf, East India Dock, this week-end laden with a cargo of foodstuffs and supplies, part of which is six tons of flour, donated by J. Lyons and Co.

CHILDREN HELP

Also many bales of clothing, among which were 22 sacks of blankets knitted by Birmingham schoolchildren and brought to London by a Cadbury van.

Trade union dockers and port workers offered to load the second London Foodship free. Unfortunately they were working on another wharf and it was not possible to arrange for their transfer.

A second Yorkshire Foodship has been chartered and it is hoped it will set sail in about ten days.

Crowded together in a narrow street in Collioure, French frontier town, are Spanish Government soldiers after their flight from Catalonia

"WE FIGHT TO A FINISH," SAYS SPANISH GOVERNMENT

Cabinet Now Plans To Rule From Valencia

SPAIN'S Republican Government is to "continue resistance to the end." This declaration was made in London last night by a Spanish Embassy official.

Dr. Negrin, Spanish Premier, and other Ministers, said the official, would probably set up Government at Valencia rather than Madrid. They would return to Spain immediately after settling the refugee question in France.

Señor del Vayo, Republican Foreign Minister, confirmed the "fight to a finish" policy in a statement at La Junquera, on the Catalan border. He added: "The means at our disposal in the central zone permit us to prolong the struggle for months. In spite of the gravity of the situation we are confident of the result, for we have the entire Spanish people with us."

Despite reliable reports that the Italian Government has renewed assurances to Britain that Italian troops will be withdrawn from Spain when Franco is victorious, Signor Gayda, "Mussolini's mouthpiece," enumerated further conditions for their withdrawal in the "Giornale d'Italia" yesterday, telephones the Rome Correspondent. They included the return of the Spanish Government's gold from France to Spain.

Light area of map shows territory remaining in Spanish Republican hands

M. Bonnet, French Foreign Minister, told the Senate last night that Britain had informed the French Government that she is solidly behind France "to assure the independence of Spain." He repeated that France would not cede an inch of her Empire.

Meanwhile, General Franco's forces, closing the Republican "pocket" in Catalonia, claim to have taken Olot, ten miles from the French frontier, north-west of Gerona, and to have reached the outskirts of Puigcerda, frontier town opposite Bourg-Madame.

February 10 1939.

Three London Printers In Spain Rescue

Lorry Dash To Save Refugees

By PHILIP BOLSOVER

BACK to Britain carrying vivid impressions of tragedy and heroism have come from Spain three members of the Printers' Anti-Fascist Movement who took to Figueras lorry loads of medical supplies and food.

The three men—L. Kenton (Reynolds News), H. Harrison (Daily Herald) and E. Williams (News of the World)—drove one lorry from the printers and one from the Amalgamated Engineering Union, and were the first to cross the Franco-Spanish frontier after the border hold-up caused by the fall of Barcelona.

Never did two lorries do better work. They

carried food which saved hundreds of lives;
transported 150 children to safety;
saved large quantities of medical supplies.

They reached the frontier at a time when roads were jammed with women, children and old men, who sat starving, cold, wet and miserable in pouring rain at the roadside.

All had been bombed and machine - gunned, many were wounded. With them were wounded soldiers wearing blood-stained bandages.

MONOPOLY OF MISERY

"We saw men," said Harrison, "who had legs and feet in plaster of Paris, but on the soles of their feet the plaster had been worn through during their struggle towards the frontier."

"It seemed," added Kenton, "as though there was a monopoly of the world's misery there."

The drivers waited three days before they could get over the border, meanwhile unloading their cargo of medical supplies, powdered milk and cod-liver oil in order to take on the bread and condensed milk that was immediately necessary.

After unloading their supplies at a Government store they picked up children to bring back.

"The kiddies were all huddled together," they said, "thousands lined up on each side of the road with nothing to keep them warm, their homes just mere bundles of clothing which they sometimes untied, trying to get comfort."

Children and people had a look of dumb resignation.

FOR NEWSPAPER

The drivers bought with money contributed by the staff of the DAILY WORKER food for the staff of Frente Rojo, the Spanish Communist Party newspaper.

"We bought bully beef, salmon, sardines, cigarettes and 100 loaves of bread, and arrived with it just when the staff of the paper was having a meeting," they said. "They were tired and unshaven, red-eyed from lack of sleep, and they looked as if

they had not had a rest for weeks. They had not seen bread for six days.

"But the food and, above all, the thought that here was support from Britain, seemed to put new life into them.

"They were carrying on. The Editorial Board of the paper, with eight members of the Central Committee of the Communist Party, had been the last active anti-Fascists to leave Barcelona.

"Armed with revolvers and expecting to have to fight their way out, they drove down one street as the Fascists appeared at the end. Two girl members actually had to fight their way to safety."

For some time after the fall of Barcelona, they added, there was no radio and no newspapers. Frente Rojo was the first out. The appearance of the paper and reorganisation of the radio had a tremendous effect.

OUR JOB

"People seem to brace up when they heard the radio and saw a newspaper," said Harrison. "When we left last Thursday, people were moving towards the fighting line instead of away from it."

"I thought," he continued, "that I was doing something as an anti-Fascist while I was in England. But when I saw Spain and the Spanish people I knew I had been doing nothing. Their spirit is indescribable."

Said Kenton: "The Spanish people will never give in. We know that, but sometimes we are too optimistic. We always believe they will win, but we sometimes forget that they can only win if they have sufficient arms and sufficient food—and it is our job to give them that."

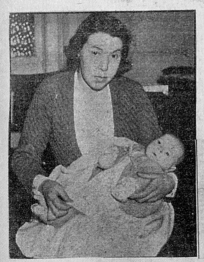

When this cute little baby boy was born his father was in Spain, in a Franco jail. Danny Gibbons had never seen his young son until Tuesday, when he came back home with the group of released prisoners who arrived here after nearly a year in jail.

His wife, Mrs. Kath Gibbons, who lives in North London, was waiting at Victoria with the baby to welcome Danny. Her husband went out to Spain for the second time in March last year.

SPANISH refugees are trudging hopelessly into the French border town of Le Perthus. And ahead of them lie days of doubt and anxiety.

One woman, luckier than many, rides on a mule with two children. The animal is laden with their few possessions.

Weary mothers cling to their babies. Their faces betray the effects of the arduous journey into France.

FRONTIER MASSACRE HALTED BY FRENCH GUNS

IN ONE OF THE MOST COLD-BLOODED MASSACRES OF THE WHOLE WAR, FRANCO'S PLANES SWOOPED YESTERDAY UPON THE DENSELY PACKED THOUSANDS OF REFUGEES AT THE FRENCH FRONTIER AND BOMBED THEM.

The whole region of Puigcerda was thronged with tens of thousands of refugees, exhausted, starving, waiting to cross into France.

At 3.30 nine bombers appeared. In three raids at short intervals they dropped approximately 200 bombs into the midst of the refugees.

Though the dead and wounded already amounted to hundreds, the bombers were still unsatisfied.

They were about to make yet another attack upon the defenceless people when the French anti-aircraft guns from the French side of the border opened fire, and drove them away.

At Le Perthus yesterday Franco's troops reached the frontier. Thousands of refugees hurriedly grabbed their few possessions and fled into France. The Fascist flag was hoisted on the frontier.

At Lambeth Baths: Miss Frances Day, who broke a bottle of "printer's ink" on the bonnet of a Spain Food Lorry, and Mr. Hannen Swaffer, photographed at the ceremony.

February 18 1939.

15 Miles Of Misery In Death Valley

By ERNIE BROWN
(Just home from Catalonia)

WE drove through a valley of death on Saturday night—the valley from Le Perthus, on the French frontier, to Figueras, 15 miles inside Catalonia.

Our five lorries were loaded with 25 tons of food and medical supplies for the relief of refugees flocking towards France. Two of the lorries were supplied by the Amalgamated Engineering Union and three by the National Joint Committee for Spanish Relief.

HORRIFIED

The lorry drivers had served with the Medical Aid units in Spain and had seen how Franco massacres civilians and refugees, but when we crossed the frontier into Catalonia we saw things that shocked and horrified ever, one of us.

For miles, on each side of the road, thousands of groups of refugees lay exhausted and helpless. They had tramped for miles with their pathetic bundles of belongings, and now they could go no further.

Among them were some Basque women and children, enduring their fourth agony of starvation and bombing. They had gone through Guernica—and Durango, some of them—and then came Barcelona, Gerona and Figueras.

At La Junquera, first village in Catalonia, we met the first of the wounded men heading a continuous line of crippled, maimed and shattered humans struggling to the frontier after hurried first-aid treatment.

Early on Sunday morning, at Port de Malins, we learned of the order for the general evacuation of the whole of the Spanish Army, and officials insisted that we return to La Junquera with the food.

It was at Port de Malins that we heard of the magnificent rearguard action being fought by the Fifteenth Army Corps under Modesta, holding up the Fascist advance to allow an organised evacuation.

Ten miles north the Duruti Divisions were hanging on like grim death.

After the food was unshipped from the lorries the convoy worked ceaselessly on the evacuation of refugees. The five lorries, and the two sent a day earlier by the Printers' Anti-Fascist Movement, are still running continuously on the job.

When I left on Monday the Spanish Army was still fighting. Spain is not beaten.

Message to Spain

IN its hour of travail the Spanish Government has received a message of sympathy and admiration from a hundred British members of Parliament.

Spain's fight against heavy odds for democracy and freedom deserved the support not of a hundred but of six hundred members of the greatest democratic assembly in the world.

Had the British Parliament done its duty at the beginning and realised in good time the full implications of the Spanish Civil War we might have been spared the recurrent crises of recent months and the menacing spectacle of a world in arms.

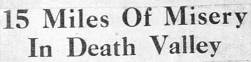

Spain's International Brigade Marches Into France

Germans, Czechs, Poles were in the 3,000 men of Government Spain's International Brigade who marched over the Pyrenees into France. A few watchers salute as they cross the border

Franco Claims To Have Complete Control in Minorca

LEADERS FLEE IN BRITISH CRUISER

GENERAL FRANCO'S troops, aided by an uprising of the local garrison, yesterday completely occupied Minorca, second largest of the Balearic Islands, which had been held by Government forces since the beginning of the Spanish civil war.

Early in the morning the British cruiser Devonshire with the Conde de San Luis, military governor of rebel-held Majorca on board, called at Minorca and took off 450 refugees—mainly Republican leaders—who will be landed today at Marseilles.

Below Vernon Bartlett states that the Spanish Government did not know of the visit of the Devonshire He reveals that Britain acted because there was strong evidence that Italy and Germany were preparing for an attack on the island.

Shortly after the Devonshire left the island with the Republican leaders on board the garrison at Ciudadela (led by Colonel Rodriguez) and, joined by civilians, seized the whole of the west coast.

Later, according to messages from Barcelona received last night in Paris, 12,000 men were landed under cover of fog from six warships anchored off Ciudadela.

Citadel Seized

The capitulation of Minorca did not take place without bloodshed.

A minority among the Republicans, who refused to surrender, seized the Citadel and barricaded themselves there ready to resist any attack.

The fort of the island opened fire against the Citadel, and in the bombardment 30 men were killed. At 11 a.m. the white flag was hoisted.

Government forces are reported to be fleeing in disorder and Republicans to be escaping from the island in fishing boats, heading for the French coast.

Berlin's Anger

Berlin Government circles show great resentment at Britain's action yesterday in the case of Minorca.

Newspapers (states the Berlin Correspondent) refer sarcastically to the "non-political services" of Britain and France in obtaining the surrender of Minorca to Spanish troops in order to save it from Italian assault.

Italy's reaction is seen in the words of Signor Gayda, writing in the "Giornale d'Italia": "It is evident that Britain and France want to keep Minorca from the Italians."

Franco Seizes Minorca

FRANCO officially claimed last night that his forces, with the aid of traitors in the Republican garrison, had seized the greater part of the island of Minorca.

It is thought in London and Paris that the rising in Minorca by the Fifth Column was organised with the help of the British Navy, which conveyed Colonel San Luiz, Military Governor of Majorca, to Minorca, 48 hours ago.

It is understood that, with the protection of the British cruiser Devonshire, he was negotiating with leading members of the military Fifth Column in the organisation of a rising in the island.

Spanish soldier is about to drop his arms after crossing the frontier into France. A mother stands by with her child, eyes downcast

British Nurses And Ambulances Will Go To Central Spain

AMBULANCES and lorries sent to Spain by the Spanish Medical Aid Committee are being transferred from Catalonia to Valencia and the central area of the country to go on with their magnificent work there as the war continues, the committee informed the DAILY WORKER yesterday.

"Ten ambulances sent out by the workers of Britain have been doing great work in rescuing refugees and wounded, and are to be sent to Valencia," the DAILY WORKER was told.

"We are intensifying our work to send supplies and medical aid, and we need all the help we can get in Britain."

British nurses sent out by the Medical Aid Committee are still working in Catalonia with their military units, while others are on the French side of the frontier tending refugees and wounded.

The motorised X-Ray apparatus and the field ambulance sent out from Britain have been brought from Catalonia and are to be sent with other apparatus to Valencia. Five lorries which have transported hundreds of refugees over the frontier are also to be sent to central Spain.

"We received this news today from Perpignan," said the Committee. "We shall carry on."

A PRESENT OF FOOD FOR SPAIN

Gordon Harker, the actor, helping to load a lorry with food for Spain to-day as a donation from members of the artistic professions.

Miaja Takes Over

General Miaja, who last night was appointed generalissimo of the Republican land, air and sea forces in Central and Southern Spain, and Deputy Defence Minister, has officially denied that he has been negotiating with General Franco.

Premier Negrin left Toulouse last night for an unknown destination.

★

Further evidence that Republican Spain will fight on in the South came yesterday from General Solchaga, leader of Franco's Navarrese, who denied that Miaja had entered into negotiations with Franco and stated that a further campaign would be necessary before Madrid fell.

★

The Spanish Embassy in London last night declared, "There have been no direct or indirect conversations of peace. The decision to continue resistance remains unaltered."

★

And in Perpignan Senor del Vayo said, "Everything is not lost. The southern zone has not surrendered and is not asking for a separate peace."

★

The war in Catalonia is all but over. Franco's troops are now along the French frontier except at Port Bou and Puigcerda, where the Government forces are holding out.

"BACK THEY WENT, BACK ACROSS OPEN COUNTRY UNDER HEAVY FIRE, BACK TO THE RIDGE, REACHED THE RIDGE .... HELD THE RIDGE"

"THE BRITISH went up to the front on February 12. Even as they were moving up, the Italians were taking Malaga and beginning a massacre that shocked the world. The battalion knew nothing of these events, but news of Malaga's fall had reached the Fascists and Moors on the Madrid front, sending their morale sky-high.

Airplanes, artillery, machine-guns, bombs, battered at the Republican lines; wave after wave of Moors and Fascists attacked.

After three days the inadequately armed Brigade fighters were forced back. The retreat looked almost as though it might become a rout, for men were beginning to move back in disorder.

Orders were given for the retreating forces to hold at all costs a ridge abutting on the main road and to make a new line there. But the troops were streaming away in scattered groups....

It was at this moment that the British Battalion proved itself—and the episode was one of the most gallant in its history. The Battalion had been scattered, like others, but it re-formed itself into two halves and, under a hail of fire, marched from two different points along the road towards the ridge.

Retreating men saw two compact

THE SPANISH PEOPLE REPEAT "NO

IT was only a month ago—though it seems like years—that we had lunch with Dr. Negrin in Barcelona. The day before, he had received a delegation of French M.P.s.

"I told them," said Negrin, "that France had better hurry up and help us, for we couldn't hold out indefinitely—not more than another two or three years."

The next time we saw Spain's Premier was at the midnight session of the Cortes in the fortress of Figueras. Barcelona had fallen to the enemy, and the Republican Army was in full retreat. Would Negrin, I wondered, still talk of a prolonged resistance?

The answer came towards the end of his speech. "We shall fight to save Catalonia," he said, "but if we cannot save it, thousands of Spaniards are waiting for us in Central and Southern Spain, by whose side we will continue the struggle. We can triumph, and we will triumph."

"How the capitulators must have shuddered when these words were reported to them, in Perpignan, or Paris, or London?

WHY does Negrin say: Fight on? In the first place, because Spain can fight on.

I think it was Jose Diaz, secretary of the Spanish Communist Party, who pointed out

Salud !

Spanish carabineers who made an orderly retreat in the face of overwhelming armaments show their still undaunted spirit with Popular Front salute. They want to go back to Government Spain and Government Spain must have the right to arm them.

the other day that in two and a half years of struggle the Spanish people have lost far less than the Czechs lost in one day of capitulation.

The Republic still has a formidable army, half a million strong, holding the central and southern fronts—Levante, Madrid, Estremadura, Andalusia. The man-power of the Army of Catalonia has not been annihilated. Four thousand men of the Catalan Army have chosen to go over to Franco, and the French authorities have facilitated their passage. Tens of thousands will demand to be sent to the Madrid Valencia zone.

All the Army leaders, in whom the Republic has placed such well-merited confidence, are still at the Republic's service. Miaja, Menendez, Casado, Duran, Campesino, are already in the field: Rojo, Cordon

Tarama ... two years ago tom

¡No pasan los invasores!

Nuestros soldados les contienen con gran heroismo en los sectores de Solsona,

Front page headlines of the Republican Army newspaper, People's Army, immediately after the fall of Barcelona. The paper defies the invaders. "Our soldiers are holding them in the Solsona Sector," it says.

PASARAN!"

Modesto, Lister, Del Barrio, Galan and a score of others have survived the Catalan disaster and are ready to renew the fight down south.

Shortage of war material rules out any possibility of offensive action: it does not, however, nullify the capacity for resistance. And Madrid and Valencia will be far tougher nuts for Italy to crack than Barcelona was. Madrid has her ring of concrete which has withstood the test of two years' siege. Valencia, menaced last summer, followed Madrid's example, and she has now had six months in which to strengthen her defences. In Barcelona they began to fortify only three days before the city fell.

SPAIN has the power to fight on.
But, more important, she has the will to fight on.
After the fall of Barcelona, Miaja toured the central fronts and came back with this message:—
"My men have told me they will stick with me to the end. Madrid and the territory under my control

Believe me, Negrin is not the man lightly to betray a trust, not the man to seek a safe hide-out in France and leave the eight million Spaniards remaining in Government territory to their fate.

THE last point is:—
Spain has the duty to fight on.
Don't misunderstand me: it is not I who stress this aspect of the situation—it would be a piece of rank impertinence for any outsider to utter the word "duty" to a Spaniard in A.D. 1939.

No, it is the Spanish people themselves who regard it as a sacred duty to carry on the struggle until Spain is rid of the foreign invader: a duty imposed by the million dead and by the generations who have fought and died in times long past to make Spain free.

Never was Spain more proudly conscious of the heritage of her history than in these agonising days. Listen to Negrin, the last time he spoke in Madrid:—

"I cannot renounce my country's history. We have inherited a magnificent history. To every generation its task. Because the task of our generation is a hard one, that is no reason for refusing to fulfil it. Noblesse oblige! Are we, or are we not, fighting for the independence of Spain?

" As long as there remains a handful of our soil, as long as there remains one breast

WHY SPAIN FIGHTS ON

y Journalist In Spain

in which a Spanish heart beats—for the sake of our country's future which is now at stake, we will die or we will conquer. And we will conquer!"

IS there anything more to be said?
If the national independence and territorial independence can be obtained by negotiation, good. But if it cannot—and how **can** it, with von Franco insisting on unconditional surrender?—the war must go on.

There is just this more to be said. The democracies of Britain and France have the **power**—far greater than that of the Spanish people—to bring victory to the Republic. They have the **duty,** too, have they not, likewise imposed on them by their history.

But the **will?** Surely they have that, too.
The task of the hour is to translate that will into effective **Action.**

bodies of troops moving in good order **towards,** instead of away, from the advancing enemy. Groups stopped . . . rallied . . . joined the marching men. . . . More and more of them; back they went, back across open country under heavy fire, back to the ridge; reached the ridge . . . held the ridge. . . .

They kept on holding the ridge. That piece of ground was never taken. And when dusk fell, the battle took an entirely different turn. The Government troops, including the British Battalion, counter-attacked along the whole front. The enemy broke, fled in disorganised retreats. Today, along that road still rumble lorries full of food, ammunition trucks — all that is vital for the defence of Madrid.

But the cost was terrible. Four hundred men were killed or wounded in the British Battalion. Four hundred of the best men this country ever saw."

THE BEST MEN THIS COUNTRY EVER SAW. Let us shout it aloud! Let pride drive out our tears. We will teach it to our children that the men of the International Brigade brought nobility to earth.

For the first time in history, free men from all countries fought side-by-side, united by a hatred of oppression. They fought heroically, but it is not for military prowess that we praise them. We praise them because their love of Liberty endured the last and fearful test: they chose to face death to defend the cause which is theirs and ours.

Comrades! The story of their sacrifice must never be marred by any stain. While we can help, children must never suffer, because their fathers died as these men did. The wounded must have care.

This is our especial task. We who are in the forefront of the fight against Fascism, must see to it that the funds are provided for the widows and children of the men who were killed in Spain and for the wounded who returned. Other appeals can be addressed more widely. This is our responsibility—ours alone.

British Moves To Recognise General Franco

THE SPANISH GOVERNMENT, HEADED BY DR. NEGRIN, MOVED INTO MADRID YESTERDAY MORNING.
FASCIST GUNS IMMEDIATELY BOMBARDED THE STREETS WHERE LARGE NUMBERS OF PEOPLE WERE TAKING THEIR SUNDAY MORNING WALK. DUE TO THE EXCELLENCE OF THE SHELTER SYSTEM, CASUALTIES WERE FEW.

Jesus Hernandez, Commissar Inspector of the Central Armies, broadcasting across the battle fronts to the scores of thousands of Republicans in the invaded areas, said:—

" The hour demands of all of us a spirit of bravery and sacrifice. Because our cause is that of justice, no one has thought for a moment we would yield to the invaders of our country.

"Our duty is to defend ourselves. The free peoples of the world, who understand why we are fighting, will not reproach us for our resistance."

In a statement in Valencia, General Miaja declared: " If anyone thinks I have any intention of selling my country to the invaders, they do not know me."

Meantime, in London and Paris the Chamberlain Government moved swiftly to press its attack upon the Republicans.

With American ships full of food and medical supplies on their way to Valencia and other Republican ports, the British Government sought to grant full " recognition " and belligerent rights to General Franco, to enable him and the Italians to blockade the coast.

It was semi-officially admitted during the week-end that the British Government is " considering " recognition of Franco "this week."

Previously semi-official messages had declared that " recognition " must wait until the Italian troops had been withdrawn.

PRETENCE ABANDONED

Now this pretence has apparently been abandoned, largely because of the convoys of foodships that are on the way to victual Central Spain.

In the same way it is hoped by "recognising" Franco as the "legitimate" Government of Spain, to get out of the necessity of sending the defeated but unbeaten Brigades of the Army of Catalonia back to the central front.

The men, under their leaders' Modesto, Lister and others, are demanding to be conveyed back to the lines immediately.

From the attitude of the British Government—and from the tone of its almost frantic attempts to convince the Republicans and their supporters that they are beaten—it was clear that this week is going to be one of the most critical in the course of the war.

The Chamberlain Government is very evidently preparing to throw all its forces into trying to secure " another Minorca ": a Republican surrender dressed up as " means of avoiding bloodshed."

Right : Loading mattresses and medical supplies aboard the French liner Patria, which is being fitted out at Marseilles as a hospital ship for Spanish refugees.

A STRETCH of sand dunes near Perpignan, where in summer French holiday-makers bask in the sunshine, is now the site of a great Spanish refugee camp. Men, women and children are living there in tents. Their only comforts are those they were able to carry with them from their homes in Catalonia.

Mother and father of girl above were killed in the rebel bombardment of Figueras. She had trudged with her brother to the frontier, was carrying him into the camp when picture was taken.

This Is A Hospital For Wounded Soldiers

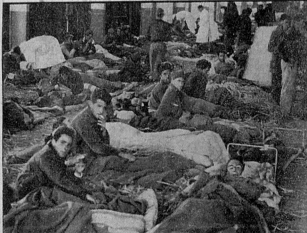

THE building is a warehouse near Bourg Madame, French frontier town. The floor has no covering.

The men are wounded Spanish Government soldiers. Some have blankets with which to cover themselves. They are the lucky ones. Others have to make do with straw bedding.

White-gowned figures are doctors giving attention to the men.

Februa[ry]

PREMIER IN VALENCIA SAYS FIGHT WILL GO ON

MADRID is once again the capital of Spain; any doubt that the war would end with the fall of Catalonia has been dispelled.

Yesterday Dr. Negrin, the Republican Premier, Senor del Vayo, the Foreign Minister, and other members of the Cabinet flew from Toulouse to Alicante and Valencia.

After talks with officials in these two cities Dr. Negrin last night made this declaration:

"Now that the evacuation of the army from Catalonia has ended, the Spanish Government is transferring to the uninvaded part of Spain and fixing its official seat at Madrid."

Independence

Defended

The Government, he said, had decided to continue the fight, defending the principles for the independence of Spain which were affirmed at the last meeting of the Cortes (Parliament) in Figueras. These were immediate evacuation of foreign troops, safety of life and liberty for all and free choice of Government by the Spanish people.

Barcelona messages state that numerous rebel divisions are being withdrawn from the Catalan front and are being rested preparatory to an advance against Central Spain.

The war in Catalonia ended yesterday with the occupation by Franco's troops of the frontier towns of Puigcerda and Port Bou.

Port Bou was dynamited by the retreating Government forces.

Daladier Hears

Socialist View

M. Daladier, the French Premier, yesterday saw M. Blum and heard the point of view of the Socialist Party on recognition of Franco.

Last night a Quai d'Orsay spokesman said it was not the intention of the French Government, which had been in communication with London on the subject, to agree to a recognition de jure of General Franco so long as a Republican Government or organisation existed in Madrid, or before all the Italian and German troops have left Spain.

The British Government proposes to make a further grant of £40,000 to the International Commission for the assistance of child refugees in Spain. If by March 1 the need still exists a further £40,000 will be available, making Britain's total contribution £120,000.

The Paris Correspondent, Reuter and B.U.P.

Recording Last Act of Retreating Army

LAST act of the Spanish Government troops, before leaving Puigcerda to cross the border into France, was to blow up their ammunition dump in the town. Cameraman is filming the explosion from the French frontier town of Bourg-Madame

1,000,000 Workers Ask Aid For Spain

PARIS, Tuesday.—Representatives of over one million metal workers and their families in Paris are to visit Leon Jouhaux, general secretary of the French General Confederation, to impress on him the need for immediate concrete action to aid Spain.

This was decided on yesterday at a meeting of the Paris bureau of the Metalworkers' Union which, following up the appeal for international unity of all forces throughout the world for aid to Spain, issued by the general secretary of the union last week, showed itself dissatisfied with the slowness of negotiations for such an international conference.

"ASTONISHED"

The Paris metalworkers, declared the statement issued after the meeting, "are astonished at the slowness to respond to the proposal of an international conference to unite all democratic countries against Fascism.

"The metalworkers of Paris, who do not intend to abandon Spain any more than they will abandon those militants condemned only because they were fulfilling their mandates, will reply by organising mass protests against the actions of those who play the game of Fascism and reaction."

Modesto Men Demand To Fight On

From SAM RUSSELL

CERBERE (French Frontier), Sunday.

"HOW soon shall we be able to get to Madrid?" was the question the men of the army of Catalonia asked me as they crossed the frontier on Friday.

And "Hurry up and get us to the Central Front" is the demand of this defeated, but unbeaten army, now enduring the humiliations of the concentration camps.

For even now the enemy has been unable to destroy the men of Modesto and Lister.

Since December 23 they have been fighting against the greatest concentration of troops and German and Italian aviation ever known in the course of the Spanish war.

Since January 26, when Barcelona fell, this army has had to combat the disorganisation of its rear, due, in the first place, to the panic of the civilian population, which refused to live under the Fascist invader.

Since the fall of Gerona it has been fighting back all the way, protecting the withdrawal of the women and children fleeing before the enemy advance.

Up to the very last moment they fought back and from the crest of the mountain at Cerbere I saw the men of the 11th and 15th divisions protect the withdrawal of the last troops and material into France.

All night long the units of the 15th and 5th army corps were entering France along the route from Port Bou to Cerbere, while in Spanish territory the leaders of the army remained to the very last.

Where it was not possible to withdraw the material, it was destroyed by special units, who, at the same time, blew up every bridge and means of communication once the Republican troops were safe across.

SING AS THEY GO

From then on, the Republican soldiers came through in a continuous stream, orderly, disciplined and singing even, in spite of the complete physical prostration that was evident on their faces.

The men that I saw pass through Cerbere are ready to continue, and this was obvious, not only from their bearing, but from the questions which many of them asked me.

Every one of these men know that he has done the best possible job under the circumstances.

They fought on till the last moment in Catalonia. And now they wish to rejoin their comrades in the central zone, to continue that resistance which will bring victory to the end.

I found among the commanders of this army the same determination to continue fighting, as I have found among others. Modesto and his Commissar Delage, were both full of praise to the army and the troops for the successful way in which they had covered their retreat to the border.

WILL FIGHT ON

With them were Lister, Commissar of the 5th Army Corps Santiago Alvarez, and the Commander and Commissar of the 15th Corps, Taguera and Fusimana.

The strain of the past weeks was evident, but more remarkable still was the firm decision to continue.

This army is the finest reply to those who have been assiduously spreading the tale that Spain is finished.

Catalonia has been captured, thanks to the German and Italian troops and material, sent with the approval of the democracies. The Central Zone is still intact, and these men of the army of Catalonia, rested and re-organised, will give further strength to the armies of General Miaja.

It is the duty of all democrats and lovers of peace to see to it that this wish is granted. At the same time proper treatment of the thousands of wounded, who, at the moment have been for days without attention, must be insisted upon.

Tom Mann speaking to the huge crowd in Trafalgar Square on Sunday during the demonstration held as part of the International Solidarity With Spain Day. Sunday was also the anniversary of the battle of Jarama.

IT WAS just after daybreak on March 31 last year that I fell into the hands of General Franco. I was a stretcher bearer in the Major Attlee Company of the English Battalion of the 15th Brigade, forming part of the 35th Division, and I was among a large number captured during the Ebro offensive.

Really our capture was due to over-eagerness. Our communications had been broken for about 24 hours and we did not know where our front line was. We had kept pushing on, and suddenly found ourselves in the Italian lines. There were four of us who were stretcher bearers and two first-aid men, and instead of being at the rear of our company we found we were practically at the front.

We saw a number of small tanks approaching and thought they belonged to our troops. All at once, to our amazement, we saw popping out the faces of Italian officers, grinning from ear to ear at their good fortune.

About half of our company had gone on patrol the previous night and had got lost, so there were only about half of us left. When it was realised that we were in the Italian lines and the order to retreat was given we found we were surrounded.

I ran straight into the arms of an Italian officer, and only one man, I think, out of the remnant of our company—about a hundred—managed to escape. The official figure of the number of Government troops captured that day was about 1,200.

* * *

Along with the other International Brigade prisoners I was taken about 30 miles by lorry to Alcaniz where we were all put in a church.

And what a church—I never saw one like it! It was used as a temporary quarters for prisoners on their way to concentration camps, and all the ornaments and decorations had been broken down.

Where the altar had been there was a row of barrels from which we had to get our drinking water. The vestry was used as a lavatory and the floor was ankle-deep with filth.

The prison was under the guard of Italian soldiers. There were a lot of Spanish prisoners and about 90 English on the first day, which number was next day made up to 120.

Captured with us were 60 Germans fighting in the International Brigade, and while they have been in our prison they have been visited about four times a week by Gestapo officers (the German secret police).

On the very day on which we left one of the officials came round and asked why the Germans had not been shot. He said they would be shot as soon as the war was over, so they might as well be shot now. The commandant of the prison simply shrugged his shoulders.

* * *

Our brigade captain, an Irishman, Frank Ryan, was captured with us. He was asked the usual question, "Are you a Communist?" and replied "I am an Irish Republican." This did not convince them, and before they marched him off between guards, which was the last we ever expected to see of him, we heard him say "If I was a Communist I shouldn't be ashamed of it, should I?"

However, two days later, he was brought back into the prison. We have heard since that he has been sentenced to 30 years' imprisonment.

We spent several days in the church and then were taken down to Sarragossa, where the military barracks were being used as a concentration camp.

After being there six days we were bundled into a train composed of cattle trucks. We were so packed that we could not sit down. We were on that train for about 50 hours and had to stand the whole of the time.

Our train kept stopping to allow other trains to pass—many of them hospital trains conveying wounded Italian soldiers. The Italians threw cigarettes to us as their trains passed.

* * *

When we arrived at Burgos we were transferred to lorries and taken about 14 kilometres to San Pedro de Cardena. There was no room in the concentration camp when we got there—it was filled with about 2,500 prisoners, most of whom were Spaniards. The actual building was formerly a convent.

We had to be accommodated in a barn. It was bitterly cold and the wind was howling through the tiles. We had no blankets and there was no straw, so we simply had to drop down on the bare floor. And there seemed to be more mice in that barn than the entire human population of the world!

Next day I woke up with a cold. I complained to the Dutch prisoner who was acting as interpreter, who told one of the officers that I had a fever. (If you had a cold it was always a fever!)

They did nothing for me, however, for two days, but I had got worse in the meantime and was sent into the "hospital," where a doctor felt my pulse and gave me an aspirin tablet. They put me in the basement of the building, on a tiled floor—where there were tiles—and I was given a mattress, which consisted of a sack filled with straw, but it was alive with lice.

I was in the "hospital" for about a month and during the whole of the time the only treatment given me consisted of aspirin tablets.

At the end of about a week my face had swollen very badly and something seemed to burst in my ear. I was stone deaf and my ear bled for a week and the only thing the doctor could do for me was to wipe the blood away with a rag dipped in cold water. I just had to put up with it, and it went right by itself about two months later.

The food given to the patients in the "hospital" consisted solely of a small ladle of diluted milk twice a day. The milk tasted like dried milk.

When I returned to the ordinary prison quarters from the hospital I found there were about 700 prisoners herded in two large rooms. There were 350 in each room, only about a quarter of whom had mattresses. I hadn't one—they didn't allow me to bring with me the one I had in hospital—and for the last ten months of my captivity I slept on the boarded floor. After about the first week they did supply us with one blanket each.

* * *

The "plates" we were given were sardine tins, fairly big and about an inch and a half deep, with the lids off. We had to eat everything from these, and as we had nothing but cold water with which to wash them out you can imagine the state they were soon in.

The food and the conditions made me ill again before long — I had suffered from a poisoned stomach before going out to Spain—and I went into the "hospital" again. This time they had got the place a little better organised and there were bandages as well as aspirins, but a complaint came through that the doctors were using too many, and the supplies were cut down.

I was in hospital a week this time, during which I managed to rearrange an enamel plate.

The ordinary prison routine started in the morning by us being marched out to give the Fascist salute to the Spanish Nationalist flag. If you did not give the salute you were taken inside and beaten by about six corporals with sticks. These beatings were so bad that after one you were little use for about a month.

* * *

For breakfast we were given water, and bread flavoured with garlick. For dinner, four times a week, we were given a helping of beans followed by a smaller helping of potatoes and what was called meat. The meat was mostly lights. A good many of us could not stomach it, but some were so wolfishly hungry that they tackled it.

On the other three days we got just beans. Occasionally we had boiled fish —one day between three men—but there was always beans, either white beans, brown beans, black beans, red beans or some other coloured beans. The black beans we used to call "beetle beans," because there was a small beetle in each bean.

On one occasion during the summer the boiled fish they brought us was full of maggots, so we organised a strike against the food. A sample was handed to the prison doctor for his verdict on it. He held it well away from his nose, sniffed in the air and pronounced it perfectly fit to eat.

We were never given any tea, but for supper each night we either had more beans, or two sardines which had not been gutted but which had had the heads cut off, and had been fried in olive oil. Each day we had two small loaves of very poor quality bread, which we calculated would together weigh about 12 ounces.

The door through which we had to pass when we went for meals was only wide enough for two to go through at once, so in order to speed things up a sergeant stood on one side to beat us through with a stick, and on the other side there was a soldier to hurry us on with the butt end of a rifle. This treatment went on for months and months, and we protested time after time, but the only answer we ever got from those in charge was that when there was better discipline we might get better treated.

There were no guards inside the large rooms in which we were confined, and as we had no work to do we were able to spend our time doing pretty well what we liked. One prisoner was very clever at carving and after he had fashioned a knife out of a piece of steel he carved a set of chessmen and a pipe for me.

When relatives and friends sent us books we organised quite a good library, and other attempts at culture included the formation of a number of classes in almost all conceivable subjects.

As there were a large number of different nationalities represented among the prisoners the formation of language classes was an easy matter, and we also had classes in practical subjects such as electrical engineering.

We got exercise, which sometimes consisted of being drilled in the yard, where, with all the prisoners in, there was room to take only about ten paces. At other times we were allowed to go in a field where we stayed sometimes for three hours and played with a baseball bat which one of the prisoners had made, and a string ball. We organised teams representing the various nationalities.

We had been going to this field about three weeks when two Austrian prisoners managed to escape. We were kept in for a month after that. The two Austrians were recaptured and given a bad beating up. Then three Germans escaped, one of whom must have got out of the country.

The other two were caught and when they were brought back to the prison were put in the "black hole," a cell where there is no window at all, and where the stone floor is always wet. They were brought out only once in about three weeks. As far as I know they are still there.

* * *

I never saw a Russian all the time I was there. There was a Chinese, a Turkish professor who spoke seven languages, Canadians, Americans and nationals of many other countries.

In July the English prisoners were told they could write home and I wrote home asking for clothing, books and money. I posted the letter on July 2 to the address I had left in Bradford-row in Doncaster. It arrived in Doncaster on October 27 and I got it back a month later, it having been returned because the family had removed.

Our clothes had fallen off us in the first two or three weeks and all I had was a pair of trousers and a pair of rope slippers. I had no shirt or jacket and we all suffered severely from the cold.

The trousers had been of the knickerbocker type, fastened below the knee, but the concentrations of lice in the bottoms of the trousers were so great that I tore the bottoms off.

My wife sent me a parcel containing a pair of trousers and a shirt, but I was informed that I could not receive the parcel until I had paid duty amounting to something like £1. Three of us got to know we had parcels coming containing clothing, in addition to cigarettes and chocolate and all were informed they had duty to pay. We had no money, so the parcels were never received.

* * *

The irony of it was that the commandant had told the prisoners that anyone caught out in the prison yard without trousers would be punished.

We had trousers waiting for us in those parcels yet we weren't allowed to get them because we had no money. So to avoid the promised punishment some of us started staying indoors. Then the guards came and beat us for not going out!

We were always able to tell when the Government forces were advancing because the beatings always became worse.

* * *

There was in another of the prisons a young artist of the name of Clive Branson, and during the time we were there his wife sold several of his pictures and sent him the money. His release came through just as the money arrived and as the English prisoners in his camp all left at the same time he left the whole of the money, amounting to something like 1,600 pesetas for the prisoners in our camp.

* * *

I never feared while I was in prison that I should not get home again, but I was upset when I learned—not until I received a letter from my wife in September—that my youngest child had died in March at the age of 16 months and that she was worrying about this loss and my absence.

Nearly 70 British volunteers were released at the same time as I was and none of us knew anything about it until the day before. After we walked over the international bridge at Hendaye we were provided with food and a bottle of wine between two of us at the expense of the British Government, but I had to travel from London wearing a pair of blue dungarees, a pullover and a pair of rope slippers.

It has been a big ordeal and I feel very weak through having insufficient food for so long—I lost 31lbs. during my imprisonment— but I would go out and fight again if the call came, in the interests of democracy against Fascism.

Ten Months In Franco Prison

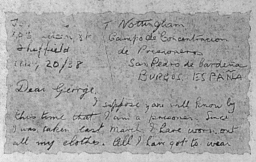

Cripple Climbed Pyrenees To Fight Franco

Returned Doncaster Volunteer's Spanish Adventures

AFTER 13 months in Spain, where he fought in the International Brigade against the forces of General Franco, one of Doncaster's volunteers, Mr. Clarence Wildsmith, of Worcester-avenue, Wheatley, arrived home in Doncaster at the week-end, in his own words, lucky to be alive.

Mr. Wildsmith had to resort to subterfuge in order to join the International Brigade. Concealing that he was a cripple (an accident left him with a very definite deformity of the leg and a stiffened ankle), he gamely tramped over the Pyrenees—about an 11-hour walk, the majority of which was undertaken under cover of darkness—to make a secret entry from France into Spain, along with about 50 other volunteers.

While physically sound men collapsed and had to be carried on the last stages of the gruelling walk, Mr. Wildsmith plodded on. He says the last downhill stretch was the worst of the whole journey, for the steepness of the descent forced them on, almost at a trot, however unwilling their feet!

There were about 50 of them on this eerie walk though the night—a heterogeneous collection of men who joined the party with secrecy at various stages of the journey from Paris. A French guide accompanied the party over the border and told them they had done the crossing in record time.

Mr. Wildsmith's deception was discovered after his uniform had been allotted to him. He was caught trying to stuff some packing inside his puttees to make his leg look normal size!

His plea not to be rejected was answered by his transfer from the infantry training base at Tarragona to the artillery training base at Almansa, and he became a telephonist with an artillery battery.

He came home with three regrets:

That he had not seen the Republican armies victorious;

That he had not been able to stay longer to help the Spanish Government in their fight for Spain for the Spaniards and

RE-UNITED—but there was one little face missing from this family gathering—the child who died two months after Mr. Nottingham left for Spain.

THE DONCASTER GAZETTE, THURSDAY, FEBRUARY 16, 1939.

WELCOME ! Group at the Doncaster Station when Mr. Nottingham returned home. The handshake is from Mr. A. E. Hall, Doncaster Divisional Labour Party chairman. Behind is Mrs. Tagg, whose husband was killed fighting in Spain. On Mrs. Nottingham's left are two more returned volunteers, Mr. Ralph Nicholas and Mr. Clarence Wildsmith.

Franco Prisoner Welcomed Home

Mr. Thomas Nottingham, of Worcester-avenue, arrived at the Doncaster Station from London on Wednesday night and among those who met him were his wife, Mr. Wildsmith, Mr. Ralph Nicholas, who returned from Spain some time ago, and Mrs. Tagg, widow of Mr. Herbert Tagg, the only Doncaster volunteer to lose his life in Spain. Mr. A. E. Hall, chairman of the Divisional Labour Party, was also there. The Mayor (Councillor E. Scargall) was unable to be present owing to a prior engagement.

Mr. Nottingham then drove home and was re-united with members of his family, including his three children. The youngest died last March while Mr. Nottingham was in Spain, and he did not learn of the child's death until September.

From six o'clock this morning (for milk for her child. The Spanish mother has been in the tins of milk roll down pavement into the gutter. The frantic mother is dragged away from the bodies.

Near me a captain, his arm in a sling, clenches his fist and says, "You murderous swine!"

Day after day week after week, Barcelona and thousands of other towns and villages of loyal Spain have to look on, while scenes such as these are repeated in all their horror...

The Truth About The Alcazar

By PHILIP JORDAN

THIS is the true story of the siege of the Alcazar. It has nothing in common with romantic and false legends written by men who were never in Toledo during the siege ; and were able to gather their "facts" only from rebel propagandists.

Read these words : read this true story ; and then see how far the B.B.C. dramatic presentation of the siege has anything in common with the truth.

★

This is what happened. Franco rose against the legitimate Government of Spain—to which he had sworn an oath of loyalty—on July 18, 1936. Four days later the Government gained control of the city of Toledo ; and the disloyal mutineers fled into the Alcazar, the mediæval fortress which dominates the city.

In their flight they kidnapped and took as hostages for their safety some 250 women and children. These 250 were the wives, sisters and children of men who were loyal to the Government.

Once inside the Alcazar the rebels telephoned to the Government commander, and told him what they had done.

Such was the first "brave" act of the legendary Cadets of the Alcazar. For legendary they indeed were.

The garrison of the Alcazar, in fact, consisted of 1,100 men. Nearly 700 were the hated Civil Guards ; there were nearly 300 Phalangists and there were about 100 men of the Foreign Legion. In addition there were some 400 women and children, of whom 250 were the unfortunate kidnapped.

Such was the setting for as sordid a gangster story as the world has seen.

★

For law-breakers who shelter behind the skirts of women and the bodies of little children we have nothing but contempt. Yet upon these men, who, on a larger and bloodier scale, were guilty of the same reprehensible cowardice, admiration has been poured out in full measure.

At no time were they in grave danger. For more than a month they were subjected to nothing but rifle fire. They were neither shelled nor bombed ; although the Government troops knew that they had but to employ such methods to achieve a speedy surrender.

But they knew also that their employment would mean the immediate massacre of their own relations.

So great was the fear for their lives that even when, after more than a month, artillery was brought into action, nothing greater than a 4 in. gun was used ; and it was turned upon nothing but the outbuildings of the fortress.

★

In the Government barracks as many photographs of the kidnapped women and children as could be collected were pasted up for all to see ; and underneath was written : "Be careful ; they are our women and our children."

It was not until nearly the end of the siege, not until the rebels had refused to allow the women and children to depart, that Government sappers began to attack the fortress in earnest ; but even then they confined their attention to the outer towers.

Not even a priest who went in, under the white flag, to beg for the freedom of the women and children, could obtain anything but a blank refusal from the rebel blackmailers.

The women and children were the best weapon the rebels had.

★

And at the end, when, after 70 days, Franco took the town and relieved the siege, what was disclosed to the world, fed as it had been on legends of bravery and death ?

Only 83 out of the garrison of 1,100 had been killed. No more than that. There were still 400,000 rounds of ammunition left.

To celebrate so glorious a victory Franco sent his brave soldiers into those military hospitals from which badly wounded cases had not been removed. They had a field day with their bayonets, and finished it off with hand grenades.

That was the measure of their splendour.

Alcazar Broadcast Protest

DEMONSTRATORS marched round Broadcasting House in the rain last night to protest against the broadcast of "The Siege," a play based on the fall of the Alcazar.

"Is the B.B.C. Franco's mouthpiece ? " demanded one of the posters.

"We feel the glorification of the Fascists in this play is just a part of the general policy of the Government

One of the banners carried in a parade outside Broadcasting House last night

to prepare British people for the recognition of Franco," one of the demonstrators, a member of Marylebone Aid Spain Committee, told the News Chronicle.

"That is why we object to it and why we are trying to persuade as many people as possible to complain to the B.B.C."

Feb. 18 1939.

FOODSHIPS GET THROUGH
British Cargoes Dodge The Bombs In Fascist Raids

"THANKS your shipments. Whole civilian population Madrid has received in last ten days free ration sugar, cod, potatoes, oil, besides proportionate allocations institutions."

"Further boat now unloading sugar, soap, peanut oil."

This is a cablegram just received by the National Joint Committee for Spanish Relief in London.

It follows a cablegram received by the Committee on February 16, which states:—

"Replying yours thirteenth on return from Madrid, where food situation improved largely thanks your recent shipments. Do utmost maintain present rate supplies.

"So far no losses due recent bombardments. All our boats unloaded before damage. All Stanlake load in Madrid, in course distribution. Stancourt milk on way. Tell friends Caonlara unloading now.

"1,500 tons food and clothing from you safely received and distributed since January 25 to date."

TWO SHIPS READY

Mr. Harold Fountain, acting secretary of the National Joint Committee, told the DAILY WORKER yesterday that two more British shiploads of food are ready for despatch, and a third will be under way in a few days.

He pointed out that there are 22,000 babies under one year in Madrid and its environs, cared for in 16 dispensaries of the Subsecretariat of civilian health.

value of its gas at 470 British thermal units. He alleged that the consumers were not getting 470 B.T.U. and that the gas was not [...]

A proud Spanish father and his child.

Feb. 23 1939

NURSING MIRROR

May 13, 1939.

English Nurse in Spain

LILLIAN URMSTON, S.R.N., T.A.N.S., an English nurse who spent 22 months nursing on the Teruel front in Spain, describes, in a series of articles specially written for the "Nursing Mirror," her personal experiences when "Nursing in War Time."

Miss Urmston, the author, outside an ambulance which has been badly damaged by shrapnel on the Teruel front.

IN Spain we had a system of first-aid (classification) posts—front-line hospitals, usually 6 to 12 kilometres behind the front lines, and second-line hospitals about 30-40 kilometres back. The base hospitals were 50 kilometres or more behind the lines. First-aid posts had often to be fixed up in farmhouses, huts, tents and even village churches. Whenever possible these posts were outside the villages. In towns there would be about four posts, near to the outskirts of the town.

Let me describe the routine of one of the many first-aid posts in which I have worked. This was a small farmhouse, just outside a small village on the Aragon front. It was September 1937. The first-aid post was the ground floor of an old house. We could not use the second storey because a shell had crashed through the roof, owing to shortage of disinfectants and general lack of material we had to clean the place as best we could, using cold water, toilet soap and dried straw fastened round twigs, which served as mops. A small kitchen, which is always a necessary part of a first-aid post, was put in a small lean-to shed in the back yard.

There was only sufficient space for fifteen stretchers, and these were placed with the heads against the walls. In one corner of the room near the door was a desk and shelves. Here the secretary and his assistant worked. Their work was to identify the patient and write particulars in a special book. On the opposite side of the room, placed mid-way between the line of stretchers, was a large table on which everything necessary for treatment was placed.

Besides the usual dressings and supplies of splints, antiseptics and bandages, we had large stocks of coaguline, camphor in oil, morphia, novocain, stovaine, adrenalin, cafeine, thrombyl, cardiazol (or

(Continued on page 234.)

A view of an improvised hospital in a cave, showing the hand-made road and the sort of country with which the medical units in Spain had to contend.

... were haemorrhaging or who had tourniquets on their limbs. In my early days in Spain, before we had a doctor with us who was solely responsible for transfusions, I gave, when necessary, blood transfusions by indirect method.

Complete with Pump.

Tubing & Needle.

Diagram of the improvised apparatus for injections.

SAM RUSSELL REPORTS ON SPAIN

HAVING followed the war in Spain since it began, I have returned to Britain to find a demoralisation among the friends of the Republic which has amazed and horrified me.

With the occupation of Catalonia and the withdrawal of the Republican armies into France, it was only natural to expect Fascists the world over to recommence their howling.

Those who do not understand the strength and determination of the Spanish people have announced in tremendous headlines that all is over.

In one-third of Spain, eight million people are mobilised as never before in support of the Negrin Government in Madrid. With an Army half a million strong at the front under the sure guidance of General Miaja and Commissar-General Hernandez, with another half a million in reserve and training, the fruit of the recent general mobilisation, Central Spain is in a position to continue resistance.

CATALONIA was unable to reap the benefit from the series of measures taken by the Government in the days immediately after the fall of Tarragona.

Catalonia had not enough time to profit by the general mobilisation. The enemy at the gates made it more difficult than ever to deal with the hydra-headed Fifth Column which, with the saboteurs, spies and Trotskyist agents was stabbing the Republic in the back.

THE magnificent six-week resistance of the Armies of Catalonia has enabled the Central Zone to benefit to the full from the measures of the Government. Giving way foot by foot in face of the overwhelming odds, the men who are now in concentration camps in France, know that every day gained was a day in which Miaja's armies would use to the full—fortifying, training the men for the front and the women for industry, weeding out the spies and traitors, doing all those things that Catalonia could not do.

While the Fascists howl of the defeat of the Spanish people, while the faint-hearted say that all is up, while the City of London tries to cash in on the tragedy of a nation, the men who with their bodies have held up all the forces of intervention for over two and a half years, have only one 'esire—to get back to Republican Spain. They know that it is not all up.

I SAW them crossing from Port Bou into Cerbere. I saw them coming into Perthus. I saw them yesterday in the concentration camps of Argeles and Saint Cyprien.

They have been subjected to every humiliation, they have been exposed to hunger and cold, they have to give up the few arms that the Government was able to smuggle past the stranglehold which the so-called non-intervention had imposed on the Republic, yet their spirit is not broken.

I saw Modesto and Lister and Delage and the other military commanders as they crossed into Cerbere. They were tired. Lister could hardly keep his eyes open. The only leave that Modesto has had since the war began has been a fortnight spent in hospital recovering from wounds.

When I arrived with the correspondent of L'Humanité Delage threw his arms round both of us.

"It's good to meet comrades at a time like this," he said.

I HAD last seen the Commissar of the 12th Brigade when the dispositions were being taken for the retreat on to Tarragona.

He reminded me how close the shells had come then. He also reminded me of his last words to me when I left: "With material we can still save the situation."

At that time his Brigade had been reduced to a Battalion. Batteries of artillery which should have had 12 guns were working with three or four.

They did their duty, but the democracies didn't do theirs. Material did not come, and that is the reason why I was watch-

JUST BACK FROM SPAIN, SAM RUSSELL, DAILY WORKER CORRESPONDENT THERE, SAT DOWN AND WROTE THIS ARTICLE. HE WENT OUT IN 1936 AS A MEMBER OF THE INTERNATIONAL BRIGADE, AND HE KNOWS WHAT HE'S TALKING ABOUT.

ing that heroic army retreating into France.

Spain's people, Spain's soldiers and Spain's leaders know that all is not lost.

Spain and world peace can still be saved providing the action of the Spanish people is seconded by the action of the peoples of Britain and France, compelling their Governments to stop intervention against the Spanish Republic.

LET us make no mistake, the arrival of the German and Italian troops at the Pyrenees frontier represents a direct menace to the security of France and Britain.

Occupation of Minorca has made France's communications with North Africa dependent on the whim of Hitler and Mussolini. Britain is threatened. By helping Spain now we are helping those who for more than two years have been keeping war away from Britain's homes.

THE hounding of the refugees from Catalonia—men, women and children—is a crime which is being encouraged by the French authorities with the approval of Downing Street.

In Argeles and Saint Cyprien nearly 200,000 men are being herded together like animals. According to the statement of the French Commandant of Saint Cyprien, all the food distributed for the 70,000 men in the camp was 30 tons of bread.

In the whole camp there were five water pumps, no sanitary arrangements, no shelter, no treatment of the wounded. This is being done in order to force the men back to Franco.

All this is being done to break the spirit of those who have come from Catalonia defeated, but not beaten. It will not succeed. The perspective in Spain today as ever, is of continued resistance.

Feb. 23 1939.

PICTURE POST

Vol. 2. No. 5.

February 4, 1939

On the Road That Leads to Safety. . . .

They lived in the country outside Tarragona. When they knew that Franco's men were coming they put all their goods into a waggon. The waggon was so heavy that they had to push. The road they had to go along was continually machine-gunned from the air. But they preferred to go.

TRAGEDY OF SPAIN

Fleeing from the war, a million human beings crowded into overcrowded Barcelona before it was cut off. As they trudged the roads, following a horse or mule if they were lucky, death came down on them from the skies.

THIS is the road from Tarragona northwards. Along it travels a pitiful procession. These people would be pitiful simply for what they have lost and for the few pathetic possessions they have left. But their losses are the smaller part of their suffering. Worse, far worse, is the death that continually swoops down upon them from the skies. These people are not "reds." They

are not "fascists," nor "anarchists," nor any kind of person one can comfortably dismiss under a label. They are old women, young women, children, just like the old women and the children in our own families.

Why have they taken to the open road? Because Italians and Germans have bombed Tarragona. Why are they hurrying? Because now and then

Italians and Germans in aeroplanes make low dives and machine-gun them from a hundred feet or so above their heads. . . .

The bundles which they carry are all their possessions. They have no home, no shelter, next to no food. What does it mean? Remember, this is not China or Turkey or South America. Somewhere we can easily say is far away. This is

a city of refuge, compared with what they feared if they remained in Franco's territory.

In Barcelona Italians and Germans carried on

"They Should Have Been Here For Us by Now . . ."

Waiting by the roadside . . . With them their bedding, a few clothes, several blankets, and the child's cot they saved up to buy last year.

15

Picture Post, February 4, 1939

IS THERE NO-ONE WHO COULD STOP THIS?

The Road They Hoped Would Lead to Safety Was Machine-gunned from the Air

This was the road to Barcelona: the road they had been at such pains to take. Some had got up while it was still dark to get started. Some had stood for hours to get a seat in a cart or lorry. Then came the enemy. . . . They flew low over the road. They saw the pathetic conveyances of the refugees. They machine-gunned them from the air, and flew away. There was nobody to stop them.

17

The Camion Arrives: But the Enemy is at the Gates

...enemy was only a few kilometres away, but there was no sign of panic. The few soldiers had to do little ordering about. The people climbed quickly in. The camion drove off.

...hostile, territory. To see France, our only certain ally, with another frontier to defend, cut off by sea from her Emp... Africa. Shall we wish... happen, that...

Will the Bus Come? Will They be Able to Escape?
At first Tarragona itself was a place of refuge. Hundreds came in from outside. Then Tarragona fell. A rising tide of refugees headed for Barcelona.

14

Still Pouring into Tarragona
While the townspeople are fleeing, country people are still pouring in.

These people, hurrying unprotected along an open road, a Spanish road bombed by Italians and Germans, are seeking a City of Refuge. In the Old Testament we read of cities of refuge to which even a criminal could flee and be safe. What is a City of Refuge like in 1939? The City of Barcelona. Normally Barcelona has a population of one million. To-day there are two million, the extra million in all people

happening on our doorstep—six hours away by plane. It is in the small piece of the earth's surface from which came Western Civilisation—our civilisation—that these massacres are taking place. This is Western Civilisation, 1939 style.

THE TRAGEDY OF SPAIN: A Mother And Her Children Set Out On Foot   One little girl carries her doll. Another has a basket with a little food—and, of all things, an umbrella. The mother supports her youngest on her lap. At her back hangs something to drink when the children get thirsty on the way.

A Mother And Her Children Sit Waiting For A Lorry
Lorries were set apart to carry all the refugees possible to Barcelona. But there were not enough lorries for all who wanted them. So they sit by the roadside with their possessions, wondering whether there will be one for them or not.

One Brings the Baby-Chair
All that remains of their peasant home is
carried in their arms or on their heads.

like these, who have travelled the open roads of Spain, bombed, machine-gunned by Italians, Germans—perhaps even here and there a Spaniard has risked killing his sister or his grandmother.

In Barcelona you got a ration of 3½ oz. of bread per day. You got 1¾ oz. of rice, 1¾ oz. of dried beans and just under 1 oz. of sugar, but these three quantities must last you the whole week. On Sundays, too, you must miss your bread ration. And yet to hundreds of thousands of Spaniards Barcelona seemed a city of refuge, compared with what they feared if they remained in Franco's territory.

In Barcelona Italians and Germans carried on

"They Should Have Been Here For Us by Now ..."
Waiting by the roadside ... With them their bedding, a few clothes, several blankets, and the child's cot they saved up to buy last year.

15

18

Waiting for the Camion: Outside the Tarragona Munitions Factory

Workers from Tarragona's biggest munition factory wait outside their factory for a lorry to carry them and their families to Barcelona.

What Lies Ahead?

children of Spain. Civilisation, as two great nations understand it, launched these attacks. Civilisation, as two other great nations understand it, did nothing to prevent them. But it could have done something had it wanted. When piracy in the Mediterranean interfered too much with British shipping, the Nyon Pact was formed. Piracy was ended. But the women and children on the roads involve no interests of ours or so it was thought till lately. To-day all

BUT THE REST GO ON: Old and Young Follow the Same Road

Like a painting by one of the old masters—the tired and puzzled child, the enduring woman of middle age, the old people who have seen much suffering but never anything like this. All of them walking; walking, they hope, to safety.

A Village Takes the Road Together

Half a dozen women and two or three men were all the war had left in their small hamlet. They take the road together, loading the belongings of all of them on to a small cart drawn by their two remaining mules.

The Camion Arrives: But the Enemy is at the Gates

enemy was only a few kilometres away, but there was no sign of panic. The few soldiers had to do little ordering about. The people climbed quickly in. The camion drove off.

Still Waiting . . .

over the country men and women are wondering whether it will be our concern to see German submarine bases in North Spain, German submarines and seaplanes in the Canaries. To see Gibraltar no longer in friendly, but in hostile, territory. To see France, our only certain ally, with another frontier to defend, cut off by sea from her Emp... Africa. Shall we wish ...
happen, tha...

1939: TO THE FREE PEOPLE OF SPAIN FROM THE REAL PEOPLE OF BRITAIN — GREETINGS AND FOOD: FOR STARVATION ALONE CAN CONQUER THEM

Montage by Reg. Bartlett

[Photo of ship by courtesy of Syren and Shipping, Ltd.

BRITISH FOODSHIP

Photos. by Robert Capa]

Dark as the hour seems, the loyalist Spaniards go on, for they remember the words of one of their leaders: "Better to die standing than to live on one's knees."

The cry is still "NO PASARAR!"

Selected further reading

Richard Baxell, **Angela Jackson** and **Jim Jump** *Antifascistas: British & Irish Volunteers in the Spanish Civil War* (London: Lawrence & Wishart, 2010)

Richard Baxell *Unlikely Warriors: The British in the Spanish Civil War and the Struggle Against Fascism* (London: Aurum Press, 2012)

Tom Buchanan *Britain and the Spanish Civil War* (Cambridge: Cambridge University Press, 1997)

Tom Buchanan *East Wind: China and the British Left, 1925-1976* (Oxford: Oxford University Press, 2012)

Jim Fyrth *The Signal Was Spain: The Aid Spain Movement in Britain 1936-39* (London: Lawrence & Wishart, 1986)

Helen Graham *The Spanish Civil War: A Very Short Introduction* (Oxford: Oxford University Press, 2005)

Angela Jackson *British Women and the Spanish Civil War* (London: Routledge, 2002)

Linda Palfreeman *¡Salud! British Volunteers in the Republican Medical Service During the Spanish Civil War, 1936-1939* (Eastbourne: Sussex Academic Press, 2012)

Paul Preston *I Saw Spain Die: Foreign Correspondents in the Spanish Civil War* (London: Constable & Robinson, 2009)

Thanks

Several people and organisations have helped with the production of this book, notably Lucie Hyndley and Sue Taylor at Unison, who were responsible for scanning Pearl Bickerstaffe's scrapbook, James Sutherland, who helped with research at the Modern Records Centre in Warwick, Marshall Mateer, who provided the pictures of Sam Lesser and Rodney Bickerstaffe taken in 2010, and Alan Slingsby, who contributed design skills and efforts well beyond the normal professional call of duty.

***Mick Jones
(1944-2012)***

Thanks must also go to the *Morning Star* and People's Press Printing Society for allowing us to reproduce so many cuttings from the *Daily Worker* and likewise to the *Daily Telegraph*. Every effort has been made to identify, contact and acknowledge all known copyright holders of any scrapbook cutting used in this book.

We are also grateful for the financial assistance given to this project by the train drivers' union ASLEF. Finally, none of this would have been possible without the help and encouragement of Rodney Bickerstaffe and without financial support from a legacy to the International Brigade Memorial Trust from Mick Jones.

International Brigade Memorial Trust

International Brigade Memorial Trust

The International Brigade Memorial Trust keeps alive the memory and spirit of the 2,500 men and women from Britain and Ireland who volunteered to defend democracy and fight fascism in Spain during the Spanish Civil War of 1936-39. We also remember those who supported the volunteers and the cause of the Spanish Republic at home. The IBMT brings together families, friends and admirers of the International Brigades, along with historians, labour movement activists and all others who share an interest in the exceptional story of the International Brigades.

The IBMT organises and supports educational, cultural and commemorative events around the country. We assist students, academics and others researching the International Brigades and the Spanish Civil War and promote the preservation of archives about the volunteers. Through the *IBMT Newsletter*, our website (www.international-brigades.org.uk) and new media platforms we keep members and the wider public informed about developments concerning the memory and legacy of the International Brigades. We also ensure that the more than 100 memorials in the British Isles to the volunteers – 526 of whom were killed in Spain – are maintained in good order and, where appropriate, new ones are erected.

The IBMT is a registered charity and relies on membership subscriptions and donations to finance its activities.